A. E. (Addison Emery) Verrill

Notes on Radiata in the Museum of Yale College

A. E. (Addison Emery) Verrill

Notes on Radiata in the Museum of Yale College

ISBN/EAN: 9783743370616

Manufactured in Europe, USA, Canada, Australia, Japa

Cover: Foto ©ninafisch / pixelio.de

Manufactured and distributed by brebook publishing software (www.brebook.com)

A. E. (Addison Emery) Verrill

Notes on Radiata in the Museum of Yale College

NOTES ON RADIATA

IN THE

MUSEUM OF YALE COLLEGE.

BY A. E. VERRILL,

PROFESSOR IN YALE COLLEGE, NEW HAVEN. CONN.

No. 8.— ADDITIONAL OBSERVATIONS ON ECHINODERMS, CHIEFLY FROM THE PACIFIC COAST OF AMERICA.

No. 9.—THE ECHINODERM-FAUNA OF THE GULF OF CALIFORNIA AND CAPE ST. LUCAS.

[FROM THE TRANSACTIONS OF THE CONNECTICUT ACADEMY OF ARTS AND SCIENCES.
VOL. I, MARCH, 1871.]

NEW HAVEN:
PRINTED BY TUTTLE, MOREHOUSE & TAYLOR.

NOTE TO THE REPRINT.

That portion of Part II which precedes page 503 of this volume of the Transactions, had been printed and the author's separate edition of 150 copies mostly distributed before the fire, by which the regular edition was destroyed, causing considerable delay in issuing the volume. A portion of the author's edition was also distributed, as soon as printed, in sheets, each bearing its date of publication, to all those Zoölogists known to be interested in the subject.

Hence it was thought undesirable to introduce in this reprint even those changes which the progress of science has rendered necessary, except when it could be done in parentheses or foot notes, without essentially changing the paging and original reading. Therefore, in the first five articles, no changes of importance, unless typographical errors, have been made, except in foot notes to which "—Reprint" is appended. In the sixth article, it being still incomplete and less extensively distributed, I have introduced changes more freely, yet without changing the paging, and have in all important cases affixed "—Reprint" to new matter. When a name has been changed the original name follows in parenthesis, in order that no confusion may arise from references to copies of the first edition. The following are the most important changes: p. 386, *Gorgonia* is changed to *Eunicella*, and *Pterogorgia* to *Gorgonia*; p. 387, *Litigorgia* to *Leptogorgia*; p. 392, *L. rutila* is made a distinct species; p. 398, *L. lævis* changed to *L. alba*; p. 398, *L. fucosa* to *L. Caryi*; p. 410, *Eugorgia Mexicana* to *E. aurantiaca*; p. 413, *Leptogorgia aurantiaca* E. and H. to *Echinogorgia*; the measurements of the spicula of *Leptogorgia* and *Eugorgia* have been corrected in accordance with the note on p. 415 (1st ed.), and in some cases additional ones given; new localities have been added from the collections of McNiel and Capt. Pedersen; p. 417, *Psammogorgia fucosa* added; p. 450, *Echinogorgia aurantiaca* added; p. 497, *Gemmaria* changed to *Epizoanthus*.

The above changes in nomenclature have also been made in the American Journal of Science, vol. xlviii, p. 419. Nov., 1869, from which they should date.

A. E. VERRILL.

NEW HAVEN, CONN., November 15th, 1869.

1. Notes on the Radiata in the Museum of Yale College, with description on new Genera and species.

No. 1. Descriptions of new Starfishes from Zealand. pp. 247-251.

No. 2. Notes on the Echinoderms of Panama and West Coast of America, with descriptions of new Genera and Species. pp. 251-322.

No. 3. On the Geographical distribution of the Echinoderms of the West Coast of America. pp. 323-351.*

No. 4. Notice of Corals & Echinoderms collected by Prof. C.F.Hartt, at the Abrolhos Reefs, Province of Bahia, Brazil, 1867. pp. 351-371.

No. 5. Notice of a collection of Echinoderms from La. Paz, Lower California, with descriptions of a New Genus. pp. 371-374.

No. 6. Review of the Corals and Polyps of the West Coast of America. pp. 377-558.

No. 7. On the Geographical distribution of the Polyps of the West Coast of America. pp. 558-567.

No. 8. Additional observations on Echinoderms, chiefly from the Pacific Coast of America. pp. 568-593.

No. 9. The Echinoderm-Fauna of the Gulf of California and Cape St. Lucas. pp. 593-596.

Trans. Conn. Acad. of Arts & Sci., Vol. I. March 1871. pls. IV-X.

V. Notes on the Radiata in the Museum of Yale College, with Descriptions of new Genera and Species. By A. E. Verrill.

Read, Jan. 16th, 1867.

No. 1. Descriptions of new Starfishes from New Zealand.

The following interesting species of New Zealand starfishes were sent from Peru by Mr. F. H. Bradley, to whom they were given for our Museum by Henry Edwards, Esq.

They afford a partial illustration of the little known Echinoderm fauna of the Southern Ocean. They contrast strongly with those of the Northern Hemisphere.

Cœlasterias, gen. nov.

Large starfishes, with four rows of ambulacral suckers, and large, swollen rays (eleven in the typical species), which are free to near the base, and are united beneath by a group of interradial plates. Interambulacral plates united directly to the first row of ventral plates, and these to a second row of larger plates without the intervention of open spaces like those seen in *Asterias*. Dorsal surface with large, strong, imbricated, irregularly arranged ossicles or plates, bearing short, very numerous spines.

This genus is more closely allied to *Asterias* (Asteracanthion) than to *Heliaster*, and approaches still nearer to *Stichaster*, but appears very distinct from either. The excessive development of the abactinal system over the ambulacral is its most remarkable characteristic. In this respect it contrasts strongly with the next genus. The form and general aspect is that of a *Solaster*.

Cœlasterias australis Verrill, sp. nov.

Rays eleven, in the only specimen seen, large, inflated, rounded, tapering rapidly to the end. Disk of moderate size, swollen; radius of disk to length of rays, measuring from the center, as 2 : 6. The triangular interradial space beneath is occupied by a cluster of irregular stout plates, mostly without spines. Ambulacral grooves relatively narrow and shallow, the pores small and crowded, in four well-marked rows. The interambulacral plates usually bear alternately one and two spines, which are long and rather slender toward the mouth, but short, thick and obtuse toward the end of the ray, and much crowded in indistinct rows. The next row of plates is united directly to these, and the plates are small, longest lengthwise of the ray, and each bears a short, thick spine, but little larger than the preceding, and forming a regular, rather open row. Exterior to these is another ventral row of large, strong, imbricated, prominent plates, each bearing at its summit two very thick, short, obtuse spines, much larger than the interambulacral ones, and arranged in a single row, and on their external side each plate usually supports two or more short, rounded, much smaller spines, the largest of which usually form a regular row. The plates of the first lateral row are much elongated transversely to the ray, imbricated and strong, and so united to the ventral as to leave large openings between; each bears about twelve small, short, rounded, clavate spines, which are placed along the plates in single or double rows transverse to the ray. The plates of the median dorsal row have a similar form, and bear a similar transverse row of spines, which are somewhat larger. Between these and the first row of lateral plates the plates are irregular in form and arrangement, but short and imbricated, with unequal openings between, forming, about five indistinct rows, all covered with groups of short sub-globular spines, giving an even appearance to the surface, but with large vacant spaces between. Madreporic plate, small, of fine texture, situated a little nearer to the center of the disk than its edge. Minor pedicellariæ few, at the bases of the spines and on the spaces between, longer than broad, obtuse, somewhat compressed, constricted near the base. A few major pedicellariæ, scattered on the dorsal surface and on the interradial surface beneath, are much larger and stouter, with enlarged bases and obtuse tips.

Greatest diameter 11 inches; disk 4; width of rays at base 1·25.
Aukland, New Zealand,—H. Edwards.

Coscinasterias, gen. nov.

Starfishes with many rays, which are elongated, slender, and united only at the base, without interradial plates beneath. Disk small. Ambulacra broad, highly developed, suckers very numerous, in four rows. Spines prominent, arranged in longitudinal rows on the rays. Dorsal surface with large, scattered pedicellariæ. Madreporic plate large, irregular, often with several accessory ones placed irregularly on various parts of the disk. Dorsal plates (ossicles) arranged much as in *Asterias*.

The excessive development of the rays and ambulacral system, compared with the disk or central cavity, is the most characteristic feature of this genus.

The *Asterias aster* Gray, probably belongs to this genus, but is too imperfectly described for identification.

Coscinasterias muricata Verrill, sp. nov.

Rays nine to eleven, slender, tapering, rounded above, flat below owing to the width of the ambulacra, narrowed at the base, five to seven times as long as the radius of the disk, which is small. Ambulacral furrows shallow and broad, with very numerous small suckers, crowded in four rows. Interambulacral plates thin, somewhat imbricated, connected with the lateral plates by a row of small, stout ossicles which alternate with small rounded pores. Each interambulacral plate usually bears a long, slender, tapering spine; these are arranged in a single close row. External to these is a row of distant, longer and stouter cylindrical spines, arising singly from the connecting ossicles between the interambulacral and ventral plates. The latter are strong and imbricated, each usually bearing two longer and stouter blunt spines, which form a crowded double row, along the sides of the arm. Ossicles of the upper surface very stout, bearing strong, acute spines, which are arranged in about five open rows, the median and two external alone reaching the base of the ray; those of the median row are somewhat larger, and all are surrounded by close wreaths of minute pedicellariæ. On the disk they are smaller and loosely scattered, often obtuse. The major pedicellariæ are numerous, scattered over the whole dorsal surface and between the ventral spines, and also form a row within the edge of the ambulacral furrow. They vary considerably in size and form upon different parts. Most of those of the dorsal surface are stout, oval, compressed, pointed, nearly twice as long as wide, about ·05 of an inch long, while with them are others of similar form not half as large. Those in the ambulacral furrows are even longer, but more acutely pointed. The madreporic plates are variable in number and size as well as position. One appears to be always in its normal position and near the edge of the disk, while the accessory ones are introduced at various points around the disk, but at about the same distance from the margin. Sometimes, when there are but two and the rays are in even numbers, they are directly opposite and in the same transverse plane. A specimen with eleven rays has two contiguous ones and another separated by four rays, each being composed of several pieces united. One specimen has but one large, convex madreporic plate.

The largest specimen is 7·5 inches in diameter across the rays, with a disk 1·25 inches in diameter; rays ·5 broad; interambulacral spines, ·15 long.

Aukland, New Zealand,—H. Edwards.

Asterina (Asteriscus) regularis Verrill, sp. nov.

Pentagonal, depressed, with the interradial spaces evenly concave, and the rays short, broad and acute; greatest radius to least as 15 : 10. Ambulacral pores large; interambulacral plates each with two slender acute spines, forming a single row. Those near the mouth larger, obtuse and flattened. Ventral plates of the first row stout and prominent, each bearing a conical, acute spine, twice as large as the preceding. Exterior to these the ventral or interradial plates are flattened and imbricated, diminishing in size as they recede from the center, each bearing an acute conical spine; these diminish in size like the plates, the larger ones being about as thick as the interambulacral spines, but shorter; near the margin these spines become very small and crowded, many of the plates bearing two. Plates of the upper surface rather large, increasing toward the center, regularly imbricated, the free margin evenly rounded and thin, bearing near the end a cluster of five to nine very small, nearly equal spines; toward the center the plates become less regular in form and unequal in size, the larger ones often bearing twelve or fourteen spines in a transverse cluster. Madreporic plate large and prominent, at about one-third of the distance from the center to the margin. The large dorsal pores are in groups on the sides and within the bases of the rays, arranged in about four rows, which run parallel with the median line of the rays, with from six to twelve pores in a row. A few irregularly arranged pores between adjacent rays connect these groups.

Color, when dried, dark olive-green above, yellow below.

From center to end of ray 1·5 inches; to edge of disk ·8.

Aukland, New Zealand,—H. Edwards.

Astropecten Edwardsii Verrill, sp. nov.

Rays five, long, regularly tapering, acute, about four and a half times as long as the radius of the disk. Ambulacra broad, interambulacral plates angular, imbricated, each bearing a cluster of three or four slender spines on the inner edge, and two or three smaller ones on the outer angle, not forming regular rows. Ventral plates densely covered with minute rough spines, each having also a central series of sharp spines, the inner ones very small, increasing outwardly to the external, marginal ones, which are strong, sharp and slightly curved upward, a quarter inch long. The lower marginal plates are opposite the upper, and project considerably beyond them. The latter are elevated and narrow, twenty-eight on each side of a ray, the two at the angle between the rays much higher and larger, covered like the rest with rough rounded granules, and each surmounted by a stout, blunt tubercle. All the others, except the next two, bear a similar, much smaller tubercle, decreasing regularly in size to the end of the ray. The two next the basal one of each ray are thinner than the rest and without a tubercle. Paxillæ largest along the center of the rays, presenting a crowded even surface.

Length of ray from center 2·6 inches; radius of disk ·6; width of ray at base ·7; of median space ·4.

Aukland, New Zealand,—H. Edwards.

No. 2. *Notes on the Echinoderms of Panama and West Coast of America, with descriptions of new Genera and Species.*

The materials for this paper have been derived chiefly from the collections made by Mr. F. H. Bradley, who has spent nearly a year in collecting the marine animals of Panama and adjacent coasts, for the Museum of Yale College, and is still engaged in that exploration. I am also indebted to the Smithsonian Institution for specimens collected at Cape St. Lucas by John Xantus, Esq., and others from Central America sent by Capt. J. M. Dow.

Order, OPHIUROIDEA.

Astrophyton Panamense Verrill, sp. nov.

The largest specimen in the collection is about 13 inches in total diameter, with the disk 1·4. The arms are irregular in their outer divisions, some of the main trunks dividing 19 or 20 times, with very small and slender terminal twigs. The entire surface above and below is closely covered with rather coarse granulations, which are rounded and even on the radial ribs and upper side of arms, but flattened and larger on the lower side of arms, especially at the base; on the interradial membrane they are less crowded, rounded, and unequal. The ten radial ribs are long and narrow (1 inch long and ·15 broad at middle) much raised and prominent, strongly arched, extending to the center, gradually enlarging outwardly to near the end, where they suddenly expand to the end, which is truncate, leaving a transverse cicatrix. Their upper surfaces are slightly convex and have no indications of spines or tubercles, being uniformly and coarsely granulated. The arms are rounded above, with a slight longitudinal groove along the center; the joints are distinctly marked by transverse lines destitute of granules; beneath they are flat and have, also, a slight central depression, and are covered with crowded, pavement-like granulations; tentacle-scales two or three, quite distinct, short, spine-like, commencing at the third or fourth forks; hooks very small, visible only on the terminal twigs. Teeth about eight, strong, blunt-pointed, diminishing in size outwardly and blending with the teeth-papillæ, which are irregular in number; mouth-papillæ small, 6 or 8 on each side, crowded toward the teeth, leaving the corners of the mouth entirely destitute of them; those farthest from the teeth are much the smallest; madreporic plates prominent, transversely elliptical, twice as long as broad (·13 inch by ·6), situated at the edge of the interradial spaces. The projecting angles of the mouth and a space on the lower side of the arms within the disk and bordering the interradial spaces all around, is covered with coarse rounded granulations like those of the upper surface. The space around the mouth and connecting with the median area of the arms is granulated like the lower side of the arms. Color, in alcohol, deep umber; when dry, yellowish brown.

The largest specimen, described above, measures as follows:

From angle of mouth to	1st fork of arms,	·72 of an inch.
" " "	2 " "	·87 "
" " "	3 " "	1·25 "
" " "	4 " "	1·65 "
" " "	5 " "	1·95 "
" " "	6 " "	2·30 "
" " "	7 " "	2·75 "
" " "	8 " "	3·10 "
" " "	9 " "	3·40 "
" " "	10 " "	3·80 "
" " "	11 " "	4·05 "
" " "	12 " "	4·40 "
" " "	13 " "	4·65 "
" " "	14 " "	5·00 "
" " "	15 " "	5·20 "
" " "	16 " "	5·52 "
" " "	17 " "	5·75 "
" " "	18 " "	5·95 "
" " "	19 " "	6·10 "

From center to edge of interradial space ·7. Width of rays, at base beneath, ·4; of 1st forks ·3; of 2nd forks ·15; from outer side of madreporic plate to end of teeth ·4; to corner of opposite mouth-slit ·62; between corners of adjacent mouth slits ·22.

A younger specimen, ·25 inch from center to edge of interradial space and ·3 to end of radial ribs, has the disk prominently five lobed, the two radial ribs of each arm being separated only by a shallow groove. The first fork of the arms is considerably outside of the disk, ·52 of an inch from center of mouth. The arms divide six times. The upper surface is uniformly and coarsely granulated, similarly to that of the larger ones. The lower surface is more uniformly granulated, the disk and region around the mouth presenting nearly the same appearance as the lower sides of arms. The mouth-papillæ are more slender and relatively longer, and extend nearly to the end of the mouth-slits. The madreporic plate is very small and inconspicuous. The hooks of the arms are more conspicuous and numerous.

Another, much younger specimen, measures from the center to edge of interradial space, ·05 inch; to end of radial ribs ·1; to first fork of arms ·18. The arms divide four times and are long and slender, with numerous hooks; the tentacle-scales extend as far inward as the first fork. The radial ribs do not reach the center, where there is a small, much depressed space; they have the form of five very prominent oblong lobes with a shallow dividing line along the top of each. The whole upper surface is covered with coarse rounded granulations, which are arranged in transverse lines on the arms.

Color of dried specimens, yellowish brown, with traces of lighter bands on the arms.

Panama and Pearl Islands, adhering to *Muriceæ*,—F. H. Bradley.[*]

Six specimens of this species, of various sizes, are in the collection.

It appears to be most nearly allied to *A. Caryi* Lyman, of San Francisco, Cal.

Ophiura teres Lyman, Catalogue Museum Comp. Zoöl., I, p. 37, 1865.

This large species is common at Panama and the Pearl Islands, at extreme low-water under stones. About 25 specimens are in the collections of Mr. Bradley.

Some of the larger specimens have rays 5 inches long, with the disk 1·4 in diameter. It is readily distinguished by its stout, round arms, with much broken upper arm-plates. The color is dark olive or purplish brown above, the arm-plates, and sometimes the disk, is thickly speckled with grayish white. Lower side of arms and chewing apparatus light yellowish brown, in life lemon-yellow.

Ophiura Panamensis (Lütken) Lyman, op. cit., p. 32.

Ophioderma panamensis Ltk., Additamenta, hist. Oph., p. 91, 1859.

This species is, apparently, more common than the preceding. Mr. Bradley has sent numerous specimens from Panama. It also occurs at Acapulco (Mus. Comp. Zoöl.), and Cape St. Lucas (Smiths. Inst.).

The larger specimens have arms 4·25 inches long; disk ·9 in diameter.

The color is dark greenish gray or brownish above, sometimes with a central light spot; arms similar in color, banded with lighter and darker. Lower surface grayish or greenish white. Mouth-shields rounded, broad-oval; side mouth-shields granulated.

This species is closely allied to *O. teres*. It may be distinguished by its longer, less convex, and more slender arms; by the upper arm-plates,

---

[*] Since received from Zorritos, Peru, and Gulf of California, at La Paz.—Reprint.

which are either entire or but little broken,—rarely into more than three pieces, which do not disturb the regular arrangement of the plates; by the radial shields, which are naked in this species and nearly always covered in the preceding.* The arm-spines in this species, near the base of arms, are usually eleven in well grown specimens; in *O. teres* of corresponding size nine, and in the largest but ten. There are, usually, one or two more mouth papillæ in the present species. The mouth-shields of *O. teres* are very broad and short, with a nearly straight outer edge, concave sides, and a rounded lobe projecting inward; in this species they are oval, about as long as broad, very convex outwardly, with a slight, rounded angle inwardly. The under arm-plates are relatively wider than in *O. teres* and somewhat different in form. In the latter the narrow space between the upper genital slits and the arms is covered with granulations like the disk; in *O. Panamensis* it is occupied by narrow naked scales, without granulations.

Ophiura variegata (Lütken) Lyman, op. cit., p. 10 (no description).

Ophioderma variegata Lütken. Vidensk. Meddelelser, March, 1856; Addit. hist. Oph., p. 97.

A much smaller number of this species than of the last was collected by Mr. Bradley at Panama. Dr. Lütken's specimens were from Realejo.

It may be distinguished from the preceding by its covered radial shields, naked side mouth-shields, and oval mouth-shields not so broad as in the last. Upper arm-plates undivided, arms depressed and more slender. It is closely allied to *O. brevispina* of the West Indies. Length of arms 3 inches; diameter of disk ·7 of an inch.

The color above is olive-green or greenish brown, with a central blotch and other irregular blotches of reddish scattered on the disk, or sometimes only five, corresponding to the interradial spaces. The arms are conspicuously banded with lighter and darker. The whole lower surface is reddish white.

Ophiura Daniana Verrill, sp. nov.

A depressed species, with short, tapering arms, and partially covered radial-shields. Upper genital openings visible from above, with elevated borders. Side mouth-shields naked. Under arm-plates broad and strongly concave outwardly. Arms speckled above with dark brown, and having a row of distant, circular spots of yellowish-white; beneath white.

Diameter of disk ·55 of an inch; arms 2 inches long; ·15 wide at base. Mouth-papillæ ten or eleven on each side of the mouth-slits;

---

* Mr. Lyman describes the young as having naked radial shields. Our specimens, both large and small, have them covered.

outer one longest, pointed, overlapping the next, which is stout, broad, blunt, and larger than the others, which decrease to the sixth and then increase to the innermost; the inner ones are more cylindrical and pointed. Mouth-shields one-third longer than broad; the outer side broadest, rounded; the sides somewhat converging, a little concave, the inner lateral edges nearly straight, forming the acute inner angle. Side mouth-shields naked, triangular, the side next the angle of the mouth concave; one of the corners reaches the genital slit, another the angle of the mouth, the inner ones are widely separated by the mouth-shields. Under arm-plates nearly twice as broad as long near the base of arms; the outer edge regularly and deeply concave; the outer corners prolonged in an acute angle, bounded on each side by short reëntering lines; the inner lateral lines also concave; the inner end regularly convex, about as broad as the concave portion of the outer edge; toward the middle of the arms they become as long as broad, but still have a similar outline. Upper arm-plates nearly twice as broad as long, the outer edge bounded by a slightly convex line, the inner edge by a parallel, concave one, sides nearly straight, converging inwardly. Side-plates encroaching but little. Disk finely and closely granulated, the granules wholly or partially covering the radial shields, and covering the scales at the base of the arms; just outside of the radial shields and about on a level with the upper side of the arms the edge of the disk rises into somewhat prominent verrucæ, perforated at top by the upper genital openings, which are surrounded with elongated, granule-like papillæ. Radial shields large, usually mostly concealed by the granules; the naked part when present is broad oval or nearly round, widely separated, often with scattered granules. Arm-spines ten at base of arms, the upper ones very small, regularly increasing in length toward the lower side of arm to the ninth; the lowest one is a little shorter than the two above it, which are of equal length, and scarcely reach the middle of the next side-plate. The spines are all acute. Tentacle-scales broad and short, the inner one considerably largest.

Color of upper surface when dried, yellowish brown, the arm-plates speckled with dark brown; along the middle of the arm there is a row of distant, small, circular, yellowish white spots, usually divided between two plates; some of the plates also have very small light spots on their outer edges. Lower surface yellowish white, extending upward in points on the sides of the arms at distances corresponding to the dorsal light spots.

La Union, San Salvador, in 6 or 7 fathoms, muddy bottom,—F. H. Bradley. Two specimens.

This species is very different from the others of this region, but resembles *O. variegata* most. The latter has, however, much longer arm-spines, of which the upper are longest; much longer arms; smaller under arm-plates, which are more hexagonal, scarcely broader than long and convex outwardly; the mouth shields are more rounded, broad oval, more prominent, and less acute inwardly; the mouth-papillæ are different in form, the outermost one being shorter and stouter and not overlapping the next; the upper ovarial openings are slits near the base of the arms, beneath, not visible from above. The color also is quite different.

The peculiarity in the form and position of the upper genital openings may hereafter require this species to be separated generically from *Ophiura*, if accompanied by corresponding internal differences in structure.

Ophiolepis variegata Lütken, Vidensk. Meddelelser, March, 1856; Addit., p.106.

Mr. Bradley has sent specimens of this species, dredged at Panama, of various sizes. From La Union he sent quite a number of very large ones, which came, however, in a badly broken condition. At the latter locality it appears to be abundant, in 6 or 7 fathoms, muddy bottom.

Dr. Lütken's specimen was quite young, agreeing well with some of our smallest ones. The adult specimens present somewhat different characters. It is closely allied to *O. elegans* Lütk. of the West Indies.

The largest specimen from Panama has arms 1·8 inches long; disk ·6 in diameter. The mouth-papillæ, eleven to each angle of the mouth, resemble those of *O. elegans*. The outer one on each side is longer and sharper than the rest, quite overlapping the next one, which, like the succeeding three, is short and broad, with a cutting edge. The mouth-shields are more than twice longer than broad, the outer end rounded; the sides reënteringly curved; the inner edge pointed, with nearly straight sides. Side mouth-shields large, quadrangular, the inner sides longest, slightly concave; the inner lateral sides in contact along their whole extent, the outer edge in contact, for three-fourths its length, with the mouth shield, the outer corner projecting into the genital slit; the outer lateral edge is a little concave, exceeding the inner lateral and about equal to the outer edge. Under arm-plates, toward base of arms, twice broader than long, the outer edge concave, the inner convex, the sides strongly concave; along the middle of the arms they are more nearly square; toward the end of the arms they become longer than broad, with a convex outer edge, concave sides and nearly pointed inner edge. Upper arm-plates broader than long, toward base of arms, the outer and inner edges nearly straight, resembling those of *O. elegans.** Plates of the disk large, very regularly arranged, precisely like those of *O. elegans*. The central one is nearly circular, surrounded by a rosette of five angular ones with convex inner margins. From the central group a row of the large plates radiate to each interradial margin; to the base of each arm radiates another row of these plates, of which the two outermost are smaller and separate the large, oval radial shields, which are pointed inwardly; between each radial shield and the base of the arm there is also a large angular plate. All the plates of the disk are bordered by a row of very small plates. Arm-spines five at the base of the arms, four farther out, short, tapering, the middle ones longest. Tentacle-scales two, short, broad, the inner one largest.

Color, in alcohol, very variable above; in the specimen above described, dark greenish, with a large central blotch of reddish white surrounded by a narrow line of dark brown; each outer interradial plate is of the same color, with a similar dark border. The other plates, both large and small, are speckled with very dark brown. The upper side of the arms are alternately lighter and darker grayish green, with frequent blotches of reddish white. The lower surface is uniformly white or pale flesh-color. Other specimens have the greater part of the upper side of the disk light grayish green, with blotches of dark brownish green, and a central patch of reddish, which appears to be the constant color of the outer interradial plate. The arms also are at times mostly reddish with irregular patches of green, or they may be very regularly banded with reddish and dark olive-green.

A small specimen with arms ·78 of an inch long, and ·25 in diameter of disk, has but three arm-spines at the base of the arms and two farther out. Another, somewhat larger, has four spines at base and three along most of the length of the arms.

Some of the specimens from La Union are ·9 of an inch in diameter of disk; arms 3·25 long; and have six arm-spines at the base of the arms, of which the uppermost ones are longest.

Ophiozona Pacifica Lyman, op. cit., p. 67.

Ophiolepis pacifica Lütken, Vidensk. Medd., 1856; Additam. hist. Oph., p. 104.

A few specimens of this species have been received from Panama and the Pearl Islands, collected by Mr. Bradley. Dr. Lutken's specimens were from Puntarenas in four fathoms.

Our largest specimen has arms 2 inches long, and a disk ·45 in diameter. It was generically separated from the last species on account of the absence of supplementary side pieces to the upper arm-plates. The disk is covered by numerous convex, naked plates, bordered by

---

* See Catalogue Mus. Comp. Zoöl., Pl. II, fig. 5.

small ones; the central one is largest, nearly circular, surrounded by a rosette of several circles of plates, from which a band of three rows of plates radiates to each interbranchial margin, and a less regluar row to the base of each arm between the radial shields; these are longer than broad, pointed at each end, irregular, placed obliquely, and widely separated at the outer edges, which are bordered next to the base of the arms by a large convex plate. The upper arm-plates are quite regular, with nearly straight outer and inner edges, widest outwardly, with slightly concave, diverging sides; near the ends of the arms they become fan-shaped, and the side-plates meet above. Near the base of the arms there are five very short arm-spines, of which the lowest two are slightly longer than the others.

Color, in alcohol, umber-brown above, with slightly indicated bands of lighter brown toward the ends of the arms; below uniformly brown, of a somewhat lighter shade. Young specimens are lighter colored, especially beneath. In another specimen the disk is grayish yellow; upper side of arms the same, with transverse bands of brownish, occupying two or three plates, and an interrupted light stripe, bordered with brown along the middle, formed by a spot of yellowish white on the outer edge of each plate. All the upper plates are mottled with lighter and darker yellowish brown. The upper edge of the side-plates also has a light spot. Beneath uniform yellowish white.

Ophiocoma æthiops Lütken, Addit. hist. Oph., p. 145; Lyman, op. cit., p. 78.

Very abundant at Panama and Pearl Islands, from whence Mr. Bradley has sent about one hundred and fifty specimens. From La Union he has also sent numerous large examples. It occurs also at Acapulco (Coll. Mus. Comp. Zöology), and Cape St. Lucas (Smithsonian Institution).

This species grows to a large size, many of our specimens measuring 8 inches in length of arms; 1·3 in diameter of disk; arms, not including spines, ·3 wide; spines ·3 long.

It is allied to *O. echinata* and *O. Riisei* of Aspinwall and the West Indies, but differs in the shape and proportions of the arm-spines and mouth-shields, as well as by having flatter arms, etc. In *O. echinata* the upper arm-spines are short, blunt, and remarkably thickened; in *O. Riisei* they are long and slender, like the rest, but considerably longer; in the present species they are stout, the lower ones shorter, and somewhat flattened, the upper ones becoming longer and stouter, the uppermost being considerably thickened. In *O. echinata* the mouth-shields are squarish, with rounded corners; in *O. Riisei* they are ovoid, the smallest end inward; in *O. æthiops* they are oblong with rounded corners.

The color, both in alcohol and when dried, is a dark, rich brown or almost black above, occasionally with distinct, broad bands of grayish on the outer part of the arms. Sometimes the disk is blotched with grayish white. Lower surface of arms and chewing apparatus grayish brown, rest like upper surface. Young specimens are lighter colored and more conspicuously banded.

Ophiocoma Alexandri Lyman, op. cit., p. 74.

Several specimens of this species were collected by Mr. Bradley at the Pearl Islands, and a single, large one, at Panama. It occurs at Acapulco (Mus. Comp. Zoöl.), and Cape St. Lucas (Smiths. Inst.).

Our largest specimen has arms about 5·5 inches long; disk ·8 in diameter. The color of the upper side, in alcohol, is yellowish brown on the disk; the arms a brighter shade of the same, with unequal transverse bars of dark brown, the lighter colored plates finely mottled with yellowish-white. Lower surface of arms light yellowish brown, with a narrow longitudinal stripe of darker brown passing along each side of the lower plates. Mouth-shields and other parts about the mouth light brownish yellow.

This species may readily be distinguished from the preceding by its relatively longer and more slender arms; by its brighter and lighter colors, and peculiar markings on the arms; by its disk covered with little spinose grains; by the arm-spines arranged in rows of five to seven, the third and fourth from the lowest being longest, the upper one smallest; by its nearly round mouth-shields, a little truncated inwardly; and by differences in the form of the upper and lower arm-plates.

Ophionereis annulata Lyman, op. cit., p. 143.

Ophiolepis annulata LeConte, Proc. Phil. Acad., v, p. 317, 1851.
O. triloba Lütken, Vidensk. Meddelelser, 1856.
Ophionereis triloba Lütken. Addit. hist. Oph., p. 112.

This species is very common at Panama and the Pearl Islands, Mr. Bradley having sent numerous specimens. It occurs, also, at Cape St. Lucas (J. Xantus, Smithsonian Inst.) and on the west coast of Central America, whence Dr. Lutken received his specimens. Mr. Bradley collected, also, a few specimens at Acajutla, San Salvador. It lives under stones and in crevices at and near low-water mark.

Our largest specimens have arms 3·3 inches long, the disk ·5 broad.

It may be recognized by its long, slender arms, with three rows of spines, of which the middle one is considerably longest. Disk covered with very small scales, larger around the edge, with small, narrow, elliptical, widely separated radial-shields. Upper arm-plates more than twice as broad as long, broadest near inner edge, with very acute lateral angles, and bordered by broad, triangular, supplementary plates.

Color, in alcohol, varying on the disk from grayish to purplish brown, usually thickly covered with light spots; arms yellowish green or greenish brown with numerous dark purplish brown bands extending entirely around the arms, and often with an interrupted dark line along the middle; lower side yellowish gray, the arms crossed by dark bands.

In one specimen the arms are olive-green above, each upper plate having a small dark brown spot in the middle and another broader one on the inner edge, while the supplementary plates have also a similar smaller spot on the upper edge. The transverse bands have the form of large rounded spots of rich, dark brown, surrounded by a ring of yellowish. The arm-spines are greenish, banded with brown. The arms are yellowish beneath, with transverse bars of reddish brown, occupying two or three plates, corresponding to the large spots above.

In other specimens, also well preserved, the disk and arms correspond in their colors, the disk being clear reddish brown, very thickly spotted with light olive-green, of the same tint as the ground-color of the arms, while the transverse bands of the arms are reddish brown, like the ground-color of the disk, but they are partially interrupted, along the median line, by a faint, yellowish band. One specimen from which part of the arms have been partially or wholly broken and again restored, has the disk and uncast portion of the arms reddish brown, the latter with narrow bands of deep brown, while the restored portions of the arms are olive-green, with broad bands of reddish brown.

Ophiocnida hispida Lyman, op. cit., p. 133.
    Ophiolepis hispida LeConte, loc. cit., p. 318, 1851.
    Amphiura hispida Lütken, Addit. ad hist. Oph., p. 119.

Two specimens of this curious species have been received from Panama in the collection of Mr. Bradley. The largest measure 3·15 inches in length of arms, and ·32 in diameter of disk.

This species is remarkable for its very long, slender arms, and its disk covered above and below by small, sharp spines.

The radial shields are narrow, tapering inward to a point, separated by a spiny strip. There are three short, rounded mouth-papillæ, of which the inner one is largest, on each side of the mouth-slits. Arm-spines regular, even, in three rows. The upper surface of arms and disk is straw-colored, with narrow transverse bars and irregular spots of deep brown or blackish; under side dull yellowish.

Amphiura geminata Lütken,* op. cit., p. 122

Ophiolepis geminata LeConte, op. cit., p. 318.
Amphiura geminata Lyman, op cit., p. 180.

Two specimens of this species have been sent from Panama by Mr. Bradley, both of which are injured.

It has long, slender arms, with four rows of spines at the base (in well-grown specimens) and three farther out, of which the middle one is largest and bluntest and somewhat rough. There are three mouth-papillæ on each side of the mouth-slits, of which the outermost is broader than both the others. Mouth-shields lance-shaped, with the inner end acute. Lower arm-plates pentagonal, broader than long, with one angle turned inward. Disk covered by small even scales, a little larger toward the edge of disk. Radial shields narrow, pointed inwardly, in contact, except at the inner ends, which are separated by a scale.

According to Mr. Lyman, a specimen had arms 1·4 inches long, with a disk ·16 in diameter. Our specimens are somewhat smaller, but have the arms broken. They are, in alcohol, yellowish white, with a few small, light brown spots on the upper arm-plates.

Amphiura violacea Lütken, Vidensk. Meddelelser, 1856; Addit. hist. Oph., p. 123.

In the collection from Panama there is a small specimen, apparently identical with this species. Dr. Lütken's specimens were from Realejo.

According to Dr. Lütken, it has the following distinctive characters: Mouth-shields small and lance-shaped; side mouth-shields large and triangular; under arm-plates as long as broad, and separated, like the upper plates, which have the same form as those of *A. microdiscus*† Lütk., but are less broad, by the side arm-plates. Diameter of disk 2^{mm}.

Amphiura Puntarenæ Lütken, op. cit., 1856; Addit. hist. Oph., p. 123.

A single specimen from Panama, too imperfect for description, is doubtfully referred to this species. Dr. Lütken's original description is as follows: The mouth-shields are a little longer than broad, and

---

* This and the other species here named *Amphiura* belong to the genus, *Amphipholis* Ljung,—Reprint.

† *A. microdiscus* Lütken, was described as follows: Disk small, arms thick, but thin at base; upper arm-plates twice as long as broad, outwardly slightly and inwardly strongly curved; lower arm-plates as long as broad, without an indentation; diameter of disk 1^{mm}. Puntarenas, 10 fathoms.

have rounded but very prominent side-angles, so as to become nearly heart-shaped; lower arm-plates longer than broad, having a slight incurvature on the outer edge; upper arm-plates regularly oval, not much broader than long; the disk has a diameter of 2^{mm}; the slender arms a length of c. 20^{mm}. Puntarenas, in 3 fathoms.

The two preceding species and *A. microdiscus* are very small species allied to *A. squamata* M. and Tr., and all have the radial shields joining each other completely; mouth-shields lengthened, rhomboidal; outermost mouth-papilla broader than the other two; lower arm-plates pentagonal with an angle turned inward; upper arm-plates transversely oblong; arm-spines three in number.

Two other species, *A. Örstedii* Lütk., from Puntarenas, and *A. marginata* Lütk. (*Ophiophragmus marginatus* Lyman) from Realejo, I have not seen.

Hemipholis gracilis Verrill, sp. nov.*

A delicate species, closely allied to *H. cordifera* Lyman, with long, slender arms; arm-spines in three rows, tapering, thickened at base; mouth-shields broad pentagonal, with rounded corners; under arm-plates octagonal with rounded corners; a single tentacle-scale.

Arms about nine times as long as the diameter of disk. Mouth-papillæ two to each mouth-slit, situated at the outer lateral edge, slender, somewhat elongated, blunt. The mouth-slits, or spaces between the jaws, are broad and regularly heart-shaped, the indentation in the outer side formed by an acute, triangular projection from the inner arm-plate, which is mostly concealed by the side mouth-shields, which meet above it. The two inner tentacles are situated on each side of this pointed inner angle of the first arm-plate, and within the mouth-slits. Mouth-shields a little broader than long, somewhat pentagonal, the outer edge nearly straight, the outer lateral edges short, the lateral angles rounded, the inner lateral sides longer, somewhat curved and forming a rounded inner angle. Side mouth-shields elongated transversely, meeting in front of the mouth-shields, and also across the arms so as to form a continuous ring around the mouth; the inner side is concave, the outer has a central, projecting, acute angle, extending to the lateral angle of the mouth-shield. Under arm-plates somewhat octagonal, broader than long, toward the base of the arms the outer and inner edges are nearly straight, the lateral edges are composed of three short sides, with rounded angles between, which farther out on the arms become merged into a curved lateral line.

---

* *H. affinis* Ljungman, Ophiur. viventia, Ofv. af Kgl. Vet. Akad. Förh., May (?) 1867, p. 322, appears to be identical with this,—Reprint.

The second, third and fourth plates have a somewhat different form, the outer edge being broader than the inner, and the sides concave. Upper arm-plates broad and somewhat irregular-oval, about twice as broad as long, the inner edge much more strongly arched than the outer, which, on some of the plates near the base of the arms, is slightly concave in the middle. Side-plates encroaching but little above and scarcely any below, except toward the ends of the arms. Arm-spines three, nearly equal, a little thickened near the base, round, slender, tapering, but not sharp. Tentacle-scale oblong, flattened, rounded at the end, hardly twice as long as wide, standing free from the sides of the lower plates, except at the second and third from the base, where they are shorter and in close contact with the lower arm-plates.

Disk, above, covered with unequal, rounded, overlapping scales; a larger, round, central, primary plate is surrounded by smaller ones, and then by five primary ones about as large as the central one, each of which is surrounded by a few smaller scales; from these five a row of primary plates, bordered on each side by smaller imbricated scales, radiates to each interbrachial margin. Radial shields pear-seed-shaped, with the point inward, the outer side strongly arched, the inner sides in contact at the outer end, separated inwardly by three scales, of which the most exterior is elongated and narrow and the most interior broad, rounded, the intermediate one somewhat triangular. Between each radial shield and the base of the arm there are two or three scales and a small papilla-like spine, not one-fourth as long as the arm-spines. Lower side of disk destitute of scales, but bearing minute, scattered granules.

Color, in alcohol, light greenish gray above, darker and more distinctly greenish toward the ends of the arms, which are banded with whitish; radial shields and primary disk-plates green; beneath white, chewing apparatus yellowish.

An average specimen has the arms 1·38 inches long with the disk ·17 in diameter. One of the larger is ·2 in diameter of disk; the arms, though broken at the ends, 1·8. The largest is ·22 in diameter of disk.

Panama,—F. H. Bradley. Eight specimens, 4 fathoms, muddy bottom.

This species very closely resembles *H. cordifera* of South Carolina, which has the habit of living buried in mud at low-water mark and thrusting out of its burrow one of its long slender arms. It differs, however, in the form of the mouth-shields and lower arm plates, as well as in several other particulars.

Ophiactis Lütken.

Of this genus there have been described four nominal species from the Panamic Province, besides one from Peru. Of these, it is probable, as has been suggested by Mr. Lyman, that *O. Örstedii* Lütken, is a synonym of *O. simplex* (LeConte sp.), no differences yet indicated being sufficient to separate them clearly.

The species of *Ophiactis* may be recognized by their rather short arms and stout disk, covered above with overlapping scales and a few, small, scattered spines; usually with separated radial shields. There are commonly four to six rows of arm-spines, which are rough, short, and stout, projecting at right angles from the arms. There is but one tentacle-scale and but one or two mouth-papillæ on each side of the mouth-slits. The species are mostly small and often have six arms.

Ophiactis Kroyeri Lütken, Vidensk. Meddelelser, 1856; Lyman, op. cit., p. 108.

Mr. Bradley has sent several hundred specimens of this species from Callao, Peru, where they were found in abundance among the interstices of *Balani, Discinæ, Mytili*, etc., scraped from the bottom of a vessel that had been a long time in that port. Some of the largest specimens have arms 1·7 inches long and the disk ·35 in diameter. Of this species I have seen no specimens having six arms.

The color varies considerably, but most frequently is dull greenish, in alcohol, with a few irregular bands of purplish brown upon the arms; beneath grayish or greenish white. Some specimens are purplish brown above, with bands of greenish on the arms, and others are yellowish gray, with or without bands of darker. Frequently the upper arm-spines have a spot of white at base. The radial shields are usually darker green or brown than the rest of the disk, and have a yellow spot on the outer end and are sometimes edged with white, or have a white spot at the inner end. In other specimens the radial shields are yellowish with a greenish disk. The disk may, also, be mottled with lighter and darker.

The number and size of the spines upon the disk are also quite variable. In some cases they are nearly or entirely absent, while in others they are quite numerous, long and sharp, scattered all over the disk, except on the large radial shields; more frequently, however, they are mostly confined to the interradial spaces of the disk, and are rather few in number. The radial shields are large, acute-triangular, with the point inward and a prominent, elevated lobe on the corner where they join their neighbors; the inner ends are separated by about four plates, of which the outermost is very narrow and the innermost rounded. The mouth-shields are short and broad, with an elongated, acute point outwardly and a slight angle inwardly. The side mouth-shields are elongated transversely and do not meet within. Mouth-papillæ one on each side of the mouth-slits, short and stout. Lower arm-plates rounded octagonal; upper plates broad-oval, a little overlapping, most convex outwardly. Arm-spines five, the middle one longest.

Callao, Peru,—F. H. Bradley. The specimens of Dr. Lütken and Mr. Lyman came, also, from the same place.

Ophiactis virescens Lütken, op. cit.; Lyman, op. cit., p. 113.

This species may readily be recognized by the upper arm-plates, which are twice as broad as long and have a distinct, projecting lobe in the middle of the outer edge. The arms are somewhat narrowed at the base and very slender at the ends. Under arm-plates as long as broad, octagonal. Mouth-shields roundish rhomboidal, with an angle inward. Two small mouth-papillæ on each side of mouth-slits. Five or six arm-spines, short and stout, rough, upper two longest. The disk-scales bear a few scattered spines, which are sometimes wanting.

Color yellowish green, with narrow dark green bands on the arms, beneath greenish gray. The radial shields are dark green and often have a light spot on the outer ends.

Our specimens all have six arms, except the very young, which lack three, on one side. The largest has arms ·75 of an inch long, with a disk ·15 in diameter. Another has arms ·4 inch, with the disk ·12.

Panama, clinging to Gorgoniæ and sponges. Occasionally adhering among the arm-spines of *Ophiothrix spiculata*,—F. H. Bradley. It occurs at Puntarenas and Realejo,—Dr. Lütken; and Cape St. Lucas,—J. Xantus, (Smiths. Institution).

In one instance I found, in a small cavity of a branching sponge from the Pearl Islands, upwards of fifty specimens of this species, of various sizes, but mostly young. Thirty-seven were quite small, and light colored, and although many had six equal arms, others, of similar size, had three upon one side, very small, appearing as if just starting to grow, or entirely wanting. From this mode of occurrence it is probable that this species, like some *Amphiuræ*, is ovo-viviparous.

In this lot were two specimens differing considerably from all the others. These are among the largest, and have the arms narrowed at base; seven arm-spines, upper ones longest; large radial shields, covering a large part of the disk; broad upper arm-plates, convex outwardly, and destitute of a distinct lobe, or with only a slight central prominence, except near the ends of the arms, where a small, distinct lobe is visible. In most other respects they agree well with the ordinary form, except that the color is light yellowish gray above, with greenish radial shields and an undefined greenish spot on each upper arm-plate, the tips of the arms faintly banded with greenish; yellowish white beneath. Diameter of disk ·17; length of arms ·75 of an inch.

Ophiactis simplex Lütken; Lyman, op. cit., p. 105.

Ophiolepis simplex LeConte, Proc. Phil. Acad., v, p. 318, 1851.
? *O. Örstedii* Lütken,Vidensk. Meddelelser, 1856; Addit. Ad. Hist. Oph., p. 129.

Eight specimens of this species occurred with the last, from Panama.

The species may be distinguished by the small, widely separated radial shields; rounded and regular disk-scales, with very few small spines, except beneath, where they become more numerous; arms longer and more slender than those of the preceding species; mouth-papillæ prominent and flat, one upon each side of the mouth-slits.

The mouth-shields are transversely rhomboidal, with an angle within and without. Five short arm-spines, of which the three middle ones are longest. Upper arm-plates broad-oval without a lobe.

Color greenish, with lighter bands on the arms.

In all our specimens there are six arms. They agree very nearly with *O. Örstedii* Lütken,* which came from Puntarenas.

Ophiactis arenosa Lütken, op. cit., 1856.

There are a few young specimens, found with the last two species, which appear to represent a third species. Whether they belong to the present one or not is somewhat uncertain, owing to their immaturity.

Mr. Lyman places this species as a doubtful synonym of *O. simplex*. Our specimens are insufficient to determine this question satisfactorily.

According to the original description by Dr. Lütken, its characters are as follows: "*O. arenosa* Lütk. Mouth-shields roundish; one mouth-papillæ; upper arm-plates broad-oval; under arm-plates rounded, quadrangular, a little broader than long; four short arm-spines, of which the two middle are the longest.

---

* Dr. Lütken's original description is as follows: *O. Örstedii* Lütk. Mouth-shields broad rhomboidal; one mouth-papilla; five arms; upper arm-plates broad-oval; lower arm-plates octagonal, a little broader than long; five short arm-spines, of which the three middle and longest are only as long as one of the arm-joints.

Color green, with bands upon the arms.

Diameter of disk 4mm. Length of arms 18mm. Puntarenas.

The color seems to have been about like that of the two preceding (*O. Örstedii* and *O. virescens*).

Diameter of disk 5^{mm}; length of arms 20^{mm}.

Puntarenas and Realejo."

In addition to the preceding species of *Ophiactis* there is a single imperfect specimen that may belong to an undescribed species.

It has larger radial shields than *O. simplex*, separated by a row of about three scales, no spines apparent on disk; five arm-spines, the upper one very short, the middle one longest; upper arm-plates short, transversely oblong, nearly three times broader than long, with nearly straight outer and inner edges and slightly rounded sides; mouth-shields rounded; one mouth papilla on each side of mouth slits; under arm-plates somewhat octagonal, outer edge convex.

It has about the size and proportions of our largest *O. virescens*, but has no lobe on the outer edge of upper arm-plates and differs in other particulars. It is probably nearest to *O. simplex*.

The color is dark greenish above.

Until more specimens have been examined, it appears undesirable to apply a new name to this form.

Ophiothrix spiculata LeConte, op. cit., p. 318; Lyman, op. cit., p. 167.

This species is very abundant at Panama and the Pearl Islands, clinging to sponges, Gorgoniæ, etc., whence Mr. Bradley has sent upwards of two hundred specimens. He has also sent it from Realejo, Nicaragua, and Acajutla, San Salvador. It occurs from low water to 4 fathoms.

Our largest specimens have arms about 3 inches long, and the disk ·5 in diameter.

The color, in alcohol, is usually light cobalt-blue or bluish purple, often with every fourth or fifth lower arm-plate red or brownish. Some specimens have spots of red on the disk and more or less on the upper side of the arms. In life the color is described as fuscous above and paler beneath; or greenish with violet upper arm-plates, and occasional red plates on the lower side of the arms.

It is allied to *O. violacea* of Aspinwall and the West Indies,[*] but differs in having longer arm-spines and in several other characters.

The disk usually has the centre and a band radiating to each interbrachial margin and to the base of each arm covered with numerous, very short, branching spines, with more or less numerous, long, slender, thorny spines scattered among them. The arm-spines are long and slender, thorny, the next to the upper one longest.

---

[*] Recently separated from the Brazilian *violacea* and named *O. Caribæa* by Lütken. —Reprint.

Ophiothrix (Ophiothela) mirabilis Verrill, sp. nov.

A small species with six arms, granulated above; disk mostly covered by the large radial shields, and in the longer specimens with central and interradial groups of simple, short, conical spines; arm-spines short, directed downward, armed with hooks. Teeth-papillæ about ten, rounded, arranged in an oval group. Mouth-shields and side mouth-shields closely united to the surrounding parts, so as to form a continuous ring around the mouth, covered with a skin which conceals their outlines, the side mouth-shields about as large as the mouth-shields. Under arm-plates about as long as broad, widest outwardly, the outer edge convex, the sides converging to the rounded inner angle, separated by the side arm-plates, and covered, like the mouth-shields, with a naked skin, which obscures their outlines even in dry specimens. Side arm-plates well developed, bearing upon the very prominent sides about five tapering spines, of which the uppermost is quite small, the next and longest about equal to the width of arm, the others decreasing in size to the lowest, which is very small. When six spines occur the third is the longest. Toward the base of the arms the spines are minutely thorny near the ends, the thorns being chiefly on the lower side of the spines, irregular, and often curved; toward the middle of the arms and beyond, the thorns become more numerous, larger and curved into well-marked hooks. Disk nearly covered above by the twelve prominent, elongated radial shields, which reach nearly to the center and are narrow and blunt at the outer ends. They are in contact, except along the inner portion, where they are slightly separated. Their surface is minutely pitted and more or less covered by scattered, unequal, rounded granules. Between the radial shields and at the center, the surface is covered by a distinct skin, without visible scales. In the interbrachial spaces at the margin of the disk there is a cluster of about six sharp, conical spines, without thorns. A cluster of similar spines sometimes occupies the center. In young specimens the spines are absent. The upper arm-plates are concealed by the skin, which is covered by numerous, rough, unequal, rounded grains, the intervals between the plates being indicated by narrow, transverse, naked spaces.

Color, in alcohol, quite variable, usually dark. One specimen has the disk grayish brown, the outer ends of radial shields bright yellow; the arms with narrow bands of grayish white, bright yellow, and black; beneath yellowish brown, the under arm-plates minutely speckled with dark brown. Another has the disk, above, deep reddish brown, with a lighter center; the outer ends of the radial shields yellowish white; the upper side of arms transversely banded with dark brown and yellowish white.

A medium-sized specimen has arms ·5 of an inch in length, with the disk ·16 in diameter; the two largest yet examined have the disk ·22 in diameter. It is quite probable that all these specimens are young.

Pearl Islands, Bay of Panama,—F. H. Bradley.* Among the interstices of a branching sponge, associated with two species of *Ophiactis*, about a dozen specimens of various sizes were found. Others occurred in colonies clinging to the branches of Gorgoniæ and Muriceæ, with the arms wound closely around the branches.

Subgenus, Ophiothela nov.†

The name *Ophiothela* is here employed to designate a group of Ophiurians, of which the preceding species is the type, agreeing together in having the upper arm-plates covered with granulations as in *Astrophyton*; in having short, rough arm-spines, mostly turned downward, and armed with roughnesses or hooks, beneath, as in *Ophiactis*; in having very large radial shields, covering most of the disk, the intervening spaces being covered with a skin and bearing simple spines; in having the lower side of arms and disk covered with a skin, more or less obscuring the plates; and in having the mouth-shields and side mouth-shields united into a ring around the mouth. The present species and another from the Fejee Islands have, in the numerous specimens observed, always six arms, and have the same habit of clinging closely around the branches of *Gorgoniæ*.

In the structure of the mouth it agrees well with the typical species of *Ophiothrix*, but it differs in having the arms distinctly covered with a membranous skin, and their upper surface granulated; and in the character of the spines of the arms and disk, which lack the glassy appearance and prominent thorny branches, and approach more nearly those of *Ophiactis* in form, structure, and arrangement. Although intermediate in some respects between *Ophiothrix* and *Ophiactis*, it is evident that these species are more closely allied to the former genus, under which I have placed them as a subgenus.

Additional Remarks on Ophiuridæ.

Owing to the small number and imperfect condition of our specimens of some of the species of *Amphiura* and *Ophiactis* I have been obliged to leave them somewhat in doubt and, in order to avoid producing any confusion, have in such cases preferred quoting the original descriptions instead of giving new ones. This seemed still more

---

* More recently from Cape St. Lucas and La Paz.—Reprint.

† This has since been regarded as a distinct genus (p 376). Besides this species and *O. Danæ* V., Feejee Is., a species occurs on *Mopsella* from Japan (Dall), and *Parisis* from Formosa (Lütken),—Reprint.

desirable, since the original descriptions by Dr. Lütken are somewhat inaccessible in this country and have not been translated before.

In the identification of some of the species I have had important assistance from Mr. W. H. Niles, of the Sheffield Scientific School.

In the preceding pages I have enumerated all the species of Ophiurans which we have hitherto received from the Panamic Zoölogical Province, with the exception of an apparently undescribed species of *Ophiura* allied to *O. Panamensis*, and as yet represented by only four specimens.*

The following species, which I have not seen, have been described from the same coast:†

Ophiostigma tenue Lütken—Realejo, West Coast of Central America.
Ophionereis Xantusii Lyman—Cape St. Lucas.
Amphiura microdiscus Lütken—Puntarenas.
Amphiura Örstedii Lütken—Puntarenas.
Ophiophragmus marginatus (Lütken) Lyman—Puntarenas and Realejo.
Ophiothrix dumosa Lyman—Gulf of California.

---

* The specimens referred to have rather slender arms, subcarinate above; radial shields mostly covered, the naked part being oval, widely separated; mouth-shields oval, the narrowest end inward, about as long as broad; side mouth-shields covered; mouth-papillæ eight or nine on each side of the mouth-slits, the innermost and three outermost stoutest; under arm-plates as long as broad, somewhat octagonal, with a slightly convex outer edge and concave sides; arm-spines eight to ten, the lowest one considerably longest; the others decreasing in length to the uppermost, which is quite short.

Color, above, dark olive-green, the disk finely speckled and the arms conspicuously banded with greenish gray. the upper arm-plates with irregular longitudinal dark streaks, and numerous light spots; lower surface yellowish white, the dark bands of the arms passing entirely around, but lighter beneath.

It appears to differ from *O. Panamensis* in having only eight or nine mouth-papillæ instead of from ten to twelve; in the outermost of them being much smaller than the next, instead of projecting beyond it; all of them being relatively larger and less crowded; the tentacle-scales being less unequal in length; the arm-spines more unequal, stouter, and more acute; in the somewhat coarser and less crowded granulation of the disk; in the larger and less sunken radial shields (which are nearly covered, however, in young specimens); and in the coloration. The outer and inner genital slits appear to be nearer together and the inner ones more transverse.

Notwithstanding these differences. I have deemed it best not to give a new name to this form until more numerous specimens can be examined.

Our largest specimen is ·75 of an inch in diameter of disk.

† *Amphipholis grisea* Ljung., Guayaquil. appears to be an additional species,—Reprint.

Order, ASTERIOIDEA.

Luidia tessellata Lütken.

Luidia tessellata Lütken Vidensk. Meddelelser, 1859, Bidrag til Kundskab om de ved Kysterne af Mellem- og Syd-Amerika levende Arter af Söstjerner. p. 16.

Several specimens of this species, of various sizes, were obtained by Mr. Bradley at Panama, and one small one at Acajutla. Dr. Lütken's specimens came from Puntarenas and Realejo.

Our largest specimen measures, from the center of disk to tip of rays, 6·5 inches; to border of disk 1 inch; width of rays at base, not including spines, 1·1. A medium sized specimen measures 3·4 inches from center to end of rays; and ·6 to edge of disk; rays ·7 wide at base.

The rays are depressed and taper regularly to the ends, which are more slender in the small than in the large specimens. The interambulacral* plates bear a slender, sharp, and strongly curved spine on the inner edge, and more externally a group of three or four longer and stouter ones, of which the inner stands singly, the two next side by side, and the outer, when present, singly. The ventral plates are covered with numerous unequal, minute, sharp spines and bear a central row of eight to ten small, stout spines, and usually three long, sharp, marginal ones, which are somewhat curved in the direction of the ends of the rays, and longer than the interambulacral spines (·3 of an inch in large specimens). The upper surface is crowdedly covered with elongated paxillæ, which are much larger along the sides of the rays than in the middle and upon the disk, where they become very small and close. Those of three marginal rows on each side are considerably largest and somewhat quadrangular, bearing at the top a central group of six to ten small, short, blunt, or rounded tubercles, surrounded by numerous, fine, slender, diverging papillæ. Toward the center of the rays and on the disk, they usually bear only one or two small, rounded tubercles, surrounded by similar papillæ.

The color of a dried specimen is yellowish green above and yellow beneath; in alcohol, brownish green above, yellowish beneath.

This species is allied to *L. clathrata* of Florida and the Carolina coast, but has broader and less slender rays; much longer and stouter interambulacral spines; more spinose ventral plates; and much larger and more numerous marginal spines; the paxillæ are not so short and thick, and bear fewer and larger central tubercles.

---

* We use the term "*interambulacral*" to designate the first row of plates bordering each side of the ambulacral furrows of starfishes, believing, as Prof. Agassiz has shown, that they are strictly homologous with the interambulacral plates of *Echini*.

Dr. J. E. Gray has given the name, *Petalster Columbiæ*, to a species from "St. Blas," collected by H. Cuming, which is, apparently, allied to this, but which cannot be the same if correctly described. The diagnosis, which is too imperfect for reliable identification, is as follows: "Rays elongated, slender, gradually tapering; tubercles short, with crowded groups of rather large, acute spines, and a fringe of very fine radiating ones."

In *L. tessellata* the rays are certainly not slender, when compared with other species of the genus, and the "spines" on the paxillæ are not acute.

It is probable that Gray's species has not yet been rediscovered, as is the case with many other starfishes described by him from the collections made by Cuming, on the same coast. But if intended for the present species, the description is so inapplicable and imperfect that it cannot be deemed sufficient to characterize it.

Astropecten fragilis Verrill. sp. nov.

A thin, depressed species, with slender, acutely tapering rays, which, measuring from the center, are about four and a half times the radius of the disk. A specimen measuring 2·3 inches from center to tip of ray has about 40 marginal plates. Each interambulacral plate usually bears three slender spines at the inner edge, the middle one being longest, and outside of these a single longer and stouter, pointed spine. The lower marginal plates are covered on their lower side with sharply pointed spinose granulations and bear numerous small sharp spines, mostly along their outer edges. At the margin these become larger and longer, each plate bearing three or four spines which may be considered marginal, of which the uppermost is usually longest. These are round, rather slender, tapering and acute, slightly curved outward, diminishing gradually in size toward the tip of the ray. The upper marginal plates are low and quite short, those at the interradial angle being shortest, those toward the tip of the rays becoming very small. These are coarsely granulated and destitute of spines or tubercles, except three or four of those at the base of the rays, which, in the larger specimens, bear at the inner edge a small, rounded tubercle, most prominent on the interradial pair of plates, which are also somewhat higher than the rest. The dorsal area is about one and a half times the width of the marginal plates. The lower marginal plates are but little produced beyond the upper.

One of the larger specimens measures 2·3 inches from center to tip of rays; ·5 to edge of disk; width of ray at base ·6; its dorsal area ·4;

height of broadest upper plates ·1, length ·07; length of longest marginal spines ·15.

Panama, at extreme low-water on sand, and Zorritos, Peru,— F. H. Bradley.

A specimen measuring 1·3 inches from center to tip of rays agrees closely with the preceding description, except in lacking the small tubercles on all the upper plates, even at the base of the rays. It has 30 marginal plates.

This species is, in many respects, allied to *A. regalis* Gray, of which I add a description for comparison, but is nevertheless remarkably distinct in form and many other important characters.

Astropecten regalis Gray, Ann. and Mag. Nat. Hist., vi. p. 178, 1840.

A depressed species with broad, short arms, a little contracted at base, scarcely acute. Radius of rays to that of disk at 3 : 1. A specimen 1·5 inches from center to tip of rays, has 23 marginal plates.

The interambulacral plates bear three slender spines at the inner edge, of which the central is nearly twice as long as the others, and outside of these a single, sharp, much stouter, but scarcely longer, spine. The lower marginal plates are closely covered with even, flat-topped granulations, and bear along the outward border from 5 to 8 nearly equal, small, conical spines, and at the upper margin, usually, two large, flattened, blunt or lanceolate spines, which are largest toward the base of the rays, but quite small in the interradial region. They are mostly channeled upon the upper side and convex beneath. The upper marginal plates are low and rather short, closely covered with unequal rounded granules, those upon the middle being largest and, on the plates toward the tip of the ray, enlarging into small rounded tubercles, two, three, or four standing in a transverse row along the middle of the plate. The plates on the basal portion of the ray are destitute of tubercles or spines, in both of my specimens, but older specimens may, perhaps, attain small tubercles even to the base of the ray, since there are fewer on the younger specimen. The dorsal area of the rays is broad, with fine paxillæ. The lower marginal plates project considerably beyond the upper.

The larger specimen is 1·5 inches from center to tip of ray; ·48 to edge of disk; width of ray at base ·5, of dorsal area ·3; length of longest marginal spines ·18.

Panama,—F. H. Bradley; San Salvador,—Capt. J. M. Dow (Coll. Smiths. Institution).

It is quite probable that the *Astropecten cœlacanthus* Martens,*

* Monatsb. der Akad. der Wiss., Berlin, Jan., 1865, and translated in Annals and Mag. Nat. History, vol. xv, p. 435, 1865.

may be the more mature condition of this species. It agrees in most of the characters, except in having small tubercles on all the upper marginal plates and in the character of the spines of the lower surface. In form and the peculiar character of the marginal spines, it agrees very closely. This specimen was considerably larger (radii of rays 49^{mm}; of disk 17^{m}) and came from Costa Rica.

Gray's original description of this species,* which, though very brief, agrees, quite well with our specimens, is as follows: " Upper plates spineless, lower produced." " Rays one-fourth longer than the diameter of the body, broad, tapering; spines broad, stout, depressed." " Like *A. marginatus*, but the arms are shorter and broader." San Blas,—Mr. Cuming.

Astropecten Örstedii Lütken, Vidensk. Meddelelsor, 1859.

Rays moderately long, rather broad at base, tapering regularly to the acute ends. Greatest to least radii as 5 : 1. A specimen measuring 3 inches from the center to the end of the rays has 36 marginal plates. Interambulacral plates each with an inner row of three slender spines, of which the central is a little longer than the others, and outside of these a single, large, blunt spine, which is somewhat flattened, and nearly twice as long as the inner ones. Exterior to these the same plates bear several slender, short spines. Lower marginal plates broad, projecting a little beyond the upper, closely covered with short, blunt, spicula-like spines, and bearing a transverse series of five or six strong, sharp spines, which bend somewhat toward the tip of the ray. The first of these spines are of about the same length as the larger interambulacral, toward the margin of the ray they increase in length, the longest being ·35 of an inch long and very strong and sharp. The uppermost row is irregular and the spines smaller. The upper marginal plates are narrow and high, the two basal ones of each ray bearing a large, conical, sharp spine, ·2 inch or more long; all the others, two subequal, smaller spines, of the same shape, which form two regular rows. Central region of the rays covered with paxillæ, which are longer and less crowded than in most species. Around the center of the disk some of the paxillæ have a cen-

---

* This species may be at once distinguished from the preceding by its broad, short rays, which do not taper to long slender points, by the broader disk and dorsal area of rays, by the stouter spines of the lower plates, which are flattened and rather blunt, instead of round and sharp, and by the even granulation of the lower surface, and much less spinose character, which gives it a smoother appearance. The small tubercles of the upper plates, also, are more developed toward the tip of the rays, while in the preceding they appear only at the base.

tral acute spine, rising above the general surface. Madreporic plate large, very near the marginal plates.

Length of rays from center of disk 3 inches; to edge of disk ·6; width of rays at base ·65; of central, dorsal area ·4 of an inch.

Panama,—F. H. Bradley.

A small specimen in the collection of the Smithsonian Institution, apparently belonging to this species, collected at Cape St. Lucas by J. Xantus, presents the following peculiarities: Radius of rays 1 inch, of disk ·3. The rays have the same form as in the preceding. The upper marginal plates are narrow and rather high, formed as in the large specimen; there are 20 on each side of the rays; the two occupying the interradial angle bear, each, a single long sharp spine; the next three or four bear two smaller spines, while the remaining plates, even to the end of the ray, bear a single small spine. The lower marginal plates are closely granulated and each usually bears five or six spines, of which the three lower are short and sharp, and the two upper long, round, sharp, and somewhat bent, resembling, except in size, those of the larger specimens.

Dr. Lütken's specimens are intermediate in size between the two preceding, and differed from the large specimen, above described, chiefly in having the inner row of upper marginal spines confined to the inner three to eight plates, instead of extending nearly to the tip of the rays.

Astropecten Peruvianus Verrill, sp. nov.

Rays narrow, elongated, acute, with the angle between somewhat rounded. Greatest to least radii as 5 : 1. In a specimen two and a half inches from the center to tip of rays there are 34 marginal plates. Interambulacral plates each with three slender spines at the inner margin, of which the central is much the longest; exterior to these each plate bears a somewhat stouter, blunt spine, of about the same length, and several very small spines. The lower marginal plates project but little beyond the upper, each bearing about five small, sharp spines, the three lower being shorter than the inner interambulacral, the two upper considerably longer and larger (about ·1 of an inch long). The upper marginal plates bear, each, a small conical spine at the inner edge, and several of those toward the ends of the rays have also a very small spine on the central part. Dorsal area of the rays narrow, depressed at the middle of the ray, somewhat exceeding the width of a marginal plate. Madreporic plate small, about its own diameter from the marginal plates.

Length of rays, from center, 2·5 inches; to edge of disk ·5; width of rays at base ·5 of an inch.

Paita, Peru,—F. H. Bradley; Dr. C. F. Winslow (Boston Soc. Natural History).

Whether *A. stellatus* Gray, is identical with this species cannot be determined by his very imperfect description, which applies equally well to several other species.

His description of *A. stellatus* is as follows: " Rays more than twice the diameter of the body; narrow central area of the rays equal to one series of marginal tubercles. Coast of South America?"

Müller and Troschel place this, with doubt, as a synonym of *A. Valenciennesii* M. and Tr., Vera Cruz.

Patiria obtusa Gray, Proc. Zoölogical Soc. London, 1847, p. 72.

In the collection of Mr. Bradley* there is a specimen, which I refer to this very imperfectly described and hitherto obscure species.

Greater radius ·95 of an inch; smaller ·60. From pentagonal, with regularly concave sides; rays short, rapidly tapering and somewhat obtuse at the end; upper side convex. The ambulacral grooves are deep and narrow, bordered by rounded interambulacral plates, which bear four or five long, rather slender spines in a single row, of which the one next to the outermost is usually the longest, and the one nearest the mouth considerably the shortest. Outside of these and parallel with them is another row of spines of about the same number, form, and size, and borne upon plates of similar character, which are connected with the inner row, and directly opposite to them. The ventral plates of each triangular area, toward the mouth, bear from four to six slender, sharp spines, a little shorter than those along the ambulacral grooves, placed in a single transverse series on each plate, or sometimes in a crescent-shaped group; toward the margin of the disk the plates and spines rapidly diminish in size, each plate bearing three or four very small and slender spines, mostly placed transversely side by side. The margin is formed by a row of small rounded plates, without a sharp edge, and closely covered with minute granule-like spines. The dorsal surface, near the margin between the rays, is covered with small, close, uniform plates, which bear closely crowded, circular or rhomboidal clusters of minute papilla-like spines, which are subdivided at the end into microscopic radiating points. The plates increase in size toward the central area, and at a short distance from the margin become crescent-shaped and separated by the dorsal pores, with other much smaller rounded plates between them, each of which bears a small rounded cluster of small spines, silmilar to those borne by the larger plates, which are longer toward

---

* The locality is uncertain, probably Panama, but perhaps Paita,—Reprint.

the center than upon the plates near the margin, but have the same character. These thorny spines in the central region are still very small and slender, two or three times longer than thick, and form densely crowded, large, crescent-shaped, or small rounded groups, according to the shape of the plates. The crescent-shaped plates extend along the middle of the rays to near the tip, and are accompanied everywhere by the dorsal pores, which are large and numerous. There is a small central area, occupied by small rounded plates, with pores between them, at the edge of which is placed the small madreporic plate, composed of but few convolutions. A narrow band, extending from the central area toward the margin, in the middle of each interradial region, is destitute of pores.

Color, in alcohol, yellowish-red.

The original description by Dr. Gray is so brief and imperfect as to render the identification of this species somewhat uncertain. It is as follows: "Brown, depressed, 5 or 6 rayed; rays depressed, rounded at the end; dorsal surface with lunate ossicules crowded with short spines; oral surface with circular groups of crowded spines in the middle of each ossicule. Panama, 6 to 10 fathoms."

This description, so far as it goes, agrees tolerably well with our specimen, except that the groups of spines on the oral surface cannot properly be called "circular." In this case, as in many others, Dr. Gray does not mention the size of the specimens described, so that no account can be taken of variations due to difference of age, which are often very great among starfishes.

Asterina (Astericus) modesta Verrill, sp. nov.

Form pentagonal with slightly concave edges and broad, very short, rounded rays. Radii as 7 : 5. The interambulacral plates bear three or four small, slender spines, forming a single row along the ambulacral grooves. The ventral plates each bear one or two sharp spines, a little larger than the preceding, in the region near the mouth, and more numerous and much smaller ones near the margin. Margin thin and sharp, with a fringe of minute sharp spines, 6 or 8 to each plate. The dorsal surface is covered with imbricated plates which are finely granulated, and each bears upon its upper margin from 5 to 15 minute sharp spines. The plates rapidly increase in size from the edge of the disk to the central region. Dorsal pores in five imperfect rows along each ray and many scattered about the central region of the disk. One of the larger specimens measures ·35 of an inch from center to end of ray; ·25 to edge of disk.

Panama and Pearl Islands,—F. H. Bradley.

Oreaster occidentalis Verrill, sp. nov.

A large species, resembling in form and character of the upper surface *O. gigas* Lütk. (*O. reticulatus* M. and Tr.), but less spinose above and not at all so beneath; marginal plates without spines, or only a few near the ends of the rays. Greater to smaller radii as 2¼ : 1.

The largest specimen has a greater radius of 4·3 inches; smaller 2. Another has the radii respectively 3·8 and 1·7 inches. Form pentagonal, with a large, elevated, angular disk, and narrowed, rather slender, short rays. The margin between the rays is regularly and deeply incurved, without a distinct angle. The interambulacral plates bear an inner row of slender spines, seven or eight on each plate near the center, and four or five toward the end of the rays, the middle ones longest, the others decreasing in length on each side to the outer ones, which are quite short, thus forming pointed groups. Outside of these there is a second row of much larger, short, flat, blunt spines, three to each plate on the inner and only two on the outer portion of the rays, the middle one, when there are three, being a little the longest and considerably largest, but when there are but two the one nearest the mouth is usually, but not always, largest. The ventral surface is destitute of spines and covered with coarse, irregular, crowded, unequal granules, among which there are scattered numerous, sessile, two-lipped pedicellariæ, with narrow, elongated openings. In one specimen the ventral plates, especially near the mouth, have a central group of larger, elevated granules, some of which become twice as high as thick, with a somewhat acute point, thus approaching the character of small spines. On each side of the rays are 18 lower and 17 upper marginal plates in the larger specimen, and one less of each in the smaller. The lower plates belong entirely to the ventral surface and are covered with coarse granules similar to those of ventral plates, becoming finer and more uniform at the outer margin. They all bear numerous small, oblong-oval, sessile pedicellariæ, and in the largest specimen are destitute of spines and tubercles, but in the smaller, from two to four of the plates nearest the end of the rays bear small, stout, obtuse spines or tubercles, which are surrounded at the base by granulations, but naked above. The upper plates, which form the margin, are thick and convex, rather rounded, much longer than those of *O. gigas*, closely covered with small, angular, convex granules like those of the whole upper surface, among which there are numerous, scattered, sessile pedicellariæ, like those of the lower plates. In the larger specimen none of them bear spines, but in the other there are from one to four that bear small, short, stout, blunt, conical spines near the ends of the rays. The upper surface of the arms and disk i reticulated with elevated plates and connecting ossicles, as in *O. gigas*, which bear at most of the nodes or intersections small, conical, naked spines of unequal size, each on a large conical tubercle, which is granulated. Around the central area there is a well-marked pentagon, with a large conical tubercle at each angle, corresponding to the rays, and a small one on each side, opposite the interradial region. Within this pentagon there are four spine-bearing tubercles around the slightly convex anal region, and a few others irregularly placed. From the angles of the pentagon a row of large, spine-bearing tubercles, from fifteen to twenty in number, extends along the middle of each ray. The spaces between the reticulations of the upper surface are pierced by very numerous pores, among which there are many small oval pedicellariæ. Other similar, but more elongated, pedicellariæ are frequent on the spine-bearing tubercles. Madreporic plate small, fine, situated considerably outside of the dorsal pentagon. Color, in alcohol, grayish brown; in life the dorsal plates are bright crimson, the spaces between, greenish brown.

Panama, two specimens, dredged, in 6 to 8 fathoms,—F. H. Bradley.

This species is allied to *O. gigas* of Florida and the West Indies, but the latter has larger and more numerous spines on the upper surface; much smaller upper marginal plates, each bearing a conical spine; more coarsely granulated lower marginal plates; ventral plates bearing one or two short conical spines; outer row of interambulacral spines formed by much larger and longer, subacute, stout spines, one to each plate, instead of flat, thin, truncate spines standing two or three to a plate, as in *O. occidentalis*. The pedicellariæ of the ventral surface are very much smaller and different in form, those on the marginal plates are less numerous and more rounded.

Under the name of *Pentaceros Cumingii*, Gray has briefly described a very small specimen, which may, possibly, have been the young of this species, but none of the characters given are applicable to our specimens, and the presence of marginal spines in so small a specimen, when they are almost entirely wanting in large ones, is a character which seems to render their identity extremely improbable.

Gray's description is as follows: "The arms are rather narrow, nearly as long as the diameter of the body; marginal spines few, small; back rather depressed, with conical protuberances, bearing small spines. Diameter 12″. Perhaps the young of a much larger species."

Punta Santa Elena, rocky ground, 12 to 18 fathoms,—H. Cuming.

Nidorellia.

This name was applied by Dr. J. E. Gray* to a section of his genus *Pentaceros* (*Oreaster* M. and Tr.), which included only the following species. Although the character of having movable spines, which he attributed to it, seems not to exist, it has so many important differences from typical *Oreaster*, in external form and structure, which we must suppose to be connected with still more important internal peculiarities, that it appears worthy of being separated as a distinct genus.

Until a comparative study of the internal structure shall have been made we can only indicate some of the more important external peculiarities for distinctive generic characters.

Such are the broad depressed disk, the short, broad, depressed rays, rounded at the ends; the elevated margin, with large plates, those at the ends of the rays largest and swollen.

Nidorellia armata Gray.

Pentaceros (*Nidorellia*) *armatus* Gray, Ann. and Mag. Nat. Hist., vol. vi, p. 276, 1840.
Oreaster armatus Müll. and Tr., System der Asteriden, p. 52, 1842.
Goniodiscus armatus Lütken, op. cit., 1859, p. 75 (p. 51 of pamphlet).
Oreaster armatus Lutken, op. cit., p. 148, 1864; E. von Martens, Monatsb. Akad.. Berlin, 1865, and Ann. and Mag. Nat. Hist., xv, p. 433, 1865.

Numerous specimens of this species were collected by Mr. Bradley at Panama and the Pearl Islands, and Zorritos, Peru. It occurs on the reefs at low-water. Prof. B. Silliman has, also, presented two specimens from Panama. It is also found at Realejo and Puntarenas,—Dr. Lütken; Punta Santa Elena,—Dr. Gray; Gulf of Nicaragua, Costa Rica,—Dr. E. von Martens.†

Our largest specimen is 6·5 inches in diameter, the smaller radius being 2·75 and the greater 3·25.

The specimens vary greatly in the number and arrangement of the large conical spines; and in the spines of the marginal plates, which may be numerous, both above and below, or entirely absent. The pedicellariæ are also very variable, sometimes being entirely absent, while other specimens have numerous large, two-lipped ones, near the mouth or scattered on the lower surface, and smaller ones on the lower marginal plates, or even on the upper ones. All these variations are too inconstant to allow the species to be divided into varieties. Sometimes the extreme variations are found on the different rays of the same specimen. The number of spines of the dorsal sur-

---

* Annals and Magazine of Natural History, vol. vi, p. 275, 1840.
† Capt. Pedersen has recently sent several large specimens from La Paz,—Reprint.

face and of the marginal plates increases with age, though not regularly, since some specimens of large size have fewer than others, which are much smaller. I have not yet seen two specimens that agree in the number of the spines.

One specimen, which may be considered as representing the *average condition* of adult specimens, has the following characters. Form pentagonal, with regularly incurved sides and short, broad, rounded rays. Greater radius 3·3 inches; smaller 2·2. Dorsal surface a little convex. Interambulacral plates, near the mouth, bear five or six flat, blunt, slender spines, forming a single row, the two middle ones longest; toward the end of the rays there are but three, of which the middle one is the longest. Outside of these there is a row of very stout, thick, rounded spines, with obtuse ends, arranged one opposite each cluster of the interambulacral spines, those near the mouth largest, the size diminishing to the end of the rays, where they become small and more pointed. The ambulacral furrows turn upward at the end of the rays and terminate between the swollen upper plates, between which there is, also, a small plate, bearing a small conical tubercle. The lower surface is covered by coarse rounded granulations, that become finer and closer toward the marginal plates, which they completely cover, and bears numerous, regularly arranged, short, stout, blunt, conical spines or tubercles, which also decrease in size from the center to the margin. Among these are scattered many short, stout, oblong, two-lipped pedicellariæ, which are more numerous near the center, but vary greatly in number upon the different rays. The lower marginal plates belong chiefly to the ventral surface, except near the end of the rays, where they form more of the margin. There are eight of these to each side of a ray, all are convex, those in the interradial spaces being smaller than those toward the end of the rays, except the last one, which is smaller than any other and somewhat triangular. Each of these plates bears a short, stout, conical spine larger than those of the lower surface. The upper marginal plates, which form the greater part of the margin, are somewhat irregular in number and form, there being either seven or eight upon each side of the rays, of these the four nearest the end of the rays, on each side, are about as long as broad, very convex, the last one largest and swollen, joining its mate on the other side of the ray. The six or seven plates that occupy the interradial portion of the margin are less convex and much broader than long, one or two of them bearing near the lower side a stout conical spine. Each of the four outer plates of the margin, except one of the outermost ones, bears a similar conical spine; these are mostly larger than those of the lower plates. In the center of the upper surface there is a stout conical spine upon a tubercular prominence, and around it are ten similar spines, five of which correspond to the interradial spaces and five to the rays, and from the latter a row of five or six similar spines extends along the median line of each ray. In the interradial regions of the upper side there are from three to five similar spines placed irregularly. The spines of the upper surface and margin are smooth and naked, except at the base, which is surrounded by a ring of crowded, polygonal, flat-topped granules, like those that cover the general surface. More than half of the upper surface is covered by large groups and clusters of pores, which occupy all the intervals between the plates and often blend together into large patches on the rays. Among the pores are scattered very numerous, small, short and stout, oblong pedicellariæ. A few similar, but somewhat larger pedicellariæ occur upon the lower marginal plates, either singly or in small groups. The madreporic plate is large (·3 of an inch in diameter), slightly convex, of fine texture, placed about an inch from the center, just outside of one of the ten spines that surround the central area.

The largest spines in this specimen are ·28 long and ·15 in diameter at base; they are united to the plates by a suture, which readily separates, when the specimens are not well preserved, leaving a smooth depression, but they do not appear to have been movable.

Color, in alcohol, deep reddish brown above, yellowish brown below. When living, bright scarlet, (F. H. Bradley).

Some of the more prominent variations from the preceding condition are as follows:

2d. A specimen with the greater radius 2·3 inches. Pedicellariæ of lower surface smaller and less numerous; marginal plates seven above and below on each side of the rays, less unequal in size and form, with small pedicellariæ, very numerous on many of the upper plates, less so on the lower; lower plates mostly bearing conical spines, but some having a group of three or four small rounded tubercles instead; upper plates mostly without spines or tubercles, one ray having two spine-bearing plates near the end on one side, another having two on each side, but not on corresponding plates, the rest without any; a few plates with groups of small tubercles, apparently where spines have been broken off. Upper side with a central large spine and a row of three or four spines along each ray, no spines in the interradial region.

3d. Greater radius 2·5 inches. Similar to the last, but the marginal plates are nearly destitute of pedicellariæ, and the lower ones all bear a spine, while the upper ones, except one or two near the ends of the rays are without spines or tubercles. Four of the interradial regions of the upper surface have each a single large spine near the margin, and one of them also a small one inside the madreporic plate; the fifth has no spine.

4th. Greater radius 3 inches. Lower surface with very few large pedicellariæ, eight lower and seven upper marginal plates, the outermost two the most swollen; all the lower plates bearing a spine; two or three of the upper ones near the ends of the rays bearing small spines, and many of them with a few scattered pedicellariæ. Central dorsal spine surrounded by ten spines, and only one of the interradial regions having a spine near the margin. Five or six spines along the middle of the rays.

5th. A specimen of the same size as the last. Lower and upper marginal plates without tubercles or spines, except two or three of each at the end of each ray, which bear small spines; most of them bearing scattered, large, oblong, sessile pedicellariæ. Interradial regions with from four to seven large, sharp spines.

6th. The largest specimen, with the greater radius 3·75 inches. Lower surface nearly destitute of pedicellariæ, a few very small ones on most of the upper marginal plates. The latter are more uniform in size and shape than usual, from three to five of the outermost bearing small spines, the rest without spines or tubercles, except that one of the middle ones, on three of the interradial margins, bears a spine. Central dorsal spine surrounded by ten spines, with two other spines irregularly placed within the ring. The median row of spines along the rays has from seven to ten spines. The interradial regions bear from nine to thirteen spines in unequal, but somewhat regular, groups.

7th. A specimen, having the greater radius 3·3 inches, has groups of from six to eight interambulacral spines in the inner row. Each of the interradial spaces beneath bears from two to six stout, unequal, irregularly placed pedicellariæ. There are eighteen lower and sixteen upper marginal plates along each interradial margin, all of which are destitute of pedicellariæ. Each of the lower ones bears a short, blunt spine, largest near the end of the rays. The three upper plates nearest the ends of the rays alone bear spines, the rest are evenly granulated. There are from seven to nine spines along the median ridge of the rays and from four to six, regularly placed, in the interradial regions. Besides the usual ten spines around the central one, there are four others, forming an imperfect inner circle around it and corresponding to four of the radial rows.

Goniodiscus stella Verrill, sp. nov.*

Form pentagonal, with short, acute rays, and regularly concave sides. Radius of rays to that of disk as 8 : 6. Marginal plates, in a specimen one half inch from center to end of rays, five on each side of rays, those above and below corresponding. These plates are squarish, about as broad as long, diminishing regularly to the tips of the rays. The interambulacral plates bear each three or four short spines of which the central one is slightly longer and larger; these form a single range along the groove. Outside of these there is a row of slightly longer and much stouter, flattened, oval, blunt spines, which do not reach the end of the rays. The ventral plates are closely granulated, those nearest the margin bearing one and sometimes two small rounded tubercles on the center. The marginal plates, above and below, are closely and finely granulated; the two of the lower series, next the end of the rays, bear each a small rounded tubercle. The dorsal surface is covered by very regular hexagonal plates, which are covered by rounded, unequal granulations, coarser and less crowded than those of the margin. These plates are nearly flat and each is surrounded by six pores, placed at the angles, except a few of those opposite the angle between the rays, which lack a part of the pores. The central area is surrounded by five somewhat larger plates, corresponding with the interradial spaces, and by five others a little more prominent outside of these, alternating with them and corresponding with the rays, which have, along the central line, a row of plates that are a little more prominent, but not appreciably larger than those of the general surface. The anus is central, surrounded by fine irregular plates. Color, in alcohol, grayish yellow.

The only specimen seen, which is probably young, is ·48 inch from center to end of rays; ·3 to edge of disk; length of largest marginal plates ·08; diameter of medium sized dorsal plates ·05 of an inch.

Cape St. Lucas, Cal.,—J. Xantus (Coll. Smithsonian Institution).

Since the above has been put in type, another large specimen has been sent us from Zorritos, Peru, by Mr. Bradley, agreeing in most of its features with the one described, but having characters that cause it to approach *Nidorellia armata*. This specimen, therefore, leads me to suspect that both may, possibly, prove to be the young of the latter.

The Zorritos example measures, from the center to end of rays, ·72; to edge of disk ·48. Six plates on the sides of the rays, above and below. Most of the ventral plates bear a small rounded tubercle; the larger spines of the row outside the ambulacral grooves are stout,

---

* This has since been ascertained to be the young of the preceding species,—Reprint.

short, and flattened, diminishing to the end of the rays. The outermost two, lower, marginal plates bear a small rounded tubercle. The plates of the upper surface are regularly arranged, polygonal, surrounded by from six to ten pores, and bearing oblong, sessile pedicellariæ, which do not rise above the granules; five of the plates around the center, corresponding to the median line of the rays, are more prominent and bear short, thick, round-topped, naked tubercles, forming a pentagon; from these a line of ten plates extends along the middle of each ray, a few of them bearing one or two very small, rounded tubercles. The middle of the disk is a little more elevated than in the smaller specimen.

Linckia.

We follow Dr. Lütken in retaining the name *Linckia* (Nardo, in part) for the group having the *Asterias lævigata* Linn. as its type, not deeming its previous use in Botany a sufficient reason for rejecting it. This genus corresponds nearly with *Linckia* of Gray and includes the typical species of Nardo. It corresponds with the section *b* of *Ophidiaster* in the "System der Asteriden" of Müller and Troschel. *L. unifascialis* departs considerably from this generic type, and may ultimately require separation.

For the genus *Ophidiaster* we take *O. ophidianus* Agassiz, as the type, as most authors have done. Thus it corresponds to the group as restricted by Gray and by Lütken, and nearly to the section *a* of Müller and Troschel.

For the group typified by *Asterias variolata* Lam., we have adopted Gray's name, *Nardoa*, which has two years priority over *Scytaster* of Müller und Troschel, and has the same species for its type, although some additional species were added to it by the latter authors. This group corresponds in part to *Linckia*, of Nardo and of Agassiz, and to *Scytaster*, as restricted by Lütken.

Linckia unifascialis Gray.

Linckia (*Phataria*) *unifascialis* Gray. loc. cit., 1840.
Ophidiaster (*Linckia*) *unifascialis* Lütken, Kritiske Bemærk. om forskj. Söstjerner, Vidensk. Meddelelser, 1864, p. 165.
? *Ophidiaster suturalis* Müll. and Troschel, System der Asteriden, p. 30, 1842.

We have received a large number of specimens of this species from Panama and the Pearl Islands, and Zorritos, Peru, collected by Mr. Bradley, and from Cape St. Lucas, collected by J. Xantus for the Smithsonian Institution. Dr. Gray's specimens were collected by Hugh Cuming in the Bay of Carracas, on rocks at low water. Dr.

Lütken received his specimens from Cape St. Lucas through the Smithsonian Institution, and one from Acapulco from the Museum of Comp. Zoölogy.

The disk is small and the rays are slender, slightly tapering, rounded-triangular. Proportion of radii as 7 or 8 : 1. The mature specimens of average size have the greater radii 3·7 inches; the smaller ·5; width of rays at base ·5.

The interambulacral plates bear an inner double row of short, crowded, papilla-like, alternately unequal spines, and an outer row, close to the inner, of similar form, but stouter and nearly uniform in size. The plates are placed obliquely and each one bears on its inner side a very small blunt spine, and a little more outwardly and to one side, a much stouter one, which is flat, broad and truncated at the end, but narrowed at base, and so arranged that the smaller ones stand within and appear to alternate with them. On its outer portion each plate also bears a still larger and stouter, but scarcely longer, truncated spine, forming the outer row. The lower side of the rays, outside of the interambulacral plates, is formed by four or five rows of small, squarish, equal, and regularly arranged plates. Beyond and joining these along the sides of the rays there is a row of similar plates, but more than twice as large. Above these, and occupying about half the width of the sides of the arms, there is a continuous longitudinal belt of pores, without intervening plates. Along the middle of the arms there is a wide belt of irregular, angular, crowded plates, larger and more convex than those of the lateral rows. The plates are everywhere covered with similar, crowded, coarse, rounded granules, which are largest near the ambulacral grooves. The poriferous belts are covered with finer, rounded granules. The madreporic plate is large, irregular in form, adjacent to the convex, central, anal area.

Color, in alcohol, light yellow or reddish.

I am unable to find anything in the description of *Ophidiaster suturalis* M. and Tr. by which it can be distinguished from this species. Its origin was unknown.

A somewhat larger specimen, without authentic locality, presented to the Boston Society of Natural History by Mr. Horace Mann, differs in having the lateral poriferous region divided into two, for one or two inches from the base of the rays, by a row of plates like those of the dorsal series, with which they unite outwardly, forming thus a wider region of plates without pores on the outer part of the rays. This specimen has also three madreporic plates, regular and normal in structure. The inner interambulacral plates, near the base of the rays, form only a single series, alternately larger and smaller, the larger ones broad, flat, truncated. Outside of these a row of larger ones, similar in form, but much stouter.

This form, which does not appear to be a distinct species, may be *Linckia bifascialis* Gray. It occurs, also, at Cape St. Lucas.

Ophidiaster pyramidatus Gray.

Ophidiaster (Pharia) pyramidatus Gray, Ann. and Mag. Nat. Hist., 1840.
Ophidiaster porosissimus Lütken, op. cit., 1859.

Mr. Bradley has sent numerous specimens of this species from Panama and the Pearl Islands. We have also received specimens from the Smithsonian Institution collected at Cape St. Lucas by J. Xantus. Dr. Gray's specimens came from the Bay of Caraccas, West Columbia, on rocks,—Hugh Cuming. Dr. Lütken received his from Puntarenas. It therefore has, like the last species, a range extending through the whole extent of the Panamic Zoölogical Province. It occurs on the reef at Panama, with the last, at extreme low-water of spring tides, among rocks.

The original description by Dr. Gray is as follows: "Rays subangular, elongate, nearly four times as long as the width of the pyramidal body, with seven rows of tubercles; the central dorsal series much the largest; spines near the ambulacra ovate, subacute."

Our numerous specimens show that the pyramidal form of the body is merely due to the state of preservation, the specimens in alcohol showing little or nothing of this character, while in a part of the dried specimens it is pretty well marked.

The ratio of the greater to the smaller radius is as 7 or 8 : 1. A specimen, with rays 4·6 inches long, has the radius of the disk ·6; width of rays at base ·7; elevation of dorsal surface of disk ·9.

The rays are rounded, somewhat swollen, tapering very slowly to the thick, obtuse, rounded ends. The rays, in small specimens, and those that are in the process of restoration after being broken, have more acute tips.

The interambulacral plates bear two elongated, blunt spines on the inner edge, of which the one nearest the mouth is a little longer than the other and twice as thick, flattened and subclavate at the ends. These form a single, crowded row of alternately larger and smaller spines along the edges of the ambulacral furrows. Outside of these there is a row of distant, short, stout spines, blunt at the ends and narrow at the bases, which arise from the outer part of every second or third plate. Joining the outer edges of the interambulacral plates there is a close row of stout, somewhat convex plates. At intervals of one or two of these plates transverse series of two or three or more smaller plates connect this row with a similar row of larger convex plates along the sides of rays, thus leaving oblong spaces which are occupied by numerous pores. Three other longitudinal belts of similar poriferous spaces, alternating with rows of convex plates, occupy the sides of the rays, while along the dorsal median line there is a broader, irregular, often double row of larger and more irregular plates.

The whole surface, above and below, is covered by coarse, short, convex granulations, with other minute ones intervening. Sessile pedicellariæ, with oval openings, scarcely raising above the granules, are scattered on the lateral plates, and numerous smaller ones occur among the pores. They often have the slit divided across the middle, so as to appear double.

Color, in alcohol, dark grayish or yellowish brown, when dry, often tinged with purplish brown above. In life variegated above with purple and brown.

Mithrodia Bradleyi Verrill, sp. nov.

Disk small; rays five, round, elongated, not rigid; dorsal surface coarsely reticulated and covered with numerous, small, scattered, papilliform spines, and with a median and about three lateral rows of large, stout spines, roughened, like the small ones, with small spinule-like granulations.

Radii as 7 : 1. Length of rays from the center 4·3 inches; radius of disk ·6; width of arms at base ·6, somewhat enlarged farther out; length of longest spines ·25, diameter ·08. The interambulacral plates bear an inner row of very slender, small, sharp spines, from five to seven to each plate, the middle ones longest, forming rounded clusters, in which the spines are connected together by a web to the ends; and close to these, on the outside, a simple series of much longer, stout, round, strongly granulated spines, one to each plate, most of which have enlarged tips. Outside of these the ventral and lateral parts of the rays are openly and coarsely reticulated and bear, on each side, three irregular rows of large, distant spines, those of the first row, near the interambulacral spines, shorter and more numerous than the others, which are separated by distances about equal to their length. All these spines are movable at base, and are round, somewhat tapering, obtuse or rounded at the ends, and covered with closely crowded, coarse, elongated grains, which become longer and more spiniform at the tips of the spines. The dorsal surface of disk and rays is less firm, and more finely reticulated, bearing very numerous, scattered, small, roughly granulated spines (some of which also occur among the lateral spines), and an imperfect median row of large, distant ones, like those of the sides, but somewhat smaller. The entire surface, between the spines, is covered with coarse, rough granules. Madreporic plate subcentral, small, narrow, elongated, composed of a few radiating lamellæ. Color, in alcohol, reddish brown.

Panama,—F. H. Bradley. One specimen, at low-water of spring tides, on rocks.*

This species is interesting as showing the propriety of retaining Gray's genus *Mithrodia*, which was established to receive *M. spinulosa* (Linck. sp.) and *M. clavigera* (Lamarck sp.). The former is said to be an *Asteracanthion* by Müller and Troschel, and the latter seems to be but little known. For these reasons the necessity of retaining this genus has been doubted by some authors. The present species, however, which agrees well with the characters assigned by Gray, and must be closely allied to *M. clavigera*,† cannot, with propriety, be united to any other genus. It is not at all allied to *Asterias* (*Asteracanthion* M. and Tr.), but approaches more nearly to *Ophidiaster* and allied genera. The ambulacral pores are large and form but two rows.

Heliaster helianthus Gray.

Asterias helianthus Lamarck; Blainville, Actinologie, tab. 23, fig. 5.
Asterias (Heliaster) helianthus Gray, Ann. and Mag. N. H., 1st series, vi, p. 180, 1840.
Asteracanthion helianthus Müll. and Tr., Syst., p. 18, 1842.

Numerous specimens of this species, both large and small, were sent from Callao, and a few from Paita, Peru, by Mr. Bradley, a part preserved in alcohol and a part dried. It occurs, also, at Caldera, Chili,—Capt. W. H. A. Putnam (Coll. Essex Institute). It is found on rocks at low-water, adhering very firmly.

Disk broad, rays short, slender, about thirty or thirty-five. Radii as 8 : 5. A medium-sized specimen measures from center to end of rays 4 inches; to edge of disk 2·5; length of rays beyond disk variable, longest about 1·5.

The interambulacral plates bear a single row of rather long, stout, blunt spines, one to each plate, a large and small one often alternating; outside of these, but near them, the ventral plates bear about

---

* Two specimens have since been sent from La Paz, by J. Pedersen.—Reprint.

† Another species of this genus, with remarkably long arms, which must be nearly allied to the *M. clavigera*, was collected at the Sandwich Islands by Mr. Horace Mann, and by him presented to the Boston Society of Natural History.

three rows of spines, which are crowded and rather indistinct, decreasing in length outwardly from the ambulacral grooves, those of the first row being of about the same size and shape as the interambulacral. Beyond these on the sides of the rays there are three, more distant, regular, longitudinal rows of short spines, those of the two lowest being conical and somewhat sharp; those of the upper flattened, and blunt, or dilated at the ends. On the dorsal side, each ray has a crowded, irregular, broad, median belt or row, and a more simple, crowded, marginal row on each side, all of which extend to the central area of the disk, where the spines become very numerous and irregularly crowded. All the spines of the upper surface are short and thick, with enlarged, rounded tips. Numerous, very small, short, pointed pedicellariæ are scattered over the surface between the spines, and beneath, among the lateral and ventral spines, there are other much larger ones, which are short, broad-oval, with pointed tips. Madreporic plate small, inconspicuous, irregular.

Color, in life, dark greenish brown, the spines reddish, yellowish, or light green.

Heliaster microbrachia Xantus, Proc. Phil. Acad. Nat. Sci., 1860, p. 568.

A few specimens that appear to be identical with this species were collected by Mr. Bradley at Panama and the Pearl Islands, on rocks at low-water, and in cavities higher up. The original specimens of Mr. Xantus were obtained at Cape St. Lucas.

Disk very broad, rays relatively shorter than in the preceding, small, slender, about thirty in number. Radii about as 3 : 2. A medium-sized specimen measures from center to end of rays 2·8 inches; from center to edge of disk 2; the free part of the rays varies in length from ·5 to 1 inch.

The interambulacral plates bear a single row of slender, blunt spines, which are quite long toward the mouth, but shorter than in preceding species on the free part of the rays; small spines frequently alternate with the larger ones. Outside of these along the lower and lateral sides of the rays there are about four regular longitudinal rows of longer and stouter spines, not clearly distinguishable into ventral and lateral, but those of the upper rows are more flattened and clavate at the ends. The dorsal side of the rays is covered with numerous, small, slender, sub-acute, nearly equal spines, arranged along each margin in a distinct row, which extends inward on the disk, but not forming a distinct median row, the surface between the marginal rows being nearly evenly covered with the spines, among which indications of five or six indistinct rows may, sometimes, be traced. The surface of the disk is thickly covered with similar spines, irregularly scattered, except toward the outer part, where they have a tendency to form radiating rows continuous with those on the rays. Minor pedicellariæ small, short and thick, thinly scattered among the spines on the disk, but becoming very numerous toward the end of the rays, less so among the lateral and ventral spines. Major pedicellariæ not observed. Madreporic plate rather large, oval.

Color, in alcohol, brownish black above, yellowish below.

This species is closely allied to the preceding, but is quite different in appearance. It may by distinguished by its relatively shorter rays; the much smaller and sharper spines of the upper surface, which are much more numerous and scattered, and do not form three distinct rows on the rays; by the larger and more uniform lateral and ventral spines, which are crowded toward the ambulacral furrows.

Heliaster Cumingii Gray.

In a collection from Zorritos, Peru, Mr. Bradley has sent several specimens of various sizes, which are, perhaps, the species described by Gray. He also collected a few specimens at Paita.

These resemble in form *H. helianthus*, but have exceedingly short rays, ranging in number from 34 to 41. One of the largest specimens measures from the center to end of rays 4·5 inches; to edge of disk 3·8, the rays being mostly about half an inch in length. A smaller one has a greater radius of 3·4 inches; lesser 2·8. The length of the rays varies from one-eighth to less than one-tenth of the entire diameter. The spines of the upper surface, also, are less numerous, and much stouter, with more swollen tips, which are rounded and capitate. They are arranged in a regular, simple, marginal row on each side, and an irregular median series, sometimes forming a regular double row, all the rows extending inward to near the center of the disk, where they become irregularly scattered, but have nearly the same form and size. The interambulacral spines form a single row, one to each plate, and are mostly rather stout, with enlarged, blunt tips. Outside of these, toward the edge of the disk, there is a row of spines of about the same length, but stouter and more clavate, and flattened at the ends. On the sides of the rays there are, in addition, two or three imperfect rows of similar, but shorter and more flattened spines.

Zorritos, and Paita, on rocks, at low-water,—F. H. Bradley.

Under the name of *Asterias* (*Heliaster*) *Cumingii* Dr. Gray* very briefly described a species, allied to or identical with this, as follows:

---

* Annals and Magazine of Natural History, 1st series, vol. vi, p. 180, 1840.

"Arms 30 or 31, very short, not one-tenth as long as the diameter of the body, conical, with blunt spines."

"Inhabits Hood's Island, on rocks at spring tides, H. Cuming, Esq."

Heliaster Kubiniji Xantus, loc. cit., p. 558, 1860.

A good specimen, agreeing well with this species, was presented to us by Mr. Horace Mann, who obtained it, with several other characteristic Panamic species, from Mr. Pease at the Sandwich Islands. It probably came from Acapulco or Mazatlan. Mr. Xantus obtained his original specimens at Cerro Blanco, off Cape St. Lucas.*

Disk relatively smaller than in either of the preceding species; rays twenty-three, longer and rounder, gradually tapering. Radii as 2 : 1. From center to end of rays 3·2 inches; to edge of disk 1·6.

The interambulacral spines are subequal and blunt, and form a single, close row, one to each plate. Just outside of these there is a row of longer and very stout ventral spines, obtuse and flattened or clavate at the ends. Beyond these there are three lateral rows of much smaller and shorter, tapering, blunt spines, regularly arranged. The dorsal surface of the rays has five regular rows of larger, short, obtuse, and mostly clavate spines, the median row having larger spines than the two on each side, which are regular and equally spaced. All the dorsal rows extend inward to the central area of the disk, where the spines become irregularly scattered, and much larger and stouter, with dilated, truncate, or even concave ends. Minor pedicellariæ very small, ovate, pointed, very numerous on the upper side of the rays near the ends, and among the lateral and ventral spines. Madreporic plate small, very convex, about half an inch from the center.

This species is very different from the two preceding. It is readily distinguished by its fewer, longer, and rounded rays; by the five regular rows of spines on their dorsal surface; by the larger, stout spines of the central part of the disk, often dilated and capitate or concave at the end; by the very stout spines of the first ventral row; and smaller and more equal interambulacral spines.

Dr. Gray has very briefly described, in the work previously cited, under the name of *Asterias* (*Heliaster*) *multiradiata*, a species that seems, in some respects, allied to this. His description is as follows: "Arms 22 or 24, cylindrical, elongated, tapering at the ends, one-third longer than the diameter of the body; the dorsal series of spines rather longer and more compressed.

Inhabits Hood's Island,—H. Cuming, Esq."

---

* Capt. J. Pedersen has recently sent it from La Paz,—Reprint.

Whether the Hood's Island referred to be the one in the Galapago Group, bearing that name, is somewhat uncertain.

In the character of the dorsal spines and the much longer rays, his description differs widely from our specimen.

Stichaster aurantiacus Verrill.

Asterias aurantiacus Meyen, Reise um die Erde, 1834.
Stichaster striatus Müll. and Trosch., Wieg. Arch., vi, B. ii, p. 323, 1840.
Tonia atlantica Gray, Ann. and Mag. Nat. Hist., vi, p. 180, Nov., 1840.
Asteracanthion aurantiacus Müll. and Trosch , System der Asteriden, p. 21, 1842.

Numerous specimens of this species were obtained by Mr. Bradley at Callao, Peru, on rocks at low-water mark. It has also been described from Chili.

Its color in life, according to Mr. Bradley, is bright orange; dried specimens are dull yellow.

The following species, which was omitted in its proper place, on page 272, following *L. tesselata*, is inserted here chiefly on account of the peculiar interest connected with its geographical distribution.

Ludia Bellonæ Lütken, Kritske Bemærkn., Vidensk. Meddelelser, 1864, p. 133.

Two specimens, apparently identical with this species, were collected at Callao, Peru, by Mr. Bradley. The specimen described by Dr. Lütken was believed to have come from Guayaquil. If this be true, it is the only instance known to me of a species of starfish common to the Peruvian and Panamic faunæ, except *Heliaster Cumingii*, but neither of these have been found at Panama.

Our largest specimen, preserved in alcohol, has a greater radius of 3·7 inches; lesser, ·5. Another dried specimen is about half as large. The five rays are narrow, more convex than usual in this genus, scarcely depressed, the edges not thin. Interambulacral plates bearing three spines (occasionally but two) the inner one slender and shorter than the others, curved, the outer one stoutest, straight, a little longer than the middle one. Ventral plates bearing very small, slender, papillary spines, and a transverse row of about five large blunt ones, increasing in size to the margin, the longest about equal to the outer ones on the interambulacral plates. The paxillæ of the upper surface are unequal in size, the large ones are arranged in transverse rows of about six on each side of the rays, and bear a short, blunt spine in the middle, surrounded by 8 to 12 very small, shorter radiating papillæ. Smaller paxillæ are scattered among these and also occupy the disk and middle of the rays.

Color, in alcohol, yellowish, mottled with dark brown above.

Order, ECHINOIDEA.

In the identification of several species of the following Echini I have been greatly aided by Mr. Alexander Agassiz, of the Museum of Comparative Zoölogy, who kindly compared with me a set of our specimens with the types of species described by himself in the Bulletin of the Museum, and also gave in exchange authentic specimens of several of those species. Without this assistance some of the identifications could not have been made with so much certainty as was desirable.

Cidaris Thouarsii Valenciennes.

Cidaris Thouarsii Agassiz and Desor, Catal. Rais. des Echinides, Ann. des Sci. Nat., vi, p. 326, 1846.

Mr. Bradley has sent numerous specimens of this species from Panama and the Pearl Islands, where it occurs among rocks and in cavities at low-water. It has been described from the Galapago Islands and California (Ag. and Des. Cat. Rais.). The Smithsonian Institution has presented specimens from Cape St. Lucas, collected by J. Xantus.[*]

This is closely allied to *C. annulata* Gray, common at Aspinwall and the West Indies, but differs in the wider and more closely granulated median area of the interambulacra and in having much stouter and relatively shorter spines, which are more coarsely sculptured on the surface. The large spines are round, largest a short distance above the base, and then slightly and gradually diminish to near the ends, which are enlarged and obtuse. A specimen 1·25 inches in diameter has the large spines 1·3 long, ·15 in diameter. The small spines at their bases are flat, thin, spatulate, obtuse at the ends. The ovarian plates form a regular five-rayed star, more distinct than in *C. annulata*. Color of the larger specimens, when dry, deep brown, with the larger spines light purplish brown. Young specimens, in alcohol, have the spines light purple, banded with white.

Diadema Mexicana A. Agassiz, Bulletin Mus. Comp. Zoöl., No. 2, p. 20, 1863.

We have received from the Museum of Comparative Zoölogy, through the kindness of Mr. A. Agassiz, a good example of this species, collected by him at Acapulco. In the Smithsonian Institution there are a few young specimens, apparently of the same species, collected at Cape St. Lucas by J. Xantus.

Our specimen has a test 2·25 inches in diameter, 1·25 high; diame-

---

[*] Sent in abundance from La Paz, by J. Pedersen,—Reprint.

ter of the actinal area, not including actinal cuts, 1·10; extreme diameter, including cuts, 1·25; of abactinal area ·3; longest spines about 5 inches in length, ·07 in diameter.

This species is allied to *D. Antillarum* Phil. of Aspinwall and the West Indies, but may be at once distinguished by its much larger actinal area, as compared to the abactinal area, or to the diameter of the test. In *D. Mexicana* the proportion of the actinal area to the diameter of the test is about 1 : 2·05, in *D. Antillarum* as 1 : 2·3. In *D. Mexicana* the large tubercles of the outer interambulacral rows continue nearly to the ovarial plates, diminishing but little in size, and there is less space, also, above the median rows than in the other species.

The sutures between the interambulacral plates are rather deep and well marked. The spines are very long and sharp, about twice as long as the diameter of the test.

Color of the dried specimen brownish black, spines black. Young specimens about half an inch in diameter, from Cape St. Lucas, have the spines regularly banded with deep purple alternating with purplish white.

Echinodiadema, gen. nov.

Test depressed, circular. Actinal cuts slight. Buccal membrane with five principal groups of oblong scales, bearing numerous slender spines and pedicellariæ. Ambulacral pores trigeminate, the poriferous zones wider beneath, where the rows of three pairs are more transverse. Tubercles arranged much as in Diadema,—two principal rows in the ambulacra, and four in the interambulacra, of which the external ones are smaller and border the poriferous zones. Anal membrane small, covered with small scales. Spines long, slender, hollow, externally resembling those of Diadema.

Echinodiadema coronata Verrill, sp. nov.

Test circular, much depressed, actinal opening one half the diameter of test, with very slight cuts, its membrane partially covered by five principal groups of large oblong scales, which support numerous slender, somewhat clavate spines, ·1 inch long, and numerous short, rounded pedicellariæ. Ambulacral pores large, in arcs of three pairs, becoming more oblique below, where the zones are wider; tubercles in two rows, rather large, with a median zigzag line of miliaries. Interambulacra about twice as wide as the ambulacra, with two rows of tubercles, somewhat larger than those of the ambulacra, reaching the abactinal region; external to these are two irregular rows of small tubercles bordering the ambulacra; and between them two imperfect rows of about the same size, arranged alternately, with smaller miliaries scattered among them. The three uppermost tubercles of both the ambulacral and interambulacral systems are very small, and the two next the last bear very small slender spines with globular, bright purple tips. The ocular and genital plates bear each a somewhat longer, slender spine. Abactinal system small, somewhat angular, depressed, spines twice as long as the diameter of the test, rather stout, with conspicuous verticillations, annulated with narrow bands of purplish brown and light brown.

Diameter of test ·85 of an inch; height ·35. Cape St. Lucas, Lower Cal.,—J. Xantus. From the Smithsonian Institution.

Astropyga venusta sp. nov.

Test circular, much depressed, nearly flat below, fragile, the ambulacra considerably elevated above the general surface on the upper side. Actinal area about one third the diameter of the test, its membrane covered with unequal scales. Ambulacral zones about one third as wide as interambulacral at the periphery, not varying much in width to the actinal area, but tapering gradually to a point on the upper surface where they are elevated and conspicuous. Pores in arcs of three pairs, which are much more oblique above than below. Ambulacral tubercles alternating in two rows, variable in size, largest on the lower surface. Interambulacral tubercles in eight principal rows, the four median not extending much above the outer curvature of the margin, leaving a naked portion above. The tubercles of the external row are largest but extend only a little further toward the center, with about three tubercles more. The row next to the external has much smaller tubercles and extends to the summit. The naked spaces radiate from the center and soon fork, one branch passing down between the second and third rows of tubercles along each interambulacral border. These spaces are much depressed toward the center and are light purple, with a row of dark purplish spots extending to the end on each side, just within the second row of tubercles, and terminating at the periphery. The color of the lower surface is light yellowish, extending upward in the center of each interambulacrum in a broad petal-like space between the purple forks of the naked area; and in other narrower lobes, embracing the ambulacra and outer interambulacral tubercles, to the ocular plates. Spines very slender and unequal in length, the longest about one half the diameter of the test, finely barbed and longitudinally striated, light flesh-color, or greenish with narrow bright purple bands. Actinal cuts not deep. Diameter 2·3 inches; of actinal area ·75; of abactinal area ·35; height of test about ·75.

A much larger specimen has a test 4·4 inches in diameter, with longest spines 3·5 inches long; anal area ·55 in diameter; genital plates ·35 in length, ·28 in breadth; ambulacra ·45 wide at the periphery.

In this specimen the ambulacra are much more elevated above the abactinal area and interambulacra of the upper surface than in the smaller ones. The genital plates are large and acutely triangular, projecting considerably into the interambulacral spaces, forming a well-marked star. The interambulacral zones are over five times as wide as the ambulacral at the periphery, where they have ten or twelve rows of large tubercles, with a few small tubercles irregularly scattered among them. Near the edge of ambulacral zones, on each side, a row of primary tubercles extends upward to the fifth plate from the abactinal area; between this row and the ambulacra there is a row of smaller alternating tubercles extending a little higher; and on the other side another similar row of small tubercles extending as far as the genital plates. The next row of primary tubercles attains only to the periphery; and the third, counting from the ambulacra, terminates two plates below; the fourth extends six plates higher than the third, and considerably beyond the outer arch of the shell; the fifth ceases two plates earlier than the fourth; and the sixth one plate sooner, or scarcely above the outer arch. The median spine-bearing area of the ambulacra has, therefore, a broad petal-like form on the upper surface, reaching about midway to the abactinal area and considerably beyond the fourth row of primary tubercles, its upper portion including only small scattered tubercles. Its outline is well defined, owing to the contrast between the light yellow color of this area, and the deep purplish brown of the naked space above and on each side of its upper portion. The ambulacral tubercles are unequal in size and form two irregular rows.

The color is nearly like that of the first specimen described, but somewhat darker. The spines of the upper surface are greenish, banded with purple; below, yellowish or reddish white with few purple bands, or quite plain.

Two specimens in alcohol, intermediate in size between those above described, agree well with the characters indicated. The buccal membrane bears a few very small and slender spines, scattered over the surface and more numerous near the mouth. The spines of the lower surface are all small, slender, rarely exceeding an inch in length, the largest ones enlarged and flattened near the ends, mostly light yellow in color, with faint bands of purple. The long spines are greenish at the base and have narrow bands of bright purple; the short spines of the upper surface are light green, with narrow purple bands.

In life, according to Mr. Bradley's observations, the spots along each side of the interambulacral zones are bright blue and very conspicuous.

Panama and Pearl Islands;* one specimen was found on the reef at low-water, the others were dredged in four or five fathoms, on shelly bottom,—F. H. Bradley.

This species has probably been confounded, hitherto, with *A. radiata* of the Indian Ocean, at Zanzibar, etc., to which it is closely allied.

Echinocidaris stellata (Blainv. sp.) Agassiz and Des., Catal. Rais., 1846.

Echinocidaris incisa A. Agassiz, Bulletin Mus. Comp. Zoölogy, No. 2, p. 20, 1863.
Echinocidaris longispina Lutken, Bidrag til Kundskab om Echiniderne, p. 62, Vidensk. Meddelelser, p. 130, 1864.

A large number of specimens of this species, of various sizes, were collected by Mr. Bradley at Panama and the Pearl Islands, where they occur at low-water mark on the reef, among stones and in crevices. At Zorritos, Peru, he obtained many specimens of large size, and, also, a few from La Union, San Salvador. From the Essex Institute we have a specimen from Margarita Bay, Lower California. It also occurs at the Galapago Islands (Agassiz and Desor), and at Guayamas (A. Agassiz), and Realejo (Dr. Lütken). Mr. Bradley obtained one living specimen at Paita, Peru.

The specimens described by Mr. A. Agassiz were not fully grown, and differ in some respects from larger ones.

A specimen from Zorritos, measuring six inches in diameter, including the spines, has spines two inches in length; others have somewhat shorter spines. The spines near the center of the upper surface are quite short, but increase rapidly in length toward the periphery, where they are longest, round, moderately slender, gradually tapering. On the lower side they diminish rapidly in size and length and have flattened tips; around the actinal area they are quite small.

A specimen having the test 2·1 inches in diameter, and 1·35 high, has the actinal opening 1 inch in diameter; the anal area ·3; from the outside of an ocular plate to the outer point of the opposite genital plate ·6; length of genital plates ·22; greatest width ·2; breadth of ambulacral zones at periphery ·42; of interambulacra ·85. Test usually regularly arched above, often a little depressed.

The genital plates are large, pointed outwardly, and project into the interambulacra so as to form a very distinct star; inwardly their

---

* More recently sent by J. Pedersen from the Gulf of California, near La Paz,—Reprint.

sides unite together for a short distance so that the ocular plates do not join the anal area; the madreporic plate is much larger than the others. The anal area is broad-oval, its four plates usually prominent. The ambulacral zones are, ordinarily, somewhat elevated and in some cases considerably so, giving a somewhat pentagonal form to the outline of the test. They bear two regular rows of tubercles, nearly as large as the interambulacral beneath and on the sides, but becoming very small above and disappearing before reaching the summit. Interambulacra with large naked median spaces, extending about half-way to the periphery; sutures between the plates rather deep and conspicuous. The plates are very broad, fifteen forming each vertical series in the specimen above measured. The tubercles are very large on the sides, forming six vertical rows, which are not crowded. The two middle rows are represented at the periphery by a few tubercles only; the two next extend from the actinal area to within about five plates of the summit; the outer row on each side continues even to the ocular plates, but the two or three upper tubercles are much smaller than the lateral. Actinal area sub-pentagonal, the cuts shallow. Auricles short and broad, the supports widely separated at the ends.

Color of test, in dried specimens, grayish or purplish brown, weathering to purplish white or rose-color; the lower half or the whole of the outer end of the interambulacral plates deep purple, in the naked spaces of the upper surface, forming a double series of conspicuous, alternating, angular spots; genital plates variegated with purple; spines dark purple.

A specimen 1·35 inches in diameter of test has but eleven interambulacral plates in the vertical series and but four rows of large interambulacral tubercles, with a very few belonging to a fifth row. In this the auricular supports are short, broad at the ends, where they are in contact or overlap.

Specimens ·4 in diameter have but eight plates in the vertical series. The outer row of interambulacral tubercles reach the summit, but the intervening rows are represented only by three or four irregularly placed tubercles on the lower surface. The spines are mostly flattened and channeled at the ends, the longest equaling the diameter of the test. Sutures more marked than in the large examples.

An examination of a large number of specimens of all ages and from various localities has convinced me that the *E. stellata* of Agassiz is the same as *E. incisa* A. Ag. Dr. Lütken's work was printed before he had received that of Mr. Agassiz. He has suggested that his species might prove identical with *E. stellata*.

Echinocidaris spatuligera Agassiz, Catal. Rais., 1846.*

Echinus spatuliger Val., Voyage Vénus. Zoöl., pl. 5, fig. 2, 1846.

Numerous specimens of this species were found by Mr. Bradley both at Callao and Paita, Peru, thrown upon the shore after storms. It has been recorded from Coquimbo (Catal. Rais.), and from North Chili (Philippi).

A specimen of the usual size has a diameter of 2·1, not including spines; height 1·3; longest spines 1·8; diameter of actinal area ·98; of anal area ·28; from the outside of an ocular plate to the outer end of the opposite genital plate ·48; length of genital plates ·13; width ·15. Test with a regularly rounded outline, often subconical, sometimes regularly arched above, usually less depressed than the preceding species.

The genital plates are rather small, with an obtuse angle outwardly, the adjacent ones usually separated completely by the ocular plates, which reach the anal area, except the two next to the madreporic plate. The ambulacral zones have two close rows of tubercles, which become very small on the upper surface and do not reach the summit. The interambulacral plates are narrower and more numerous than in the preceding species, 18 forming a vertical series: those near the outer parts and beneath, except near the actinal opening, bear four tubercles, forming obliquely transverse rows on the plates and eight vertical rows in each interambulacral zone, of which the two middle rows are irregular and consist of smaller tubercles. The primary tubercles, below and on the sides, are crowded, subequal, of moderate size. The row next the ambulacra reaches the ocular plates, the upper tubercles, like those of all the other rows, being very small; the next row ceases at the fourth plate from the summit; the third, two plates sooner; the fourth, two or three plates sooner than the third. The median naked spaces of the upper side are, therefore, narrow and less distinctly bounded than in *E. stellata*, owing to the smallness of the surrounding tubercles.

The color of dried specimens is dark reddish brown, much lighter beneath; spines reddish or purplish brown. Young specimens have purplish poriferous zones, and grayish brown interambulacral spaces.

A specimen ·9 of an inch in diameter has five rows of interambulacral tubercles with rudiments of a sixth. The outer rows reach the summit, but the next cease at the sixth plate from it.

A young specimen, ·5 in diameter, has but four rows of interambulacral tubercles, the two outer rows reaching the summit, the others scarcely extending above the outer curvature of the sides.

* A recent examination of this species confirms its identity with that of Valenciennes, but the latter differs in its flatter spines, which in ours is variable,—Reprint.

This species is readily distinguished from *E. stellata* by much more numerous, more crowded, and smaller interambulacral tubercles; by the narrower and more numerous plates; by the much smaller genital plates, which are outwardly obtuse instead of acute, so that they do not form a well marked star, and are broader than long, while in *E. stellata* they are longer than broad. The lateral union of the genital plates in front of the ocular plates is a good distinctive character for the latter species, as well as the greater size of the abactinal star; deeper sutures between the plates; and the variegation of the test.

This species in some respects corresponds with *E. Davisii* A. Ag., found from Long Island Sound to Virginia, while *E. stellata* may be considered the Pacific representative of *E. punctulata* of the Carolina coast and Florida.

Arbacia nigra Gray.

Echinus niger Molina, Hist. Nat. du Chili, p. 175.
Echinus purpurescens Val., Voy. Vénus, pl. 5, fig. 1, 1846.
? *Echinus grandinosus* Val., op. cit., pl. 11, fig. 1.
Echinocidaris (*Tetrapygus*) *nigra* Agassiz, Catal. Rais., 1846.

This species was found at Callao, Peru, in great abundance by Mr. Bradley, thrown upon the beaches, and also living at low-water mark among rocks. It has been recorded from Paita, (Ag. and Desor).

The Essex Institute has specimens collected at Caldera, Chili, by Capt. W. H. A. Putnam, who also collected it at Mejillones.

Psammechinus pictus Verrill, sp. nov.*

A small species with a regularly rounded profile, somewhat hemispherical in form, but slightly depressed. Spines slender, moderately long, one fourth the diameter of the test. Actinal region large, nearly one half the diameter of the test, its membrane covered with small irregular scales. Ambulacral zones about two thirds as broad as interambulacral. Pores in regular arcs of three pairs, which become much narrower beneath. Ambulacral tubercles in four series, those of the two exterior relatively large and prominent, not crowded; between these the miliaries form two somewhat irregular rows. In the poriferous zones a small tubercle separates the successive arcs, forming a regular row of distant tubercles, not larger than the largest miliaries. Interambulacral spaces with two principal rows of tubercles, near the exterior, about the same size as the principal ones of the ambulacra. Exterior to these are two outer rows of much smaller tubercles that do not reach the summit; in the space between the two principal rows similar secondary tubercles are distantly scattered; miliaries numerous around the larger tubercles. Ocular and genital

---

* Mr. A. Agassiz thinks this the young of *Lytechinus semituberculatus* V.,—Reprint.

plates each with a group of small, unequal tubercles. Abactinal area small, closed by five principal plates of unequal size.

Color of spines, on a specimen dried from alcohol, bright purple, test light purple with yellowish white bands extending from the actinal area along the poriferous zones and covering the adjacent tubercles as far as the outer curvature of the sides, forming thus a ten-rayed star. An undefined space around the ocular and genital plates is also yellowish white. A narrow black ring surrounds the teeth. Diameter of the largest specimens about one inch.

Cape St. Lucas, Cal.,—J. Xantus, (Smithsonian Institution).

Lytechinus A. Agassiz, Bulletin Mus. Comp. Zoöl., p. 24, 1863.

Hemiechinus (*pars*) Girard, MS. (Coll. Smithsonian Inst.).
Psilechinus Lütken, Bidrag til Kunskab om Echin., p. 25, 1864.

This genus agrees with *Psammechinus* in having the pores in oblique rows of three pairs, and in the scales of the buccal membrane, but differs in having deeper actinal cuts, with thickened, or sometimes revolute, edges; and in having partially naked median spaces on the upper part of the ambulacral and interambulacral zones. The species also attain a much greater size than is usual in *Psammechinus*.

The *Echinus variegatus* may be regarded as the type. In the Smithsonian Institution there are specimens of *L. Carolinus* Ag. under the name of *Hemiechinus nobilis* Girard MS., but I cannot find that such a genus has ever been published.

Lytechinus roseus Verrill,

Boletia rosea A. Agassiz, op. cit., p. 24.

Numerous large specimens of this fine species were dredged in Panama Bay, in 6 to 8 fathoms, shelly bottom, by Mr. Bradley. Mr. Agassiz described specimens from Acapulco.

The largest specimen has a test 3·6 inches in diameter; 1·8 high; diameter of actinal opening, not including cuts, 1·25; depth of cuts ·27; from outside of madreporic plate to outer edge of opposite ocular plate ·52; diameter of anal membrane ·2; length of longest spines ·5.

Test thin, fragile, low, subconical, lower side concave, outline somewhat pentagonal. The ambulacral zones are two thirds as wide as the interambulacral, and slightly raised above them, with a narrow, somewhat sunken, median naked space on the upper side. On the lower side there are six rows of ambulacral tubercles, which diminish in size upward, the outside rows attaining the summit, the others ceasing successively sooner. Interambulacral tubercles on the lower side in ten rows, subequal in size; the third row from each margin alone extending to the summit; the outside one hardly reaching the upper surface; the second reaching about half way from the outer curvature to the genital plates; the inner rows successively shorter than the third. The tubercles in all the rows diminish rapidly on the upper side, those of the third row less so than others; naked median space narrow, depressed, sutures conspicuous.

Genital plates large, the outer end subacute, projecting into the interambulacral spaces. Ocular plates tridentate on the outer side, usually only two of them touching the anal membrane. The anal area is covered with irregular, unequal plates. The poriferous zones are rather broad, the pores large, in oblique rows of three pairs, which become more nearly transverse at the outer margin. Actinal cuts very deep, with elevated callous margins, which, on the side next the interambulacra, are elevated and sharp, slightly revolute, and bounded externally by a shallow groove. The spines are short and stout, on the lower side numerous, blunt, and subequal; on the upper side shorter, more unequal, and not so numerous. The major pedicellariae in this species are numerous, especially among the spines of the lower side, and are remarkable for their great size, the heads often ·13 long; and 0·0 broad at base; with a pedicel ·3 or more long. The three branches are slender, somewhat smaller just above the enlarged base. Other short, thick, rounded, and very much smaller pedicellariae are scattered among the spines, and there is a thick wreath of similar ones around the mouth. The buccal membrane is covered with numerous scattered scales, which become smaller and crowded, near the mouth.

Color, in life, light purple or rose-color; when dried or in alcohol dull purplish white, the test sometimes dull greenish above.

This species, which appears to be beyond question a true *Lytechinus*,* is allied to *L. variegatus* of the West Indies, but still more so to *L. Atlanticus* A. Ag. of Bermuda. The latter differs, however, in having very slender and longer spines, much smaller and more slender pedicellariae, more uniform tubercles on the upper side, narrower poriferous zones, shallower actinal cuts, a more elevated form, and deep purple color. The specimens of this species were identified by Mr. Agassiz as the *Boletia rosea* by direct comparison with his original specimens. A comparison with the *Psammechinus semituberculatus* will, however, be necessary before it can be definitely ascertained whether they be really distinct.

---

* By more recent comparisons I have been led to consider it nearer *Boletia pileolus* than here indicated. It is very near, if not identical with *B. depressus*, figured in Voy. Vénus, Pl. 3, fig. 7,—Reprint.

Boletia viridis Verrill, sp. nov.*

A single specimen of this species was obtained by Mr. Bradley at Callao, Peru.

Diameter of test 2·7 inches; height 1·3; diameter of actinal area ·8; from outer end of madreporic plate to outside of opposite ocular plate ·38; diameter of anal area ·18; length of longest spines ·65.

The test is rather thick, depressed above, sides regularly arched, lower side concave, nearly circular in outline. The ambulacra have two rows of primary tubercles extending to the summit, with an irregular row of much smaller ones between them. The interambulacral zones have about six principal rows of tubercles on the lower side, of which the next to the outermost are much the largest on the upper side, and reach the genital plates; the outermost rows have small unequal tubercles. The secondary and large miliary tubercles are numerous on the central part of the interambulacra. The poriferous zones are rather wide, a little narrower beneath. The pores form a nearly regular vertical row on the inner side of the zones, separated from the others by a vertical row of small tubercles, outside of which the pores are rather irregularly placed, but apparently form two irregular alternating, vertical rows. The genital plates bear spines; they have a rounded angle outwardly, and are longer than broad; the openings are large. The ocular plates are small, most of them excluded from the anal area. Anal membrane covered by numerous, angular plates, which bear small spines. Spines short, stout, tapering, very unequal in size. Actinal cuts moderately deep; buccal membrane thin, with a few small widely separated scales. Color of spines bright green, the smaller ones often with light yellow tips; test brown.

Euryechinus Verrill. Proc. Boston Soc. Nat. Hist., x, p. 341.

Echinus (*pars*) Lamark; Agassiz, Monog. d'Echinod., 2me liv. (Introduction), July, 1841, and liv. 4me (Introduction), Dec., 1841.

Toxopneustes (sub-genus, *pars*) Agassiz and Desor, Catal. Rais., 1846.

This name was proposed, in the work cited, for a group of *Echini* having *E. Dröbachiensis* as the type, and including, in addition, *E. granulatus* of New England, *E. lividus* of Europe, *E. gibbosus*, Galapago Is., and *E. Delalandii* of New Holland. Since that time, however, I have received an authentic specimen of the last species and have satisfied myself that it does not belong to the same group,

---

* Mr. A. Agassiz considers this the *Echinus chloroticus* Val. If so the specimen described was probably from the New Zealand collection of Mr. Edwards, and accidentally misplaced in packing at Callao,—Reprint.

but rather to the genus, *Toxocidaris* of A. Agassiz, where he had already placed it.

The reasons for not adopting the name, *Toxopneustes*, for this group, are these:

1st. When this name was *first proposed* "*Echinus pileolus*" was mentioned, without description or reference, as its type, (Monog. Ech., 2me liv., p. 7).

2nd. When next mentioned and *first described*, *Echinus tuberculatus* Lamarck was given as its type, and the description applies to such species as are now named *Toxocidaris* by A. Agassiz, (Monog. Ech., 4me liv., p. ix).

3rd. In the work last named the typical species of *Euryechinus* were described under *Echinus proper*, as restricted by the removal of *Tripneustes*, *Toxopneustes*, etc., and therefore were evidently not regarded as belonging to the latter genus.

4th. In a work published five years later (Catal. Rais.) *Toxopneustes* was placed as a sub-genus of *Echinus*, and a variety of forms were referred to it, amounting to thirteen nominal species, among which are several types now regarded as generically distinct. Of these species the 1st, 2nd, and 4th are now placed in the genus *Sphærechinus* Desor; the 3rd, 5th, 7th, and 10th belong to *Euryechinus*; while the 8th (*T. Delalandii*) and 9th (*E. tuberculatus*) are true *Toxopneustes*, now referred to *Toxocidaris* by A. Agassiz; the 6th, 11th, 12th, and 13th are doubtful species, the last fossil.

It is, therefore, evident that if *Toxopneustes* be taken in its original sense, *when first described*, it must be restricted to that group having *T. tuberculatus* as its type, a group apparently equivalent to *Toxocidaris* A. Agassiz, which is represented by several East Indian and Pacific Ocean species, as well as by two species upon the Pacific coast of N. America (*T. mexicana* and *T. franciscana*). These species have the characters originally assigned to *Toxopneustes* in an eminent degree, while to *E. pileolus*, as now understood, neither the name nor description would apply. Therefore there seems to be grave objections against restricting it to the latter species, and its allies, even were it certain that the species now known as *Boletia pileolus*, was the one referred to as *Echinus pileolus*, without authority.

Euryechinus imbecillis Verrill.

? *Echinus gibbosus* Val. MS.; ? *Echinus* (*Toxopneustes*) *gibbosus* Agassiz, Catal. Rais.
Euryechinus gibbosus Verrill, Proc. Boston Soc. Nat. Hist., x, p. 341, 1866.

This species was found thrown upon the beach abundantly at Callao and Paita, Peru, by Mr. Bradley. At the latter locality living specimens were obtained at low-water. *E. gibbosus* was originally described from the Galapago Islands.

The larger specimens have a test about 2 inches in diameter, and 1 in height; spines ·9 long; diameter of actinal area ·7; of abactinal area, including genital plates, ·6.

The form is rather depressed, the abactinal area somewhat sunken, the sides regularly arched, the lower surface nearly flat. The test is rather thin. The actinal area is small, with slight cuts. The ambulacral zones are nearly as broad as the interambulacral, and slightly elevated above them. The poriferous zones are broad, becoming a little wider beneath; the pores, arranged in oblique, slightly curved rows of four or five pairs above, form on the lower surface more transverse and nearly straight rows of four pairs, with rows of very small tubercles intervening. The ambulacra have two rows of primary tubercles, with an irregular median row of small tubercles between them. The interambulacra have two primary rows of somewhat larger tubercles, midway between the sides and median line, and a row of smaller ones, on each side, bordering the poriferous zones, and a median double row of alternating tubercles of still smaller size. The genital plates are small, broader than long, uniting so as to separate the small ocular plates from the anal area. Madreporic plate small, transversely oval. Spines not very numerous, long, slender, with fine longitudinal striations, the ribs crossed by fine lines. Color, in alcohol, dark purplish brown, when dry test often variegated with light green and whitish; spines dark green, often tipped with purple.

Nearly every specimen examined is irregular in the form of the shell above, near the abactinal area, which is, also, generally distorted or enlarged on one side, where the shell is thinner. This distortion, which often amounts to gibbosity, is irregular and inconstant, and is caused by a parasitic crustacean (*Fabia Chilensis* Dana) allied to the *Pinnotheres*, which inhabit oysters and other bivalve mollusca. This curious parasite* appears to force an entrance into the anal orifice when quite small, and, having effected a permanent lodgment there, causes a dilation and malformation of the intestine, which eventually forms a large membranous cyst or sac, often in the larger specimens extending from the summit to the lower side of the shell, along one side, to which it is attached by fibrous tissues. In one instance the cyst was an inch in length and nearly half an inch in diameter, enclosing a female crab of corresponding size, with large numbers of eggs attached to its abdominal appendages. A large opening is

---

* *Pinnaxodes hirtipes* Heller, appears to be the same species.

always maintained externally, out of which the claws of the crab may be thrust, but is apparently not large enough to allow it to go entirely out, when fully grown. By this parasite the anal area is so distorted and displaced that among ninety specimens I have not found one in which it is in its natural state, every specimen giving evidence, by distortion or otherwise, of having been infested by it. But as most of these were found dead upon the beach it is probable that they were individuals that had been killed or weakened by the parasite, while specimens unattacked by them may be found in deeper water.

It is probable that the irregularity or gibbosity of the *Echinus gibbosus* Val. was caused by the same or a similar parasite, but whether that name applies to the present species of *Euryechinus* I am unable to determine, the description being too imperfect for reliable identification. But should it prove to be the same, the name is inapplicable, referring only to an accidental, or diseased condition, which is not constant even in the diseased specimens. For these reasons I have thought it necessary to apply a new name to the present species.

The original description of *E. gibbosus* is as follows :* "Espèce irrégulière voisine de l'*E. lividus* par les détails de son test. Quatre paires de pores légèrement arquées. Des iles Gallapagos,—Mus., Paris."

The *Euryechinus imbecillis* can scarcely be said to be near *E. lividus* in the character of the test, since in the latter there are eight or ten rows of subequal interambulacral tubercles, which are larger and far more numerous than in this species, besides many other differences. It approaches much more nearly, in the character of its test and arrangement of its tubercles, *E. Dröbachiensis* and, especially, *E. granulatus* Verrill, of the coast of New England, but is quite distinct from all, in the thinness of its test; in its smaller and weaker genital and ocular plates, and larger size of the anal area and, consequently, of its abactinal system; in the flatness of the lower surface and somewhat widened poriferous zones; fewer tubercles; and more slender spines.

Toxopneustes sp.

Toxocidaris mexicana A. Ag., Bulletin M. C. Z., p. 22, 1863, (no description).

Mr. Agassiz has identified a specimen from Acapulco, in the Museum of Comparative Zoölogy, as the *Heliocidaris Mexicana* Ag. The latter species was originally described (Catal. Rais.) as coming from Vera Cruz. Dr. Lütken refers it to *Echinometra*. In our col-

---

* Agassiz and Desor, Catal. Rais., in Ann. des Sci., vi, p. 367, 1846.

lection there are two specimens,* received from the Boston Soc. Nat. Hist., and collected by different persons, labeled "Gulf of Mexico?" which I have considered the *Heliocidaris Mexicana* Agassiz. But these belong to the genus *Anthocidaris* of Lütken. Should this identification prove correct, the name, *Anthocidaris mexicana*, may be applied to this species, while the species from Acapulco, since it apparently belongs to a distinct genus, might be allowed to retain the same specific name, but until described this name can only be considered as provisional, and not entitled to priority. For these reasons I leave this species without a name, for the present.

Echinometra rupicola A. Agassiz, Bulletin M. C. Z., p. 21, 1863.

Mr. Bradley sent numerous examples of this species from Panama and the Pearl Islands, where it occurs on the reefs at low-water mark, and in rocky pools. It has the habit of forming excavations in the rocks in the same manner as *Eurychinus lividus* of Europe, most of the larger specimens occurring in such cavities. He also obtained specimens at La Union, San Salvador, and Zorritos, Peru. From the latter locality the specimens are very large and beautiful.

Our largest specimen measures, in the greater diameter of its test, 3·2 inches; smaller diameter 2·8; height 1·5; diameter of actinal opening 1·1; of abactinal area, including genital plates, ·45. The spines are variable in length; usually the longest, in large specimens, are from 1 to 1·5 inches long. In a specimen having the test 1·5 inches in diameter some of the spines are 1·6 long.

The test is broad oval, or subcircular, depressed above, regularly arched on the sides, rather flat beneath. Actinal cuts deep and narrow. Interambulacral zones are a third wider than the ambulacral, with at least six rows of large tubercles, those in the next to the outer one largest, continuing to the genital plates. Ambulacra with four rows of smaller tubercles, those of the two median rows largest and regularly arranged, about equal in size to those in the outer row of the interambulacra. In the largest specimen there are 24 ambulacral, and 18 interambulacral tubercles in the principal rows. Poriferous zones rather wide, with seven or eight pairs of pores in well curved arcs. The upper pair in each arc is between the outer and median rows of ambulacral tubercles. Genital plates of moderate size, outward edge acutely angular, openings large; ocular plates reaching the anal area. Spines slender for this genus, regularly tapering to the acute ends, more equal in size than usual, the second series being less numerous. Color dark purple throughout.

---

* Mr. A. Agassiz considers these, *Echinometra plana* A. Ag.,—Reprint.

Echinometra Van Brunti A. Agassiz, op. cit., p. 21.

Several large specimens of this species, collected at Cape St. Lucas by J. Xantus, have been presented by the Smithsonian Institution. The examples originally described were from Acapulco.

The largest specimen has a test 2 inches across the longest diameter; 1·7 wide; ·8 high; actual opening ·85 in diameter; longest spines, which are somewhat broken at the end, 1·6.

In the form of the test this species resembles the preceding, but it is often even more depressed. The interambulacra, in a specimen 1·6 inches in diameter, have two rows of large primary tubercles, with a row of much smaller ones outside of them on each side, bordering the ambulacra, and two imperfect median rows of similar secondary tubercles. The ambulacra have two rows of tubercles, which are smaller than the principal tubercles of the interambulacra. The poriferous zones are very narrow on the upper surface, having nearly vertical arcs of about seven pairs of pores; on the lower side the arcs become more nearly transverse, and the zones are much wider. The genital plates are less acute outwardly, and less prominent than in the preceding species. The spines are large and strong, and when perfect taper to a sharp point. They seldom equal in length the greatest diameter of the test. Color, dried from alcohol, deep ashen brown, or purplish.

This species may be easily distinguished from *E. rupicola* by the fewer and larger interambulacral tubercles; stouter spines; and the very narrow poriferous zones above, with their rapid dilation beneath.

Encope occidentalis Verrill.

Encope tetrapora Agassiz, Monog. d'Ech., Scutelles, p. 49. Tab. 10ᵃ, figs. 1-3, 1841. (*non* Gmelin).

Plate X, figures 4, 4ᵃ.

Numerous specimens of this species are in our museum, which were dredged in the Bay of Panama in 5 to 8 fathoms, shelly bottom, by Mr. Bradley. He also obtained one large specimen at Zorritos, Peru. The specimen described by Prof. Agassiz came from the Galapago Islands.

The largest specimen is 5·5 inches long; with the extreme breadth 5·7; height ·6; from center to anterior opening 1·9; to anterior-lateral 1·8; to posterior-lateral 2; to posterior 1·5; from center to anterior margin 2·6; to posterior margin 2·9; from center to end of anterior ambulacral rays 1·7; of lateral 1·5; of posterior 1·72; breadth of anterior ray ·67; its median region ·3; breadth of lateral ·7; its middle ·35; breadth of one of the posterior pair ·7; the middle area ·3; length of posterior foramen ·5; center of mouth to anus ·65.

Test much depressed, becoming gradually very flat toward the margin; highest part at the middle of the anterior ambulacrum. Margin broadly rounded posteriorly, the widest place opposite the middle of the posterior ambulacra; sides wavy, converging somewhat toward the anterior side, which is slightly emarginate in the middle. The posterior opening is rather oblong, relatively nearer to the center than in most species; the other openings are elliptical, the anterior one shortest. The rays are broad, shorter than usual, especially the anterio-lateral pair. The genital openings are large, and form a regular pentagon. The anal opening is situated about midway between the mouth and posterior foramen. The sulcations of the lower surface are very distinct and much branched.

Color deep reddish brown, or dark greenish brown.

This species can readily be distinguished from *E. emarginata*, and its varieties, and *E. Michelini* of the West Indies, by its broader form, narrowing anteriorly; by the relatively broader and more equal, ambulacra; and by the position of the posterior foramen, it being half its length nearer the center than the posterio-lateral ones.

Dr. Lütken, apparently with good reason, refers the *Echinus tetrapora* Gmelin to the *E. emarginata* of the West Indies. Our species appears to be the one well figured and described by Prof. Agassiz under the former name, and will, therefore, require a new designation.

The specimen figured by Agassiz is smaller than any of ours, and had the posterio-lateral lunules still open, while in all the specimens that I have seen they are completely closed, unless opened by reason of some injury.

Encope grandis Agassiz, op. cit., p. 37, Tab. 6.

Two specimens, apparently belonging to this species, are in our collection, one of which, received from the Boston Society of Natural History, is labeled as coming from the Gulf of California, and the other, presented by Mr. Horace Mann, was obtained by him from Mr. Pease, with several other characteristic Panamic and Californian Echinoderms, but without any authentic locality.*

The latter agrees perfectly with the figure and description by Agassiz. The origin of his specimen is unknown, but it was supposed to have come from the Antilles. Owing to lack of perfectly authentic localities, I prefer to avoid confusion and possible error by omitting descriptions until more authentic specimens can be obtained.

---

* Several dozens of large and fine specimens have recently been sent from La Paz by J. Pedersen.—Reprint.

Astriclypeus Verrill, gen. nov.

Ambulacral star as in *Encope;* four genital openings, the posterior one wanting, as in *Mellita;* with five lunules or perforations in the prolongations of the ambulacra, as in *Encope;* but destitute of any perforation or indentation in the posterior interambulacrum, like *Lobophora.* Anal opening round, about midway between the mouth and margin. Sulcations of the lower side more simple than in *Encope*, a primary branch passing along close to the openings, on each side, and sending off numerous inconspicuous branches to the interambulacra. Actinal opening as in *Encope.*

This genus presents a remarkable combination of characters belonging to other allied genera, but has an assemblage of characters entirely unique. It appears to be most nearly allied to *Lobophora*, from which it differs chiefly in possessing five ambulacral lunules or openings, instead of but two; and in the sulcations of the lower surface.

Astriclypeus Mannii Verrill, sp. nov.*

Test subcircular, about as long as broad, with the posterior side slightly truncate, and a slight prominence of the edge opposite each opening. Summit central, considerably elevated.

Length 4·2; breadth the same; height ·65; from center to anterior opening 1·2; to the lateral ones 1·1; to end of anterior ambulacral ray 1·2; to lateral ·98; breadth of anterior ambulacral ray ·42; of its median area ·16; of the anterior lateral ·45; its median area ·2; length of three anterior openings ·6; breadth ·18; length of posterior openings ·7; breadth ·18; center of mouth to anal opening 1 inch; from the latter to the margin the same.

The anterior ray of the ambulacral rosette is a little longer and narrower than the others, with the widest part near the end, which is not closed; lateral rays nearly equal in length, the anterior pair a little wider, increasing in width to near the end, which is broad and rounded. Openings oblong, the posterior pair a little longer. Anal opening nearly circular, midway between the mouth and margin.

Locality West Coast of North America (?). (Japan,—Reprint).

The single specimen of this curious species was presented by Mr. Horace Mann, of Cambridge, Mass., in honor of whom I have named it. It was obtained by him, with several other West Coast Echino-

---

* Dr. F. H. Troschel has well described and figured this species under the name of *Crustulum gratulans* in Niederrh. Gesells. fur Naturg. und Heilkunde, Universität Bonn, Aug. 3, 1868, p. 1, Pl. I. In Archiv fur Naturg. 1869, p. 52, he has identified it with our species and described specimens from Japan (E. von Martens),—Reprint.

derms,* from Mr. Pease of the Sandwich Islands. Its origin is entirely doubtful. It is destitute of spines and in the same state of preservation as a *Dendraster excentricus,* which came with it.

Echinoglycus Stokesii Gray; A. Ag., Bulletin M. C. Z., p. 26, 1863.

Encope Stokesii Agassiz, Mon. Scutelles, p. 59, Tab. 6a, figs. 1 to 8, 1841; Lütken, Bidrag til Kundskab. om Echin., p. 65, 1864.

This species was found abundant on a sandy beach near Panama, at low-water mark. Dr. Lütken's specimens were from Punta Arenas, whence he has sent examples to us. It has also been described from Guayaquil and the Galapago Islands.

The larger specimens from Panama are two inches long; 2·15 broad; ·25 high at center; from center to end of anterior ambulacral ray ·55; to end of anterior-lateral ·5; posterior-lateral ·48; center to genital openings ·08; width of anterior ambulacral ray ·25; its central area ·11; width of the four lateral rays ·27; central area ·11; center to anterior lunule ·8; to anterior-lateral ·73; to posterior-lateral ·67; to posterior perforation ·68; its length ·2; breadth ·1; mouth to anal opening ·42. The form is nearly circular, the posterior interambulacrum usually slightly truncated. Lower surface flat, upper side most elevated at the center of the rosette, which is behind the middle; test rather thin and brittle. Six lunules or perforations, the posterior one, even in very young specimens, is a rounded oblong perforation, in the adult specimens becoming twice as long as wide; the lateral ones appear at first as shallow notches in the edge, which gradually become narrow, long or oval, and in the larger specimens all, except the anterior one, become closed at the edge. In young specimens the posterior-lateral notches appear first, the anterior one not being apparent in a specimen ·6 of an inch in diameter; in the larger specimens its outer edges are in contact and doubtless finally unite. Ambulacral rays short and broad, a little elevated above the general surface; the anterior odd one longer and narrower than the others; posterior pair shortest, but about equal in width to the anterior pair; along the middle of each there is a narrow naked line. Genital openings usually five, large and regular, sometimes the posterior one is double or irregular. Spines of the upper surface crowded, uniform, very slender, enlarged or clavate at the tips; the edge fringed with larger and

---

* The species received in this collection are as follows: *Linckia unifascialis* Gray, *Nidorellia armata* Gray, *Oreaster occidentalis* Verrill, *Heliaster Kubiniji* Xant., *Culcita,* sp., *Dendraster excentricus* Ag., *Encope grandis* Ag., *E. occidentalis* V., *Astriclypeus Mannii* V.

longer ones, not clavate; lower surface with three kinds, the median region of each interambulacrum with crowded spines, which are longer and stouter than those of other parts and slightly enlarged toward the ends; on the median area of the ambulacra, in line with the lunules, the spines are similar in form, but much fewer and smaller; between these two kinds the surface is covered with very small crowded, clavate spines, similar to those of the upper surface, but less enlarged at the tips. Color, when dried, dull greenish brown.

Mellita Pacifica Verrill, sp. nov.

A depressed, subcircular species, with six perforations; allied to *M. hexapora*, but having a large, round posterior, and small, narrow ambulacral perforations; spines of the upper side short and crowded.

Length, not including spines, 2·2 inches; greatest breadth 2·3; height ·25; from center to end of anterior ambulacral ray ·58; to end of anterior-lateral ·55; of posterior-lateral ·61; width of anterior ambulacral ray ·27; its central area ·13; of anterior-lateral ·25; its central area ·12; of posterior lateral ·25; its central area ·10; from center to anterior perforation ·83; to anterior-lateral ·81; to posterior-lateral ·8; to posterior ·4; length of latter ·25; its width ·2; mouth to anal opening ·25; length of marginal spines ·15.

The outline is nearly circular; broadest a little behind the center, where the outer edges of the posterior-lateral interambulacra are somewhat prominent beyond the rest of the outline; center of abactinal rosette a little behind the middle; edges thin. The five ambulacral perforations are small and narrow, elliptical; the posterior one is large and broad oval; its inner half within the ends of the posterior ambulacral rays. The ambulacral rays are elongated-oval; the posterior pair longest; the anterior-lateral pair shortest; each with a well-marked naked median line. Plates of the upper surface relatively more numerous than in *M. hexapora*, and narrower in the direction of the radii; four ambulacral plates intervening between the perforations and the ends of the rays, while in *M. hexapora* of similar size there are but two. Spines of the upper surface close and short, slender at base, with greatly enlarged, rounded tips; those of the marginal fringe long, tapering, often acute; those of the median regions of the interambulacra are similar in form to those of the margin, but much more slender and delicate; those of the areas enclosed by the primary radiating grooves are very small and slender, not clavate.

Color, deep green when dried.

Zorritos, Peru, at low-water mark,—F. H. Bradley.

This species is allied to *M. hexapora* of the West Indies, but the latter is very distinct in the form of the posterior perforation, which is much more elongated and narrow, in adult specimens; in the ambulacral perforations, which are longer and larger; in the smaller number and larger size of the plates of the upper surface; in the longer spines of the upper surface, which have smaller tips; in the broader posterior-ambulacral rays; and in the more angular outline, which is distinctly truncate posteriorly.

Mr. A. Agassiz has mentioned by name *M. longifissa* Mich.,* as coming from Panama (Bulletin M. C. Z.), but whether his specimens are the same as the species here described I am unable to say, not having seen them. Dr. Lütken refers *M. longifissa* Mich., described without locality, to *M. pentapora*, with which it appears to agree far more nearly than with *M. Pacifica*. If the specimens of Mr. Agassiz prove to be distinct from our own, they probably will belong to a Pacific representative of *M. pentapora*, while *M. Pacifica* is the analogue of *M. hexapora*.

Stoloniclypeus rotundus A. Agassiz. Bulletin M. C. Z., p. 25, 1863.

Clypeaster Riisei Lütken, op. cit., p. 132. 1864.

Mr. Bradley collected numerous specimens of this species in Panama Bay, on shelly bottom in 6 to 8 fathoms, with *Encope occidentalis* and *Lytechinus roseus*. Mr. Agassiz collected his specimens at Acapulco. Dr. Lütken's example was from Panama.

One of the largest specimens is 5·4 inches in its longest diameter; 4·9 broad at the middle; ·75 high at center; ·3 at margin; from center to end of posterior lateral ambulacral rays 1·52; breadth of same ·8; of median area ·52; center to posterior margin 2·8; to anterior margin 2·6 The test is thin, somewhat oblong, depressed, except at the center, which is a little elevated. The margin is slightly undulated, curving somewhat inward at the interambulacral zones, and extending farther out in broad, slightly prominent lobes at the ambulacra, which are about three times as broad as the interambulacra at the margin. The posterior portion of the test is somewhat broader than the anterior; a slight lobe on the posterior margin, opposite the anal opening, which is circular and close to the edge. Ambulacral rays broad, subequal, forming a very regular rosette. The anterior one slightly narrower, and the anterior lateral pair slightly shorter than the posterior pair. The genital pores are close to the center, in the angles of a small pentagon. The ocular openings are scarcely visi-

---

* Specimens of this species have been received from Gulf of California and Nicaragua,—Reprint

ble to the unaided eye, nearer to the center than the genital pores. Spines uniformly crowded above and beneath, short and slender, the larger ones of the upper surface mostly with slightly enlarged tips. Color, in alcohol, dark ash-brown.

This species is allied to *S. prostratus* (Rav. sp.) of the West Indies, but has a thinner margin, broader ambulacra, a larger rosette, and a thinner test.

Pygorhynchus Pacificus (Ag. MS.) A. Agassiz, Bulletin M. C. Z., p. 27.

We have received from the Museum of Comparative Zoölogy, two specimens of this very interesting species, collected by Mr. A. Agassiz at Acapulco; and young specimens, from the Smithsonian Institution, collected at Cape St. Lucas by J. Xantus.

One specimen is 1·8 inches long; 1·4 broad; ·9 high; from center to anterior margin 1; to posterior margin 1·22; to anal orifice ·9; to end of anterior ambulacral ray ·75; to end of anterior-lateral ·7; to end of posterior-lateral ·8; width of ambulacral rays ·18; the median area ·1; width of actinal opening ·2; length ·12. Another specimen is 1·9 long; 1·6 wide; 1 high.

Test thin, concave beneath, the sides most prominent opposite the mouth; above regularly arched except at the anal region; marginal outline oblong, the ends obtusely rounded, the posterior portion broadest. Anal area transversely oval, situated in a depression above the margin. Ambulacral rays nearly equal in width, the posterior ones longest; the anterior poriferous zones in the anterior-lateral ambulacra and the posterior zone in the posterior ones, shorter and narrower than the others. From the ends of the ambulacral rays two single rows of pores may be traced around to the mouth, in most of the ambulacra. The actinal opening is wider than long, with five angles alternating with prominent lobes. One of the angles is on the anterior side, with a lobe opposite. A rosette of pores surrounds the mouth, each ray having two short rows of double pores and two rows of few, larger, single pores within them, and in the center another very short row of double pores, the pair next the mouth larger. The "naked space" beneath is broadest anteriorly, enclosing the mouth, and narrowing posteriorly. In life it is covered by minute spines. The spines of the upper surface are short and delicate, crowded; on the sides of the lower surface they are longer and larger, tapering, sharp at the ends, longitudinally fluted. Tubercles of the upper side small and regular; on the lower surface they are larger and sunken on the lateral parts; very small and unequal on the median area. Genital openings four, near the center. Color, when dried, brownish yellow. In alcohol, darker yellowish brown.

In form and general appearance this species resembles *Cassidulus Carribœarum* Lamk.,* of the West Indies. The positions of the mouth and anal openings are nearly the same, and the latter is situated in a similar transverse depression surmounted by an arched, lip-like projection of nearly the same form, in each.

The *Cassidulus* differs, however, in several structural features of importance,—such as the number and arrangement of the pores in the rosette around the mouth, and in not having the pairs of pores in the dorsal rosette connected by transverse grooves, which, in *P. Pacifica*, are deep and conspicuous and separated by rows of small tubercles.

Brissus obesus Verrill, sp. nov.

Closely allied to *B. columbaris* of the West Indies, and *B. Scillœ*, Mediterranean, especially to the latter, from which it differs chiefly in its proportions (as seen in profile) and the position of the vertex.

The largest specimen is 2 inches long; 1·35 broad; 1·15 high, at the most elevated point; 1·35 from abactinal center to posterior margin; ·92 to anterior margin; ·55 to end of anterior-lateral ambulacra; ·80 to end of posterior; ·65 to end of anterior odd one (where crossed by fasciole); sub-anal fasciole ·75 broad, ·25 long; "plastron" 1·20 long; ·70 broad at posterior end; mouth ·40 broad.

Viewed from above the form is regularly ovate, except the narrower, posterior end, which is somewhat truncate and slightly emarginate at the anal area. Distance from abactinal area to posterior end one and a half times that to anterior end. The abactinal region is small and scarcely depressed. The posterior interambulacrum is elevated and swollen from its origin to the anal area, and subcarinated between the posterior ambulacra, causing the latter to appear unusually sunken. The region in front of the anterior lateral ambulacra is regularly and pretty uniformly rounded, lacking the flattened, somewhat depressed anterior area seen in *B. Scillœ*, and bears larger tubercles than the rest of the test, as in the allied species. The anterior odd ambulacrum is very narrow and scarcely depressed, with rather indistinct pores. Those of anterior pair are moderately long, lanceolate, nearly transverse, their ends curving somewhat toward the anterior end. Posterior-lateral ambulacra longer than anterior

---

* This species, which has recently been referred to *Rhyncopygus* by Dr. Lütken, was the type of the genus *Cassidulus* when it was first established in the Système des Animaux sans Vertébres, p. 348, 1801. Therefore it seems most proper to restrict the genus *Cassidulus* to species like this.

(This name is preoccupied in mollusca. Mr. A. Agassiz has recently united this and *Pacificus* in a new genus, *Rhyncholampas*, Bulletin M. C. Z., p. 270,—Reprint.)

(in the ratio of 16 to 15) diverging at a smaller angle than in *B. Scillæ*. In a side view the anterior end has a regularly convex outline to the abactinal area, which forms a slight depression, from thence the outline rises gradually to a point about half way to the posterior end and then curves rapidly downward to the truncate anal region, which makes more than a right angle with the lower surface. Subanal region obtuse, high and inflated, very convex; posterior median region of the "*plastron*" inflated, rising into a prominent point. The sub-anal fasciole is broad, transversely reniform, its longitudinal diameter to its breadth as 1 : 3. The "plastron" is shield-shaped, rather broad, a little narrowed posteriorly, its length to breadth of posterior end as 12 : 7. Color of test, in alcohol, uniform yellowish gray; of spines, dark gray.

Gulf of California,—E. Samuels (Coll. Boston Soc. Nat. Hist. and Museum Yale College); Cape St. Lucas,—J. Xantus (Coll. Smiths. Institution).

This species is more liable to be confounded with *B. Scillæ* Ag. than with any other known to me. It may be distinguished readily, however, by its evenly rounded outline between the anterior margin and ovarial plates; by its more swollen posterior region, which is due both to the elevation of the posterior interambulacrum and the increased convexity of the sub-anal and ventral areas; by the less anterior position of the abactinal areas; by the relatively shorter and broader plastron and sub-anal fasciole; and by the latter being placed rather upon the posterior than upon the lower surface, while in *B. Scillæ* it is more nearly continuous with the plastron.

Meoma nigra Verrill.

Kleinia (*Ryssobrissus*) *nigra* A. Agassiz, Bulletin M. C. Z., p. 27, 1863.

This large species is closely allied to *M. grandis* Gray, from Australia.

Length four inches; breadth 3·6; height 1·9; length of anterior lateral ambulacra 1·9; of posterior 2; length of anal area ·7; breadth ·45.

Its outline is broad ovate, somewhat cordate anteriorly, and truncate and slightly emarginate posteriorly. The upper surface is rather depressed, but not flattened, covered with scattered larger tubercles and very numerous small ones. The tubercles are largest within the peripetalous fasciole and beyond it on the posterior interambulacrum. The anterior ambulacral area is but little sunken, with rudimentary pores. The anterior-lateral ones are rather broad and deep, curving forward, especially at the ends. The two posterior are somewhat longer, strongly divergent, obtuse at the ends. The posterior interambulacrum and the lateral pair are about equally swollen, within the fasciole, but the former is somewhat inflated beyond it, near the posterior end, which is obliquely truncated, the upper surface projecting considerably beyond the lower. The anal area is large, elliptical, acute above, and occupies the greater part of the truncated posterior end.

The peripetalous fasciole is nearly transverse anteriorly, but forms two abrupt, angular bends between the anterior and lateral ambulacra, of which that next to the lateral extends much farther toward the summit. In the rest of its course it agrees very nearly with that of *M. grandis* as figured by Gray.* The sub-anal fasciole is nearly transverse between the posterior ambulacra; at a distance from the anal area about equal to the length of the latter, each end bends obliquely upward laterally and becomes irregular and gradually disappears opposite the sides of the anal area and at some distance from it, without enclosing a sub-anal area. Genital openings four, the two posterior largest and farthest apart.

Acapulco, Mexico,—A. Agassiz. In exchange from the Museum of Comparative Zoölogy.†

I am indebted to the kindness of Mr. A. Agassiz for a typical specimen of this interesting species. It seems to be a true *Meoma*.

Metalia Gray.

Brissus (subgenus *Metalia*) Gray, Catalogue of the Recent Echinida of the British Museum, p. 51, 1855.

Xanthobrissus A. Agassiz, Bulletin M C. Z., p. 28, 1863.

The first division of the genus *Brissus*, as limited by Dr. Gray, contained only one species, the *B. sternalis* Ag. This group, to which he applied the name *Metalia*, he characterized as follows: "Subanal area heart-shaped, edged by a broad subanal fasciole; the disk radiated, striated, with a series of marginal pores, and with a short fasciole, branched up and edging the sides of the vent; the hinder part of the peripetalous fasciole slightly bent, but not margined to the hinder edge of the hinder ambulacra; spines on the side of the ambulacra larger, elongate."

This division appears to be perfectly equivalent to *Xanthobrissus* A. Agassiz. The type of the latter, *M. Garretii* (Ag. sp.), from the Kingsmills Islands, is closely allied to *M. sternalis*, as I have ascertained by an examination of typical specimens of the former, belong-

---

* Catalogue of the Recent Echinida of the British Museum, Part 1, pl. 5, fig. 2, 1855.

† More recently sent by J. Pedersen from La Paz,—Reprint.

ing to the Boston Society of Natural History and the Essex Institute, received from the Museum of Comparative Zoölogy. Whether it be really distinct can be ascertained only by an actual comparison of authentic specimens of each, the descriptions of *M. sternalis* not being sufficient to distinguish it from *M. Garretii*.

Metalia nobilis Verrill, sp. nov.

Test depressed above, most elevated at the abactinal pole and upper part of posterior interambulacrum; anterior end arched; posterior end obliquely truncated; lower surface but little convex. In a view from above the form is very broad oval, the anterior end a little emarginate, the posterior truncate, but prominent.

Extreme length 4·5 inches; breadth 4; height 2·2; from abactinal pole to anterior end 2; to posterior end 3·1; to end of anterior ambulacral rays 1·7; to end of posterior 1·92; to peripetalous fasciole in posterior interambulacrum 1·5; in lateral interambulacra 1·3; in anterior ambulacrum 1·7; length of anal area ·62; breadth ·52; length of subanal fasciole ·88; breadth 1·35; from anal area to fasciole ·25; mouth to subanal fasciole 2·45; breadth of plastron 1·25; length of spines of lower surface ·55; of upper surface bordering ambulacra ·22.

The anterior ambulacrum is but slightly sunken; the lateral ones in deep grooves, nearly uniform in width; the anterior pair nearly straight; the posterior curving slightly outward. The lateral and posterior interambulacra are convex within the peripetalous fasciole, but beyond this the latter is suddenly depressed, causing a slightly concave place, behind which it is slightly convex, and slopes gradually to the posterior end. The peripetalous fasciole is nearly transverse in front, bending upward for a short distance, nearly at a right angle, about at the middle of the anterior-lateral interambulacra, and then turning back again at a similar angle, passes close by the end of the ambulacral rays. In the lateral and posterior interambulacra it bends but slightly upward, and does not margin the ambulacra. The sub-anal fasciole is rather large, broader than long, broad heart-shaped, the lower end terminating in a slight point, the lower sides rounded to the extreme lateral lobes; the upper or posterior side with a straight line in the middle, and slightly concave ones running to the lateral lobes. From each end of the straight, posterior part a narrow fasciole passes outward and upward in a broad curve and terminates about opposite the middle of the anal area. The anal area is broad-oval, longer than broad. The plastron is elliptical, but little convex, the most prominent points being at the posterior end, where the subanal fasciole crosses it, and at the mouth. Pores around the mouth large, in five conspicuous rays. The spines are long and slender on the lower surface, short and fine above, except on the borders of the ambulacra and within the fasciole, where the tubercles are considerably larger.

Color of test dark ash-brown, a yellowish white line or narrow band passing from the ambulacral petals or rays to the outer margin, along each border of the ambulacral zones. Color of spines very dark gray, or blackish.

A small specimen from Cape St. Lucas is 1·55 inches long; 1·4 broad; ·88 high; from center to end of anterior ambulacral rays ·52; of posterior ·57; width of latter ·12; center to anterior end 1·7; to posterior end 1·3; length of area within subanal fasciole ·4; breadth ·45.

In form this agrees nearly with the large specimen, except that the posterior interambulacral region is depressed within the peripetalous fasciole and the lower surface is more convex, the plastron being subcarinated and most prominent in the middle. The anterior, odd ambulacrum is scarcely depressed below the general surface.

The form of the peripetalous fasciole is the same as in the large specimen. Color of test and spines, in alcohol, is white, the spines transparent.

Panama Bay, dredged in 6 to 8 fathoms, shelly bottom,--F. H. Bradley. Cape St. Lucas,--J. Xantus (Coll. Smithsonian Inst.).

This species is allied to *M. Garretii* of the Kingsmills Islands, but the latter differs in having a more elevated and convex form, especially posteriorly; in having the anterior end high and abruptly descending, with the imperfect ambulacrum in a deeper groove; in having relatively shorter and broader ambulacral rays, which are not so uniform in width, and the posterior ones more curved; in the form of the anal area, which is pointed below, instead of rounded; in the subanal fasciole, which is smaller, narrower, and more rounded, being about as long as broad. The peripetalous fasciole bends up in an abrupt angle in the lateral interambulacra, instead of crossing in a broad, slightly concave curve.

Agassizia ovulum Lütken, Vidensk. Medd., p. 134, tab. II, fig. 8, 1864.

Mr. Bradley sent one specimen of this species, found on the beach at Panama. Dr. Lütken's specimens came from Boccones, Central America.

Order, HOLOTHURIOIDEA.

A large number of Holothurians, representing numerous species, from Panama, San Salvador, etc., were collected by Mr. Bradley. But since it is very difficult to properly characterize animals of this order from specimens preserved in alcohol, most of these species are here omitted. The Holothurians of other localities have, also, been so imperfectly described that descriptions of those of this region would at present afford but little additional evidence upon questions of Geographical Distribution.

Most of the species in the collection belong to the restricted genus *Holothuria*, and allied genera, having twenty peltate tentacles.

Two of the more interesting and unusual forms are described below. It is to be hoped that examinations of the living animals will soon afford material for completing the descriptions of these, as well as of the remaining species.

Pentacta Panamensis Verrill. sp. nov.

Body somewhat fusiform, pentagonal, the angles prominent, both ends turned upward. Length, in alcohol, 1·4; diameter at middle ·28. Suckers not entirely retractile, arranged along the angles. In the three lower ambulacra there are two alternating rows on each angle, along the middle of the body, but toward each end they become more distant, smaller, and form but a single row; on the two ambulacra of the upper side they are less numerous and form a single row along the whole length of the body. The suckers are stiff at the lower part, and filled with calcareous grains; the ends are soft and extensible, with well developed disks. The interambulacral zones are smooth and without papillæ; the skin thin, coriaceous, filled with very numerous, minute, calcareous grains or plates. The anal opening is surrounded by ten small papillæ. Tentacles ten, the two lower ones much the shortest, all arborescently branched, the numerous ultimate divisions forming, in contraction, clusters of small rounded papillæ on the branches.

Color, in alcohol, grayish brown, the tentacles yellowish brown.

Panama,—F. H. Bradley, one specimen.

The extensive group of Holothurians referred to *Pentacta* by some authors, and by others to *Cucumaria*, appears to include several distinct generic types. The present species is closely allied to *P. pentactes* Jæg., of Europe, properly the type of the genus *Pentacta*, which should, therefore, be restricted to those species which have a pentagonal form, with suckers confined to the angles, and smooth interambulacra. In the same manner *Cucumaria* may be restricted to the group having *C. frondosa* as its type. In these the form is more swollen and rounded; the suckers wholly retractile, in five zones; the interambulacral zones provided with few scattered papillæ.

Anaperus Peruanus Troschel, Wieg. Arch. xii, p. 61, 1846.*

Holothuria peruviana Lesson, Cent. Zool., pl. 46, p. 124.
Thyone peruana Selenka, Zeitschrift für Wissenschaft. Zoologie, 1867, p. 354.

Several large examples of this species were obtained by Mr. Bradley both at Paita and Callao, Peru.

This species may be regarded as the type of the genus *Anaperus* of Troschel, it being the first species mentioned by him. It is allied to *A. Briareus* (*A. Carolina* Tr.) from the Carolina coast, Long Isl. Sound, etc.

Lissothuria Verrill, gen. nov.

Allied to *Psolus*, but having the upper surface of the body covered with a soft, smooth skin in which are imbedded minute perforated plates. Lower surface flat, with three broad rows of crowded suckers. Anal area elevated, the opening surrounded by calcareous papillæ. Tentacles ten, arborescently branched, the two lower ones smallest.

Lissothuria ornata Verrill, sp. nov.

Body elongated, depressed, the flat lower surface broad; the anterior end elevated; the anal area near the high posterior end, little elevated above the surface of the back. Length 2·1; breadth ·85; height ·35; length of lower surface 1·7; breadth ·85.

The anterior end, bearing the tentacles, rises considerably above the level of the back, and where it joins the naked part below the tentacles there is a ring of calcareous plates, with pointed ends, and on the upper side four, elongated, flexible papillæ rising from enlarged bases having calcareous grains, apparently corresponding to four of the ambulacra. The tentacles are arborescently branched, not large, the subdivisions in contraction forming a rounded cluster, on a stout pedunculated base. Anal region conical, opening posteriorly. Suckers of the lower surface small and very numerous, crowded, six or eight series in each ambulacrum. The skin above is soft, but filled with minute calcareous grains and fewer, somewhat larger, perforated ones.

Color, in alcohol, light purple, whitish beneath, disk purple, with a yellowish white ring around the mouth; tentacles purple at base, the subdivisions yellowish.

Panama, one specimen,—F. H. Bradley.

---

* This belongs to the genus *Pattalus* (see page 376),—Reprint.

No. 3. *On the Geographical Distribution of the Echinoderms of the West Coast of America.*

Published July, 1867.

Although a large proportion of the Echinoderms inhabiting this coast were long since described, very little has been done toward the study of their distribution, and comparisons with the Echinoderm Faunæ of other regions.

It is certain that our knowledge of the species inhabiting the various districts upon this coast is still quite imperfect, for even the collection of Mr. Bradley contains several undescribed species from Panama, which was the region previously best known. But since the collections which he has made, and those made by Mr. J. Xantus at Cape St. Lucas, have contributed a large amount of new and authentic materials for such investigations, it is thought proper to introduce here a brief account of what is already known concerning this interesting and important subject.

The distribution of the species of the West Coast of America should be studied with reference to several questions:—

First.—To ascertain the range of each species along the coast, both geographically and in the depth.

Second.—To ascertain the extent and boundaries of the several faunæ, which occupy the coast.

Third.—To compare these faunæ with those of other regions,—especially the tropical fauna of the West Coast with that of the East Coast and West Indies, and with that of the Pacific Islands and East Indies.

Fourth.—To compare the living species with those found fossil in the Tertiary and more recent formations of the neighboring coasts, and of the West Indies and Eastern North America.

Very little material is now accessible for the investigation of the subject included under the fourth head, but since prolific fossiliferous deposits are known to occur near Aspinwall, as well as along the western coast of South America,* many important results may be expected when such localities shall have been fully investigated.

The principal sources of information concerning the existing faunæ of the coast have, hitherto, been the works of Brandt[1] for the north-

---

* A deposit abounding in fossils was examined by Mr. Bradley near Zorritos, Peru, which is apparently of late Tertiary age, but the collection has not yet been examined with care. (See vol. ii,—Reprint).

[1] Prodromus descriptionis animalium ab II. Mertensio in orbis terrarum circumnavigatione observatorum. Recueil des Actes de la séance publique de l'académie impériale de St. Petersbourg, 1825.

ern district; Dr. William Stimpson[2] for the Coast of Oregon and California; D. J. E. Gray,[3] Dr. Chr. Lütken,[4] and Mr. A. Agassiz[5] for the tropical region; Valenciennes[6] and Agassiz and Desor[7] for the Galapago Islands and coast of Peru; Philippi[8] for the coast of Chili and southward to the Straits of Magellan. Dr. Lütken has given lists of all the species of Echini and Starfishes known upon the whole coast at that time, but numerous discoveries have been made since the publication of his valuable papers. Mr. Theodore Lyman[9] has given a list of all the known Ophiurians, with descriptions of all the America species which he has personally examined.

From these and other works, and from the collections of the Yale College Museum, the Smithsonian Institution, the Boston Society of Natural History, and the Essex Institute, the following lists have been complied.

Care has been taken not to admit doubtful species, and those apparently without sufficiently authentic localities. The few species included in the lists of which the localities are questionable or suspected are preceded by a mark of doubt, thus, (?); those that I have personally studied are marked thus, (!).

List of species found at Sitcha.

ASTERIOIDEA.

Asteropsis imbricata Grube.
Patiria miniata (*Asterias miniata* Brandt). Extends south to Monterey.
Solaster decemradiatus (Brandt sp.) Stimpson.
Pycnopodia helianthoides (Brandt sp.) Stimpson. Extends to Tomales Bay, Cal.

---

[2] The Crustacea and Echinodermata of the Pacific Shores of North America. Journal of the Boston Society of Natural History, vol. vi, 1857. Proceedings Bost. Soc. N. H., vol. viii, p. 261, 1861.

[3] Synopsis of the genera and species of the Class Hypostoma (*Asterias* Linn.). Annals and Magazine of Natural History, vi, 1840. Numerous starfishes from the collection of Hugh Cuming are briefly described in this paper.

[4] Videnskabelige Meddelelser fra den naturhistoriske Forening i Kjöbenhavn. Bidrag til Kundskab om Ophiurerne ved Central-Amerikas Vestkyst, 1856. Bidrag til Kundskab om de ved Kysterne af Mellem-og Syd-Amerika levende Arter af Søstjerner, 1858. Bidrag til Kundskab om Echiniderne, 1864. Kritiske Bemærkninger om forskjellige Söstjerner (Asterider), med Beskrivelse af nogle nye Arter, 1864.

[5] Bulletin of the Museum of Comparative Zoölogy, No. 2, 1863.

[6] Voyage autour du Monde sur la frégate la Vénus par Petit-Thouars, Atlas de Zoologie, Zoophytes, 1846.

[7] Catalogue raisonné des familles, des genres et des espéces de la classe des Echinodermata. Annales des sciences naturelles, 3me serie, Zoologie, t. 6, 7, 8, 1847.

[8] Vier neue Echinodermen des Chilenischen Meeres. Archiv fur Naturgeschichte, Bd. xxiii, 1857, p. 130.

[9] Illustrated Catalogue of the Mus. Comp. Zoölogy, No. I, 1865.

Asterias ochracea Brandt. Found also at San Francisco and Tomales Bay.
Asterias epichlora Brandt.

ECHINOIDEA.

Dendraster excentricus (Esch. sp.) Ag. From Unalaschka to Monterey, Cal.
Eurychinus Dröbachiensis V.? (*E. chlorocentrotus* Brandt sp.). Mr. A. Agassiz considers this the same as *E. Dröbachiensis* of the North Atlantic. It is found as far south as the Gulf of Georgia.

HOLOTHURIOIDEA.

Chirodota discolor Esch.
Leptosynapta verrucosa* (nobis), (*Chirodota verrucosum* Esch., Zoöl. Atlas, Tab. X. fig. 3).
Liosoma Sitchænse Brandt.
Psolus Sitchænsis Duj. et Hupé, (*Cuvieria* Brandt). Whether this be a true *Psolus* can be ascertained only by reëxamination.
Pentacta albida (Brandt sp.) Stimp.
P. nigricans (Br. sp.) Stimp.
P. miniata (Br. sp.) Stimp.
Aspidochir Mertensii Brandt.
Diploperideris Sitchænsis Brandt, (? *Holothuria*).

Six species included in the above list reach Puget Sound, and five extend to Tomales Bay and San Francisco. The species now considered peculiar are chiefly Holothurians and probably many of them will hereafter be found farther south, while others may prove identical with the arctic species of the North Atlantic.

List of species found in Puget Sound and along the coast to Cape Mendocino, Cal.

OPHIUROIDEA.

Ophioglypha Lütkenii Lyman. Puget Sound.
Ophiopholis Kennerleyi Lyman! Puget Sound; Dungenes, Or. (Yale Mus.); Mendocino.
Amphiura Pugetana Lyman. Puget Sound and Mendocino.
A. occidentalis Lym. Puget Sound to Monterey, Cal.
A. urtica Lym. Puget Sound.
Astrophyton sp. (? *A. Crayi* Lym.). Puget Sound (Dr. Stimpson).

---

* Under the generic name, *Leptosynapta*, I propose to separate from the typical species of *Synapta* (*S. mammillosa* Esch.), such species as *S. tenuis* Ayres of New England, and *S. inhærens* of Europe. These are distinguished by their more slender form, the absence of prominent verrucæ, fewer (12), shorter and more digitate tentacles, etc. *L. tenuis* may be regarded as the type. Eschscholtz himself referred such species to his genus *Chirodota*, from the typical species of which they differ in having minute calcireous hooks in the skin for adhesion. The typical species of *Synapta* have fifteen tentacles, and prominent verrucæ.

ASTERIOIDEA.
Mediaster aequalis Stimp. Puget Sound to San Francisco.
Patiria miniata (Brandt sp.). Sitcha to Isl. San Miguel.*
Cribrella leviuscula (Linckia leviuscula Stimp.). Puget Sound; Dungenes, Oregon (Coll. Yale Mus.).
Pycnopodia helianthoides Stimp.
Asterias epichlora Brandt. Puget Sound (Stimpson); mouth of Columbia River (*A. Katherinae* Gray).
A. ochracea Brandt.
A. conferta Stimpson. Puget Sound.
A. fissispina Stimp. Shoalwater Bay, Oregon.
A. Lutkenii Stimp. Oregon.
A. paucispina Stimp. Puget Sound.
A. Troschelii Stimp. Puget Sound.
A. hexactis Stimp. Puget Sound.

ECHINOIDEA.
Dendraster excentricus Agassiz.
Eurycchinus Dröbrachiensis Verrill. (?) (*E. chlorocentrotus* Brandt). Gulf of Georgia; Vancouver's Island.

HOLOTHURIOIDAE.
Pentacta piperata Stimp. Puget Sound.
P. populifera Stimp. Puget Sound.
P. albida Stimp. California (Selenka).
P. quinquesemita (Selenka sp.) Mendocino.
Synapta albicans Sel. Mendocino.

Of the 25 species in this list, 16 have not been recorded from south of Mendocino; and 18 are not known north of Puget Sound; 15, so far as yet known, are peculiar to this district.

List of species found between Cape Mendocino and San Diego, Cal.

OPHIUROIDEA.
Ophiopholis Caryi Lym. San Francisco.
Amphiura occidentalis Lym. Monterey and northward.
Ophiothrix dumosa Lyman. San Diego, Cal.
Astrophyton Caryi Lym. San Francisco.

ASTERIOIDEA.
Mediaster aequalis Stimp. San Francisco.
Patiria miniata (Brandt sp.). Tomales (or Bodega) Bay; San Francisco; Isl. San Miguel.

---

* This Island is one of the most northern of the Santa Barbara group.

Pycnopodia helianthoides Stimp., Tomales Bay.
Asterias gigantea Stimp., Tomales Bay.
A. brevispina Stimp., San Francisco (10 fathoms, sandy bottom).
A. ochracea Brandt, San Francisco at low water! Tomales Bay! northward.
A. capitata Stimp., San Diego, Cal.
A. æqualis Stimp., Monterey, Cal.

ECHINOIDEA.
Dendraster excentricus Ag., from Monterey northward!
Loxechinus purpuratus A. Ag., San Francisco, on rocks at low-water!
Toxopneustes Franciscana (*Toxocidaris franciscana* A.Ag.), S. Francisco!

HOLOTHURIOIDEA.
Liosoma arenicola Stimp., San Pedro, Cal.
? *Cucumaria frondosa* Bv., San Francisco.
Holothuria Californica Stimp., Tomales Bay.

Of the 18 species in this list, 10 do not appear to have been, as yet, found north of Tomales Bay, while 6 extend northward to Puget Sound. *Astrophyton Caryi* may, also, prove to be the same species as the one indicated from Puget Sound. "*Cucumaria frondosa*" may prove identical with one of the species from Sitcha, described by Brandt, but if correctly identified it is a true circumpolar species and must be supposed to exist along the whole coast northward from San Francisco. Two species have not been found north of San Diego.

None of the species in the above list have been found at Cape St. Lucas, except *Ophiothrix dumosa*.

Concerning the Echinoderms found between San Diego and Margarita Bay, Lower California, we have no information whatever.

The special localities of the following species are unknown. It is quite probable that some of them belong to the fauna of Lower California.

Chætaster Californicus Grube, "California."
Cidaris Danæ Ag., California (Ag. and Des. Catal.).
Astriclypeus Mannii Verrill, West Coast of America (?)*

List of species found at Margarita Bay and Cape St. Lucas.

OPHIUROIDEA.
Ophiura Panamesis Lyman.
O. teres Lyman.
Ophiocoma æthiops Lütken.
O. Alexandri Lyman.
Ophiactis virescens Lütken.

---

* Dr. F. H. Troschel gives Yokohama, Japan, as the locality of this species,—Reprint.

Ophionereis Xantusii Lyman, Cape St. Lucas.
O. annulata Lyman.
Ophiothrix spiculata LeC.
O. dumosa Lyman, Cape St. Lucas, San Diego, Guayamas.

ASTERIOIDEA.
Astropecten Örstedii Lütken!
Nidorellia armata Gray!
Oreaster occidentalis Verrill, Cape St. Lucas and Panama!
Linckia unifascialis Gray!
 Do. var. *bifascialis* Gray!
Ophidiaster pyramidatus Gray!
Heliaster microbrachia Xantus, Cape St. Lucas and Panama.
H. Kubiniji Xantus! Cape St. Lucas.
Asterias sertulifera Xantus, Cape St. Lucas.

ECHINOIDEA.
Cidaris Thouarsii Val.!
Diadema Mexicana A. Ag., Cape St. Lucas and Acapulco!
Echinodiadema coronata Verrill, Cape St. Lucas!
Echinocidaris stellata Agassiz, Margarita Bay! Cape St. Lucas! Guayamas, and south to Paita, Peru!
Psammechinus pictus Verrill, Cape St. Lucas.
Echinometra Van Brunti A. Ag., Cape St. Lucas and Acapulco!
Encope sp.*
Pygorhynchus Pacificus Ag., Cape St. Lucas and Acapulco!
Metalia nobilis Verrill, Cape St. Lucas and Panama!
Brissus obesus Verrill, Cape St. Lucas and Gulf of California!

Species given in this list without special localities extend as far southward as Panama or beyond. Of the 27 species here recorded, 17 reached Panama; 3 have been found elsewhere only at Acapulco; 2 only at Cape St. Lucas and in the Gulf of California; and 5 have, as yet, been recorded only from Cape St. Lucas. The only species known to me from Margarita Bay is *Echinocidaris stellata*, which has also the most extensive range southward. *Ophiothrix dumosa*, alone, is included both in this and the preceding list.

List of species found at Acapulco, Mazatlan, and in the Gulf of California.

OPHIUROIDEA.
Ophiura Panamensis Lym., Acapulco and southward!
O. teres Lym., Acapulco and southward!

---
* Since described as *Encope Californica* V. Common at La Paz, J. Pedersen.—Reprint.

Ophiocoma æthiops Lütk., Acapulco and southward !
O. Alexandri Lym., Acapulco and southward !
Ophiothrix dumosa Lym., Guaymas to San Diego.

ASTERIOIDEA.
Nidorellia armata Gray, Guaymas! (Bost. Soc. N. H.)
Linckia unifascialis Gray, Acapulco and southward !
Heliaster sp.=(*H. Kubiniji ?*). Acapulco and Mazatlan. Dr. Stimpson records *H. helianthus* from Mazatlan, but this is probably an erroneous identification.

ECHINOIDEA.
Diadema Mexicana A. Ag., Acapulco ! Cape St. Lucas !
Echinocidaris stellata Ag., Guaymas and southward !
Lytechinus roseus Verrill, Acapulco and Panama !
Tripneustes depressus A. Ag., Guaymas ! La Paz !
Toxopneustes sp. (*Toxocidaris mexicana* A. Ag.), Acapulco.
Echinometra VanBrunti A. Ag., Acapulco! and Cape St. Lucas !
Stoloniclypeus rotundus A. Ag., Acapulco (A. Ag.), Panama !
Encope grandis A g., Head of the Gulf of California !
Pygorhynchus Pacificus Ag., Acapulco and Cape St. Lucas !
(?) *Mora clotho* Mich., Mazatlan.
Lovenia sp., Gulf of California !
Meoma nigra Verrill, Acapulco !

HOLOTHURIOIDEA.
Stichopus Kefersteinii Selenka. Acapulco.
Holothuria lubrica Selenka. Acapulco.
Stolus ovulum Selenka. Acapulco.

This list, which is doubtless very imperfect,* includes 23 species, of which 9 are found also at Panama; 5 are found at Cape St. Lucas; the remaining 9 are, so far as known, peculiar to this district, but future researches will probably reduce the number, since the coast of Mexico and Central America has been little explored.

List of species of the West Coast of Central America and the Bay of Panama.

OPHIUROIDEA.
Astrophyton Panamense Verrill, Panama and Zorritos, Peru !
Ophiura teres Lyman, Cape St. Lucas to Panama !
O. Panamensis Lym., Cape St. Lucas to Panama !
O. variegata Lym., Realejo and Panama !
O. Duniana Verrill, La Union !

---
* Many additional species have recently been sent from La Paz by J. Pedersen, lists of which will be found in articles 5 and 8,—Reprint.

O. sp. nov. (see page 270), Panama!
Ophiolepis variegata Lütk., La Union! Realejo. Panama!
Ophiozona Pacifica Lym., Punta Arenas. Panama!
Ophiocoma æthiops Lütk., Cape St. Lucas to Panama!
O. Alexandri Lym., Cape St. Lucas to Panama!
Ophionereis annulata Lym., Cape St. Lucas to Panama!
Ophiocnida hispida Lym., Panama!
Ophiostigma tenue Lütk., Realejo.
Amphiura geminata Lütk., Panama!
A. violacea Lütk., Realejo. ? Panama!
A. Puntarenæ Lütk., Punta Arenas. Panama!
A. microdiscus Lütk., Punta Arenas.
A. Örstedii Lütk., Punta Arenas.
Ophiophragmus marginatus Lym., Realejo.
Hemipholis gracilis Verrill, Panama!
Ophiactis virescens Lütk., Punta Arenas. Panama!
O. simplex Lütk., Nicaragua. Panama!
(?) *O. Örstedii* Lütk., Punta Arenas.
O. arenosa Lütk., Punta Arenas. Realejo. ? Panama!
Ophiothrix spiculata LeC., Cape St. Lucas to Zorritos, Peru!
Ophiothela mirabilis Verrill, Panama!
Ophiomyxa sp., Punta Arenas (Lütken).

ASTERIOIDEA.
Luidia tessellata Lütk., Acajutla to Panama!
(?) *Petalaster Columbiæ* Gray, San Blas.
Astropecten fragilis Verrill, Panama and Zorritos!
A. regalis Gray, San Salvador! Panama! San Blas.
A. Örstedii Lütk.,* Cape St. Lucas to Panama!
Patiria obtusa Gray, Panama!
Asteriscus modestus Verrill, Panama!
Gymnasteria spinosa Gray, Panama.
G. inermis Gray, Panama.
Nidorellia armata Gray, Guayamas to Zorritos!
Oreaster occidentalis Verrill, Cape St. Lucas and Panama!
Linckia unifascialis Gray, Cape St. Lucas to Zorritos!
Ophidiaster pyramidatus Gray, same range as last!
Mithrodia Bradleyi Verrill, Panama!

---

* A typical specimen of this species received from Dr. Lütken, while agreeing in most characters with those described in the preceding article (page 274), differs in having much smaller and shorter spines both above and below, the inner row on the upper marginal plates not reaching beyond the seventh or eighth plate, and in having the terminal papillæ of the paxillæ considerably finer, while the paxillæ are also smaller and shorter. This specimen being somewhat smaller (greater radii 2·15 inches), these differences may be due to age.

Echinaster aculeatus (Gray, sp.) Lütk., Guacomajo.
Heliaster microbrachia Xantus, Cape St. Lucas and Panama!

ECHINOIDEA.
Cidaris Thouarsii Val., Cape St. Lucas to Panama! Galapagos.
Astropyga venusta Verrill, Panama.
Echinocidaris stellata Ag., Guayamas to Zorritos and Paita!
Lytechinus roseus Verrill, Acapulco and Panama!
Echinometra rupicola A. Ag., Acajutla and La Union to Zorritos!
Encope occidentalis Verrill, Panama and Zorritos! Galapagos.
Echinoglycus Stokesii Gray, Punta Arenas! Panama! Galapagos.
Mellita longifissa Mich., Panama, A. Ag.*
Stoloniclypeus rotundus A. Ag., Acapulco. Boccones. Panama!
Metalia nobilis Verrill, Cape St. Lucas and Panama!
Agassizia ovulum Lütk., Boccones. Panama!

HOLOTHURIOIDEA.
Holothuria languens Selenka. Panama.
H. subditiva Sel., " Panama (Florida?)."
(?) *H. glaberrima* Sel., Panama, West Indies.
(?) *H. botellus* Sel., Panama, also Florida, Sandwich Is., Zanzibar, etc. (Selenka).
Pentacta Panamensis Verrill, Panama!
Lissothuria ornata Verrill, Panama!
Stolus gibber Sel., Panama.

The above list includes 61 species, of which 6 are known to extend from Cape St. Lucas to Zorritos, Peru, and one of these even from Guayamas to Paita; 36 species range from Panama northward along the Coast of Central America; 12 at least, extend from Panama southward to Ecuador and northern Peru, but this number will, doubtless, be greatly increased by farther explorations, for only two Ophiurians are known to me from the region between Panama Bay and Paita. 15 species are, as yet, known only from Panama Bay;† and 9 have been found only on the coast of Central America.

These figures must be taken only as an indication of the present state of our knowledge of this fauna,—not as representing the actual condition, for it must be remembered that while the Echinoderms have as yet been but partially collected at any point, the collections from Panama have been most complete, but those from Central America have also been much more so than those made south of Panama.

The Holothurians, considered by Selenka as common to Panama and the West Indies, or the Indian Ocean, need reëxamination, from

---

* This species with *Encope occidentalis* and *Echinometra rupicola* were collected at Corinto, Nic., by J. A. McNiel.—Reprint.

† This number has since been reduced to 9,—Reprint.

authentic specimens, before all doubt can be removed concerning these conclusions, which are at variance with the distribution of the other Echinoderms.

List of Species from the West Coast of Ecuador and southern part of New Granada.

Ophiuroidea.
  Astrophyton Panamense Verrill, Zorritos and northward!
  Ophiothrix spiculata LeC. This and the preceding are introduced here because found both at Panama and Zorritos.

Asterioidea.
  Luidia Bellonæ Lütk., Guayaquil (Lütk.). Callao! (Yale Mus.).
  Astropecten armatus Gray, (non Müll. and Tr.), Puerto Portrero.
  A. erinaceus Gray, Punta Santa Elena.
  A. fragilis Verrill, Zorritos and northward! (Yale Mus.).
  Paulia horrida Gray, Puerto Portrero.
  Nidorellia armata Gray, Punta Santa Elena.
  Oreaster Cumingii (Gray sp.) Lütk., Punta Santa Elena.
  Ophidiaster pyramidatus Gray, Bay of Caraccas.
  Linckia unifascialis Gray,   "   "
  L. Columbiæ Gray, West coast of Columbia.
  Cistina Columbiæ Gray,   "   "   "
  Dactylosaster gracilis Gray, West coast of Columbia.
  Ferdina Cumingii Gray.   "   "   "
  (?) *Acanthaster Ellisii* (*Echiniaster Ellisii* Gray), "South America."

Echinoidea.
  Echinocidaris stellata Ag., Paita and northward!
  Echinometra rupicola A. Ag., Zorritos and northward!
  Echinoglycus Stokesii Gray, Guayaquil and northward!
  Encope occidentalis Verrill, Zorritos and northward!

The Asterioidea in the above list are inserted upon the authority of Dr. Gray, from the collection of H. Cuming, unless otherwise indicated. The Echinoidea, although mostly unrecorded from this region, are found beyond it upon both sides and are, therefore, inserted here. The Ophiurans and Holothurians are almost unknown. Of the 20 species enumerated, 10 are found at Panama; 2 are doubtful inhabitants of this district, and the remaining 8, unless some of them be synonymous with Panama species, are still known only from this coast. These peculiar species, which are all Asterioidea, were mostly obtained by Mr. Cuming by dredging, and may hereafter be found by similar search at Panama.

List of Species found at Zorritos, Peru.*

OPHIUROIDEA.
Astrophyton Panamense Verrill!
Ophiothrix spiculata LeC.!

ASTERIOIDEA.
Astropecten fragilis Verrill!
Nidorellia armata Gray!
Linckia unifascialis Gray!
Ophidiaster pyramidatus Gray!
Heliaster Cumingii Gray, Zorritos! Paita! Galapagos.

ECHINOIDEA.
Echinocidaris stellata Ag.!
Echinometra rupicola A. Ag.!
Mellita Pacifica Verrill!
Encope occidentalis Verrill!

Of the 11 species in this list, 9 are found as far north as Panama, or beyond,—5 even occurring at Cape St. Lucas.† *Mellita Pacifica* is not yet known elsewhere; *Heliaster Cumingii* and *Echinocidaris stellata* are also found at Paita. All the species of this list are in the Museum of Yale College.

List of species recorded from the Galapago Islands.

ASTERIOIDEA.
(?) *Culcita Schmideliana* Gray, "Lord Hood's Island on Reefs, H. Cuming" (Gray).
Heliaster Cumingii Gray, "Hood's Island" (Gray).
H. multiradiata Gray, "Hood's Island" (Gray).
(?) *Acanthaster Ellisii* Gray. *Stilifer astericola* Brod., is recorded as parasitic in "*Asterias solaris*" from Lord Hood's Island, Gal., Proc. Zoöl. Soc. London, 1832, p. 60.

ECHINOIDEA.
Cidaris Thouarsii Val., Panama! etc.
Echinocidaris stellata Ag., Panama! etc.
(?) *Lytechinus semituberculatus* Val., (? *L. roseus*).
(?) *Euryechinus imbecillis* Verrill, (*Echinus gibbosus* Val.).
Anthocidaris homalostoma (Val sp.) Lütk.
Temnopleurus botryoides Ag.
Amblypneustes pallidus Ag.
A. formosus Val.

---
* Zorritos is situated 25 miles south of Tumbes, Peru.
† Eight of these species are found at La Paz,—Reprint.

Echinoglycus Stokesii Gray, Panama! etc.
Encope occidentalis Verrill, Panama! etc.

In this list are 14 species, of which 6 do not appear to have been found on the American coast, and three others are doubtful; 4 occur at Panama, and are species of wide range along the coast, while *Heliaster Cumingii* is found at Zorritos and Paita. "*Echinus gibbosus*," if correctly identified, occurs also at Paita and Callao.

This list, though very incomplete, indicates that the Echinoderm fauna of the Galapagos is of a mixed character, having the closest relations with that of Panama Bay, but at the same time including species belonging to the more temperate waters of Peru, and a large proportion that are peculiar to the group. Most of the peculiar species resemble Pacific and East Indian forms rather than American. Such are the species of *Amblypneustes*, *Temnopleurus*, *Culcita*,— genera which have not been found upon either the East or West coast of America. On the contrary, *Heliaster*, *Echinocidaris*, *Lytechinus*, *Echinoglycus*, *Encope* are very characteristic American genera.

List of species found on the coast of Peru, at Paita and southward.

OPHIURIOIDEA.

Ophiactis Kroyeri Lütk., Callao!
Ophiothrix magnifica Lym., Peru (Lyman). Paita!

ASTERIOIDEA.

Luidia Bellonæ Lütk., Callao! (Yale Museum).
Astropecten Peruanus Verrill, Paita!
Asteriscus (*Patiria*) *Chilensis* Lütk., Callao! (Yale Mus.). Valparaiso! (Lütken).
Stichaster aurantiacus V. (Meyen sp.), Callao! Valparaiso (Gray), Chili (M. and Tr.).
Heliaster helianthus Gray, Paita and Callao! Caldera, Chili! Valparaiso.
H. Cumingii Gray, Paita and Zorritos!

ECHINOIDEA.

Echinocidaris stellata Ag., Paita and northward!
E. spatuligera Ag., Paita and Callao! Coquimbo (Ag. and Des.).
Arbacia nigra Gray, Paita and Callao to Caldera, Chili! Coquimbo.
(?) *A. grandinosa* (Val. sp), Peru, Carthagenia, (Ag. and Des.).
Loxechinus albus Ag. and Des., Mejillones! Callao to Chili (Ag. and Des.).
Euryechinus imbecillis Verrill, Paita and Callao!
Boletia viridis Verrill, Callao!*
Agassizia scrobiculata Val., Peru (Ag. and Des).

---

* Probably from New Zealand, see footnote, p. 304,—Reprint.

HOLOTHURIOIDEA.
Anaperus Peruanus Trosch., Paita and Callao !(=*Pattalus Peruvianus* V.).
Pentacta sp., Paita !

In this list are 18 species, of which only 3 have been recorded from north of Cape Blanco, and two of these apparently find their southern limit at Paita; 2 are known only from Paita, and 2 from Callao. Six of the species extend southward to northern Chili, and several even to Valparaiso.

List of species from the coast of Chili.

OPHIURIOIDEA.
Astrophyton Chilense Phil., Chili.
Ophiolepis Atacamensis Phil., Isla Blanca, Chili.
Ophiactis asperula Lütk., Chili, Isle of Philoe.
Amphiura Chilensis Lütk., Chili.

ASTERIOIDEA.
Goniodiscus verrucosus Phil., Chili, Valparaiso and Rio Maipu.
G. singularis Müll. and Tr., Chili.
Astrogonium Fonki Phil., Chili.
Asteriscus (Patiria) Chilensis Lütk., Valparaiso and northward !
Heliaster helianthus Gray, Valparaiso and northward.
Stichaster aurantiacus V. (Meyen sp.), Valparaiso and northward.
Asterias gelatinosa Meyen (*A. rustica* Gray), Valparaiso.
Asterias echinata Gray, Valparaiso. Perhaps identical with one of the following.
Asterias Germanii nobis (Philippi sp.), Chili.
Asterias lurida nobis (Philippi sp.), Chili.

ECHINOIDEA.
Echinocidaris spatuligera Ag. and Des., Coquimbo and northward.
Arbacia nigra Gray, Coquimbo and northward.
Loxechinus albus Ag. and Des., Chili northward to Callao.
Anthocidaris erythrogramma (Val. sp.) Lütk., Chili, Ag. and Des.
Colobocentrotus pediferus Ag., Valparaiso !

Of the 19 species in this list, 6 occur also on the coast of Peru, at Callao or farther north. The remaining species are peculiar to the district so far as known. It is probable that northern Chili, perhaps as far as Valparaiso, belongs to the Peruvian Fauna, while the shores of southern Chili, and Patagonia, are inhabited by a distinct Fauna. The absence of exact localities for many of the species prevents a satisfactory solution of this question.

List of species from the Southern extremity of South America, and the neighboring Islands.

ASTERIOIDEA.
  Ganeria Falklandica Gray, Falkland Islands.
  Asterias antarctica (Lütk. sp.), Straits of Magellan.
  Asterias rugispina Stimp., Orange Harbor, Terra del Fuego.

ECHINOIDEA.
  Echinocidaris Scythei Phil., Straits of Magellan.
  Echinus Magellanicus Phil., Straits of Magellan.
  Abatus australis (Phil. sp.) Trosch., South America, Statten Land.
  A. cavernosus (Phil. sp.) Trosch., Statten Land.
  A. antarcticus (Gray sp.) Lütk., South Polar Seas.
  Tripylus excavatus Phil., Southern extremity of South America.
  (?) *T. Philippii* Gray, South America.

HOLOTHURIOIDEA.
  Lepidopsolus? antarcticus (*Cuvieria antarctica* Phil.), Straits of Magellan.

An analysis of the preceding lists shows that the distribution of Echinoderms on the West coast of America agrees very nearly with that of the Crustacea, as determined by Prof. Dana;* with that of Mollusca, as elucidated by Carpenter;† and with the general facts determined for the Fishes, Mollusca and Radiata by Forbes.‡ But at the same time there are some disagreements in subordinate points which demand attention, and additional evidences are obtained concerning the actual limits of the several faunæ.

The comparatively small number of species of Echinoderms and the definiteness of their characters, except among Holothurians, renders this class well adapted to illustrate the faunal divisions, while the localities for the species described from these coasts are generally more authentic than in many other regions.

The faunal divisions, indicated by the information already in our possession, are as follows:

THE SITCHIAN PROVINCE.—This fauna was believed by Forbes to extend southward to Oregon, including Puget Sound, while by Dana the latter region was named as a distinct region, the Pugettian Province. The Echinoderms now known indicate that in this class Puget Sound agrees nearly with the fauna of Oregon. The limits of the Sitchian fauna are not yet known. To the north it appears to pass into the Arctic, or Circumpolar Fauna, while several of the arctic

---

* Report upon the Crustacea of the U. S. Expl. Exp., by J. D. Dana, 1852.
† Report of the British Association, 1856.
‡ Johnston's Physical Atlas, p. 99, Pl. 31, 1856.

species have a range even southward of this fauna to the coast of Oregon. It apparently corresponds to the Syrtensian Fauna of Packard,* on the Atlantic coast of America.

THE OREGONIAN PROVINCE.—This division includes Puget Sound, in part at least, and the Coast of Oregon, extending to Cape Mendocino, Cal. It appears to be the western representative of the Acadian Fauna on the northeast coast of America. This is not equivalent to the Oregonian Province of Forbes, which extended from Columbia River to San Diego, including, therefore, this and the following.

THE CALIFORNIAN PROVINCE.—This occupies the coast from Cape Mendocino to Santa Barbara, and perhaps farther southward, and includes the Santa Barbara Islands, corresponding therefore with the limits assigned by Dana, while later this name was applied by Forbes to the fauna occupying the coast of the peninsula of Lower California.

It appears to represent the Virginian Fauna of the Atlantic coast. Many species are common to this and the Oregonian, while a large per cent, so far as now known, are peculiar to each. Numerous representatives of the genus *Asterias* give a peculiar character to both; and the genus *Dendraster* is not known elsewhere, except in the Sitchian Fauna. *Loxechinus purpuratus* and *Toxopneustes Franciscana* are peculiar and characteristic species of the Californian Province.

The Diego, and the Sonora Provinces, indicated by Prof. Dana, are almost unexplored for their Echinoderms. The former extends, according to Dana, from latitude $28\frac{1}{2}°$ to $34\frac{1}{2}°$, and the latter occupies the coast southward along the peninsula of Lower California, nearly to Margarita Bay. It is probable that some of the species described as from "California" belong to this almost unexplored region.

THE PANAMIAN PROVINCE.—This includes the Gulf of California, and on the coast extends from Margarita Bay, Cal., to Cape Blanco, Peru. It corresponds with Dana's Tropical Sub-kingdom and includes three subdivisions: The Mexican District or Province, including the Gulf of California, Cape St. Lucas, and the Mexican coast to Acapulco or beyond; the Panama District, including the coast of Central America and the Bay of Panama; the Ecuador District, occupying the coast southward from Panama Bay to Cape Blanco, Peru. These correspond nearly with those given by Dana, who considered them three distinct Provinces. Concerning the northern limit of this fauna there has been a pretty close agreement. Its southern limit, however, has not been so well established. Forbes included the coast only to Guayaquil, while

* Memoirs Boston Society of Natural History, vol. i, page 254; and Proceedings B. S. N. H., 1866, p. 333.

Dana placed the boundary farther south, at Cape Blanco. Mr. Bradley's collection made at Zorritos, a short distance north of Cape Blanco near Tumbez, shows a remarkable agreement with the fauna of Panama, not only in the Echinoderms, but also in all other classes, and especially in the Mollusca, Polpys, and Crustacea, while his Paita collection shows quite as remarkable an agreement with the Peruvian Fauna. There is thus a very abrupt change in the faunæ between Zorritos and Paita, and Cape Blanco may properly be considered as the point of division.

The large proportion of species that have a range throughout the whole extent of this Fauna, induces me to consider the three subdivisions proposed by Dana, as of secondary importance, yet in the present state of our knowledge there are several species peculiar to each of these subdivisions. The number, however, has been materially reduced by the late explorations.

THE GALAPAGOS PROVINCE.—It is somewhat uncertain whether this should not be united to the preceding, as a district or sub-province, many of the species being characteristic Panamian forms. At the same time some Peruvian species occur, which even caused both Dana and Forbes to unite this Fauna with that of Peru. Possibly the southern part of the Islands belong rather to the Peruvian and the northern to the Panamian Fauna. The recorded localities are not sufficiently exact to determine this question.

The large percentage of species peculiar to this region and belonging in most cases to Pacific rather than American types has induced me to consider it a distinct fauna, with an intermixture of Peruvian and, especially, Panamian forms.

THE PERUVIAN PROVINCE.—The region from Cape Blanco southward to northern Chili is inhabited by a very distinct and characteristic Fauna. One species only (*Echinocidaris stellata*) has been found in this Province, and that only in the extreme northern portion, which occurs also at Panama. The northern limit is well marked, but the southern is not yet accurately known. It appears to extend as far, at least, as Coquimbo, while even at Valparaiso many of the characteristic species occur. Dana considered Copiapo to be near its southern limit.

THE CHILIAN PROVINCE.—The middle coast of Chili, from near Coquimbo to Valdiva, appears to be inhabited by a peculiar Fauna, although at the same time several of the Peruvian species are mingled with those characteristic of this region. By Forbes the Peruvian Fauna was joined directly to the Arancanian.

THE ARAUCANIAN PROVINCE.—This appears to extend from near Valdiva to the south-western coast of Patagonia, but its southern portion is very little known. Dana places its southern boundary at lat. 50°, which would make its length about 900 miles.

THE FUEGIAN PROVINCE.—This includes southern Patagonia and the adjacent Islands. Several peculiar and interesting Echinoderms have been described from this Fauna, some of which, as *Asterias antarctica* and "*Cuvieria antarctica*," recall the forms of the Arctic regions, while there are other genera, as *Tripylus*, that are quite peculiar.

Comparison of the Tropical Echinoderm Faunæ of the East and West Coasts of America.

The question of identity between certain species found upon the Atlantic and Pacific coasts of Central America is of great interest both to the Zoölogist and Geologist, and has received much attention from various writers. That the two Faunæ are remarkably similar in many respects, and have large numbers of closely allied, representative or analogous species, is admitted by all who have written upon the subject. Several authors also admit a certain number of species which are identical or undistinguishable. Thus of Mollusca, Dr. P. P. Carpenter* admits 35 species as identical between the two coasts; 34 additional ones that may prove to be identical; 41 that are "really separated, but by slight differences;" 26 that are "analogous but quite distinct species." In addition to these he admits 15 species as probably common to the west coast of America and the west and south coasts of Africa. Prof. C. B. Adams† did not admit any species as common to Panama and the West Indies, except *Crepidula unguiformis*.

Prof. Dana, Dr. Stimpson,‡ and others admit several species of Crustacea as common to the two coasts. In the collections of Mr.

---

* Report of the British Association for the advancement of Science, 1856.
† Annals of the Lyceum of Natural History of New York, v, 1852.
‡ Notes on North American Crustacea. Annals Lyceum Nat. Hist. of N. Y., 1858 and 1860. In these papers the following species are indicated from both coasts:

Petrolisthes armatus Stimp.   Cronius ruber Stimp.
Ozius perlatus Stimp.   Nautilograpsus minutus M. Edw.
Eriphia gonagra M. Edw.   Acanthopus planissimus Dana.
Callinectes diacanthus Stimp. Domecia hispida Souly.

Mr. Albert Ordway has satisfactorily separated the western species of *Callinectes* from those of the West Indies, (Boston Journal Nat. History, vol. vii, 1863). Concerning some of the other species Dr. Stimpson, himself, expresses doubt, owing to the want of sufficient specimens for ascertaining the constancy of slight differences.

Bradley there is a species of *Eriphia** from Panama that appears to be undistinguishable from specimens collected at Aspinwall, but many allied species, which are clearly distinct, occur on the opposite coasts.

Of Fishes, Prof. Theodore Gill† and Mr. F. W. Putnam both admit one species, at least, that appears to be common to both coasts, or in which no characters have has yet been found by which to separate them. The Fishes as a rule are nearly allied and many analogous or representative species occur.‡

The Polyps, as we have shown in a former paper,§ are entirely distinct, many of the genera and families being peculiar to each coast. The Panamian Fauna includes *Pavonia*, *Pocillipora*, *Ulangia*, *Cœnopsammia*, genera which are peculiar to the Pacific and Indian Oceans, while a few of the peculiarly American or Atlantic genera are represented by analogous species, as *Renilla*, *Phyllangia*, etc., but most of the characteristic West Indian genera and families are entirely absent. Several peculiar genera also occur, as *Stylatula* and *Stephanaria*.‖ The genera *Muricea*, *Gorgonia* (*Rhipidogorgia*),¶ *Astrangia*, are represented by more species in the Panamian Fauna than elsewhere, but have analogous species in the Caribbean Fauna.

In the following list all the known Echinoderms of the Atlantic and Pacific Tropical American coasts are placed side by side, in order to show the similarity of the two faunæ, as well as their remarkable distinctness. When special localities are not given for a Caribbean species, it is to be regarded as inhabiting the West Indian Islands, most frequently the Antilles. A mark of exclamation (!) has been added after the names of those species that I have personally studied, as well as after localities from which I have had specimens for examination. For the Panamian species I have in most cases omitted special localities, because they have been given in the preceding lists, but have added remarks upon their stations, etc., derived from the notes of Mr. Bradley. (Localities introduced in the Reprint are in italics.)

---

* This proves to be distinct. It is the *Eriphia squamata* St. *E. gonagra* has not been confirmed from Panama,— Reprint.

† Proceedings Philadelphia Academy Nat. Sciences, vol. xiv, p. 249, 1862. (*Brachyrhinus creolus* Gill).

‡ Dr. Gunther regards 78 out of 303 species of Central American fishes as identical on the opposite coasts. Of these 173 are truly marine species with 57 identical,— Reprint.

§ Proceedings Boston Soc. Nat. History, x, p. 323, 1866.

‖ This name is proposed instead of *Stephanocora*, which was previously used by Ehrenberg in 1834 for a genus of *Oculinidæ*.

¶ We have since ascertained that these species are generically distinct from the West Indian "*Rhipidogorgia flabellum*," and belong to *Leptogorgia* and *Eugorgia*,—Reprint.

CARIBBEAN FAUNA.	PANAMIAN FAUNA.
Crinoidea.*	
Pentacrinus asterias (Linn. sp.)	None known.
P. Mülleri Örsted (P. caput-medusæ Müll.).	
(?) *P. decora* Thomson.	Other described species probably occur in the West Indies, but the lack of authentic localities prevents their admission here.
Antedon Dubenii Bolsche, Rio Janeiro.	
A. Braziliensis Ltk. Rio Janeiro.!	
(?) *A. Milbertii* Müll. North America.	
Ophiuroidea.†	
FAMILY, ASTROPHYTIDÆ.	
Astrophyton muricatum Ltk.! Charleston, Bahamas, Florida! St. Croix.	*Astrophyton Panamense* Verrill! Panama! Zorritos, Peru, at 4 fathoms depth, clinging to Muricea! *La Paz!*
A. cæcilia Ltk. St. Croix, *on Thesea*!	
A. Krebsii Ltk. St. John (Ltk.)	
FAMILY, ASTROCHEMIDÆ.	
Asteroporpa annulata Örs. and Ltk.	
A. affinis Ltk.	
A. dasycladia Duj. and H.	
Astrochema oligactes Ltk. St. Johns, 20 fathoms.	
A. affinis Duj. and H.	
FAMILY, OPHIOMYXIDÆ.	
Ophiomyxa flaccida Ltk.! Florida to St. Thomas.	*Ophiomyxa* sp.
FAMILY, OPHIOCOMIDÆ.†	
Ophiocoma echinata Ag.! Florida! Aspinwall! St. Thomas and Cumana.	*Ophiocoma æthiops* Ltk.! Low-water to quarter tide, under stones and in crevices.
O. Riisei Ltk.! Florida! Aspinwall! St. Thomas and Cumana.	
O. pumila Ltk.! Bahamas! Florida! Aspinwall! and St. Thomas.	*O. Alexandri* Lym.! Low-water, in crevices of the reef at Panama.
Ophiopsila Riisei Ltk.!	
Ophiactis Krebsii Ltk.! Bahamas! Florida, Charleston, St. Thomas.	*Ophiactis Örstedii* Ltk.
O. Mulleri Ltk.! Florida to St. Thomas.	*O. arenosa* Ltk.
	O. virescens Örs. and Ltk.!
	O. simplex Ltk.!
Amphiura Riisei Ltk.	*Amphiura geminata* Ltk.!
A. Stimpsonii Ltk.	*A. violacea* Ltk.!
A. tenera Ltk. Charleston, St. Thomas.	*A. Örstedii* Ltk.

* *Antedon Hagenii* Pourt., *A. meridionalis* (Ag. sp.) Verrill, *A. armata* Pourt., *A. cubensis* P., *A. rubiginosa* P., *A. bervipinna* P., and *Rhizocrinus lofotensis* Sars are additional species from the deep sea explorations of Pourtales,—Reprint.

† *Amphipholis albida* Ljung, and *A. subtilis* Lj., Rio Janerio; *A. Januarii* Lj., Brazil; *Ophionephthys limicola* Ltk. and *Ophionema intricata* Ltk.. St. Thomas; *Ophiacantha Pentacrinus* Ltk., Antilles, have since been described. See also Mr. Lyman's descriptions of 7 new genera and 21 new species from the deep sea collections of Pourtales off Florida, in Bulletin Mus. Comp. Zoöl., p. 316, 1869,—Reprint.

CARIBBEAN FAUNA.	PANAMIAN FAUNA.
A. limbata Ltk. Rio Janeiro.	*A. microdiscus* Ltk.
A. gracillima Stimp.!	*A. Puntarenæ* Ltk.*
Ophiophragmus septus (Ltk. sp.)Lym.	*Ophiophragmus marginatus* Lym.
O. Wurdemanni Lym. Charlotte's Harbor, Florida.	
Ophiocnida scabriuscula Lym.	*Ophiocnida hispida* Lym.!
Hemipholis cordifera Lym. Carolina!	*Hemipholis gracilis* Verrill!
Ophioblenna Antillensis Ltk.	
Ophiostigma isocanthum Ltk. Florida, St. Thomas, St. John.	
Ophionereis reticulata Ltk.! Bermuda! Florida! Bahamas! St. Thomas. Cumana.	*Ophionereis annulata* Lym.!
(?) *O. porrecta* Lym.† Florida (?) (Lym.)	*O. Xantusii* Lym.
Ophiothrix violacea M. and Tr.‡! Florida, Aspinwall! West Indies! and Brazil!	*Ophiothrix spiculata* LeC.!
O. Örstedii Ltk.! Bahamas! Florida, St. Thomas, Cumana.	*O. dumosa* Lym.
O. Suensonii Ltk.! St. Thomas! Carthagena, N. G.	
O. lineata Lym.! Aspinwall! Florida (Lym).	*Ophiothela mirabilis* Verrill! Panama to La Paz!

FAMILY, OPHIOLEPIDÆ.

Ophiolepis elegans Ltk. Florida, Charleston, S. C. (Lym).	*Ophiolepis variegata* Ltk.!
O. paucispina M. and Tr.! Florida to St. Thomas.	
Ophioceramis Januarii Lym. Rio Janeiro.	
Ophiozona impressa Lym. Florida to St. Thomas.	*Ophiozona Pacifica* Lym.!

FAMILY, OPHIURIDÆ.

Ophiura cinerea Lyman! Florida! Aspinwall! St. Thomas.	*Ophiura teres* Lym.!
O. appressa Say! Florida! Aspinwall! St. Thomas and Cumana.	*O. Panamensis* Lym.!
O. rubicunda Lym.! Aspinwall! Florida! to St. Thomas.	*O.* sp. nov.!
O. squamosissima (Ltk. sp.) Lym.	
O. elaps (Ltk.) Lym. Bahamas!	
O. brevicauda Lyman! Florida! Aspinwall! St. Thomas.	
O. guttata (Ltk. sp.) Lyman.	
O. brevispina Say! Florida and Bahamas to St. Thomas.	*O. variegata* Lym.!
O. Januarii Lym. Rio Janeiro!	*O. Daniana* Verrill!

* *Amphipholis grisea* Ljung., Guayaquil, is an additional species,—Reprint.

† This species proves to be from the Hawaiian Islands,—Reprint.

‡ Dr. Lütken has separated the West Indian from the Brazilian form under the name of *O. Caribæa*,—Reprint.

Asterioidea.*

Family, Astropectenidæ.

Luidia clathrata (Say sp.) Ltk.!
  S. Carolina! Florida! St. Thomas (Ltk.).
L. alternata (Say sp.) Ltk.
  Florida (Say), St. Thomas (Ltk.).
L. Macrgravii Stp. Brazil!
  Jamaica (Browne), Cotinquiba.
Astropecten articulatus (Say sp.) Ltk.!
  E. Florida and Georgia (Say).
(?) *A. ciliatus* Grubé.
  Porto Cabello (Grubé).
A. variabilis Ltk.!
  Florida! St. Thomas (Ltk.).
A. Antillensis Ltk.! St. Thomas.
(?) *A. Valenciennesii* M. and Tr.
  Vera Cruz.
(?) *A. Braziliensis* M. and Tr. Brazil.
(?) *A. dubius* Gray.

Luida tessellata Ltk.!
L. Bellonæ Ltk.!
(?) *L.* (*Petalaster*) *Columbiæ* (Gray sp.).
Astropecten regalis Gray!
A. fragilis Verrill!
A. Örstedii Ltk.!
(?) *A. armatus* Gray.
(?) *A. erinaceus* Gray.

Family, Goniasteridæ.

Oreaster gigas (Linn.) Ltk., = *O. reticulatus* M. and Tr.
  Florida! Hayti! St. Thomas (Ltk.), Curacas, Barbados, Abrolhos, Brazil!
(?) *O. aculeatus* M. and Tr.
  Probably the same as the preceding.

A. stellifer Mob. (*A. Braziliensis* Ltk.)
  Rio Janeiro.
Asteriscus folium Ltk.!
  Aspinwall! St. Thomas (Ltk.).

Oreaster occidentalis Verrill!
  Panama to La Paz!

(?) *O. Cumingii* Gray sp.

Nidorellia armata Gray!
(?) *Goniodiscus stella* Verrill!
  Perhaps young of the preceding.†
Paulia horrida Gray.
Gymnasteria inermis Gray.
G. spinosa Gray. *La Paz!*
Patiria obtusa Gray!
Asteriscus modestus Verrill!
  Under stones at low-water mark.

Family, Echinasteridæ.‡

Echinaster spinosus M. and Tr.
  Florida! Hayti! St. Thomas (Ltk.).
E. Braziliensis M. and Tr.
  Puerto Cabello, Jamaica, Rio Janeiro.
E. serpentarius M. and Tr. Vera Cruz.

(?) *Acanthaster Ellisii* (Gray) *La Paz!*
Echinaster aculeatus (Gray.)

Mithrodia Bradleyi Verrill! *La Paz!*
Ferdina Cumingii Gray.

---

* Mr. Pourtales has dredged *Pteraster militaris* off Florida in 120 to 125 fathoms,—Reprint.

† This proves to be the case, (see page 372),—Reprint.

‡ *Echinaster crassispina* V., Abrolhos Reefs and *E. spinulosus* V., West Florida, are additional species.—Reprint.

| CARIBBEAN FAUNA. | PANAMIAN FAUNA. |

FAMILY, OPHIDIASTERIDÆ.

(?) *Linckia Guildingii* Gray.	*Linckia Columbiæ* Gray.
L. ornithopus Ltk.	*L. unifascialis* Gray !
St. Thomas, etc. (Ltk.), Vera Cruz (M. and Tr.). Probably identical with the last.	*Cistina Columbiæ* Gray.
	Dactylosaster gracilis Gray.
Ophidiaster flaccidus Ltk.	*Ophidiaster pyramidatus* Gray !
St. Thomas (Ltk.).	

FAMILY, ASTERIDÆ.

Asterias Mexicana (Ltk. sp.) Verrill.	*Asterias sertulifera* Xantus.
(?) *A. tenuispina* Lam.*	*Heliaster microbrachia* Xantus !
Bermuda !	*H. Kubiniji* Xantus !
	H. Cumingii Gray !

Echinoidea.†

FAMILY, CIDARIDÆ.

Cidaris annulata Gray !	*Cidaris Thouarsii* Val. !
Florida ! Aspinwall ! Rio Janeiro (Ltk.).	Cape St. Lucas, Panama ! Galapagos !

FAMILY, DIADEMIDÆ.

Diadema Antillarum Mich. !	*Diadema Mexicana* A. Ag. !
Florida ! Aspinwall ! Hayti ! Bahamas !	*Echinodiadema coronata* Verrill !
Antilles and Surinam (Ltk.).	*Astropyga venusta* Verrill ! *La Paz !*

FAMILY, ARBACIDÆ.

Echinocidaris punctulata Desml. !	*Echinocidaris stellata* Ag. !
S. Carolina to W. Indies.	Guayamas to Paita ! Galapagos Islands.
(?) *E. Dufresnii* Desml.‡	
Cumana (Ag. and Des.).	
(?) *Arbacia pustulosa* (Lam. sp.).	
Brazil (Ag. and Des.).	

FAMILY, ECHINIDÆ.

Lytechinus variegatus A. Ag. !	*Lytechinus roseus* Verrill !
Yucatan to Bahia (Ltk.), Hayti ! Florida !	Acapulco to Panama !
L. Atlanticus A. Ag. (? *L. excavatus* Bl. sp.) Bermuda !	
(?) *Psammechinus aciculatus* Hupé.	*Psammechinus pictus* Verrill !
Brazil.	

---

* Since described under the name, *Asterias Atlantica* Verrill, from Brazil, Cuba, and Bermuda,—Reprint.

† Mr. A. Agassiz records 19 additional species, including 9 new genera and 14 new species, from the deep-sea collections of Pourtales, in Bulletin M. C. Z., No. 9,—Reprint.

‡ The Essex Institute, Salem, Mass., has two specimens, beautifully variegated with green, and agreeing entirely with the description of this species. One is labelled as coming from the "West Coast of Africa," the other from the "Sandwich Islands." The former locality is most likely to prove to be the true one.

CARIBBEAN FAUNA.	PANAMIAN FAUNA.

FAMILY, ECHINOMETRIDÆ.

Echinometra Michelini Des. (*E. lucuntur, pars,* auth.)! Florida! Aspinwall! Hayti! Brazil! *E. viridis* A. Ag. (*E. Michelini* Ltk.)! Florida! Aspinwall! Antilles (Ltk.). *E. plana* A. Ag. Hayti. (?) *Anthocidaris Mexicana* (Ag. sp.)* Vera Cruz (Ag. and Des)	*Echinometra Van Brunti* A. Ag.! Acapulco, Cape St. Lucas, and *La Paz!* *E. rupicola* A. Ag.! Acajutla to Zorritos. *Toxopneustes* sp. (*Toxocidaris Mexicana* A. Ag.), Acapulco.

FAMILY, HIPPONOIDÆ.

Tripneustes ventricosus Ag.! Florida! Yucatan to Surinam (Ltk.).	*Tripneustes depressus* A. Ag. Guayamas, *La Paz!*

FAMILY, CLYPEASTERIDÆ.†

Clypeaster rosaceus Lamk. Florida to Antilles (Ltk.). *Stoloniclypeus prostratus* A. Ag.!	*Clypeaster speciosus* Verrill! *La Paz!* *Stoloniclypeus rotundus* A. Ag.!

FAMILY, SCUTELLIDÆ.‡

Mellita hexapora Ag.! Florida! Mexico, Barbados, Surinam (Ltk.) *M. pentapora* Ltk.! W. Indies, Cumana, Brazil. (?) *M. testudinea* Klein! N. Carolina! Florida! Texas! *Encope emarginata* Ag.! Florida! to Rio Janeiro. (?) *E. quinqueloba* (Esch. sp.) Grubé! Florida! to Brazil. *E. Michelini* Ag.! Florida! *Moulinia cassidulina* Ag. Martinique.	*Mellita Pacifica* Verrill! *M. longifissa* Mich. Panama (A. Ag.), *La Paz!* *Echinoglycus Stokesii* Gray! *Encope occidentalis* Verrill! *E. grandis* Ag.! Gulf of California, *La Paz!* *E. Californica* Verrill! *La Paz!*

FAMILY, CASSIDULIDÆ.

Echinoneus semilunaris Lamk.! Cuba to Trinidad (Ltk.). *Cassidulus Caribæarum* Lamk. Jamaica, etc., St. Thomas (Ltk.).	 *Pygorhynchus Pacificus* Ag.!

FAMILY, SPATANGIDÆ.

Brissus columbaris Ag. and Des.! Florida! Antilles (Ltk.). *Meoma ventricosa* Ltk. Honduras, Antilles (Ltk.). *Plagionotus pectoralis* Ag. and Des.! Mexico, Antilles, Bahia, Turks Island!	*Brissus obesus* Verrill! *Meoma nigra* Verrill! *Metalia nobilis* Verrill!

---

* Mr. A. Agassiz considers this his *Echinometra plana,*—Reprint.

† *Clypeaster speciosus* V., from La Paz, is an additional species,—Reprint.

‡ *Encope Californica* V., from La Paz, is here added,—Reprint.

CARIBBEAN FAUNA.	PANAMIAN FAUNA.
Agassizia excentrica A. Ag. *Florida.**	*Agassizia ovulum* Ltk.!
Mœra atropos Mich. N. Carolina! Texas! Antilles (Ltk.).	*Mœra clotho* Mich. (A. Ag.).
	Lovenia sp. Gulf of California.

Holothurioidea.†

FAMILY, SYNAPTIDÆ.

Synapta lappa Müll.
Leptosynapta hydriformis nob.‡ (LeS.)
  Guadaloupe.
L. Pourtalesii Selenka (S. viridis Pourt., *non* LeS.).
  Biscayne Bay, Florida. Perhaps the same as the last.
Heterosynapta viridis nob.§ (LeS. sp.)
Synaptula vivipara Örst.
Chirodota pygmæum Müll.
C. rotiferum (Pourt. sp.) Stimp.
  Biscayne Bay, Florida, (Pourt.).

FAMILY, CUCUMARIDÆ.

Phyllophorus (?) *lepadifera* V. (*Holothuria lepadifera* LeS.). St. Bartholomew.	*Stolus ovulum* Selenka. Acapulco. *Stolus gibber* Sel. Panama.
Urodemas sp. nov. Bahamas!	*Pentacta Panamensis* Verrill! *Lissothuria ornata* Verrill!

FAMILY, HOLOTHURIDÆ.

Holothuria botellus Sel.
   Tortugas, Florida. etc.
	Holothuria botellus Sel.
	   "Panama, Sandwich Is., Zanzibar, Florida."

H. princeps Sel. Florida, *Egmont Key*!	*H. languens* Sel. Panama.
H. maculata LeS. St. Bartholomew.	*H. subditiva* Sel. Panama (Florida?)
H. unicolor Sel. Barbadoes.	*H. lubrica* Sel. Acapulco.

H. glaberrima Sel.
   "Hayti, Bahama Is., Panama."
	H. glabberrima Sel.
	   Panama, Hayti, etc.

H. grisea Sel. Hayti.	
H. Floridiana Pourt. "Florida, Zanzibar, Sandwich Is., Java," &c., (Sel.).	

---

  * This species, from the dredgings of Pourtales, and *Mœra clotho* are introduced on the authority of Mr. A. Agassiz,—Reprint.

  † Mr. Pourtales reports *Cuvieria* (? *Lepidopsolus*) *operculata* (Pourt.), *Thyonidium conchilegum* P., *T. gemmatum* P., *Echinocucumis typica* Sars, *Cucumaria frondosa* Gunner, and *Molpadia borealis* Sars from his deep-sea collections,—Reprint.

  ‡ See note page 325 for the genus *Leptosynapta*.

  § The name *Heterosynapta* is here proposed for a new genus having *H. viridis* LeS. sp. as its type. It is remarkable in having four simple and eight pinnate tentacles. Its skin contains small calcareous hooks, as in *Leptosynapta*. It has the habit of clinging to algæ, etc., instead of burrowing like most others of this family.

CARIBBEAN FAUNA.

Stichopus rigidus Sel.
Florida, Zanzibar, etc.
S. *badionotus* Sel.
" Florida (Acapulco?)"
Actinopyga (*Mulleria*) *parvula* (Sel.sp.)
Florida.
A. (M.) *Agassizii* (Sel. sp.)
Florida, Tortugas, Hayti.
A. (M.) *obscura* (LeS. sp.)
St. Bartholomew. This and the next two species may prove identical with some of the preceding.
Bohadschia agglutinata (LeS. sp.)
St. Bartholomew.
B. *fasciata* (LeS. sp.)
St. Bartholomew.
Sporadipus gigas Örst.!
Perhaps identical with one of the preceding species.

PANAMIAN FAUNA.

Stichopus Kefersteinii Sel.
Acapulco.

These lists contain 125 species from the Caribbean, including a few that are marked as doubtful, and 82 from the Panamian Fauna. Of these none have ever been indicated as common to the two coasts, except two species of Holothurians which Selenka records from both coasts, and another (*Stichopus badionotus* Sel.) from Florida and, doubtfully, from Acapulco. The Holothurians being very difficult to identify with alcoholic specimens, it is not improbable that these few apparent exceptions to the rule among the Echinoderms will prove to be errors in determining the species. In the other orders the species are often very closely allied in structure and appearance, yet the differences are in all cases sufficiently apparent. There are, however, so many analogous or representative species in the two faunæ, and so general an agreement in the genera and families represented, that the general features of the faunæ have a remarkable similarity, while they stand in strong contrast with the tropical fauna of the Pacific and Indian Oceans.

In this respect the Echinoderms agree with the observations, previously made upon the Crustacea and Mollusca, and confirm the statement that both coasts of America belong to one grand Zoölogical Realm, in distinction from all other regions, and that America has therefore a remarkable insular character, and may be regarded zoölogically as a great "Island in the Atlantic Ocean," the deep oceanic basin west of the Galapagos limiting the western extension of the American or Atlantic forms.

Among the types peculiar to the American Realm the genus *Ophiura* is one of the most remarkable instances, since it abounds on both sides of America, being represented by numerous species. But with the exception of one Mediterranean species, the genus is unknown elsewhere, no representatives of it having been discovered in the Indian or Pacific Oceans, where it appears to be replaced by *Ophiopeza*, *Ophiarachna*, etc., which have a similar appearance, but with only ten ovarial openings, instead of twenty. Among other genera, occurring on both coasts of America, but unknown in the great Indo-Pacific Fauna, are the following: *Ophiozona*, *Ophiostigma*, *Hemipholis*, *Ophiophragmus*, *Ophiomyxa*, *Lytechinus*, *Encope*, etc. The following, although represented in other regions, appear to have their greatest development upon the American coasts: *Ophiactis*, *Amphiura*, *Echinaster*, *Luidia*, *Echinocidaris*, *Arbacia*, *Mellita*.

Several genera, which occur in the West Indies and appear to be peculiar to the Atlantic, or have there their greatest development, have not yet been found in the Panamian Province. Such are, *Pentacrinus*, *Ophioblenna*, *Asteroporpa*, *Asterochema*, *Clypeaster* (also Pacific), *Cassidulus*, *Plagionotus*, *Mœra*.*

A few genera are found in the Panamian Fauna, which occur also in the Indo-Pacific, but have not been met with in the Caribbean Fauna. Among these are the following: *Ophiothela*, *Mithrodia*, *Acanthaster*, *Astropyga*, *Metalia*, *Lovenia*. The following genera seem at present peculiar to the Pacific coasts of America: *Nidorellia*, *Gymnasteria*, *Heliaster*, *Echinodiadema*, *Echinoglycus* (restricted), *Pygorhynchus* (also fossil in Europe), *Agassizia*; and in the temperate regions, *Pycnopodia*, *Loxechinus*, *Dendraster*.†

There are, also, numerous species in each Fauna belonging to cosmopolitan genera, or to genera found in all tropical seas, but none of these species, excepting the doubtful Holothurians, are common to both coasts, or to the Panamian and Indo-Pacific Faunæ, or to the latter and the Caribbean. Among cosmopolitan genera, represented on each coast, are: *Ophiolepis*, *Ophiocoma*, *Amphiura*, *Ophiactis*, *Ophionereis*, *Ophiothrix*, *Astrophyton*, *Astropecten*, *Luidia*, *Asteriscus*, *Oreaster*, *Ophidiaster*, *Linckia*, *Cidaris*, *Diadema*, *Psammechinus*, *Echinometra*, *Toxopneustes*, *Stoloniclypeus*, *Brissus*, *Meoma*.

From the preceding analysis of the genera, it is evident that while the Panamian Fauna has several truly Indo-Pacific types, and some that are peculiar, it is nevertheless most closely related to the Carib-

---

* *Clypeaster speciosus* V., and *Mœra clotho* Mich., are now known from the west coast; *Cassidulus* is now regarded by A. Agassiz as the same genus with *Pygorhynchus Pacificus*, and he refers *Metalia nobilis* to *Plagionotus*,—Reprint.

† *Astriclypeus* (Japan), *Pygorhynchus* and *Agassizia* (W. Indies) must now be omitted,—Reprint.

bean Fauna, by a large number of peculiar American genera, having allied species in each, and by many analogous species in cosmopolitan genera. This close relation between the two faunæ may, also, be well shown by the large number of Indo-Pacific genera that are equally absent from both, although widely diffused through the Pacific and Indian Oceans, of which the following are examples : *Ophiopeza, Ophiarachna, Ophiomastix, Ophiarthrum, Ophioplocus, Trichaster, Culcita, Anthenia, Archaster, Nardoa* (*Scytaster*), *Goniocidaris, Phyllacanthus, Echinothrix, Salmacis, Temnopleurus, Heliocidaris* (restricted), *Heterocentrotus, Acrocladia, Hipponoë, Laganum, Rumphia, Lobophora, Echinolampas,** *Moretia, Desoria.*

The apparent absence of *Comatulidæ* and other Crinoidea is, at present, a remarkable feature of the Panamian Fauna. It is quite probable, however, that species of this group will be discovered hereafter, since they occur in considerable numbers, both in the Indo-Pacific and Caribbean Faunæ, as well as in the temperate and arctic portions of the Atlantic.

Future discoveries are likely to modify to some extent the details in the distribution of the genera here given, but it is not probable that the general arrangement of the generic types will be essentially changed, or that the conclusions arrived at can be much modified, for species that may hereafter be discovered are quite as likely to belong to West Indian or cosmopolitan genera, as to those peculiar to the Pacific and Indian Oceans.

In the above discussion the Holothurians have been omitted because quite a number of the species known to me from each fauna are still undescribed, and because there are good reasons for supposing that there are many Panamian forms that have not yet been collected, such as *Synapta, Chirodota,* and other species that burrow, or seek hiding places. Nor have the Holothurians of other tropical regions been so thoroughly collected as to make detailed comparisons possible.

To the geologist one of the most interesting questions connected with the study of the Atlantic and Pacific faunæ of tropical America, is the possibility of a direct connection of the two Oceans, across the Isthmus, during late geological periods. Such a connection has been suggested by some Geologists, upon theoretical grounds, to account for the coldness of the climate in North America and Europe, during the glacial period. The only direct, geological evidence of such a connection, that has been adduced, so far as known to me, is the

---

* Mr. A. Agassiz has described *Echinolampas caratomides* dredged by Pourtales off Florida,—Reprint.

occurrence in the miocene strata of San Domingo* of several species of shells having the closest affinity to those of the Panamian Fauna, and in some cases belonging to genera not now living in the Caribbean Fauna.† The majority of the associated species are peculiar, so far as known, to the formation, while nearly all of those identified with recent forms (14 species) still inhabit the West Indies. In the same formation 10 species of corals occur, none of which appear to be living, but most of them belong to European and Atlantic, rather than Pacific groups, except a species of *Pocillipora*, a genus not now living in the Atlantic, but common at Panama and throughout the tropical Pacific. In the paper referred to, it is stated that the Isthmus of of Darien is less than 1000 feet high,‡ while the tertiary beds of San Domingo have been elevated nearly twice that amount.

A similar formation, and probably of the same age, occurs near Aspinwall in a railway cut, 15 feet above the sea-level,§ from which nine species are recorded as identical with those of San Domingo, and others are probably so. In the museum of Yale College there is a small collection from near Aspinwall, probably from the same locality, in which are specimens of a Clypeastroid, apparently identical with *Stoloniclypeus prostratus* of the West Indies, but certainly not with *S. rotundus* of Panama. So far, therefore, as the direct geological evidence bears upon this question it would indicate a passage of Pacific forms into the Atlantic during the Tertiary period, rather than the contrary. Yet Mr. Carpenter says,‖ "As the level of the Atlantic is higher than the Pacific, any such communication must have poured the treasures of the Atlantic into the Pacific, and scarcely allowed an

---

* On some Tertiary beds in the Island of San Domingo; from Notes by J. S. Heniker, Esq., with remarks on the fossils by J. C. Moore. Quarterly Journal Geol. Soc. of London, vi, p. 39, 1849. On some Tertiary Deposits in San Domingo by T. S. Heneken, with notes on the fossil shells, by J. C. Moore, and on the fossil Corals by W. Lonsdale, op. cit., ix, p. 115, 1853.

(Mr. Duncan has since described the fossil corals in the same work,—Reprint.)

† The shells quoted as having close analogy with Panamian species are as follows:
"*Cassis*, scarcely distinguishable from *C. abbreviata*, Acapulco. *Malea*, closely resembling *M. ringens*, Coast of Peru (Panama, Yale Mus.), if it be not identical. *Columbella*, very like *C. pavona*, Gulf of California. The genus *Phos* of which several species are known in the Bay of Panama and none in the West Indies, is here represented by four species, all closely related to shells of the Pacific. *Venus*, nearest to *V. gnidia*, California (Mazatlan, etc.). *Arca*, a large species very like *A. grandis*, Bay of Panama: no large *Arca* is now found in the Atlantic."

‡ The lowest pass on the Isthmus of Panama is said to be but 287 feet,—Reprint.
§ Journal Geol. Soc. Lond., ix, p. 132.
‖ Report of the British Association, 1856, page 363.

exchange in the other direction. Such is found to be the case; no species fairly belonging to the exclusive Pacific fauna being found in the West Indies."

The higher level of the Atlantic Ocean is, however, denied by others, and in consequence of the slight tides of the Atlantic side and their great rise and fall on the Pacific side, it is quite as probable that in case of a communication by means of a shallow or narrow channel, currents would flow alternately in each direction.

It is nevertheless very apparent that an intercommunication more or less remote between the two oceans cannot of itself account for the relations between the two faunæ, for should we assume that the small per-cent of identical species can be accounted for in this way, the occurrence of very large numbers of closely allied but distinct species, and also the agreement in generic and family types, already pointed out, still remain to be explained. This part of the subject presents much greater difficulties than the identity of a few species.

Two entirely distinct theories have been, and will doubtless long continue to be, adopted by naturalists in explanation of these facts and similar ones in various other regions:

1st. That the species and genera were created as we find them, and were originally adapted to the physical conditions and peculiarities of their respective districts. Consequently we should expect to find similar regions inhabited, to a greater or less extent, by similar genera and species.

2nd. That an extensive intercommunication took place at a remote period, and that the similar and allied species found upon the opposite coasts have originated by gradual differentiation from common ancestors, after the separation of the two oceans.

No. 4.—*Notice of the Corals and Echinoderms collected by* Prof. C. F. HARTT, *at the Abrolhos Reefs, Province of Bahia, Brazil*, 1867.

Published, February, 1868.

THE collections of Radiata made by Mr. Hartt during the summer of 1867, while examining the coral-reefs which he had previously discovered upon the coast of Brazil,* having been submitted to me for examination, were found to contain so many species yet undescribed

---

* Mr. Hartt was a member of the party that accompanied Prof. Agassiz, in his celebrated Expedition to Brazil and, while making a special exploration of the coast, at that time first discovered some of the reefs near Santa Cruz and Porto Seguro.

or not previously known to occur upon that coast, that it is believed to be of interest to publish a complete list of all the species observed.

Mr. Hartt has also greatly increased the value of the catalogue by adding notes upon the distribution and stations of the species.

It appears somewhat remarkable that while the Echinoderms, with few exceptions, are common West Indian or Florida species, the corals are nearly all, so far as known, peculiar to the coast of Brazil. This is, however, in accordance with similar facts observed in the Pacific and Indian Oceans, where the greater part of the tropical Echinoderms have a vast range, in some cases even from the Hawaiian Islands to the Coast of Africa, while the corals are much more local, all the principal groups of Islands having many peculiar forms.

This is, perhaps, chiefly due to the much longer time during which the young of most Echinoderms remain in the free, swimming condition, liable to be carried great distances by currents.

A suite of the duplicates, including all the species enumerated, with the exception of two, has been presented to the Museum of Yale College by Mr. Hartt. The first set he has retained in his own collection.

Class, POLYPI.

Order, MADREPORARIA.

Agaricia agaricites? Edw. and Haime, Coralliaries, vol. 3, p. 81.

Two young specimens that may belong to this species occurred adhering to *Mussa Harttii* from the Abrolhos Reefs. They are, however, too young to be satisfactorily determined.

This species never grows to be more than two or three inches in diameter. It is very frequently found attached to *Mussa* in shallow water. Occasionally it occurs in the holes in the reefs and is almost laid dry at low water.—C. F. H.

Siderastræa stellata Verrill, sp. nov.

Corallum forming rounded or hemispherical masses, often flattened above, cells polygonal, rather large (about ·15 inch), deep, the central part rapidly descending. Septa in four cycles, those of the first two cycles considerably broadest, all of them evenly crenulated, rather thin, thickness less than that of the intervening spaces, slightly projecting, the inner edge evenly rounded. Columella inconspicuous, represented only by one or two tubercles. Wall between the cells thin, represented by a single line. Trabicular processes between the septa very plainly visible from above.

Differs from *S. radians* in having larger cells, which appear more open; thinner septa, and consequently wider intervening spaces; and four complete cycles of septa. Most of the specimens are about six inches in diameter. Color dark ash-gray when unbleached.

Abrolhos Reefs,—C. F. Hartt.

> This is one of the commonest species of Brazilian corals, and may be collected abundantly from the reefs and rocky shores everywhere northward of Cape Frio. It flourishes in the pools of rocks and reefs left by the tide, in company with *Favia gravida* V., and seems to be a very hardy species, enduring not only great changes of temperature, but also great variation in the degree of saltness of the water. It frequently lives in large ponds on the top of the stone reefs, which are only filled at high tide, and are exposed to be much heated by the sun and much freshened by heavy rains. I have found it also in little ponds above the sea level, to which the waves had access only at high tide. It sometimes grows on the level surface of the reefs, and I have seen it exposed to a hot sun for an hour or more, at very low tides. This species occasionally forms elongated masses, 8—12 inches in length. When alive it varies much in color, usually being of a very pale pinkish tint, almost white, but sometimes blotched with deepened spots of the same color. On the border of the reef, I have collected it at a depth of 3—4 feet, at low tide.—C. F. H.

Var. conferta.

Some of the specimens show a curious deformity of the cells, arising from crowding, especially in the central portions. These have the septa and walls between the cells more elevated and convex, and in many places broken through, so as to unite adjacent cells. The cells, consequently, are irregular and appear deeper. But near the basal margins of such specimens, cells of the normal form may usually be found.

Pectinia Braziliensis Edw. and Haime, Coralliaires, ii, p. 209.

One small specimen of this elegant species was obtained at the Abrolhos Reefs by Mr. Hartt. It is distinguished by its turbinate form and by having the exterior obsoletely costate and covered with short conical spines. The cells are deep and narrow, the ridges slightly sulcate at top, sometimes with separated walls. Septa rather numerous, slightly projecting, the upper part regularly arched, perpendicular within. Coral 1·5 inches high; 1·25 wide; 2 inches long.

> This species appears to be quite rare in the vicinity of the Abrolhos. The above specimen was found growing on the border of the *Recife do Lixo*, in about two feet of water at low-tide. It also occurs at Victoria, in the Province of Espirito Santo, to the southward, where it is thrown up on the beach by the waves, but I could not find it alive.—C. F. H.

Favia leptophylla Verrill, sp. nov.

Corallum rather cellular, forming large hemispherical masses, evenly rounded above, with a thin, imperfect, concentrically wrinkled epitheca beneath. Cells subcircular, or deformed, open and deep, of medium size (about ·25 inch), smaller at the central part of the upper surface, where they are crowded, with prominent, thin walls, which are mostly separated about ·08 inch, and united by a coarsely vesicular exotheca. Septa in three cycles (24 to 30), distant, very thin, exsert, the summits angular or somewhat rounded, the costæ or portion outside the walls, very thin, elevated, deeply and unevenly toothed, abruptly descending, so as to leave deep interstices between the cells, except where they are crowded, when the costæ of adjacent cells unite, but the wall remains distinct. The septa, at summit and within the cells, bear few distant slender teeth, descend perpendicularly within, and have at the base a broad, thin, but not prominent paliform lobe. Columella but little developed, of a loose, open texture. In a vertical section the walls are thin and continuous; the exotheca is composed of large rectangular, mostly simple vesicles, which are horizontal and broader than high. The endotheca consists of irregular, smaller, thinner-walled vesicles, which are often compound and incline strongly downward toward the columella, which is continuous, and coarsely spongiform in texture.

Diameter of the only specimen obtained 5 inches; cells ·20 to ·30.

Abrolhos Reefs, Brazil,—C. F. Hartt.

This is very distinct from all other American species. The very open, deep, rounded cells; few, thin, projecting septa; and thin, distinct walls are very peculiar.

Favia gravida Verrill, sp. nov.

Corallum solid and heavy, encrusting or hemispherical, with strong epitheca beneath, evenly rounded above, with unequal, rounded, oval, and often deformed, deep cells, which are somewhat prominent above the general surface, separated at unequal distances, leaving concave interstices between them, which are strongly costate. Costæ thickened, alternately larger and smaller, irregularly and roughly spinose-dentate. Septa in four complete cycles (48) in the larger cells, unequal in width and height according to the cycles, those of the first and second being nearly equal, the summits angular, projecting somewhat, and deeply toothed, the teeth and sides of the septa rudely granulous. Paliform tooth well developed, rough. Columella very little developed, open. Diameter of cells from ·15 to ·30 of an inch; their prominence about ·10. Diameter of the masses about three inches, thickness half as much.

Abrolhos Reefs, Brazil,—C. F. Hartt.

This species is allied to *F. ananas* and *F. fragum*, but has stouter and more spiny costæ and narrower and sharper septa than either. From *F. fragum* Edw. and Haime (*Favia ananas* Pallas, Dana and most authors), which is the most common West Indian form, it differs also in having more prominent and larger cells, thicker and rougher septa, which project more and are not rounded at the summits, and both the septa and costæ more coarsely dentate.

Common in tide-pools of the reefs and rocky shores from Cape Frio to Pernambuco, with *Siderastræa stellata*, which see.—C. F. H.

Favia conferta Verrill, sp. nov.

Corallum compact, forming broad convex or hemispherical masses, two to four inches in diameter, and one or two thick, covered beneath by a strongly wrinkled epitheca. Cells crowded, deep, unequal and irregular, mostly elongated, often sinuous and somewhat mæandriniform, with three or four centers, sometimes nearly circular, not projecting, the walls united to their summits, showing only a slight sulcation between the adjacent cells, which are, therefore, separated only by a narrow ridge, which at times becomes simple, as in *Goniastræa*. Septa crowded, in the circular cells in four cycles, the last usually incomplete (36 to 48), all except those of the last cycle subequal, narrow within, obtusely rounded or truncate at the summits, which project somewhat and are regularly serrate, inner edge perpendicular. Pali in front of the principal septa, little developed, roughly serrate. Columella well developed, with a roughly spinose, uneven surface. In a transverse section the walls between the cells are compact, united into a narrow, nearly solid ridge, showing only a few very small, scattered vesicles. Breadth of the cells ·12 to ·15; length ·2 to ·8 of an inch.

Abrolhos Reefs, Brazil,—C. F. Hartt.

This interesting species is, in many respects, intermediate between *Favia* and *Mæandrina*, and has relations with *Goniastræa*, yet its proper place appears to be in the genus *Favia*. It is somewhat allied to *F. deformata* Edw. and Haime. It also resembles, in general form, *F. incerta* Duch. and Mich. (? = *Goniastræa varia* Verrill), but appears quite distinct in the form of the septa and intervening ridges, as well as in the remarkably elongated and narrow cells.

Common in tide-pools from Cape Frio to Pernambuco.—C. F. H.

Acanthastræa Braziliensis Verrill, sp. nov.

Corallum large, hemispherical or subglobular, regular. Base surrounded at the margin by a strong epitheca. Cells large, usually ·3 to ·7 of an inch, irregular, polygonal, often an inch in length and containing two or three centers, moderately deep (·15 inch), with a small, depressed center. Columella rudimentary or slightly developed, of loose convoluted processes. Septa in five cycles (the last imperfect), rather thin, slightly thickened outwardly, the summits projecting subequally (about ·05 inch), the upper part divided into from three to five sharp, elongated, unequal teeth; the lower part unevenly serrate, and presenting usually a distinct, broad, paliform lobe, which is strongly serrate. Between the cells the wall is often double, with vesicles between, but it is also frequently simple and nearly solid. Color of unbleached coral deep umber. Diameter of some of the masses upward of a foot.

This is one of the most abundant corals at the Abrolhos Reefs, and on account of its large size and solidity, doubtless one of the most important entering into their structure.

Rare in tide-pools at the Abrolhos, and usually only in the deeper ones on the edges of the reef, never in stations uncovered at low tide. Very abundant on the submerged borders of the reefs in the Abrolhos region, at Porto Seguro, Sta. Cruz, Bahia, Maceió. At the Island of Sta. Barbara and on the Recife do Lixo, it grows in large sub-spherical masses, on the edge of the reef, from a few inches below low-tide level to a depth of 15 or more feet. Some of the corals are two feet or more in diameter. In the water they have a pale grayish tint.—C. F. H.

Heliastræa aperta Verrill, sp. nov.

Corallum forming large rounded masses, a foot or more in diameter, of rather light, open texture. Cells circular, large (about ·3 of an inch), moderately deep (·1 inch), with a broad central area, the margins projecting about ·08 of an inch above the general surface; septa in three complete cycles, narrow, thin, subequal, the summits considerably projecting, angular, acute, the inner edges nearly perpendicular, finely toothed, often with a distinct paliform tooth at the base. Columella well developed, of loose open tissue. Costæ elevated and thin, rising obliquely upward to the summits of the septa, finely serrate. Walls very thin, inconspicuous. In a vertical section the columella is large, composed of loosely reticulated, convoluted and often fenestrated, lamelliform processes, with large irregular cells between. The cells of the endotheca are mostly simple, broader than high, inclining slightly downward, formed by very thin lamellæ. The cells of the exotheca are larger, more irregular, alternately overlapping, often compound, about as high as broad, formed by stouter lamellæ, which curve downward. Walls very thin, but continuous. Septa longitudinally roughened, scarcely granulated. Color of the unbleached coral dull umber-brown.

Resembles in the size and prominence of the cells *H. cavernosa* Edw. and Haime, but is very distinct in its more cellular texture; fewer septa, which are also much thinner and more acute at summit; thinner and more elevated costæ, etc.

> Found with *Acinthastræa Braziliensis*, but appears to be quite rare on the Abrolhos reefs. My specimens were obtained at a depth of 3 to 4 feet, at low tide. It is quite abundant in the bay of Bahia, and is brought to the City of Bahia from the island of Itaparica, with other corals, for burning into lime. The coralla are, occasionally, a foot and a half in diameter.—C. F. H.

Mussa Harttii Verrill, sp. nov.

Corallum forming circular clumps, often a foot in diameter and half as high, consisting of numerous short, rapidly forking, subcylindrical branches, ·5 to ·8 of an inch in diameter; seldom more than an inch between the successive branches; the summits alive for about half an inch, often less, and separated from the dead portion by a well-marked epitheca, above this with numerous strong, subequal costæ, which bear strong, sharp, recurved spines; cells from ·5 to 1·2 inches in diameter, sub-circular, often with lobed margins, none of them remaining united into series, rather deep (·4 to ·5 of an inch), septa in five cycles, the last incomplete, thin, projecting subequally at summit (about ·1 inch); the upper part divided into from four to seven unequal, sharp, diverging teeth, below which they are lacerately divided into irregular, smaller teeth; sides of the septa roughened by lines of distant, small, conical spines. Columella slightly developed, consisting of slender, interlocking processes, arising from the inner part of the septa. Color of the unbleached coral, yellowish brown.

Abrolhos Reefs, Brazil,—C. F. Hartt.

This species is very distinct by its regular cells, strongly echinate costæ, etc.

> One of the commonest as well as one of the most beautiful of the corals of the Brazilian reefs. It forms splendid bouquets on the submerged borders of the reefs, seeming to prefer the very edge, where the clusters of branches are, sometimes, two feet in diameter. Most abundant in 3–6 feet of water at low tide. This is a very fragile species, and one which seems to prefer rather sheltered localities. It it very abundant at Victoria, where, however, I have never seen it alive. It appears to grow there in rather deep water, and is thrown up by storms. This species is always encrusted with several species of Bryozoa. It is rare on the stone reef at Porto Seguro, but exceedingly common on the inner side of the coral reef at that locality. It is abundant on the Recife do Lixo, Abrolhos. I have seen specimens from Pernambuco. Color, when alive, whitish.—C. F. H.

Symphyllia Harttii Verrill, sp. nov. (?)

This coral, although having the walls of the cells united laterally, and presenting all the characters of the genus *Symphyllia*, presents in the form and structure of its cells, septa, and costæ, such a close agreement with the preceding species that it may ultimately prove to be only a peculiar form of it. On this account, I have thought it best to give it the same specific name. In Mr. Hartt's collection, however, there are no intermediate forms.

Corallum forming low hemispherical masses, attached by a broad base, which is covered by a strong epitheca, extending to about ·3 inch from the margin, beyond which there are numerous strong, subequal costæ, covered with many strong, sharp spines. Cells subcircular, not united in series, ·5 to ·8 inch in diameter, moderately deep, the walls united to near the summits, bearing on the space between the cells, spinose costæ, like those of the exterior margin. Septa agreeing in the form of the teeth, and spinous lateral processes, with those of the preceding species, but differing in being considerably thickened next to the wall and at the summit, and, therefore, bearing stouter upper teeth. Columella loose, convoluted, a little more developed than in the last species.

Abrolhos Reefs, Brazil,—C. F. Hartt.

Occurs with *Mussa Harttii* on the always submerged border of the Recife do Lixo, Abrolhos.—C. F. H.

Porites solida Verrill, sp. nov.

Corallum, remarkably firm and heavy for a *Porites*, encrusting or massive, forming rounded masses with an uneven surface; base with a spreading margin, covered with a strong epitheca. Cells unusually large and deep for the genus, well defined, subcircular, separated by a rather thick wall, which is acute and divided into strong, rough, spinous processes. Septa twelve, nearly equal, well developed, rather wide, the inner edge perpendicular and irregularly toothed, sides scarcely roughened; pali not distinct. Columella well developed, at the bottom of cell solid and uniting the septa, surmounted by a small tubercle.

Diameter of the cells about ·08 of an inch.

Abrolhos Reefs,—C. F. Hartt.

This species approaches more nearly to *P. Guadaloupensis* Duch. and Mich. than to any other West Indian form; but differs in its deeper cells, thicker walls, wider septa, and more solid structure. The same characters, together with the large size of the cells and non-crispate septa, will serve to distinguish it from the other West Indian species.

Occurs in patches 6 or 8 inches in diameter, occasionally, on the submerged border of the Recife do Lixo. Abrolhos, but abundantly on the coral reef of Porto Seguro. The color is, generally, of a rather bright yellow, but it varies much.—C. F. H.

Order, ALCYONARIA.

Hymenogorgia quercifolia Edw. and Haime, Coralliaires, i, p. 181.

Plate IV, figures 1, 1^a, 1^b.

This curious species is abundant in the collection from the Abrolhos Reefs.

It forms broad, fan-shaped fronds, often two feet high and a foot broad, consisting of broad, foliaceous branches, often resembling oak leaves in form; but at other times large, oval, and irregularly incised or palmate. The branches of the axis are slender and rounded, and pass through the fronds like the midribs of leaves. The rather conspicuous flat cells are scattered over the sides of the fronds. Color light yellow, usually purplish at base.

Spicula light yellow and bright purple, of three principal forms. The most abundant are "double-spindles," fusiform, with very acute ends and a naked space around the middle, showing a slender, transparent axis, the ends covered with prominent, separate, rough papillæ, of which eight are visible from a side view, on each end. Another less common form are shorter and stouter "double-spindles," with obtuse ends, narrow naked space at the center, and crowded, rounded papillæ. The crescent-shaped spicula are smaller and more slender than the others, with the convex side nearly smooth and strongly arched, usually with a slight indentation at the center. There are, also, some slender, blunt spicula, smaller than the others, and with fewer distant papillæ.

This is a very common species on the Brazilian coast, and ranges from Cape Frio northward to Pernambuco. It is very abundant at the entrance to the Bay of Victoria, as well as at the Abrolhos, Porto Seguro, and Bahia. It sometimes occurs in some of the larger tide pools on the surface of the reefs at low-tide level, but its usual station is on the edges of the reef, and ranging from low-water mark downward, to a depth of 5–6 feet or more. It is sometimes laid bare by spring tides. The color, when alive, is yellowish or pinkish; the latter tint is apt to fade in drying. A small *Ovulum* (*O. gibbosum*) is parasitic on this species.—C. F. H.

Gorgonia (Pterogorgia) gracilis Verrill, sp. nov.

Plate IV, figures 2^a, 2^b, and 3.

Very slender and delicate, sparingly branched; the branches irregular, sometimes forked, oftener arising alternately at the distance of one or two inches apart, and abruptly spreading for half an inch or more before curving upward; branches and branchlets of nearly the same size; the terminal and some of the lateral branches often long, slender, and undivided, somewhat compressed or quadrangular; the cells arranged along the edges in a single series on the smaller branches, but in two alternating series on most of them. Cells oval, rather large, mostly prominent, forming slight verrucæ. Sides of the branches mostly smooth, sometimes with a slight groove. Height 6 to 8 inches; diameter of branches, ·08 to ·10. Color various, lemon-yellow, reddish purple, or orange. The cells are often yellow on the purple specimens.

Abrolhos Reefs, Brazil,—C. F. Hartt.

The size of the branches varies somewhat in different specimens, as well as the number of the cells and distance between them; the cells are usually crowded along the sides of the larger branches.

In the non-pinnate mode of branching, slenderness of the few branches, and prominence of the cells, this species is quite peculiar. In size and form of the branches, it somewhat resembles *P. bipinnata* Verrill,[*] from Cumana; but has an entirely different mode of growth. The latter has, also, much smaller cells.

Spicula light purple, lemon-yellow, and yellowish white, having the same forms and variations as those of the preceding species, which they closely resemble, except in being about one-third smaller. The fusiform spicula are not quite so acute. The crescent-shaped ones are thicker, and often as long as the others, or even longer, and have the convex side a little roughened and more strongly rounded than in *H. quercifolia*. The slender spicula are more numerous and relatively larger.

Grows abundantly in little tufts on the edges of the reefs of the Abrolhos region below low-tide, with *Hymenogorgia quercifolia*. When alive, the colors are much deeper and clearer than in the dried specimens. Some of the branches are of a bright amethystine tint. It is occasionally found in some of the larger tide-pools on the reefs.— C. F. H.

Eunicea humilis Edw. and Haime, loc. cit. p., 149, pl. B², fig. 1.

Gorgonia citrina Lamarck, (*non* Esper).

Plate IV, figures 4, 4ᵃ, 4ᵇ.

This is a common form at the Abrolhos Reefs, and it varies considerably in the size and form of the branches. It usually forms low, densely branched clumps, with short, round, often clavate, and sometimes crooked branches. Occasionally the branches are longer and more slender, or even less than half as thick, and tapering at the ends,

---

[*] Bulletin of the Museum of Comparative Zoölogy, p. 31, 1864.

but agreeing in color, form of cells, etc. Intermediate specimens are frequent. The cells are sometimes prominent on the main branches, near the base; but on the terminal branches are but little prominent, opening upward. They are usually closely crowded on all sides. Color lemon-yellow. Height 4 to 6 inches; diameter of branches, ·10 to ·24 of an inch, usually about ·15.

Spicula mostly large, lemon-yellow and yellowish white, with a few very small, deep purple ones. The forms are very diverse; the largest are mostly stout fusiform, often crooked, not very acute "spindles," thickly covered with rough papillæ; other fusiform spicula are less than half as long, slender, acute at the ends, with fewer separated papillæ. The purple ones are still smaller, slender, acute spindles, with prominent papillæ. Club-shaped spicula are numerous, of various sizes, the large end very thick and covered with prominent sharp papillæ; others have such papillæ only on one side. Various intermediate forms of spicula are abundant.

Very abundant below low-tide on the borders of the coral reefs of the Abrolhos and at Porto Seguro, where it also occurs on the stone reef, and in shallow water along shore. It is abundant at Bahia. Occasionally found in the larger tide-pools —
C. F. H.

Pl. xaurella dichotoma Kölliker.

Icones Histiolog., p. 138, Taf. xviii, f. 11, 1866.
Gorgonia dichotoma Esper, Tab. xiv.
Plexaura dichotoma Dana, Zoöph., p. 669.

Plate IV, figures 5, 5^a, 5^b.

Several specimens of a *Plexaurella*, closely allied to this, if not identical, were collected at the Abrolhos, by Mr. Hartt. These are about a foot in height, consisting of 4 to 8 large, round, elongated branches, which originate from near the base and seldom divide, of nearly uniform diameter, about ·5 inch throughout, except at the ends, where they are often enlarged or capitate. Cells large, rather numerous, often slightly raised, but usually flat, with a broad oval opening, or with contracted narrow ones, which are linear and at various angles to one another. All these variations may occur in one specimen.

The spicula are of several forms, many having four stout branches, forming thick, stout-armed crosses, agree well with Dr. Kölliker's figure; others occur with three or even six branches; but a large proportion are short fusiform, with a naked band around the middle. All are thickly covered with rough papillæ, and have tapering, rather blunt ends. Spicula of the typical *P. dichotoma*, prepared and sent to the author by Dr. Kölliker, do not appreciably differ.

A very common form, occurring all along the coast north of Cape Frio. It is always associated with *Hymenogorgia quercifolia*, with which it appears to agree in station.— C. F. H.

Pleuxaurella anceps? Köll., op. cit., p. 138, Taf. xviii. f. 14.

? *Eunicea anceps* Duch. and Mich., Corall. des Antilles, p. 25, tab. 3, fig. 1 and 2.

Plate IV, figures 6, 6ª.

This form, which may be distinct from the last, although intermediate specimens occur, is represented by two examples. These have branches about ·3 of an inch in diameter, which are more divided and less fasciculated than in the preceding species. The cells are a little smaller and mostly contracted and linear, often slightly raised.

The spicula agree in most characters with those of *P. dichotoma*, but appear to be a little smaller and sharper and not quite so thickly covered with papillæ. The cross-shaped ones are less numerous and smaller, the majority are fusiform and of various sizes, rather acute, and covered with rough papillæ. Abrolhos reefs, with the last.

Several additional species of polyps were observed by Mr. Hartt. Among them were eight species of *Actinidæ*, at the Island of Sta. Anna; a *Zoanthus* with emerald green disk and tentacles; a spreading, brown *Palythoa*; an *Astrangia*, common on dead shells at Rio and Victoria; a *Sympyllia* at Victoria; a nodose, slender branched *Gorgonian* at Rio and Victoria; and *Renilla*, perhaps both *R. Danæ* Verrill and *R. violacea* Quoy and Gaim., in the harbor of Rio.

The following species, previously described from Brazil, were not obtained by Mr. Hartt at the Abrolhos Reefs:

Gorgonia pumicea Val., in Edw. and Haime, Corall., vol. i, p. 160.
Phyllogorgia dilitata Edw. and Haime, op. cit., p. 181.
Juncella hystrix Val., in Edw. and Haime, op. cit., p. 186.
Eunicea Castelnaudi Edw. and Haime, op. cit., p. 148.

Class, ACALEPHÆ.

Order, HYROIDEA.

Millepora nitida Verrill, sp. nov.

Corallum forming low rounded clumps, four to six inches high, consisting of short, rapidly forking, rounded or slightly compressed branches, about ·4 to ·8 of an inch in diameter, which have remarkably smooth surfaces, and are obtuse, rounded, or even clavate at the ends. The larger pores are small, very distinct, round, evenly scattered over all the surface, at distances of about ·06 to ·1 of an inch apart. The small pores are very minute, numerous, scattered between the larger ones, and often showing a tendency to arrange themseleves around them in circles of six or eight. The tissue is, for the genus, very firm and compact.

Abrolhos Reefs,—C. F. Hartt.

The form of the branches, distinctness in outline of the cells, and smoothness and firmness of texture, distinguish this species very clearly from any of the numerous varieties of *M. alcicornis*, and other West Indian species.

<small>Quite common on the border of the reef at the "Lixo," Abrolhos, below low-tide, also on the coral reef of Porto Seguro, in 3–4 feet water, low-tide. Color, when alive, light pinkish.—C. F. H.</small>

Millepora Braziliensis Verrill, sp. nov.

Corallum forming large, irregularly lobed and branched masses, the branches erect, angular or flattened, or forming broad, convoluted and folded, rough plates, with acute edges and summits, the sides covered with sharp, irregular, angular, crest-shaped and conical prominences, varying much in size and elevation, often becoming continuous ridges, usually standing at right-angles to the sides of the branches; cells small, circular, distantly scattered; texture firm and compact; height about one foot; breadth one foot and a half; branches and plates ·5 to ·8 of an inch thick, sometimes 6 inches wide.

Pernambuco, Brazil,—C. F. Hartt.

In texture and the character of the cells, this resembles the preceding species, and possibly it may eventually prove to be only a variety of it. It differs, however, very remarkably in the mode of growth and form of the branches. On the edges and sides of the branches there are often pits of various sizes up to an inch in diameter and depth.

<small>Small specimens occur also on the reefs at the Island of Sta. Barbara dos Abrolhos. Color, when alive, pinkish.—C F. H.</small>

Millepora alcicornis Linn., var. cellulosa Verrill.

Corallum consisting of numerous, irregular, rather short branches, arising from a thick base. Branchlets proliferous, or digitate at the ends, the last divisions short, mostly compressed, and acute at the tips. Some of the branches occasionally coalesce, so as to leave small openings. Cells numerous, crowded, rather large for the genus, each sunken in a distinct depression, the wall rising up into an acute ridge between them. Texture rather open and coarsely porous.

Pernambuco, Brazil,—C. F. Hartt.

This agrees pretty closely with a specimen from Florida (Maj. E. B. Hunt), in which, however, some of the branches do not have sunken cells.

Millepora alcicornis Linn., var., **digitata** (?) Esper

Several specimens, differing widely from all the preceding, approach so nearly some of the varieties of *M. alcicornis* as to render their identity highly probable. They do not, however, agree precisely with any West Indian specimens in my possession. The most important differences are the somewhat more porous texture and the greater regularity and more scattered arrangement of the cells. The branches are round and digitate, the branchlets with three to five, short, compressed divisions at the ends.

This variety forms large clusters of flat branches, erect or horizontal, fringing the submerged edges of the reefs, and sometimes two or three feet across. It is light yellowish brown or pinkish in color. Abundant at Cape Frio, Abrolhos, Porto Seguro, Bahia, Maceió, and intermediate localities.—C. F. H.

Millepora alcicornis Linn., var. **fenestrata** Duch. and Mich.

With the preceding are a few specimens, agreeing in all respects, except that the branches are in a single plane and coalesce so as to leave numerous openings. The terminal branchlets are longer and more slender.

Abrolhos Reefs,—C. F. Hartt.

Remarks on the Brazilian Coral-fauna, by C. F. Hartt.

The following general conclusions may be added with reference to the coral-fauna of Brazil.

1st. The species are, as Prof. Verrill above remarks, almost without exception, peculiar to the Brazilian coast, along which they have quite a wide distribution; the most of the species ranging from Cape St. Roque to Cape Frio, which seems to be the southern limit of the fauna. In the Bay of Rio de Janeiro, where the conditions appear to be very favorable for coral growth, I have been able to find only one or two species of madreporarian corals, and these were *Astrangiæ*.

2d. The Brazilian fauna bears a close resemblance to the West Indian, and there are many representative species. Thus the *Siderastræa stellata*, *Heliastræa aperta*, *Favia gravida*, and *Porites solida* are representatives of West Indian forms; and among the Halcyonoids, *Hymenogorgia* represents the *Rhipidogorgiæ* of the West Indian fauna.

3d. The absence, in the Brazil fauna, of the genera *Madrepora, Mæandrina, Diploria, Manicina, Cladocora, Oculina*, genera so characteristic of the West Indian fauna, is noteworthy.

4th. The Brazilian corals form extensive reefs, which occur along the coast, from the "Roccas," north of Cape St. Roque, to the Abrolhos. The genera which contribute most to the reefs are *Acanthastræa, Favia, Heliastræa, Siderastræa, Porites*, and *Millepora*, but the *Mussa* and other species add a more or less notable share.

South of the Abrolhos region, there are no known coral reefs. Very extensive ones occur in the Abrolhos region, at Itacolumi, Porto Seguro, Sta. Cruz, and in the vicinity of Camamú, and elsewhere south of Bahia. In the Bay of Bahia are large coral banks, and off the town of Maceió, in the province of Alagôas there are large irregular coral patches, uncovered at low tide, which are seen extending northward along the coast toward Pernambuco. Coral patches occur frequently on the coast farther north, and the extensive reef of the Roccas, in the latitude of the Island of Fernando de Noronha, is formed of coral.

Around the Abrolhos Islands are *fringing* reefs. Between these Islands and the shore is a large area of shallow sea, full of irregular reefs. On the Brazilian shore, in open water, the corals grow in small patches on the sea-bottom, and rise vertically to the surface like towers. These structures are termed, in Brazil, *chapeirões* (sing. *chapeirão*). In some instances they are only a few yards in diameter, while their height may be 40 to 50 feet or more. These *chapeirões* usually grow close together and sometimes coalesce to form reefs of several square miles in area. The larger reefs are usually surrounded by chapeiroes. Ordinarily the reefs reach a level a little above low-tide. They are remarkably level topped. Occasionally sand is heaped upon them and they become islands, but instances of this kind are very rare.

Class, ECHINODERMATA.

Order, CRINOIDEA.

Antedon Dubenii (?) Bölsche, Wieg. Archiv. fur Naturg., 1866, p. 92.

One specimen, apparently identical with this species, was obtained at the Abrolhos. Its color is deep purple with large spots of yellowish white on the sides of the rays.

It is very different from a specimen of *A. Braziliensis* Lütk., from Rio de Janeiro, sent to the Museum of Yale College by Dr. Lütken, with which I have compared it.

Rare, occasionally occurring in the shallow water on the borders of reefs and rock ledges.—C. F. H.

Order, OPHIUROIDEA.

Ophiomyxa flaccida Lütken.

Ophiura flaccida Say, Journal Phil. Acad., v, p. 151, 1825.
Ophiomyxa flaccida Lyman. Illustrated Catalogue of the Museum of Comparative Zoölogy, i, p. 178, Pl. ii, fig. 6, 1865.

One large specimen was obtained at the Abrolhos Reefs. It does not appreciably differ from a specimen from the West Indies, sent by Dr. Lütken, except in having slightly longer and sharper arm-spines.

It has been found previously at Florida, St. Thomas, and various parts of the West Indies.

Ophiactis Krebsii Lütken; Lyman, Catal., p. 111, figs. 10, 11.

Several fine specimens of this species occurred at the Abrolhos Reefs, nearly all of them had six rays, with three of them usually shorter. Two specimens differ slightly from the others in having more slender arms, longer and more oval upper arm-plates, and radial shields less separated. They have, however, four mouth-papillæ, like the typical form, and agree very well in color with the others.

Its previous localities are Bahamas,—Dr. H. Bryant; off Charleston, —L. Agassiz; Florida,—Maj. E. B. Hunt, J. E. Mills, etc.; St. Thomas, —A. H. Riise; Aspinwall,—F. H. Bradley.

Ophionereis reticulata Lütken; Lyman, Catal., p. 141.

Ophiura reticulata Say, op. cit., p. 148, 1825.

This species was found in considerable abundance by Mr. Hartt, at the Abrolhos Reefs.

There are specimens in the Museum of Yale College from Bermuda (J. M. Jones); Bahamas (Dr. H. Bryant); Florida; "West Indies;" and St. Thomas. The specimens from all these localities are remarkably constant in their characters, and show scarcely any local variations.

Ophiothrix violacea Müller and Troschel, Syst. Asterid., p. 115, 1842: Lyman, Catalogue, p. 164.

This species occurred in abundance at the Abrolhos Reefs, among corals and Gorgoniæ.

In color there are two principal variations, most specimens have the light dorsal stripe on the rays very clearly defined and bordered with dark brown. Others have the stripe obscure, or lack it entirely. In the character of the spines of the disk there are also two varieties, not coincident, however, with the differences in color; most commonly the disk is covered with minute, short, forked spines, with few or numerous long, slender, thorny ones among them; but in many specimens the long spines are entirely wanting. The general color is sometimes flesh-color or pink instead of violet.

The previously recorded localities are from Florida and Aspinwall to Brazil.

Ophiolepis paucispina Müll. and Trosch., op. cit., p. 90; Lyman, Catal., p. 55.

Ophiura paucispina Say. op. cit., p. 149, 1825.

Three specimens, agreeing exactly with those from Florida and West Indies, were collected by Mr. Hartt at the Abrolhos Reefs.

Ophiura cinerea Lyman, Catal., p. 27.

Ophioderma cinereum Müll. and Tr., Syst., p. 87, 1842.
Ophioderma Antillarum Lütken, Add. ad Hist. Oph., p. 88.

Numerous large and fine specimens of this species were collected by Mr. Hartt at the Abrolhos Reefs. They were found living in crevices under corals.

Some of these measure 6·5 inches from the center to ends of rays; 1·25 in diameter of disk.

All the *Ophiurans* from the Abrolhos were collected in shallow pools on the reefs from under dead corals or stones.—C. F. H.

Order, ASTERIOIDEA.

Oreaster gigas (Linn. sp.) Lütken, Vidensk. Meddel., 1859, p. 64.

Pentaceros reticulatus Gray, Ann. and Mag. N. H., p. 275, 1840.
Oreaster reticulatus Müll. and Tr., Syst. Asterid., p. 45, 1842.

Two large and fine specimens of this species were collected by Mr. Hartt at the Abrolhos reefs.

Its previous localities were Florida, Bahamas, St. Thomas, Hayti, Barbadoes, and throughout the West Indies.

The Brazilian specimens agree perfectly with those from Florida and St. Thomas.

Linckia ornithopus Lütken.

Ophidiaster ornithopus Müll. and Trosch., op. cit., p. 31, 1842; Lütken, op. cit., p. 80.
? *Linckia Guildingii* Gray, op. cit., 1840.

Several specimens of this species from the Abrolhos Reefs present curious malformations due to the restoration of lost rays. Two consist of a single large ray, from the end of which four or five new ones have begun to grow. Two specimens are regularly five rayed.

A specimen from Bermuda (J. M. Jones) does not appreciably differ.

Echinaster (Othilia) crassispina Verrill, sp. nov.

Plate IV, figure 7.

Rays short, somewhat angulated. Radii of disk and rays as 1 : 4. Interambulacral spines, two to each plate, the outer ones being large and short, forming a close, regular row along the border of the ambulacral groove; the inner one much smaller, not half so long, and forming an inner row concealed by the others. Along the lower side of the rays and well separated from the interambulacral spines, there is a row of distant, large, conical, sharp spines, about fifteen in number, which do not extend upon the disk, and gradually diminish in size toward the end of the rays, where they are very small. Upon the sides and back of the rays there are four or five less regular rows of similar large, sharp, distant spines, arising from the swollen nodes of the reticulated plates. Disk naked beneath, above with few large spines, like those of the rays. Surface smooth, in the spaces between the spines pierced by many small pores. Color bright crimson when living; in alcohol, dull reddish brown; when dry, deep purplish brown.

Radius of disk ·5 of an inch; of rays, 1·9.

Bahia, Brazil,—C. F. Hartt. Three specimens.

This remarkable species differs widely from *E. spinosus* in its shorter and more angulated rays, coarser plates, and much fewer and stouter spines. Also in the spineless disk beneath, and much larger and more crowded outer interambulacral spines bordering the grooves. It differs from *E. multispina* Gray sp. (*E. Braziliensis* M. and Tr.) in having much fewer and larger spines above, and different interambulacral spines.

Asterias Atlantica Verrill, sp. nov.

A small specimen having eight rays, four of which are smaller than the others, was obtained at the Abrolhos Reefs by Mr. Hartt. Another specimen with six equal rays, which is in my possession, collected at Bermuda by J. Matthew Jones, Esq., does not appreciably differ in structure. Two other specimens, one of which has seven unequal rays, and the other, which is much larger, five regular ones, appear to belong to the same species. These are believed to have been collected at Remedios, Cuba.

This species may be recognized by the very slender, blunt interambulacral spines, which form a single row along the edge of the ambulacral groove; by the crowded double row of larger ventral spines, very near the interambulacral, the spines being long, round, tapering, not pointed, and arranged two upon each plate; by the regular lateral row of distant, long spines, larger than the ventral, and mostly only one upon a plate; by the fewness of the smaller dorsal spines, which form an irregular, often double median row along the rays, with a few scattered on each sides, which sometimes form lateral rows, and on the disk surround a pentagonal area, enclosing a few small spines. The spines are surrounded at base by dense wreaths of small rounded pedicellariae. No major pedicellariae were found on any part. The specimen with five arms has but one madreporic plate. The others two or three. The rays are rather long and slender, somewhat angulated when dry.

Radii as 1 : 5½.

Radius of disk of largest specimen, ·35; of rays 2 inches.

The specimen from Bermuda has somewhat longer and sharper spines than the others of similar size, and those upon the back of the rays form three regular rows. The disk is also covered uniformly with similar spines.

This species is allied to *A. tenuispina*, but appears quite distinct from the Mediterranean specimens that I have examined. It has shorter and more angulated rays when mature, and less numerous and shorter spines upon the back. Its pedicellariae are somewhat different in form, and the large scattered ones, common on *A. tenuispina*, I have been unable to find upon this, although they might occur on other specimens.

Order, ECHINOIDEA.

Lytechinus variegatus A. Agassiz, Bulletin Mus. Comp. Zoöl., p. 24, 1864.

Psammechinus variegatus Agassiz and Desor, Catal. Rais.
Psilechinus variegatus Lütken, Vidensk. Meddelelser, 1865.

This species is common at Bahia, where Mr. Hartt obtained numerous specimens. These examples agree very well with the common Florida and West Indian form, but are a little more depressed than usual, and have more numerous tubercles on the interambulacral zones.

Quite common in the vicinity of Cape Frio; also at Victoria and Porto Seguro.— C. F. H.

Echinometra Michelini Desor, Catal. Rais.

Echinus lucuntur (*pars*) Linn.; Lamarck, etc.
Echinometra lucuntur Lütken.
Echinometra Michelini A. Ag., op. cit., p. 21.

The large specimens of this species, brought from the Abrolhos by Mr. Hartt, do not appreciably differ from those of Bermuda, Florida Reefs, and West Indies.

Common on all rocky shores and reefs along the Brazilian coast. At Rio, Victoria, Bahia, and elsewhere, where the rocks are gneissose, these sea urchins are found in holes in the rocks, which they excavate for themselves. They also excavate the coral reef-rock, and sandstone.—C. F. H.

Encope emarginata (Leske sp.) Agassiz, Monog. Scut., ii, p. 37, tab. 10.

Scutella emarginata Lamarck; Blainv.; Desmoul., etc.
Echinoglycus frondosus Gray, Catal. Ech. of Brit. Mus., p. 24, 1855.

The specimens are mostly 3 or 4 inches in diameter, with thin edges. The openings vary considerably in size and the degree of closing at the margin. In most cases all are closed, but often the two posterior remain more or less open. The green and brown colored specimens are about equally common.

Very common on the sandy beaches in some localities along the coast from Rio, northward to beyond Bahia. One of these localities near the mouth of the Rio Sant. Antonia, in the Province of Bahia, is mentioned in the work of Prinz Max zu Neu Wied. Along the shores of the bay of Bahia, at Itapagipe, Periperi, and elsewhere, it may be collected in great abundance.—C. F. H.

Order, HOLOTHURIOIDEA.

Thyone (Sclerodactyla) Braziliensis Verrill, sp. nov.

Plate IV, figure 8a.

Form in contraction oval. The lower side indicated only by the lighter color. Suckers not very numerous, scattered over the whole surface, but somewhat more numerous along the ambulacral zones, where there is a tendency to form two rows. Anal orifice armed with five small, calcareous papillae. Tentacles ten, elongated, arborescently branched, chiefly near the end, the divisions short and not very numerous; the two lower tentacles slightly smaller and more divided. Plates of the oral circle closely united laterally, forming a very short ring, with ten acute points projecting backward and ten forward, the latter with wide rounded spaces between them. Distance between the anterior points ·1 inch, equal to their length and to the distance from the posterior points to the angle between the anterior points. Tentacles somewhat rigid, from the abundance of calcareous plates. Color, in alcohol, yellowish gray, with fine brownish spots and an ill-defined dark brown zone along the middle of the interambulacral spaces. Length of a contracted specimen, in alcohol, 1·3 inches; of tentacles ·4. Abrolhos Reefs,—C. F. Hartt.

This species is allied to *T. Briareus*, from the Atlantic coast of the United States, but is very distinct in the form of the ring of oral plate, which, in the latter, is relatively about three times longer, and composed of long, stout plates, with the posterior points longest. The suckers scattered over the surface are, also, much less numerous than in *T. Briareus*.

Occurs under dead corals in the shallow tide pools and holes in the reefs at the Abrolhos and elswhere.—C. F. H.

Chirodota rotiferum Stimpson, Amer. Journ. Sci., 29, p. 134, 1860.

? *Synapta rotifera* Pourtales, Proc. Am. Assoc., 1851, p. 15.
Chriodota rotifera Selenka, Zeitschr. fur Wiss. Zoöl., 1867, p. 367.

Plate IV, figures 9, 9ª.

Elongated and slender, the whole surface thickly covered with small, white, slightly prominent verrucae. Tentacles 12, short, with about five digitations upon each side, the two terminal ones longest. Color, in alcohol, light purplish brown. The specimens, which are not entire, are two or three inches long, and about ·25 in diameter.

The calcareous, wheel-shaped bodies in the skin, are all very minute, but variable in size, provided with 6 spokes, which are often thinner along the middle, so as sometimes to appear almost as if double, rim narrow, center not perforated. With these there are larger, oblong, irregularly shaped, calcareous bodies, mostly enlarged and truncated at the ends.

Abrolhos Reefs, with the preceding,—C. F. Hartt. Florida,— Pourtales.

The two specimens obtained appear to agree perfectly with the description by Pourtales. Whether *C. pygmaea* Müller be the same species, can be ascertained only by a comparison of specimens from the different localities. Should this prove to be the case, Müller's name will have priority.

No. 5.—*Notice of a Collection of Echinoderms from La Paz, Lower California, with Descriptions of a new Genus.*

Published April, 1868.

THE Museum of Yale College recently received a small but very interesting collection of Echinoderms, collected by Capt. James Pedersen, in the lower part of the Gulf of California, which gives us some additional knowledge of the marine fauna of that very prolific region. In these Transactions, I published last year a descriptive catalogue of the Echinoderms contained in the Yale Museum from the west-tropical coast of America; but in this small lot there are two species, not known to me at that time, one of which appears to be a new and remarkable genus of starfishes.

OPHIUROIDEA.

Ophiactis virescens Lütken.

Ophiactis virescens Lyman, Catal., p. 113 ; Verrill, Trans. Conn. Acad., i, p. 265.

A few specimens of this species were found adhering among the laminated scales of the pearl-oyster (*Margaritophora fimbriata*).

ASTERIOIDEA.

Linckia unifascialis Gray (*var. bifascialis*), Verrill, op. cit., p. 286.

Dr. Gray considered this form a distinct species, but the specimens that I have hitherto seen do not appear to warrant their separation from the ordinary *L. unifascialis*, unless as a variety. Yet it may eventually prove to be distinct when more and better specimens can be examined. The only difference observed between them, is the division of the lateral band of pores into two bands toward the base of the rays, in the variety, while it is simple in the normal form.

This variety appears to be common at Cape St. Lucas and in the Gulf of California, while at Panama it is very rare.

Occurs from the Gulf of California to Zorritos, Peru.

Nidorellia armata Gray.

Pentaceros (*Nidorellia*) *armatus* Gray, Ann. and Mag. N. H., vol. vi, p. 276, 1840
  Synopsis Starfishes in the British Museum, p. 7, pl. 14, 1866.
Oreaster armatus Müller and Tr., Syst. Ast., p. 52, 1842.
Goniodiscus conifer Mobius, Neue Seesterne des Hamburg und Kieler Mus., p. 10,
  Tab. iii, fig. 5. 6, 1859.
Goniodiscus armatus Lütken, Vidensk Meddel., 1859, p. 75.
Nidorellia armata Verrill, Trans. Conn. Acad., vol. i, p. 280.
Goniodiscus stella Verrill, op. cit., p. 284, (young), (*non* Mobius).

Additional specimens prove that our *Goniodiscus stella* is merely the young of this species, while in the flat, spineless condition. The characters of the young show the close affinity that this genus has with *Goniodiscus*.

There is but one specimen from La Paz. Its range is from Guayamas to Zorritos, Peru.

AMPHIASTER, gen. nov.

Disk moderately developed, flat above and below, with five broad, triangular rays, and two well developed series of marginal plates. Skeleton of the upper side formed by regular, polygonal, spine bearing, tessellated plates, with pores between them; on the lower side composed of smaller granulated plates, each bearing a tubercle. Marginal plates granulated around the margin, smooth at center, or bearing a large, smooth spine. Interambulacral plates bearing a row of smaller, inner spines, several on each plate, and an outer series of larger ones, one to each plate.

This genus is nearly allied to *Oreaster*, and still more so to *Nidorellia*. From the former it differs in its depressed form, tessellated, polygonal plates, the character of the spines, etc.; from the latter, in the larger and less numerous plates of the upper surface, consisting mainly of the three median rows of the rays, with very few in the interradial regions, while in *Nidorellia* they are much more numerous and the interradial regions of the upper surface are well developed. The marginal plates, also, in the single known species, are granulated only around the margin.

Amphiaster insignis Verrill, sp. nov.

Plate IV, figure 10.

Proportion of the radii of rays to those of the disk, nearly as 2 : 1. Rays broad at base, small, but not acute, at the tips, with the interradial margin deeply and regularly incurved in young specimens, slightly angular in larger ones. Along the upper side of the rays, there are three rows of regular plates, which are rather large and somewhat prominent, and each normally bears a large, sharp, conical spine, smooth above, but surrounded by granules at the base. These spines form, therefore, three regular rows on the rays, except near the tips, where the lateral ones become obsolete. The spines increase in size toward the center. The five inner ones of the median rows are often absent, the corresponding plates presenting a smooth, rounded surface, as if the spines had been broken off and the scars had healed over; frequently, also, several of the other median spines are wanting in the same way; but the number and positions of the naked plates differ on the different rays of the same individual, and on different specimens. In each angle between the inner ends of the median rows, and terminating the lateral ones, there is a larger spine, forming the angles of a pentagonal area, enclosing from three to five similar spines. The large madreporic plate is outside this area, close to the base of one of the spines. In the interradial regions, and surrounding the ovarial openings, there are about five small plates, one or two of which often bear spines in the larger specimens. The margin is rounded, and formed by both the upper and lower series of plates, those of each row alternately approaching and receding from the margin. These plates are variable in size, those of the upper series much the largest, somewhat rounded, and in the intervals between those that are separated there are often small accessory plates, and at the angle there is usually a cluster of such small plates, while the two inner plates of the upper series are removed from the margin to the upper surface. Ordinarily the alternate marginal plates, of both the upper and lower series, bear large conical spines, like those of the back; these are always placed upon the plates that approach the margin, while those that are placed farther back toward the upper and lower surfaces have convex and naked centers, surrounded by a margin of granules. There are about ten or twelve lower marginal plates upon one side of each ray, and eight or nine upper ones. The plates of the lower surface are nearly regular, polygonal, evenly covered with short, angular, flat-topped granules, and each bears a short, stout, blunt central spine, those near the interradial margin longer and sharper. The interambulacral plates bear an even outer row of blunt, flattened spines or papillæ, one to each plate, which are nearly as long as the spines of the adjacent surface, but much smaller; and an inner row of very slender spines, which are cylindrical and blunt and rise nearly as high as the others, forming groups of three to five upon each plate. When there are but three, as is most common, the central one is slightly longer or they are all equal; when four, as often happens toward the mouth, the inner one is much the shortest; when five, which rarely occurs, the outer one is also much shorter than the middle ones.

In the largest specimen, the radius of the rays is 2 inches; of disk ·95; length of largest dorsal spines ·30; diameter at base ·17; length of spines of lower surface ·15; diameter ·10; length of outer interambulacral spines ·12; diameter ·05. Another specimen has the greater radius 1·60; lesser ·80; with dorsal spines of the same size. The smallest specimen has the greater radius ·93; lesser ·47; length of dorsal spines ·15; diameter ·08. Color light brownish red, when dry.

This species appears to be not uncommon at La Paz, since there are eight specimens in the present collection.

Oreaster occidentalis Verrill, op. cit., p. 278.

One large specimen of this interesting, and as yet rare species, was received in this collection. It agrees, in all respects, with those from Panama.

ECHINOIDEA.

Cidaris Thouarsii Val.; Verrill, op. cit., p. 294.

One large specimen, agreeing perfectly with those from Panama.

Echinometra Van Brunti A. Ag.; Verrill, op. cit., p. 309.

Common at La Paz.

Tripneustes depressus A. Ag., Bulletin M. C. Z., p. 24, 1863.

Large and ventricose, slightly concave beneath, regularly arched above, the outline in a vertical view nearly circular, with the ambulacral zones a little swollen. Peristome larger in proportion to the diameter of the test than in *T. ventricosus*. Primary tubercles of interambulacra less numerous, especially in the vertical series, owing to the greater vertical width of the plates; secondary tubercles few and small, miliaries very numerous and minute. Tubercles of the ambulacra similar in size and appearance. Diameter of test 4·9; height 2·85; diameter of peristome, not including cuts, 1·15: of abactinal area ·70; width of ambulacral zones at circumference 1·30; of interambulacral 1·70.

This species is closely allied to *T. ventricosus* of the West Indies. The only reliable characters for separating it, that I have been able to find, are the greater relative size of the buccal opening, and the fewer primary tubercles, with much less numerous secondary ones, which, combined with the smallness of the miliaries, gives the surface a less closely tuberculated appearance.

It was characterized by Mr. A. Agassiz, only as follows:—" There is in the collection of the Smithsonian, a species from Guayamas, *T. depressus* A. Ag., closely allied to *T. ventricosus*, which differs from it in the flatness of the test, the large and uniform size of the tubercles, and the stoutness of its spines."

The spines in our specimen are removed, but in form it is less depressed than many specimens of *T. ventricosus*, and the primary tubercles are scarcely larger.

Encope grandis Agassiz, Monog. Scut., p. 37, Tab. 6.

A large and fine specimen, which was certainly collected at La Paz, came with the collection, thus confirming the Gulf of California nativity of this species, which has been erroneously attributed to the West Indies.

Brissus obesus Verrill, op. cit., p. 316.

This species is represented only by a single specimen, which agrees well with those originally described.

Supplementary Note on Echinoderms of the West Coast of America.

Ophiura variegata Lyman (see p. 254), and *Ophiolepis variegata* Lutken (see p. 256).
Numerous large and fine specimens of these two species, with a few of *Ophiocnida hispida* Lyman. were dredged by Mr. Bradley on a shell-bank in 4-6 fathoms of water, Panama Bay.

Ophiothela mirabilis Verrill (see page 268).
Numerous additional specimens of this species, some of them much larger than those first described, have been found clinging to *Gorgoniæ* and *Muriceæ* from Panama Bay. Also on *Muricea* from Cape St. Lucas. These confirm its rank as a distinct genus.

Echinometra rupicola A. Ag. (see page 308).
Several fine specimens of this species were obtained by Prof. B. Silliman near San Juan del Sur, Nicaragua, where they burrow in a hard argillaceous rock, forming cavities sometimes 5 or 6 inches in diameter.

Pattalus Peruvianus Verrill, = *Anaperus Peruanus*, p. 322 (non Troschel).
The large specimens referred to, from Callao, when dissected proved to be a species allied to *P. mollis* Sel., the only known species of the genus, from Chili and Peru.

It has 20 long arborescent tentacles, some of which are shorter. The oral ring consists of ten loosely articulated, long plates; five slender ones, having the posterior part broad triangular, with the angles rounded and edges concave, connecting anteriorly by a narrow middle with a long fusiform process, alternating with five much larger ones, having a short posterior portion, emarginate behind, narrowing somewhat anteriorly, and then expanding into a broad deeply excavated portion, ending in two points anteriorly. The large plates in a large specimen are ·7 of an inch long, ·25 broad. Polian vesicles long and slender, numerous, in large clusters. Color uniform deep crimson when living. The tentacles are 4-6 inches across in expansion. In alcohol deep purple. Anal orifice round, unarmed.

This is, probably, the *Holothuria Peruviana* Lesson. *P. mollis* Sel.,[*] as figured, differs in its smaller oral plates and fewer Polian vesicles.

EXPLANATION OF PLATE IV.

Figure 1. Spicula of *Hymenogorgia quercifolia* Edw.; 1a, double-spindles; 1b, crescent-shaped spicula,—enlarged 150 diameters.

Figure 2. Spicula of *Pterogorgia gracilis* Verrill; 2a, double-spindles; 2b, crescents,—enlarged 150 diameters.

Figure 3. A part of a branch of the same,—natural size.

Figure 4. Spicula of *Eunicea humilis* Edw.; a, spindles from cœnenchyma,—enlarged 50 diameters; b, club-shaped spicula,—enlarged 100 diameters.

Figure 5. Spicula of *Plexaurella dichotoma* Köll.; 5a, a cross-shaped spiculum with unequal branches; 5b, a cross with two of the branches undeveloped,—enlarged 100 diameters.

Figure 6. Cross-shaped spicula of *Plexaurella anceps?* Köll.; 6a, one of the larger spindles,—enlarged 100 diameters.

Figure 7. *Echinaster crassispina* Verrill; part of ray,—natural size.

Figure 8. *Thyone Braziliensis* Verrill; a, oral plates,—natural size.

Figure 9. *Chriodota rotiferum* Stimp.; calcareous wheels of the skin,—enlarged 150 diameters.

Figure 10. *Amphiaster insignis* Verrill; ray and part of disk,—natural size.

---

[*] Zeitschrift für Wissensch. Zool., Dec. 1867, p. 113, Taf. VIII, Fig. 4-5.

No. 6.—*Review of the Corals and Polyps of the West Coast of America.* By A. E. VERRILL.

Presented, April, 1868.

RECENT explorations of the west tropical coast of America, principally by Mr. F. H. Bradley for the Museum of Yale College, have contributed so much to the knowledge of the Polypi of that region and have so increased our store of specimens, that a new and much more complete catalogue of the species has become indispensable for a proper understanding of the geographical distribution of the animals of this class. The Smithsonian Institution has contributed the species collected by John Xantus, Esq., at Cape St. Lucas.

In a paper published two years ago,* the writer enumerated nearly all the species then known from Panama and called attention to the remarkable contrast between the polyp-faunæ of the Atlantic and Pacific coasts of Central America, and the bearing of these facts upon the supposed former connection between the two oceans, across the Isthmus of Panama.

The additional forms now presented make these contrasts still greater and more remarkable, and add greater force to the evidence then brought forward to show that no deep or extensive water connection, sufficient to modify the ocean currents, can have taken place since the existence of the species now living upon each coast.

The Panamian fauna proves to be remarkably rich in *Gorgonacea*, no less than 43 species having already been obtained. The genus *Muricea* appears to attain here its greatest development, since 15 species, besides several peculiar varieties, perhaps distinct, are in our collection from Panama Bay, and others from Acapulco and Peru, while from the West Indies there are but four well-ascertained species. The occurrence of two peculiar, gigantic species of *Pavonia*, a genus of corals hitherto known only in the Indo-Pacific fauna, is noteworthy, and also the presence of a peculiar new form of *Dendrophyllia*.

The classification here followed is that proposed by the writer three years ago† with a few changes that have become necessary by a better knowledge of the anatomy of some groups and the discovery of new forms.

---

* Proceedings of the Boston Society of Natural History, vol. x, p. 323, 1865.
† Proceedings of the Essex Institute, vol. iv, p. 145, 1865. See also Memoirs of the Boston Society of Natural History, vol. i, 1864.

Order, ALCYONARIA.

Sub-Order, PENNATULACEA.

Family, RENILLIDÆ.

Renilla.

The polyps arise from the upper surface of a flat, reniform, cavernous disk or frond, having a sinus on one edge, near which there is upon the lower surface a locomotive peduncle, which is muscular and greatly extensible and divided in the interior into two longitudinal chambers, which communicate with two large cavities at its base, and through these with the smaller cavities of the disk, and thus with the bodies of the polyps. The integument of the lower surface, peduncle, and upper surface, is filled with numerous, slender, prismatic spicula, and around the bases of the polyps there are pointed, projecting groups of similar spicula. The polyps originate by budding around the edge of the disk, and are therefore regularly arranged, alternately both in consecutive circles and in radiating lines, which are symmetrical upon the right and left side of a median plane passing through the sinus, and they are smaller and more crowded toward the edge than on the central parts. The polyps are rather large, much exsert in expansion, but wholly retractile.

Besides the ordinary form of polyps, there are in this, as in other genera of Pennatulacea, a second kind, having a different structure and appearance. Or, in other words, the polyps are dimorphous in a manner analogous to that observed in many Hydroids. In Renilla, the second kind of polyps are scattered thickly over the upper surface between the others, and appear in alcoholic specimens like little papillae, with clusters of whitish spots on their surface, and surrounded with spicula similar to those around the ordinary polyps, but less numerous and smaller. They are also asexual.

The writer first described these peculiar dimorphous forms of the polyps of *Renilla*, in 1864,[*] as "rudimentary polyps," and afterwards those of *Leioptilum undulatum*, *Ptilosarcus Gurneyi*, *Veretillum Stimpsonii*, etc.[†]

---

[*] Revision of the Polyps of the Eastern Coast of the United States, Memoirs of the Boston Society of Natural History, vol. i, p. 12.

[†] Proceedings of the Essex Institute, vol. iv, p. 182–5, 1865.

Dr. Albert Kölliker has recently investigated this interesting subject much more completely, both among *Pennatulacea* and *Alcyonacea*, and has already published a short notice,* preliminary to a more extended memoir upon it. For these reasons it will be passed over in the following pages with only such descriptions of the external appearance of the two forms of polyps as may be useful for the determination of the genera and species.

Renilla amethystina Verrill.

Bulletin of the Museum of Comp. Zoöl., p. 29, Jan. 1864; Proceedings Boston Soc. Nat. History, 1866, p. 326.

Plate V, figure 1.

Frond large, rather thin, broad reniform, broader than long, proportion of breadth to length about as 1·3 : 1; sinus extending more than one third across the length of the frond, about equal to one third of its breadth; the posterior lobes broad and rounded, meeting behind. Peduncle placed at about its own diameter from the end of the sinus; length, in contraction, equal to about a third of the breadth of the frond. Lower surface and peduncle rough with spicula, which are arranged somewhat in radiating lines, upper surface slightly convex, covered with very numerous, rather closely set, small polyps, which are surrounded at base by slightly projecting, rigid calicles, strengthened by numerous spicula, which rise up in angular clusters. Thickly scattered between the ordinary polyps are those of the second or rudimentary kind, which form, in the contracted state, much smaller verrucæ, surrounded by a lower border of spicula, and consisting of clusters of from eight to thirty, small, round papillæ, each with a dark point in the centre.

According to Mr. Bradley's observations upon the living polyps, these are mostly ·25 of an inch long, and about ·12 across the expanded tentacles, the bodies of the polyps being about ·06. "They are transparent, with an opaque stomach, the eight radiating lamellæ showing through the walls; around the small mouth, which is edged with white, are eight radiating white points, corresponding to the intervals between the tentacles; around the base of the tentacles is a brown ring, which runs down in points opposite the spaces between them. Opposite the base of each polyp are two (rarely four or five) bunches of little white rays. The frond is nearly transparent, but highly colored by very numerous purple spicula, evenly distributed on the

---

* Verhandlungen der physik-medicin Gesellschaft in Würzburg, Dec., 1867. Also, Annals and Mag. Nat. Hist., March, 1868.

peduncle and lower surface, but on the upper side arranged along the edges of the polypiferous radiating lines, and especially concentrated about the five (rarely six or seven) white points that surround the closed polyps. The polyps are arranged somewhat in quincunx, in lines that radiate from the attachment of the peduncle, and curve outward on the sides to the lobes. The tentacles are narrow and tapering, ·04 to ·06 long, bearing, especially in young specimens, well marked pinnæ at the tip and edges, which in old ones often become reduced to a mere fringe."

In alcohol the usual color is deep rich purple, due to the color of the spicula, with the tip of the peduncle light yellowish; but some specimens are light, reddish purple, and one is pure white, due perhaps to disease or injury, for it has become deformed. The polyps, when expanded, usually show the eight white lobes around the mouth, and the brown band below the tentacles.

The spicula are all slender and irregularly prismatic in form, sometimes bent, a little thickened in the middle, tapering slightly to near the ends, which are somewhat enlarged and bluntly truncated. They vary considerably in size, those of the upper surface around the polyp-cells and in the integument of the lower surface being the largest; many others are about half as long, and others not more than a fourth. The largest spicula of the upper surface are about ·810^{mm} long and ·064^{mm} thick; some the larger ones from the lower surface are ·544^{mm} long by ·056^{mm} thick, and ·608^{mm} long by ·048^{mm}; with these are many small ones about ·350^{mm} by ·048^{mm}. Some of the larger spicula from the white specimen are ·640^{mm} long by ·064^{mm} thick, and the smaller ones ·240^{mm} by ·024^{mm}. The color of the spicula in the darker specimens is deep amethystine purple; in the lighter specimens, light purple or silvery white. The spicula all reflect light in a peculiar manner, which gives them a silvery lustre. They do not appear to have such well marked triangular sections as those of "*R. americana*," figured by Dr. Kölliker,[*] the angles being less prominent, without reëntrant angles between them. In many cases the section is nearly round, or quadrangular with rounded corners, but toward the ends of the spiculum, usually triangular with rounded angles.

When contracted in alcohol, one of the largest specimens measures 3·75 inches in breadth; 3·30 long, from posterior lobes to front; 2·20 from sinus to front; ·35 in thickness; diameter of polyp-cells ·06. When living, some specimens were more than 6 inches in breadth.

---

[*] Icones Histiologicæ, ii, Taf. xix, fig. 16.

Panama, north of the railroad-wharf, on sand at extreme low-water, abundant on one occasion only,—F. H. Bradley; Panama,—J. H. Sternbergh, Capt. J. M. Dow, T. Rowell, Esq.; Pearl Islands, dredged on muddy bottoms, 4 to 6 fathoms,—F. H. Bradley; Acajutla, San Salvador,—F. H. Bradley; Zorritos, Peru, dredged on muddy bottom,—F. H. Bradley.

The single white specimen, referred to above, was found at Panama with the ordinary variety. The frond, apparently owing to injury or disease and subsequent restoration, is divided into three nearly equal lobes by two deep lateral notches and the sinus. The polyps are not retracted and appear a little larger than usual. The spicula are pure white and apparently somewhat smaller than in other specimens. This species has but little resemblance to *R. reniformis* of the southern Atlantic coast of the United States, being much larger, with smaller, more crowded, and far more numerous polyps, while the frond is broader than long, instead of longer than broad. The color is also much deeper and brighter, and the under surface rougher. It resembles *R. patula* Verrill, from Cumana, Venezuela, more than any other species, but can scarcely be confounded even with that, since it differs considerably in form and color and in the size of the polyps, and has a thicker frond.

Family, PENNATULIDÆ.

Leioptilum undulatum Verrill.

Proceedings of the Essex Institute, iv, 1865, p. 182.

Basal portion smooth, pointed at the end, swelling into a large bulb just below the pinnæ. Posterior part of the body, except along a narrow median band, covered with large verruciform rudimentary polyps, forming rounded papillæ, some of which are a tenth of an inch in diameter. Pinnæ large, very broad and rounded, with narrow bases, the edges thrown into undulations or frills. Polyps rather large, arranged in three alternating rows along the edges of the pinnæ. Axis very slender, about two inches long, extending from about an inch above the basal end to about the middle of the pinnate portion. The naked base, of a specimen 4·25 inches long, is 1·75; the largest pinnæ ·75 long and 1·12 wide. This specimen has twenty-five pinnæ on each side.

Pinnacati Bay, Gulf of California,—Mr. Stone. (Smithsonian Institution).

Ptilosarcus Gurneyi Gray.

Sarcoptilus (Ptilosarcus) Gurneyi Gray, Ann. and Mag. N. H., vol. v, p. 23, pl. iii, fig. 2, 1860.
Pennatula tenua Gabb, Proc. Cal. Acad. Nat. Sci., ii, p. 166, 1862.
Ptilosarcus Gurneyi Verrill, Proc. Essex Inst., 1865, p. 183.

Puget Sound, Washington Territory,—Dr. C. B. Kennerly.

Family, VIRGULARIDÆ.

Stylatula Verrill, 1864.

Polyps forming clusters upon the upper side of the lateral processes, which are supported beneath by conspicuous, sharp, radiating, spine-like spicula, which are much expanded at the base and divided into a number of irregular teeth. Besides these there are numerous, much smaller, acicular spicula imbricated at the base of the large ones and imbedded in the cœnenchyma. The stem is long and slender, as in *Virgularia*, and the lateral processes become obsolete below. The basal portion is naked, enlarged and bulbous at the base. The axis is almost cylindrical, stony, with a radiated fibrous structure, and passes through nearly the entire length. This genus is, as yet, known only from the west coast of America.

Stylatula gracilis Verrill.

Bulletin Mus. Comp. Zoöl., p. 30, Jan. 1864.
(?) *Virgularia gracilis* Gabb, op. cit., iii, p. 120, March, 1864.

Plate V, figure 2.

Stem very slender, cylindrical; base smooth, swollen and bulbous for a considerable distance relative to the length; above this a row of transverse processes (or wings) commences on each side, which are at first very narrow and slightly prominent, and leave between them, on both the front and back, a longitudinal naked space; the lateral processes gradually become wider and more prominent upward, and the naked bands becoming linear, the one on the back side is soon obliterated by the over-lapping of the lateral wings, while that on the front side finally disappears by the meeting of the processes in front. The lateral transverse processes at first bear very small rudimentary polyps in the form of small papillæ, higher up they become more elevated and supported beneath by sharp, white, radiating spines, 10 or 12 to each wing, while on the upper edge they bear a single row of 15 to 18 moderately large polyps, which in contraction are papillæ about equal in length to the spines. In the middle region the wings are close together, about 30 to an inch, arranged alternately upon the sides and regularly overlapping behind. Near the upper end they become more oblique and less crowded, about 15 to an inch, but overlap strongly. These wings are everywhere evenly rounded outwardly and more or less crescent-shaped. The axis is white, solid and very calcareous, subcylindrical, with three slight longitudinal grooves, diameter ·03 of an inch in the middle of the largest specimens. The radiating spines of the wings are smooth and sharp at the outer end, longitudinally striated toward the base, which is enlarged to a greater or less extent, flattened, and usually divided by several irregular incisions into unequal lobes. In the largest specimens, several of these spines measure respectively 1·57^{mm} long by ·20^{mm} wide; 1·47^{mm} long by ·25^{mm} wide; 1·36^{mm} long by ·13^{mm} wide. The small spicula among the bases of these and in the coenenchyma are slender, somewhat prismatic, and acicular; those of average size measure ·59^{mm} long by ·05^{mm} thick, but many are smaller than this. The entire diameter of the largest specimen from Panama Bay, from which the above measurements are taken, in the middle portion is ·10 of an inch; its length is unknown, both ends being broken off.

A nearly perfect specimen from Cape St. Lucas, having much smaller wings and spines, measures 6·8 inches in length; diameter in middle ·07; of bulbous base ·14; length of bulb to commencement of wings (much contracted) 1·30; length, or elevation, of wings ·08. Color, in alcohol, yellowish white.

Pearl Islands, Bay of Panama, dredged in 4 to 6 fathoms,—F. H. Bradley; Cape St. Lucas,—J. Xantus.

Virgularia gracilis Gabb.

Virgularia gracilis Gabb, appears to be near the preceding, but no mention is made of spines below the lateral wings, which are said to be *acute*. It may be a different species or even a different genus. The specific names, *gracilis* and *elongata*, were, by a singular coincidence, independently given to these forms by Mr. Gabb and myself at about the same time. The following is the original description:

"Polypidom long and very slender. Decorticated stem circular or elliptical in section, smooth on the surface. Polypiferous lobes slender, exsert, lunate, acute at the tips and broad at the base; arranged obliquely and alternately on the antero-lateral face of the stem. These lobes occupy the upper half of the polypidom; retaining their full size to the extreme apex, but diminishing below, so that on the middle of the stem they are exceedingly minute; and an inch or two below, are only represented by a slight ridge on the sheath, in which are two or three cells. The lower fourth of the sheath is dilated to about three times the thickness of the rest of the stem.

Length 19 inches; diameter of the naked stem ·03 in.; smallest diameter of stem, with the sheath, ·04 in.; diameter of expanded base ·13 in.; length of largest lobes ·15 inch.

Locality, Bay of Monterey, 20 fathoms. Collected by Dr. J. G. Cooper, of the State Geological Survey.

This species can be at once distinguished from *V. elongata* G. (Proc. Cal. A. N. S., vol. ii, p. 167) by its more slender form, its proportionally large polypiferous lobes, its cylindrical stem, without any grooves, and the comparatively smaller portion of the stem bearing the lobes."

Stylatula elongata Verrill.

Bulletin Museum Comp. Zoölogy, p. 30, 1864.
Virgularia elongata Gabb. Proc. Cal. Acad. Nat. Sci., ii, p. 167, 1863.

This species is larger and stouter than the preceding. The pinnæ are broader and more overlapping, leaving a naked space between the lateral rows for only a short distance from the base. In the middle twenty of the lateral wings, on each side, occupy an inch. The spines are larger and less numerous.

Near San Francisco, Cal.—A. Agassiz.

Sub-Order, GORGONACEA.
Family, GORGONIDÆ.

Gorgonia.

This genus, which formerly included the entire sub-order, has been repeatedly restricted to narrower limits by successive authors, until in the work of Milne Edwards and Haime* it is limited to those species allied to *G. verrucosa* of the Mediterranean. Yet even they, as it now appears, united with it some species† allied to *Muricea*, etc. Dr. Albert Kölliker, who in a recent work‡ has very thoroughly investigated the microscopic structure of the Alcyonaria, reunites with *Gorgonia* several of the genera established by Milne Edwards, Valenciennes, and others, viz: *Rhipidogorgia*, *Pterogorgia*, *Xiphigorgia*, *Hymenogorgia*, *Phyllogorgia*, *Phycogorgia*, *Leptogorgia*, *Lophogorgia*, and part of *Gorgonella*. As thus enlarged, the genus *Gorgonia* of Kölliker includes all the Gorgonidæ having a horny axis and thin cœnenchyma, with small and simple spicula.

---

* Histoire naturelle des Coralliaires, 1857, vol. 1, p. 157.

† *Muricea rutricosa* Köll., *Thesea exserta* D. & M., *Echinogorgia arida*, etc.

‡ Icones Histiologicæ, o Ier Atlas der vergleichenden Gewebelehre, ii, Leipzig, 1866, 4to, with xix plates.

He sub-divides the genus, however, into three groups, as follows:
1. Species having only spindle-shaped spicula.
2. Species having spindles and bracket-shaped spicula (Klammern).
3. Species having spindles, and in a peculiar external layer, singular club-shaped spicula.

The last group contains *G. verrucosa* and closely allied species, and corresponds partly with *Gorgonia* as restricted by Milne Edwards. It appears to be a very natural and well-defined group, approaching, by its smooth external layer composed of club-shaped spicula, the genus *Eunicea*. All the ascertained species belong to the Mediterranean and African coasts.*

The second section is also a natural and clearly defined group, corresponding to a great extent with *Gorgonia* and *Pterogorgia* of Ehrenberg, though a few species of the latter go into the first section (*P. sarmentosa* and *P. petechizans*). It includes the typical species of *Pterogorgia*, *Xiphigorgia*, and *Hymenogorgia* of Edwards and Haime, and two species of *Leptogorgia*, as well as the type of *Rhipidogorgia* Val. (*R. flabellum*). All the species, so far as known to me, are Atlantic, and nearly all are confined to the West Indies and Atlantic coasts of North and South America, not one having yet been found upon the Pacific coast of America.

The first section, however, appears to include several natural groups, two of which appear quite as distinct as the two preceding. Among the species enumerated by Dr. Kölliker are several species referred by Edwards and Haime to *Gorgonia*, *Rhipidogorgia*, *Gorgonella*, *Leptogorgia*, *Pterogorgia*, and the typical species of *Lophogorgia*.

The numerous species of *Gorgonia* from the west coast of America, would all fall into the first of Dr. Kölliker's sections, but among them there are two well-defined groups, characterized best by peculiarities of the spicula, each including numerous species.

In the first of these divisions the spicula of the cœnenchyma are mostly small, warty or papillose double-spindles† of two kinds,—a longer and more slender sort, mingled with those that are shorter and thicker. (*Litigorgia* V.).

In the second division there are, in addition to the two forms of double-spindles, a large number of "double-wheels," or short spicula

---

* *G. papillosa* Esper, formerly supposed to be from the East Indies, was collected at the Cape of Good Hope by the United States Exploring Expedition (Coll. Smithsonian Inst. and Yale Museum).

† Those spicula having a fusiform shape, more or less pointed at the ends, with a narrower and usually smooth space in the middle, are termed "double-spindles" (Doppelspindeln) by Dr. Kölliker. Those without the median constriction are "spindles."

with a slender axis, smooth in the middle, but surrounded toward each end with a circular and usually sharp ridge, like a little wheel. These spicula are often broader than long, and then, when seen endwise, resemble disks or circular beads with an apparent depression or perforation at the centre, owing to the transparency of the axis. In addition to the six species described below, this group includes *G. fusco-purpurea* Kölliker, the spicula of which he has well figured (Taf. xviii, figs. 28–31), and perhaps other described species. (*Eugorgia* V.).

In each of these two groups there are species with virgate, pinnate, bipinnate, and reticulated branches. There are also, in each, species with flat and with prominent cells. It is therefore evident that such external characters as the mode of branching and degree of prominence of the cells, cannot be considered as of generic importance, and that such genera as *Rhipidogorgia* Val. and *Leptogorgia* Edw., founded only on such characters, are unnatural and heterogeneous groups, which should be dropped from our system of classification.

It is probable, however, that more than the two natural groups above described, are included in the first of Dr. Kölliker's sections, represented by species that I have not been able to study satisfactorily, and among those groups that are most likely to prove distinct types, is that embracing *G. palma* and allied species, corresponding partly to the genus *Lophogorgia* Edw. and Haime.

The species of Gorgoninae which I have been able to study, may be arranged, in accordance with the above considerations, in the following manner:

Gorgonia.—Species having spindles in the coenenchyma, and an external layer of peculiar, small, club-shaped spicula, producing a smooth surface. Type, *G. verrucosa* L.* (now *Eunicella* V.—Reprint).

Pterogorgia.—Species having in the coenenchyma small double-spindles and also crescent or bracket-shaped spicula, nearly smooth on the convex side. Type, *P. acerosa* Ehr. (now *Gorgonia.*—Reprint).

Eugorgia.—Species having longer and shorter double-spindles, and numerous double-wheels; surface decidedly granulous, with naked spicula. Type, *E. ampla* V.

---

* It is not improbable that upon further study this group will be found to belong to the *Plexauridae*, near *Eunicea*, with which Ehrenberg, indeed, united it. So far as my examinations have gone this appears to me to be more in accordance with its true affinities. If this suggestion prove correct, the group should receive a new generic name, and *Gorgonia* should be restricted, partially in accordance with Ehrenberg's work, to the second group (now *Pterogorgia*) with *G. flabellum* as its type, and including, also, the true *Pterogorgia*; and in fact these are also the most common and well-known Linnaean species. (Later studies having confirmed this view, I have since adopted it, in Am. Jour. Sci., xlviii, p. Nov., 1869.—Reprint).

Litigorgia.—Species having the two forms of double-spindles and often a few small double-heads; surface somewhat granulous, but less so than in the last. Type, *L. Floræ* V. (now *Leptogorgia*.—Reprint).

Neither of the two groups belonging to the Pacific coast of America can be referred to any of the generic divisions defined by Edwards and Haime, and if classified by their system, each group would have to be dismembered and distributed among *Gorgonia, Leptogorgia, Pterogorgia,* and *Rhipidogorgia.*

Consequently I have thought it necessary to give distinctive names to the two groups already characterized, which I believe to be natural and well defined, and of generic importance, although others may consider them as subgenera merely. But in the present state of the science there appears to be no way to determine whether a certain natural group be a genus or subgenus, except by the arbitrary decisions or opinions of writers.

Leptogorgia Edw. and Haime, sens. mod. (LITIGORGIA, 1st Edition).

Leptogorgia (*pars*), *Gorgonia* (*pars*), *Pterogorgia* (*pars*), *Rhipidogorgia* (*pars*), *Gorgonella* (*pars*), and *Lophogorgia* Edw. and Haime, Corall., vol. I.—Reprint.

Spicula of the cœnenchyma mostly small double-spindles of two forms, longer and shorter. Branches usually slender, subdividing in various ways; often reticulated, pinnate, or bipinnate. Cells usually prominent, sometimes flat, mostly in lateral rows or bands.*

A.—*Flabelliform, branches bipinnate or tripinnate, not reticulated.*

Leptogorgia Floræ Verrill. (LITIGORGIA FLORÆ, 1st Ed.).

Plate V, figure 3; and Plate VI, figure 1.

Corallum very much subdivided, forming elegant, fan-shaped tufts. Several slightly flattened, slender, principal branches usually arise from near the base and spread divergently in a single plane. Each of these gives off, at intervals of about a quarter of an inch, very slender, nearly uniform branchlets, which are alternate, or sometimes opposite, and arranged pinnately. Most of these, especially in large specimens, are again pinnate in the same manner, and some of their

---

* Having recently received from Dr. Kölliker the spicula prepared from the original specimens of several of the species of *Leptogorgia* of Edwards and Haime, including the type (*L. viminalis*), I have ascertained that of the fourteen species referred by them to *Leptogorgia*, at least five, including the first, belong to the group which I had named *Litigorgia*. Therefore it seems, on some accounts, best to restore the earlier name, although a complete change in the definition and limits of the genus will be necessary. Of their other species, two belong to *Echinogorgia*, two to *Pterogorgia*, one apparently to *Gorgonella*, while three are unknown to me.—Reprint. (See Am. Jour. Sci., vol. 48, p. 325, November, 1869).

pinnæ again subdivide, but less regularly. The branchlets are all of nearly uniform size, slender and short, somewhat flattened and enlarged at the ends, which are tridentate. The cells are very small, but form well marked conical verrucæ, arranged in two alternate rows on most of the branchlets, but sometimes forming only single marginal rows on the terminal ones. The front and back sides of the branches are destitute of cells, and on the principal ones usually show a well-marked longitudinal furrow. Color bright red, sometimes tinged with yellowish. Height of the largest specimens 6 inches; breadth 12; diameter of the main branches at base ·12 of an inch; of the secondary ones ·06; of the terminal ones ·04; length of the terminal branchlets usually about ·35, rarely ·75.

The spicula are bright red with a few yellow ones intermixed. The longer double-spindles are rather slender, with acute ends, and covered with close warts arranged in about six distinct whorls, besides the terminal clusters; stouter ones smaller, with blunt ends; polyp-spicula bright yellow, slender, with few, distant, small warts or papillæ.

The longer double-spindles measure ·132^{mm} by ·048^{mm}, ·132 by ·036, ·120 by ·048, ·120 by ·042, ·108 by ·048, ·108 by ·042, ·108 by ·030; the stouter ones ·095 by ·042, ·084 by ·048, ·084 by ·042, ·078 by ·036, ·060 by ·030; the polyp-spicula ·108 by ·033, ·108 by ·030, ·096 by ·024, ·072 by ·018.

Panama and Pearl Islands,—F. H. Bradley, J. H. Sternbergh.

This species resembles, in its mode of branching, *Eugorgia Mexicana* V. and *E. Daniana* V., but is much more slender and delicate, with a smoother surface and denser coenenchyma, and is very distinct in its spicula, its color is also very different. The spicula resemble closely those of *L. eximia* V. but are somewhat more slender with the warts not so close. The external characters are very different.

I have named this elegant species in honor of the excellent wife, whose sympathy and encouragement were the chief causes that induced me to devote my life to the study of Nature.

B.—*Flabelliform, the branchlets mostly coalescent and reticulated, the terminal ones free.*

Leptogorgia Agassizii Verrill. (Litigorgia Agassizii, 1st Ed.)

Rhipidogorgia Agassizii (*pars*) Verrill, Bulletin Mus. Comp. Zool., p. 32, Jan., 1864.
Gorgonia Agassizii (*pars*) Verrill, Proc. Boston Soc. Nat. Hist., x, p. 327, 1866.

Plate V, figure 4.

Corallum forming very finely and regularly reticulated fans, usually rounded in outline. Several flattened main branches arise from the large, thickened and very short base and radiate across the fan, subdividing so rapidly and regularly that they cannot often be traced more than half way across, before becoming lost in the small, even branchlets. These form small, angular meshes, usually about a tenth of an inch across, but often smaller, ordinarily about as high as broad, but sometimes twice as high; at the outer edge the branchlets are free for about an eighth of an inch, with expanded tips, and have a diameter of about ·05 inch. The cells are small but conspicuous, in the form of small oval openings at the summits of small verrucae. They are thickly scattered over the whole surface of the frond, except upon the large branches and base, where they are few and distant. Color deep red mingled with bright yellow, or red with yellow cells, the relative amount of red and yellow varying. Height of the largest specimen 12 inches; breadth about as much; width of main branches near the base ·32; diameter of branchlets ·04 or ·05 of an inch.

Spicula deep red and bright yellow; those of the polyps pale amber. Most of the spicula are rather short, thick, and blunt, with relatively large, crowded warts, and a very narrow median space. The longer spicula are not so blunt as the others, and have smaller and more numerous warts. The longer ones measure ·120^{mm} by ·048, ·110 by ·048, ·108 by ·042, ·102 by ·054, ·084 by ·036; the stouter ones ·090 by ·084, ·084 by ·048; the double-heads ·048 by ·030, ·036 by ·033; polyp-spicula ·060 to ·084 long by ·012 to ·024. The openings of the cells are from ·21^{mm} to ·35^{mm} in diameter.

Acapulco,—A. Agassiz; Cape St. Lucas,—J. Xantus; La Paz,—J. Pedersen.

Leptogorgia media Verrill. (LITIGORGIA MEDIA, 1st Ed.).

Rhipidogorgia media Verrill, Bulletin M. C. Z., p. 33, Jan., 1864.
Gorgonia media Verrill, Proc. Bost. Soc. N. H., x, p. 327, 1865.

Corallum regularly reticulated throughout, with larger meshes, forming broad fans, often higher than wide, and frequently lobed and more or less subdivided, strengthened by large midribs. Several principal branches, which are large and compressed, arise from near the base and pass divergently through the greater part of the breadth of the frond. The branchlets are round and small, and nearly all coalescent, except the short terminal ones, forming meshes that are mostly nearly square and usually ·20 of an inch in diameter, but often not more than ·12, and sometimes up to ·80 in height, with the width ·20. The branchlets are from ·06 to ·08 of an inch in diameter. The cells form very small verrucae, with oval opening about ·005 in diameter. The largest specimens are about 15 inches high and 12 broad. Color red or brownish, often tinged with yellow, especially on the midribs.

Spicula very small and blunt, bright red and deep yellow intermingled. Longer double-spindles covered with numerous, close warts, with a narrow but well defined median space, the ends blunt; stouter ones nearly as large and with similar warts. The longer double-spindles measure ·102^{mm} by ·042^{mm}, ·096 by ·042, ·084 by ·042, ·084 by ·036; the stouter ones ·084 by ·048, ·072 by ·042, ·072 by ·036, ·060 by ·036, ·048 by ·024; the polyp-spicula ·060 to ·084 by ·018 to ·024.

Acapulco,—A. Agassiz; Cape St. Lucas,—J. Xantus; La Paz,—Maj. Wm. Rich; San Salvador,—Capt. J. M. Dow; Corinto, Nicaragua,—J. A. McNiel; La Paz,—J. Pedersen.

This species resembles *L. Agassizii* more than any other species.

Leptogorgia eximia Verrill. (LITIGORGIA EXIMIA, 1st Ed.).

Plate V, figure 20. Plate VI, figure 2.

Frond broad and rounded, composed of slender, round branches, which are openly riticulated throughout, except the short terminal branchlets at the edges. There is no distinct midrib, all the branches being nearly uniform in size, except very near the base, which rapidly subdivides into a large number of nearly equal primary branches, not distinct from the secondary. Occasionally secondary fronds start out from the sides of the frond, and one specimen has irregular, crooked, simple branchlets, arising from the sides, with a hollow axis, apparently the habitations of some parasite.

The reticulations are quite irregular in size and form, frequently squarish or rhomboidal, from ·20 to ·25 of an inch across, but more commonly with about the same width and three or four times higher than wide. Many short free branchlets often project into the larger meshes. The terminal branchlets are sometimes free for an inch, but usually much less. The cells are small and usually closely arranged on all sides, forming small, rounded verrucæ, which are slightly prominent. Color bright red or vermilion. The largest specimens are about 10 inches high and broad; diameter of branchlets ·06.

Spicula bright red, with a few light yellow ones; those of the polyps light yellow. The longer double-spindles rapidly taper to the acute ends, and are covered with rather large warts, which are not crowded; stouter ones much smaller, blunt at the ends, with fewer and more crowded warts. Polyp-spicula very slender, with few distant warts. The longer double-spindles measure ·138^{mm} by ·060, ·132 by ·054, ·132 by ·048, ·120 by ·054, ·108 by ·048; the stouter ones ·108 by ·054, ·090 by ·048, ·060 by ·030; double-heads ·060 by ·048, ·038 by ·036; polyp-spicula ·072 to ·120 by ·012 to ·024.

Pearl Islands, 6 to 8 fathoms, by divers,—F. H. Bradley.

This beautiful species resembles in its reticulations *L. media* V., but the meshes are usually larger and the coral has a more open and flexible appearance. It also differs, in all the specimens seen, in having no distinct midribs or large branches. The spicula are quite distinct, and resemble those of *L. Floræ* much more closely.

Leptogorgia Adamsii Verrill. (LITIGORGIA ADAMSII, 1st Ed.)

Rhipidogorgia Agassizii (pars) Verrill, Bull. Mus. Comp. Zoöl., p. 32, 1864; Proc. Bost. Soc. Natural History, x, p. 327, 1866.

Rhipidogorgia ventalina Duch. and Mich., Supplement aux Mem. sur Coralliaries des Antilles, 1864, p. 20, Tab. iv, fig. 3, (*non G. ventalina* Linn., Pallas, Esper, etc., *nec R. ventalina* Edw. and Haime).

Gorgonia (*Litigorgia*) *Adamsi* Verrill, Am. Jour. Sci., xlv, p. 415, May, 1868.

Plate V, figure 5. Plate VI, figure 4.

Corallum forming large, broad, rounded fans, with very small reticulations. Very young specimens, with fronds one to four inches across, usually have a rounded outline, nearly as high as broad, often very regular and almost circular, and in this stage have a few principal branches, radiating from close to the base, scarcely compressed, and traceable about half way across the frond, but often for not more than a fourth of the breadth. The branchlets are all very slender and uniform in size throughout, producing, by their fine, regular reticulations, a very elegant effect. The terminal branchlets are free and usually project about a tenth of an inch. The reticulations are mostly square or polygonal, sometimes rounded, and average ·06 to ·10 of an inch across, and the branchlets are ordinarily about ·03 in diameter, but often less.

Adult specimens have large, slightly compressed principal branches, which arise from near the base, and diverging through the frond, throw off large secondary branches which spread often at nearly right angles. Sometimes these coalesce, forming large, somewhat quadrangular areas, two or three inches across, and filled, like the rest of the frond, with fine reticulations. Occasionally secondary fronds arise from the sides and spread at right angles, other secondary fronds occasionally appear, like nearly circular rosettes, attached only by the centre to the side of the primary frond.

The largest specimens are 20 to 22 inches high, and 20 to 25 broad; the large branches ·3 to ·4 thick; the trunk at base 1 inch to 1·5.

Color light purple, usually with the terminal branchlets light yellow, sometimes yellowish over the whole surface. In life, one specimen was "bright crimson, polyps deep orange,"—F. H. B.

Spicula light purple and yellow, sometimes the same spiculum has its opposite ends of these two colors. Longer double-spindles with slender and acute ends, the warts rough and not very close, though more so than in *L. eximia* V.; the warts nearest the narrow median space are considerably largest. The stouter ones are much smaller, and also acute. Polyp-spicula light amber, very slender. With the larger spicula are many small, short ones, with only a single wreath of warts at each end.

The longer spicula are ·156^{mm} by ·036, ·156 by ·048, ·120 by ·036, ·132 by ·042; stouter ones ·096 by ·048, ·072 by ·036; the smaller ·048 by ·024.

Panama,—C. B. Adams, J. H. Sternbergh, F. H. Bradley; Pearl Islands, 6 to 8 fathoms by divers, large; and Zorritos, Peru,—F. H. Bradley; Punta Arenas and Corinto, Nic.,—J. A. McNiel.

This is, when well grown and perfect, a very elegant and beautiful species. The reticulations are of about the same size as those of *L. Agassizii*, but the branchlets are more slender and the cells smaller. The character of the midribs is also different, but the best characters for distinguishing them are found in the forms and structure of the spicula, which are very different in the two species. It has some resemblance in form and color to *Pterogorgia flabellum* of the West Indies, but the spicula separate them generically.

I have dedicated this to the memory of the lamented Prof. C. B. Adams, who was, perhaps, the first to bring it to this country. His specimens are in the museum of Amherst College.

Leptogorgia rutila Verrill. (LITIGORGIA ADAMSII, VAR. RUTILA, 1st Ed.).
Rhipidogorgia Agassizii (*pars*) Verrill, op. cit., p. 32.

Plate VI, figure 5.

The specimens from Acapulco are bright light red in color (between minium and vermillion) and differ in several other respects. The branches are not so slender and the reticulations are smaller and more regular, the cells also are more crowded, prominent, and distinctly bilobed. In these external characters it resembles *L. Agassizii*, but the cells are not quite so large and the branchlets more slender. The axis is amber-color and translucent in the branches.

The spicula are mostly light red, variable in size and shape, mostly rather slender. Long double-spindles rather slender and acute, with a wide median space; each end has three or four whorls of warts, those next to the median space considerably largest, the others diminishing to the ends. Stouter double-spindles about as thick but shorter, blunt, mostly with but two whorls at each end, the inner ones much the largest, the outer ones close to the ends; median space rather wide. There are numerous much smaller spicula, with a well marked median space, and a whorl of warts on each end, which are more or less confused with a cluster of terminal warts. Sometimes the terminal warts form a small terminal whorl. Polyp-spicula light red, slender, acute, slightly papillose.

The long double-spindles measure ·156^{mm} by ·048, ·121 by ·048, ·144 by ·042, ·103 by ·030; the stouter ones ·090 by ·042, ·078 by ·042, ·072 by ·036; the small ones ·054 by ·028, ·048 by ·024, ·036 by ·024.

C.—*Flabelliform, loosely and coarsely reticulated; terminal branchlets free. Cells flat or but slightly raised.*

Leptogorgia stenobrochis Verrill. (LITIGORGIA STENOBROCHIS, 1st ed.).

Gorgonia stenobrochis Val.,* Voyage de la Vénus, pl. 12, fig. 1, 1ª.
Rhipidogorgia stenobrochis Val.; Edwards and Haime, Corall., i, p. 176, 1858; Verrill, Bulletin M. C. Z., p. 32; and Proc. Bost. Soc. N. H., x, p. 327. (Misspelled.)
R. Englemanni Horn, Proc. Phil. Acad., 1860, p. 233. (Perhaps distinct).
Gorgonia (Eugorgia) stenobrachis Verrill, Am. Jour. Sci, xlv, p. 414, May, 1868.

Corallum forming large, openly reticulated fans, with stout, subparallel, upright branches, and long, oblong or rectangular meshes.

In young specimens the trunk is divided close to the base into two or more principal branches, which give off irregularly numerous branches of nearly the same size, so that the main branches very soon blend with the others and can be traced only for a short distance. The secondary branches and the branchlets start out nearly at right angles, and then suddenly bend upright and become parallel with the preceding branches. The cross branchlets project nearly at right angles, connecting the branches together at intervals varying from ·5 to 2 inches, so that the meshes have openings of these lengths, and about ·20 to ·25 wide. The terminal branches are of about the same size as the other branches and free for the distance of one or two inches. The branches and branchlets are often nearly round, at other times compressed in the plane of the frond, or even at right angles to it.

The cells are small, very numerous, arranged closely in many rows along each side of the branches and branchlets, but nearly covering the latter. They are mostly flat, but occasionally the borders are slightly raised. Median naked space well marked and often having strong longitudinal furrows. Color dull yellow, often tinged with purple, frequently stained dark umber-brown in drying. In life, " brownish yellow to faint salmon, polyps light yellow,"—F. H. B.

---

* The locality given (New Zealand) is probably an error. Spicula of the original type agree well with the ordinary forms.—Reprint.

Height of the largest specimens about 2 feet; breadth about the same; diameter of branchlets ·15 of an inch.

The spicula are reddish purple and light yellow intermingled, both colors sometimes occurring on one spiculum. Long double-spindles somewhat slender, acute at the ends, with a rather wide median space; warts distant, forming about three whorls around each end, those next the middle much the largest. Shorter double-spindles thick and blunt, with a wide median space, on each side of which there is a whorl of large thorny warts; beyond these is a small wreath of much smaller warts, close to the ends, and often confused with the terminal cluster of few small warts. In addition to these there are many much smaller double-spindles, with two well separated whorls of small warts on each end, one of which is nearly terminal and much the smallest.

The long double-spindles measure ·121^{mm} by ·036, and ·108 by ·036; the stouter double-spindles ·084 by ·048, ·072 by ·048, ·061 by ·048, and ·084 by ·042; the small ones ·036 by ·024.

Zorritos, Peru; Panama; and Pearl Islands, in 6 to 8 fathoms, by divers, large,—F. H. Bradley; Panama,—J. H. Sternbergh, A. Agassiz; Corinto and Punta Arenas,—J. A. McNiel; San Salvador,—Capt. J. M. Dow; Acapulco,—A. Agassiz.

Leptogorgia stenobrochis, var. Englemanni. (LITIGORGIA, 1st Ed.).

The original specimen, described by Mr. Horn, and others from Acapulco and Panama differ slightly from the ordinary forms from Panama in having smaller and usually less elongated reticulations. The branches are also more compressed and in some specimens thicker, though not constantly so. The cells are very numerous, thickly scattered over the whole surface of the branches, but sometimes leaving a narrow median space. They are oblong and slightly prominent.

The color is reddish brown, yellowish brown, or dull brownish yellow tinged with reddish.

The spicula are light yellow and deep red intermingled, and agree nearly with those of the ordinary variety in form, but are smaller.

D.—*Imperfectly flabelliform, the branches pinnate or imperfectly bipinnate, not reticulated; branchlets rather short. Cells somewhat prominent.*

Leptogorgia ramulus Verrill. (LITIGORGIA RAMULUS, 1st Ed.).

Gorgonia ramulus Val., Comptes-rendus, t. xli, p. 12; Edwards et H., Coralliaires, i, p. 160, 1857; Verrill, Bulletin M. C. Z., p. 38; Proceedings Boston Soc. Nat. Hist., x, p. 326, 1866.

Gorgonia humilis Verrill, Mem. Boston Soc. Nat. Hist., i, p. 6, 1864, (*non* Dana).

? *Lophogorgia Panamensis* Duch. and Mich., Supl. Corall. des Antilles, p. 19, Tab. iv, fig. 1, 1864, (the red variety).

Corallum very branching, often in the form of a densely branched shrub or bush, but frequently, especially when young, more or less flabelliform. The base is usually large and spreading, and quite frequently several distinct trunks arise from the same base, forming a thick clump. The trunk is very short and soon divides into several large, divergent branches, which are nearly round, but sometimes a little flattened, often more or less crooked, and give off from their sides, at distances of about a fourth of an inch apart, numerous short, irregular, crooked, and nearly quadrangular branchlets. Many of these become longer and larger than the rest, and again subdivide in the same way. The ultimate branchlets are usually about ·08 of an inch in diameter, and from half an inch to an inch long, but occasionally 2 inches. The terminal branchlets are mostly somewhat acute at the ends. The cells form small rounded verrucæ, which are quite prominent and closely arranged in two series on each side of the branches, giving them a quadrangular appearance. On the larger branches the verrucæ are more scattered and irregularly arranged. The openings are mostly on the upper side of the verrucæ, and laterally compressed. The branches and most of the branchlets have, along the naked median space, a well-marked longitudinal furrow, in which there is usually a slender longitudinal ridge. The axis is light wood-color at the base, blackish in the main branches, slender and light wood-brown in the branchlets. The cœnenchyma is almost always either uniformly greyish white or deep purplish red, but occasionally pink specimens occur. One specimen has the lower branches and base white, the middle part of the trunk and the branches arising from it purplish red, and the upper part of the trunk and terminal branches white, showing conclusively that the white and red specimens are all one species. A large specimen of the red variety is 8 inches high and 16 broad, with the main branches ·15 in diameter; another is 13 inches high and 10 broad, with the main branches ·22 in diameter. Most specimens do not exceed 6 inches in height and about the same in breadth.

Small dwarfed specimens sometimes occur that are 3 or 4 inches high, with the main branches ·08, and the branchlets ·05 of an inch in diameter, but agreeing in other respects with the ordinary forms.

The spicula in the white variety are all white; in the red variety light purple, the polyp-spicula bright yellow. The long double-spindles are but little longer than the others, not very acute at the ends, thickly covered with distinctly separated, large, warty tubercles, axis small. The stouter double-spindles are more blunt and more closely covered with warts, which are still separate. Polyp-spindles slender, distantly papillose. The longer double-spindles measure ·108^{mm} by ·042^{mm}, ·102 by ·042, ·096 by ·036, ·090 by ·042, ·084 by ·036; the stouter ones ·084 by ·048, ·078 by ·036, ·072 by ·042.

Panama and Pearl Islands.—F. H. Bradley; Panama,—J. H. Sternbergh; Zorritos, Peru,—F. H. Bradley; Acapulco,—A. Agassiz; (?) Cape St. Lucas,—J. Xantus; San Salvador,—Capt. J. M. Dow; Corinto,—J. A. McNiel.

The two very distinct colors assumed by this species are somewhat remarkable and may serve to divide it conveniently into two varieties: 1st, the ordinary white form; 2nd, the red variety. But as shown above these colors may be found on a single specimen, and are not accompanied by any other constant differences. The red variety is possibly the form described as *Lophogorgia Panamensis* by Duchassaing and Michelotti, but does not agree well with their figure.

Their brief and very imperfect diagnosis is as follows: "Ramosa, ramis distinctis sub-compressis, majoribus 4, minoribus 2 millimetris latis, colore rubro. In insula Flamenco, prope Panama."

All the specimens from Zorritos are of the red variety, and agree well with those of Panama, except that they are mostly somewhat smaller and more slender.

The specimens from Acapulco and Cape St. Lucas differ considerably in appearance from those of Panama. The branchlets are shorter and thicker, length ·2 to ·5 of an inch, thickness ·08, often somewhat clavate. Cells nearly uniformly distributed on all sides of the branchlets, smaller and less prominent, distinctly bilobed. Color deep red, some of the spicula bright yellow. This may possibly prove to be a distinct species when a good series can be examined.

The specimens in the Museum of Comparative Zoölogy, formerly described as *Gorgonia humilis*, and supposed to have come from Charleston, S. C., appear to be identical with specimens from Panama. The former locality is probably altogether erroneous.

Leptogorgia pumila Verrill, sp. nov. (LITIGORGIA PUMILA, 1st Ed.).

Plate V, figure 8.

Corallum low, densely branched, imperfectly flabelliform, a few of the branchlets coalescent, forming irregular, coarse reticulations. Several crooked principal branches arise near the base and subdivide in an irregularly pinnate manner, the branchlets being about a fourth of an inch apart and from a fourth to one inch long. These are rather thick, rounded, quadrangular, mostly curved, and spread at a wide angle. The cells form small, rounded verrucæ, which are but little prominent and not crowded, alternating in two rows along each side of the branches. The largest specimen is 5 inches high and the same in breadth; diameter of the main branches ·15; of the branchlets ·08. Color bright red, the surface sometimes fading to yellowish red.

The spicula are mostly light purplish red, mixed with a few light yellow ones; polyp-spindles light amber-color. The longer double-spindles resemble those of the preceding species, but are relatively larger and more acute. They are closely covered with large warts, with a rather wide median space. The stouter double-spindles are similar, but blunter at the ends; with them are many small, white double-spindles with only one wreath of warts near the ends. The longer double-spindles are ·138^{mm} by ·048, ·132 by ·054, ·120 by ·048, ·120 by ·042, ·114 by ·039; stouter ones ·132 by ·060, ·108 by ·048, ·102 by ·048, ·096 by ·054, ·084 by ·042.

Zorritos, Peru,—F. H. Bradley.

This species is allied to the last, and branches in a similar manner, but has thicker branchlets, with larger and more widely separated verrucae, which are less prominent and open outward. The branchlets are scarcely quadrangular, the spicula different in form, and the coalescence of the branches, common in this, is very rare in *L. ramulus*.

Leptogorgia diffusa Verrill, sp. nov. (LITIGORGIA DIFFUSA, 1st Ed.).
Plate V, figure 6. Plate VI, figure 3.

Corallum loosely ramose, the branchlets subpinnate, producing an open, shrub-like form. The trunk divides near the base, in the original specimen, into two main branches and these again fork. The branches give off pinnately, at distances of half an inch to an inch apart, slender branchlets, which are flattened and spread at nearly right angles, varying in length from a quarter inch to three inches before subdividing, as some of them do, into secondary pinnae. The main branches are round, but the branchlets are much compressed and slender. The cells form rather large verrucae, which are enlarged at base and quite prominent, not crowded, and arranged in two alternating rows on each side of the main branches, but in only one row on each edge of the branchlets, which therefore appear serrate on account of the broad-based cells. There is a very distinct sulcus on the larger branches. The specimen is 5 inches high and 6 broad; diameter of the main branches ·10; width of branchlets ·06. Color bright red.

The spicula are all bright red, resembling those of *L. ramulus*, but larger and relatively stouter. The longer double-spindles are long, covered with large papillae or warts, those next to the median space largest. Stouter double-spindles decidedly blunt, closely covered by large, rounded, rough warts. Polyp-spicula slender, bright yellow.

The longer spicula are ·144^{mm} by ·042, ·132 by ·054, ·120 by ·054, ·108 by ·048; stouter ones ·114 by ·054, ·084 by ·048, ·072 by ·054; polyp-spicula ·180 by ·036, ·144 by ·030, ·114 by ·024.

Pearl Islands, Bay of Panama,—F. H. Bradley; Gulf of Nicoya, by divers, larger,—J. A. McNiel.

Readily distinguished by its lax branches, and distant, slender, flattened branchlets, serrated by the distant, uniserial verrucæ.

Leptogorgia Californica Verrill, sp. nov. (LITIGORGIA CALIFORNICA, 1st Ed.).
Plate V, figure 10.

Corallum somewhat flabelliform, low, subpinnately branched, the branchlets ascending, not coalescent. The branchlets are nearly round and usually curve outward at first. They are from 1 to 2 inches long, before branching, and from ·08 to ·10 thick. Cells flat, scarcely rising above the general surface, arranged in about three rows along each side of the branchlets. The apertures in contraction often appear stellate. The naked median region is quite narrow. Color reddish purple, often with a narrow yellow streak along the centre of the median space. Height 4 to 6 inches.

The spicula are mostly reddish purple, some are half yellow, others entirely so. The longer double-spindles are slender, scarcely acute, with a wide median space, which is bordered by two whorls of large, rough, distant warts. Close to each end and distant from the preceding, there is a much smaller whorl of small warts, while the ends terminate with two or three similar small warts. Stouter double-spindles thick and blunt, with two wreaths of warts on each end, closely crowded together, those next the narrow median space much the largest. Polyp-spicula slender, light yellow, with few, small, distant papillæ. Compound cross-shaped spicula occasionally occur, which have short blunt rays, with rough, irregular warts. The longer double-spindles measure ·108 by ·048^{mm}, ·090 by ·042, ·084 by ·040, ·084 by ·036; ·096 by ·036; stouter double-spindles ·096 by ·048, ·072 by ·036, ·078 by ·042, ·084 by ·048; the crosses ·072 by ·066, and ·054 by ·048.

Cape St. Lucas,—J. Xantus; Margarita Bay,—A. Garret.

E.—*The terminal branchlets slender and elongated. Cells scarcely prominent.*

Leptogorgia alba Verrill. (LITIGORGIA LEVIS, 1st Ed.).

? *Lophogorgia alba* Duch. and Mich., op. cit., p. 19, Tab. IV, fig. 2, 1864 (*non Gorgonia alba* Lam.).

Gorgonia rigida, var. lævis Verrill, Proc. Bost. Soc. Nat. Hist., x, p. 327, 1866.

Plate V, figure 7.

Corallum flabelliform, with long, slender, virgate, somewhat fasciculated branchlets. The trunk is small, often nearly round, sometimes compressed, and has a small, thin base. It soon gives off from each side, in a somewhat pinnate manner, several main branches, nearly as large as itself. Those nearest the base are usually about a quarter of an inch apart, and spread at a large angle; those higher up are more distant and curving outward at the base afterwards bend upward. The branches subdivide in a similar manner, and some of the branchlets again subdivide. The smaller branches and branchlets are of about the same size and all have a tendency to become parallel by bending upward. The terminal branchlets are from 1 to 5 inches long without subdivisions, but mostly 2 or 3 inches long in ordinary specimens, with a diameter of about ·05, but often smaller. The cells are often perfectly flat, but usually form small, slightly prominent verrucae, with a small oblong opening. They are not crowded and arranged alternately in two rows on each side of the branchlets, but on the large branches they become more crowded and often form four rows on each side. The axis is slender, light-wood color at the base, dark brown in the branches, yellowish and setiform in the branchlets. Cœnenchyma thin. The largest specimens are about 12 inches high and 15 broad, with the trunk and main branches ·10 and ·12 in diameter. Ordinary specimens are about 4 to 6 inches high and broad. Dwarf specimens occur in which the trunk is only ·05 in diameter, and the branchlets ·03. The specimens in all cases appear to be white; the colored forms, referred to it formerly, prove to be a distinct species (*Eugorgia Bradleyi*). In life, "the stem is very light pink, heads deep pink, polyps transparent,"—F. H. B.

The spicula are white, resembling those of *L. ramulus*, but longer and more acute, with the papillae less crowded. The longer double-spindles are variable in size, some of them being ·138^{mm} by ·048^{mm}, ·144 by ·036, ·120 by ·048, and ·168 by ·060; the stouter double-spindles ·108 by ·060, and ·102 by ·048; some of the small ones are ·048 by ·024, and many are still smaller.

Panama and Pearl Islands,—F. H. Bradley; Gulf of Nicoya and Corinto,—J. A. McNiel; San Salvador,—Capt. J. M. Dow.

This species resembles in form *Eugorgia Bradleyi*, from which, by its color and very different spicula, it may be readily distinguished. In color it is like the white variety of *L. ramulus*, but differs in its mode of branching, in its long, slender, rounded branchlets, and less prominent cells.

Whether the *Lophogorgia alba* Duch. and Mich. be this species or the white variety of *G. ramulus*, I am unable to determine with certainty, but have referred it to this mainly on account of the size of the branches. Their brief diagnosis is as follows: "Ramosa, ventalina, alba, calycibus prominulis, sparsis. Hab. prope Panama."

"Height 10 centim., branches all, as well as trunk, 2 mill. broad."

The name, *alba*, was used by Lamarck for a "*Gorgonia*," of which the generic affinities are still unknown,* and, therefore, cannot with propriety be used for this, even if it was intended for the present species. Esper also gave the name, *Gorgonia palma*, *var. alba*, to a form which proves to be distinct from his *G. palma*.

Leptogorgia flexilis Verrill, sp. nov. (LITIGORGIA FLEXILIS, 1st Ed.).

Plate V, figure 11.

Corallum when young flabelliform, with slender, elongated, erect branches; when large scarcely flabelliform, often bushy or fasciculated, with long, slender, drooping branches. The trunk gives off at distances varying from a quarter inch to an inch, alternately from each side, large primary branches, some of which are often nearly as large as the main stem. These arise mostly at an acute angle and give off secondary branches in the same way, but at greater distances, mostly 1 or 2 inches. These branches again subdivide, giving off in a subpinnate, often secund manner, a few very long, round, slender, nearly parallel branchlets, nearly as large as themselves, and from 10 to 12 inches in length without subdivisions. These diminish very gradually toward the ends and in full grown specimens droop somewhat like the branches of the weeping-willow. Possibly, however, this may not be the case while living.

The trunk and main branches are frequently somewhat compressed, but often round, and are marked by several strong longitudinal grooves. The cells are broad-oval, rather large for the genus, not prominent, usually open, arranged upon the branchlets in four or five irregular longitudinal rows on each side, leaving very narrow, naked median spaces; on the larger branches they form two broad lateral bands, made up of many rows. They are not crowded, the spaces between them being mostly three or four times their own diameters. Color dull reddish brown, uniform throughout. Height of largest specimen about 2 feet; breadth 10 inches; diameter of trunk ·25; of main branches ·15 to ·20; of branchlets at origin ·10 to ·12; near tips ·04 to ·08; of cells ·015.

A Panama specimen, owing doubtless to an unfavorable location,

---

* Dr. Kölliker has sent spicula from the original type, which indicate that it is a *Plexaura*, therefore I have adopted *alba* for this.—Reprint.

grew in an oblique or creeping position, the branches being nearly all secund and crooked, and the branchlets much shorter and erect.

The spicula include several forms and sizes of double-spindles. The larger double-spindles are slender and acute, with a wide median space; each end with three or four whorls of well separated, nearly simple warts; the whorl next to the median space is largest, the others diminishing regularly to the ends. Stouter double-spindles much shorter and thicker, blunt at the ends, of several sizes; largest ones with a wide median space bordered by whorls of large rough warts; beyond these, and close to the warty end, there is a much smaller whorl, with small crowded warts; the shortest ones have the two whorls on each half and the terminal cluster of warts crowded together into a sort of rounded triangular head; some very small ones have the second whorl well separated from the median and close to the end. Other small spicula, approaching the form of double-heads, have a very narrow median space bordered by close whorls of very small, crowded, rough warts, which are confused with the terminal cluster; in an end view the whorls show four or five close warts. Cross-shaped spicula occasionally occur, which have four nearly equal, club-shaped arms, covered with rough warts. The longer double-spindles measure $\cdot 102^{mm}$ by $\cdot 036^{mm}$, $\cdot 096$ by $\cdot 042$, $\cdot 096$ by $\cdot 036$, $\cdot 090$ by $\cdot 042$, $\cdot 084$ by $\cdot 036$; the stouter ones $\cdot 078$ by $\cdot 042$, $\cdot 072$ by $\cdot 036$, $\cdot 066$ by $\cdot 042$, $\cdot 066$ by $\cdot 039$, $\cdot 060$ by $\cdot 036$, $\cdot 054$ by $\cdot 031$, $\cdot 048$ by $\cdot 030$, $\cdot 036$ by $\cdot 030$; the crosses $\cdot 060$ by $\cdot 048$.

Panama and Pearl Islands, 6 to 8 fathoms, by divers, large,—F. H. Bradley; San Salvador,—Capt. J. M. Dow.

The spicula, though much smaller, resemble most those of *L. rigida* and *L. cuspidata*, from which it differs in the length and slenderness of the branchlets, etc. When young it branches much like *L. alba*.

F.—Imperfectly flabelliform. Branches free, rather stout, rigid when dry. Terminal branchlets elongated. Cells in lateral bands, flat or slightly prominent.

Leptogorgia rigida Verrill. (Litigorgia rigida, 1st Ed.).

Plate V, figure 9.

Leptogorgia rigida (*pars*) Verrill, Bulletin M. C. Z., p. 32, 1864.
Gorgonia rigida (*pars*) Verrill, Proc. Boston Soc. Nat. Hist., vol. x, p. 327, 1866.
Gorgonia (*Eugorgia*) *rigida* Verrill, Amer. Jour. Sci., vol. 45, p. 414, May, 1868.

Corallum scarcely flabelliform, except when young. Trunk dividing very near the base into several stout branches, which are often strongly sulcated and much compressed. These give off, in a more or less second manner, at distances of a quarter inch to an inch, somewhat smaller secondary branches, most of which again subdivide. The branches and branchlets mostly arise obliquely, at an acute angle, but occasionally curve outward somewhat at the base. The branchlets are from one to five inches long without subdivision, rather stout, rigid when dry, irregularly compressed, often crooked, and scarcely taper toward the ends, which are often even somewhat enlarged and blunt. The cells are oval, a little prominent, rather large for the genus, and arranged in quincunx, about three or four times their own diameter apart on the branchlets, in four to six longitudinal rows, forming broad, somewhat prominent lateral bands of verrucæ. On the large branches the cells are in many more rows forming broad lateral bands; sometimes, on the same specimen, part of the cells are prominent, while the rest are flat. The median spaces are distinct throughout, with a median groove that often becomes wide and conspicuous on the larger branches.

Color deep bluish purple, or violaceous, occasionally reddish purple, sometimes with streaks of yellow, or with yellowish surface. Height of largest specimen about 15 inches; breadth 10; diameter of main branches ·18 to ·25; of secondary ·12 to ·15; of branchlets ·10 to ·12; breadth of verrucæ ·04; openings of cells ·02.

Spicula of several sizes and forms, with many intermediate, all deep purplish red in the typical variety. Longer double-spindles thick and stout, regularly tapering to the somewhat acute ends; with a narrow median space; each end with three or four crowded whorls of rough irregular warts, those next to the median space much the largest, the others rapidly decreasing to the ends. Other more slender forms occur, with distant warts and a wide median space, and having only two whorls of warts on each half, the ends acute.

The shorter double-spindles are short, thick, blunt, with a wide median space, which is bordered by prominent wreaths of large rough warts, another much smaller whorl of warts is placed just outside of each of these, and close to the ends. Many small, short double-spindles occur, which have only a single wreath of warts on each side of the median space, with a small cluster terminating each end. Occasionally compound cross-shaped spicula occur, which have the four rays about equal, short, blunt, closely covered with rough warts. Longer double spindles measure ·132^{mm} by ·036^{mm}, ·132 by ·048, ·126 by ·048, ·120 by ·042, ·114 by ·048, ·108 by ·042, ·095 by ·036; stouter double-spindles ·120 by ·060, ·095 by ·048, ·090 by ·048, ·078 by ·048, ·072 by ·048, ·060 by ·048, ·054 by ·048; the small ones ·048 by ·030, .042 by ·024.

Cape St. Lucas,—J. Xantus; Acapulco,—A. Agassiz; San Salvador,—Capt. J. M. Dow; La Paz,—J. Pedersen.

This species and the next approach *Lophogorgia palma* E. and H. in the character of the spicula, more nearly than do any of our other species of *Leptogorgia*.

The existence of numerous small, short, double-spindles, with but two whorls of warts, gives the spicula of these species an appearance quite different from those of the more typical species of *Leptogorgia*, but similar spicula occur in *L. stenobrochis*, and, to a less extent, in several other species.

Leptogorgia cuspidata Verrill. (LITIGORGIA CUSPIDATA, 1st Ed.).

Leptogorgia cuspidata Verrill, Proc. Essex Inst., iv, p. 186, 1865.
Gorgonia (*Eugorgia*) *cuspidata* Verrill, Amer. Jour. Sci., vol. 45, p. 414, May, 1868.

Corallum broad, sub-flabelliform, irregularly branching nearly in one plane. The trunk divides near the base into several principal branches, which subdivide in an irregularly dichotomous manner, forming a somewhat fasciculated clump; sometimes the branches are subpinnate. Branchlets moderately elongated, thick, rigid, nearly straight, tapering to the ends. Cells numerous, rather large, rounded, covering the surface of the branchlets, except along a narrow median space on each side. Longitudinal grooves scarcely distinct, except near the base. Color deep purple, the cells surrounded by bright yellow, and the median space sometimes streaked with yellow.

Height about 6 inches; breadth about the same; length of branchlets 1 to 3 inches; diameter ·10 to ·13.

A specimen from Cape St. Lucas, referred with doubt to this, resembles *L. rigida* in its subpinnate mode of branching. The branchlets are from ·75 to 1 inch long, and ·12 in diameter, and less cuspidate than in the typical form. As I have not had an opportunity to examine the spicula of the original specimen, I add a description of those from this doubtful variety, which may, perhaps, belong rather with *L. rigida*. Spicula of various forms and sizes, deep red and bright yellow mingled. Longer double-spindles large, with acute ends, median space rather wide, warts well separated, forming 3 or 4 whorls on each end, the whorl next to the median space much the largest, consisting of large, ragged warts; the others diminish toward the ends, the last warts becoming very small and simple. Stouter double-spindles thick and blunt, with a deeply sunken median space, bordered by whorls of large, crowded, rough, compound warts; outside of these, but close to them, there is a whorl of much smaller warts on each end, and usually another subterminal whorl of very small simple warts. Many small, short spicula have the form of double-heads, with a well-defined median space, and two closely crowded whorls of small warts on each end. Cross-shaped spicula occasionally occur, having acute points, with well-separated rough warts.

The longer double-spindles measure ·144^{mm} by ·042, ·132 by ·048, ·120 by ·048, ·120 by ·042, ·114 by ·054; the stouter ones ·096 by ·052, ·090 by ·054, ·078 by ·054, ·078 by ·042, ·072 by ·039; the double-heads ·048 by ·033, ·054 by ·036, ·042 by ·024.

The specimens from Zorritos belong to this variety but are dwarfed. Height 3 or 4 inches, branchlets ·25 to ·75 long, ·08 in diameter. Color purple, with the surface streaked and stained with yellow. Spicula much like those of the specimen described above.

Cape St. Lucas,—J. Xantus; Acapulco,—A. Agassiz; Corinto,—J. A. McNiel; Zorritos, Peru,—F. H. Bradley.

This species is closely allied to *L. rigida*, yet the typical specimens from Cape St. Lucas have a very different appearance, due mainly to the larger, straight, cuspidate branchlets, and the peculiar color, which is seen, however, to a less extent in some specimens of *L rigida*. Possibly it may ultimately prove to be only a variety of that species, when a larger series of specimens can be examined. Owing to the doubtful affinities of the peculiar specimen from which the spicula above described were taken, no reliable conclusions can, as yet, be based upon the slight differences observed in the spicula.

Leptogorgia Caryi Verrill. (LITIGORGIA FUCOSA, 1st Ed.).

Plexaura fucosa Verrill, Bulletin M. C. Z., p. 45, (*non* Val.).

Corallum dichotomous, subdividing some distance above the base. Terminal branches stout, two to four inches long, as large as the main stem, nearly round. Cells very little raised, scattered on all sides of the branchlets. Color bright orange-red.

Spicula yellowish red. Longer double-spindles rather stout, scarcely acute, with a wide median space; two or three whorls of large, compound, rough warts on each end, those nearest the middle much the largest. Stouter double-spindles short and blunt, with a wide median space, each end with two or three crowded and usually somewhat confused whorls of large rough warts, forming a large terminal cluster. Some approach the form of double-heads, with a narrow median space and a large cluster of closely crowded warts on each end. Other "heads" are shorter, lack the median space, and are entirely covered with crowded warts. Crosses, with four short, roughly warted branches frequently occur.

The longer double-spindles measure ·150^{mm} by ·060^{mm}, ·144 by ·066, ·144 by ·060, ·132 by ·054; stouter double-spindles ·120 by ·060, ·114 by ·054; double-heads ·156 by ·078, ·144 by ·071, ·120 by ·060, ·114 by ·066; heads ·120 by ·060, ·114 by ·060, ·072 by ·048; crosses ·144 by ·120, ·120 by ·078, ·096 by ·084, ·084 by ·072.

California,—Maj. Wm. Rich; near San Francisco,—T. G. Cary, (Coll. Mus. Comp. Zoölogy).

The original description (of *G. fucosa*) is so imperfect as to render the identity of the later specimens with it somewhat uncertain.*

G.—*Densely ramose, low and fruticose; branchlets short, irregular.*

Leptgorgia Peruana Verrill. (LITIGORGIA PERUANA, 1st Ed.).

? *Plexaura reticulata* Ehrenberg, Corall. des rothen Meeres, p. 141, 1834.
Plexaura reticulata Philippi, Wieg. Arch., 1866, p. 119.

Corallum low and shrubby, very densely branched, the branches short, irregular, and crooked, often irregularly coalescent. Several stems often arise from the same large base, close together. They at once divide and subdivide irregularly into numerous crooked branches; these give off very numerous short and crooked branchlets, which are sometimes distinctly pinnate. The branches and branchlets are rather thick and round. The cells are small, not raised, and very numerous, arranged in a broad band on each side of the branches. Axis dark wood-brown, brittle and rigid, often hollow in the branchlets, due perhaps to some parasite. The cœnenchyma is thin and brittle. Color whitish. The largest specimens are about 6 inches high and broad; the branches ·25, and the branchlets ·10 in diameter. The spicula are pure white; the longer double-spindles are slender and acute, with numerous close warts, and a rather wide median space. The stouter double-spindles are much shorter, with a narrow median space and blunt ends, the warts forming a single wreath on each side of the middle and a rounded cluster at each end. The longer spicula are ·120^{mm} by ·048^{mm}, ·120 by ·042, ·108 by ·048; the stouter ones ·084 by ·048, ·078 by ·048, ·072 by ·042, ·084 by ·042.

Callao, Peru,—F. H. Bradley.

I have thought it necessary to give a new name to this species for several reasons:

1st. It is not the *Gorgonia reticulata* Ellis.
2d. It may not be the *Plexaura reticulata* Ehr.

---

* Dr. Kölliker has sent the spicula prepared from the original specimen of *Plexaura fucosa* Val. It proves to be very different from the present species, and belongs to *Psammogorgia*, (see p. 414).—Reprint.

3d. Although "*reticulata*" might be a somewhat appropriate name for it if considered a *Plexaura*, it becomes very inappropriate when referred to a genus in which there are so many species that are *actually reticulated* throughout, while in this the reticulations are few, irregular, and often entirely absent.

The following species, which I have not seen, are here referred to this genus with doubt.

? Gorgonia sanguinea Lam. (LITIGORGIA (?) SANGUINEA, 1st Ed.).

? Gorgonia sanguinea Lamarck, An. saus verteb., 2d edit., p. 495, (Loc. unknown).
Plexaura sanguinea Val., Comptes-rendus, xli, p. 12.
Leptogorgia sanguinea Edw. and Haime, Corall., vol. i, p. 165.

In the latter work this species is described as follows: Corallum rigid, more branched than *L. virgulata*, and with branches still more slender. Calicles scarcely visible. Color carmine-red. Callao.*

Leptogorgia (?) arbuscula V. (LITIGORGIA (?) ARBUSCULA, 1st Ed.).

Plexaura arbuscula Philippi, Wieg. Arch., 1866, p. 118.

"Pl. 4-6 pollicaris, a basi inde in formam fruticuli divisa, roseo-coccinea; ramis subdichotomis, omnibus libris; ramulis ultimis 1⅓ lin. crassis."

Isl. Santa Maria, Bay of Arauco.

Leptogorgia (?) Chilensis Verrill. (LITIGORGIA (?) ROSEA V., 1st Ed.).

Plexaura rosea Philippi, l. c., p. 118 (*non Leptogorgia rosea* E. & H.).

"Pl. 1½ pedalis, roseo-carnea, subflabellato-dilitata; ramis virgatis, subnodosis liberis; ramulis ultimis elongatis, cylindricis, 1¼ lin crassis, sæpe 6 poll. longis."

Algarrobo, somewhat south of Valparaiso, Chili.

Leptogorgia (?) platyclados V. (LITIGORGIA (?) PLATYCLADOS, 1st Ed.).

Plexaura platyclados Philippi, l. c., p. 119.

"Pl. roseo, flabellatim ramoso; ramis latissimis, valde compressis, loriformibus."

Isl. Santa Maria.

It seems very doubtful whether this species be a *Leptogorgia*, but it cannot be a *Plexaura*.

Eugorgia Verrill.

Amer. Jour. Sci., xlv, p. 414, May, 1868.

Cœnenchyma composed chiefly of three forms of small spicula, which are naked at its surface. There are two kinds of warty doublespindles,—longer and usually sharper ones, and stouter and blunter ones. These are intermingled with numerous double-wheels, which are usually shorter; sometimes one of the wheels is smaller than the other, or rudimentary, frequently there are four wheels developed.

---

* The original *G. sanguinea* is, by its spicula, a true *Gorgonia* (*Pterogorgia*); the Callao species is probably distinct and may be one of the following.—Reprint.

The polyp-spicula are small, slender spindles. The axis is horny. Branches either round or compressed, variously subdivided, much as in *Leptogorgia*, surface finely granulous. Cells mostly in a band along each side of the branches, sometimes prominent, usually flat.

A.—*Flabelliform, branches subparallel, dichotomous, usually stout. Cells flat or very slightly raised.*

Eugorgia ampla Verrill.
Leptogorgia ampla Verrill, Bulletin M. C. Z., p. 32, 1864.

Plate V, figure 12.   Plate VI, figure 6.

Corallum large, flabelliform, with numerous elongated, subparallel branches and branchlets. Several main branches, which are large, rounded or slightly compressed, and nearly equal, arise from close to the base, the lateral ones curving out at first and then becoming upright and nearly parallel. The branches give off from each side distant, long, and often slightly flexuous, branches and branchlets, which bend outward and then become parallel like the main branches. The branchlets are rigid, from 2 to 6 inches long without dividing, and but little more slender than the branches from which they arise, usually slightly compressed and tapering but little to the obtuse ends. They arise from 1 to 3 inches apart and are often alternate, but at other times only arise from one side of the branch. The cœnenchyma is quite thick and firm, granulous at the surface. The cells are flat, very numerous, crowdedly arranged in two broad lateral bands, separated by a very narrow, naked median space, which forms a slight groove. The cells are usually so contracted as to appear very small and inconspicuous, but when the surface is removed they are seen to be rather large, oval, and so closely arranged that they are separated only by thin walls. The axis is horn-like, blackish in the main branches, but in the branchlets amber-yellow and translucent. Color, in the typical specimens, bright yellow, in the variety light purple. The largest specimens are 18 inches high and nearly as broad; diameter of the main branches ·30; of the branchlets at base ·12; at tips ·10.

Spicula, in the typical specimens, bright yellow. Long double-spindles very acute, distantly warted, with about three wreaths of warts on each end, those next the middle much the largest; median space wide. Shorter double spindles obtuse and more densely covered with warts. Double-wheels nearly or quite as broad as long, the "wheels" large, rather thin, their edges often acute; median space narrow; axis small. The ends of the axis are also terminated by small, thin, wheel-like disks. The polyp-spicula are of several kinds, the most common are small but not very slender double-spindles, with few, distant, thorny papillæ.

The longer double-spindles are ·132ᵐᵐ by ·048, ·120 by ·048, ·108 by ·048; the stouter ones ·120 by ·060, ·108 by ·060, ·108 by ·054, ·096 by ·054, ·096 by ·048, ·072 by ·054; the double-wheels ·054 by ·060, ·054 by ·054, ·054 by ·048, ·054 by ·042, ·048 by ·054, ·048 by ·048.

Margarita Bay, Lower California,—A. Garret; La Paz, Gulf of California,—Maj. Wm. Rich.

Var. purpurascens Verrill.

Similar in form to the preceding, with the branches and branchlets, even in large specimens, not more than half as large. Color light purple, spicula similar in form, but usually with the double-wheels smaller and their edges less acute. The colors of the spicula are deep purple, light purple, and white. Height of the largest specimens 2 feet. This form may prove to be distinct, but our specimens are too few to satisfactorily determine. It is near *Eugorgia fusco-purpurea* (? Ehr. sp.) and may be identical with it. The spicula of the latter are well figured by Dr. Kölliker,* and agree very well in form with those of this supposed variety.

Pearl Islands and Zorritos,—F. H. Bradley; Corinto,—J. A. McNiel.

Eugorgia nobilis Verrill, sp. nov.

Plate V, figure 13.

Large, flabelliform, with large, divergent, compressed branches, and numerous short, thick, curved branchlets. Several very large flattened branches arise close to the base from the broad trunk, and spread divergently in the plane of the frond, giving off at short distances (usually about half an inch, often less) numerous sub-parallel, undulate branches, which are strongly compressed at their bases. These give rise to numerous secondary branches and branchlets, which arise at distances of from ·25 to 1 inch apart, and are short, thick, and strongly curved, scarcely tapering, rarely more than an inch long without dividing. The cœnenchyma is thick and persistent. The cells are larger and less crowded than in the preceding species, usually flat, sometimes a little prominent, forming two broad bands, which are separated by a narrow, sterile sulcus on each side, corresponding to a large longitudinal duct. Color brownish yellow, or reddish brown. The largest specimens are 18 inches high and 2 feet broad; diameter of main branches ·35 to ·75; of branchlets ·12 to ·15.

Spicula light purple, yellow, and white. Long double-spindles somewhat acute, thickly covered with warts. Stouter ones more densely

---

* Icones Histiologicæ, Taf. xviii, figs. 28 to 31.

warty, blunt, quite variable in form and size. Double-wheels small, about as long as broad, with small wheels very close together, and with the axis projecting but slightly at the ends. The long double-spindles are ·120^{mm} by ·048^{mm}, ·120 by ·042, and ·120 by ·036; the stouter double-spindles ·084 by ·054, ·084 by ·048, and ·096 by ·054; the double-wheels ·042 by ·042, and ·048 by ·042.

Pearl Islands, 6 to 8 fathoms by divers,—F. H. Bradley; La Paz,—J. Pedersen (var. *excelsa*);* Corinto,—J. A. McNiel.

This species resembles *E. ampla*, but is more densely ramulous, and has shorter, curved branchlets, instead of long, erect ones. Its spicula are similar, but the double-wheels are smaller and more rounded.

B.—*Flabelliform. Branches bipinnate and tripinnate, not coalescent. Cells prominent.*

Eugorgia Daniana Verrill, sp. nov.

Plate V, figure 14.   Plate VI, figure 7.

Corallum densely ramose in one plane, forming broad, rounded, fan-shaped fronds. Near the base the short, thick, compressed trunk divides into several large, divergent, compressed, main branches. These give off, pinnately from each edge, at intervals of a quarter of an inch or less, short, slender branchlets, and occasional longer branches, which are similar to the primary ones. These again subdivide pinnately, in the same manner, part of the pinnae remaining short and simple, while others elongate into branches, which again subdivide, producing similar simple branchlets, and some branches that subdivide again. The final branchlets are slender and short, varying in length from ·15 to ·30 of an inch, very seldom ·50, with a diameter of about ·06. The verrucae are small, prominent, higher than broad, conical, crowded on all sides of the branchlets. Surface of the branches and cells distinctly granular with the naked spicula. Color bright yellow, streaked and blotched with dark red both upon the branches and cells. Axis strongly compressed, black in the main branches, setaceous and rigid in the branchlets, where it becomes translucent and brownish.

Height 10 inches; breadth 14; diameter of trunk ·22; of main branches ·15. The spicula are deep red and bright yellow, intermingled. Long double-spindles slender, acute, with a wide median space, and about four whorls of well separated warts on each end, those next to the median space considerably the largest, the others diminishing toward the ends, where they become very small. Some are less slender, but similar in length and structure. Stout double-spindles

---

* The La Paz specimens (*var. excelsa*) are large and tall, with elongated branches, but the spicula are smaller and more slender. Color brown or yellowish-brown.—Reprint.

short and thick, with two whorls of large warts on each end, the outer ones terminal. Double-wheels large, little longer than broad, with a rather wide median space; inner wheels thin, with sharp edges; outer ones terminal, not half as large, sharp-edged, about as far from the median ones as these are apart. The long double-spindles measure ·120^{mm} by ·042^{mm}, ·114 by ·045, ·117 by ·034, ·096 by ·042; the stouter double-spindles ·090 by ·054, ·072 by ·048, ·078 by ·054, ·096 by ·060; double-wheels ·072 by ·060, median space ·018, diameter of axis ·024, terminal wheels ·036, space between outer and inner wheels ·017. Other double-wheels measure ·066 by ·060, and ·072 by ·054.

Panama and Pearl Islands, 6 or 8 fathoms,—F. H. Bradley; Gulf of Nicoya,—J. A. McNiel.

Eugorgia aurantiaca Verrill. (Eugorgia Mexicana V., 1st Ed.).

Lophogorgia aurantiaca Horn, Proceedings Philadelphia Acad. Nat. Sciences. 1860, p. 233 (*non Loptojorgia aurantiaca* Edw., 1857).
Gorgonia aurantiaca Verrill, Bulletin Museum of Comp. Zoölogy, 1864, p. 33.
Eugorgia Mexicana Verrill, Amer. Journal of Sci., xlv, p. 415, May, 1868.

Plate V, figure 15. Plate VI, figure 8.

Corallum forming large densely branched fans, the branches subdividing in the same manner as in the preceding species, but the main branches are longer and less compressed, and the pinnate branchlets are not so close together (usually ·25 inch). The branchlets are also larger and somewhat longer, the length being from ·25 to 1 inch, the diameter ·10 inch. The cells are crowded on all sides of the branchlets, but form irregular lateral bands on the larger branches. They form rounded prominent verrucæ, that are a little larger but not so prominent as in the preceding species, mostly bilabiate. The main branches have a well marked median groove, surface granular, cœnenchyma thin and friable. Color bright orange, streaked with red; interior of the cœnenchyma red. Axis yellowish brown in the larger branches, light yellow and translucent in the smaller branches and branchlets, where it is very slender and rigid. Height 15 inches; breadth 20; diameter of the trunk ·18; of the main branches ·15.

The spicula are light red and bright yellow. Longer double-spindles slender, acute, with three or four whorls of well-separated warts; stouter double-spindles short and thick, with about two whorls of large, separate warts, the outer whorl nearly or quite terminal, median space wide. Double-wheels small, resembling the stouter double-spindles in size and proportions, with a rather wide median space; inner wheels not large, with rounded edges, sometimes crenulated or a little warty, especially on one side; terminal wheels much smaller, close to the inner ones, with rounded edges.

The long double-spindles measure ·108^{mm} by ·038^{mm}, ·108 by ·036, ·102 by ·034, ·096 by ·030; the stouter double spindles ·084 by ·042, ·078 by ·039; the double-wheels ·060 by ·042, ·066 by ·042, ·054 by ·042, with the terminal wheels ·021, axis ·021, length of median space ·009.

La Paz, Gulf of California,—J. Pedersen, Maj. Wm. Rich; Mazatlan,—Dr. Horn; Acapulco,—A. Agassiz, Rev. J. Dickinson.

In the mode of branching, the size and structure of the branchlets, and color, this closely resembles the last species, which I have separated chiefly on account of the very different size and form of the spicula, and especially of the double-wheels.*

Eugorgia rubens Verrill, sp. nov.

Corallum slender, bipinnate and tripinnate. The small branches and branchlets arise at distances of a quarter to half an inch apart, and are either alternate or sub-opposite. Branchlets very slender, rather short, the edges dentate by the prominent cells. Axis slender, setiform in the branches, pale amber-color, translucent. Cells prominent, forming small conical verrucæ, arranged in a single row along each edge of the branchlets. Color pale red or rose-color. Diameter of the branchlets ·08 inch; of terminal branchlets ·06; length of branchlets ·35 to ·60; entire specimen 2 or 3 feet across.

The spicula are pale red, and mostly short and stout. The longer double-spindles are rather small, slender, not very acute, with about three distant whorls of crowded warts on each end, the median ones a little larger; median space moderately wide. Stouter double-spindles short and thick, blunt, with two or three close whorls of crowded rough warts. Double-wheels rather large, with thick, round-edged wheels, the outer ones terminal; median space narrow.

The longer double-spindles measure ·120^{mm} by ·048, ·096 by ·042 ·096 by ·036; the stouter double-spindles ·096 by ·048, ·084 by ·036, ·072 by ·048, ·072 by ·036; double-wheels ·066 by ·048, ·066 by ·042, ·060 by ·042, ·060 by ·036.

Paita, Peru,—F. H. Bradley, from Mrs. George Petrie.

C.—*Dichotomous, terminal branchlets slender, elongated. Cells scarcely raised.*

Eugorgia Bradleyi Verrill, sp. nov.

Corallum small, slender, more or less flabelliform. The round, slender trunk arises from a flat, expanded base, and at the height of

---

* Since Valenciennes' species (see p. 413) proves to belong to a distinct genus, I have restored the earliest name,—Reprint.

one or two inches divides into two equal branches. These subdivide either immediately or at various distances up to 1·5 inches in a similar dichotomous manner. The tertiary branches are again unequally dichotomous. The branchlets are mostly secund, slender, spreading outward from the branches in a wide curve, varying in length from 1 to 4 inches, tapering toward the tips, which are very slender. The cells are small, oblong, flat or very little raised, arranged closely in one or two rows on each side of the branchlets, but in broad bands of four or more, irregular, crowded rows on the larger branchlets. Median groove very distinct. Axis slender, blackish in the trunk and larger branches, brown and translucent in the smaller branches, yellowish and setiform in the branchlets. Color bright purplish red, bright lemon-yellow, or light yellowish brown. Height 7 inches; breadth 5; diameter of trunk ·13; of branches ·10; of branchlets ·03 to ·05.

Spicula light purple, or bright yellow. Longer double-spindles rather slender, very acute, sometimes curved, often with the ends unequal, median space wide, warts numerous, in 4 to 6 whorls, those toward the ends very small, the median ones much larger, occasionally several sharp points terminate one of the ends. Stouter double-spindles much smaller, stout and thick, with about 3 whorls of very prominent, rough warts; the last whorl is sometimes terminal, in other cases the end is formed by a single rough wart; some have the warts so crowded that they resemble double-heads. Double-wheels variable in size, about as long as broad, mostly with a narrow median space, small axis, and thin wheels; terminal wheels small, close to the inner ones. Cross-shaped compound spicula occasionally occur, having slender branches, covered by small but prominent warts.

The longer double-spindles measure ·175^{mm} by ·042^{mm}, ·138 by ·042, ·132 by ·048, ·126 by ·036; the stouter double spindles ·096 by ·054, ·090 by ·048, ·072 by ·054, ·072 by ·048; the double-wheels ·036 by ·036, with median space ·009, diameter of terminal wheels ·018; and ·048 by ·042, with the median space ·012, terminal wheels ·024; others ·048 by ·042, ·043 by ·043; crosses ·084 by ·084, and ·060 by ·060.

Panama and Pearl Islands, rare,—F. H. Bradley; Gulf of Nicoya,—J. A. McNiel.

This species resembles in form, mode of subdividing, and slenderness of trunk and branches, *Leptogorgia alba*, but is very distinct in the character of the spicula. Its color, though variable, is probably also sufficient to separate them, since this has not been observed *white*, which is the constant color of *L. alba*, so far as can be judged from an examination of over 200 specimens.

The following species, which I have not seen, is placed here with much doubt. In its external characters it appears to resemble some species of *Eugorgia*, but the form of the spicula, if correctly stated, would indicate affinities with *Psammogorgia* or *Plexaura*. Edwards and Haime describe it as follows:*

Echinogorgia aurantiaca Verrill. (LEPTOGORGIA AURANTIACA, 1st Ed.).

Plexaura aurantiaca Val., Comptes-rendus, xli, p. 12.
Leptogorgia aurantiaca Edw. and Haime, Corall., i, p. 165, 1857.

Corallum rather branching, branches pretty stout, the last elongated. Calicles crowded and very distinct throughout. Spicula in the form of warty clubs ("slérites en massue"). Color ferruginous yellow. Callao ("Calloa").

Phycogorgia Val.; Edw. and Haime, Corall., i, p. 182.

Axis lamellar and dilated in the form of membranous leaflets, similar to a fucus, and covered with a thin sclerenchyma, perforated by poriform calicles. (Edw. and Haime).

Phycogorgia fucata Val.; Edw. and Haime.

Gorgonia fucata Val., Voyage de la Vénus, Zoöl., Pl. 11, fig. 2.

Corallum thin, expanded, divided into ramose fronds, the branches of which are contracted at their base and enlarged toward the summit. Calicles small and close. Color rosy. Mazatlan. (E. and H.)

Family, PLEXAURIDÆ Gray.

Annals and Mag. Nat. Hist., 1859, p. 442.
Eunicidæ Kölliker, Icones Histiologicæ, p. 137, 1865.

Corallum usually dichotomous and more or less arborescent. Axis horn-like, or more or less calcareous, especially at base. Longitudinal ducts equal, arranged regularly all around the axis. Cœnenchyma usually thick. Cells scattered over all parts of the surface, flat, or elevated on prominent verrucæ. Tentacles at base, and sides of the polyps stiffened with large fusiform spicula. Spicula of the cœnenchyma usually large, of various forms, most frequently there are large warty spindles mingled with clubs or crosses.

The three principal genera of this family, *Plexaura*, *Plexaurella*, and *Eunicea*, which are each represented by numerous large and common species in the Caribbean Fauna, appear to be entirely absent from the Pacific coast of America.

The following genus, which is scarcely a typical representative of the family, appears alone to replace the larger forms of the Atlantic.

---

* Spicula from the original specimen, sent by Dr. Kölliker, show that it is an *Echinogorgia*,—Reprint.

Psammogorgia Verrill.

American Jour. of Sci., vol. xlv, p. 414, May, 1868.

Corallum dichotomous or subpinnate, with round branches. Axis horn-like. Cœnenchyma moderately thick, the surface finely granulated with small rough spicula. Cells scattered, sometimes flat, more frequently raised in the form of rounded verrucæ. Polyps with rather large, elongated, slender, warty spindles at the bases of the tentacles. Spicula of the cœnenchyma mostly short, thick, and very rough, warty spindles and rough, warty clubs of moderate size.

Psammogorgia arbuscula Verrill.

Echinogorgia arbuscula Verrill, Proc. Boston Society Natural Hist., vol. x, p. 329, April, 1866.

Psammogorgia arbuscula Verrill, Amer. Jour. Science, xlv, p. 414, May, 1868.

Plate V, figure 17. Plate VI, figure 9.

Corallum low, irregularly dichotomous, subflabelliform, several stems often arising from one base. Base broad, encrusting, covered with a thin cœnenchyma, which usually bears polyps. From this, one to twelve stems arise, which, when numerous, form rather dense clumps of branches. The young stalks are often 2 to 4 inches long before subdividing, enlarging upward to the obtusely rounded tips. In other cases they subdivide dichotomously very near the base, the main branches being about as large as the trunk. These again subdivide in a similar manner into secondary and tertiary branches and branchlets, which curve outward at base and then become subparallel, but are often crooked and irregular, and sometimes coalesce. The terminal branchlets are round, obtuse, scarcely tapering, often enlarged at the tips, from 1 to 4 inches long, about as large as the main branches. Cœnenchyma moderately thick. Surface of the cœnenchyma roughly granular. Cells large, more or less prominent, at the summit of rather large verrucæ, which are often as high as broad, uniformly scattered over all parts of the branches, arranged somewhat in quincunx, the summits frequently eight-rayed. Color dark red. In life, "stem bright red, polyps bright yellow." Height of largest specimens 4 to 8 inches; breadth 3 to 6; diameter of main branches ·15.

Spicula bright red, mostly rather stout thorny spindles. Longer spindles stout, with acute ends, covered with large thorny warts, which are largest about the middle; stouter spindles blunt at the ends, and more thickly covered with similar rough warts. Other stout, thick spicula, or "heads," about as thick as long, and crowdedly covered with thorny warts, are abundant, especially in the superficial layer, mixed with the last. Also much smaller and more slender spindles, with few large warts. The club-shaped spicula are not numerous and are variable in form; the larger end is not much expanded, but covered with sharp and thorny warts, which decrease to the somewhat acute, smaller end. The polyp-spicula from the bases of the tentacles are relatively large, very long, slender spindles, with acute ends, often curved, and covered uniformly with small, sharp, conical warts. Some of the smaller ones are but slightly warted.

The longer spindles measure $\cdot 264^{mm}$ by $\cdot 096^{mm}$, $\cdot 240$ by $\cdot 108$, $\cdot 240$ by $\cdot 084$, $\cdot 204$ by $\cdot 072$, $\cdot 192$ by $\cdot 084$; the stouter ones $\cdot 144$ by $\cdot 084$, $\cdot 144$ by $\cdot 072$; the "heads" $\cdot 108$ by $\cdot 102$, $\cdot 144$ by $\cdot 126$, $\cdot 120$ by $\cdot 096$, $\cdot 108$ by $\cdot 084$; the "clubs" $\cdot 180$ by $\cdot 084$, $\cdot 180$ by $\cdot 078$, $\cdot 168$ by $\cdot 078$, $\cdot 156$ by $\cdot 072$; the polyp-spindles $\cdot 264$ by $\cdot 054$, $\cdot 240$ by $\cdot 048$, $\cdot 240$ by $\cdot 042$, $\cdot 227$ by $\cdot 054$, $\cdot 204$ by $\cdot 042$, $\cdot 204$ by $\cdot 024$.

Panama and Pearl Islands, in pools at extreme low-water mark,— F. H. Bradley; Gulf of Nicoya, by divers,—J. A. McNiel.

This species is very variable in form, and especially in the prominence of the cells, or else there are two or more species here included. The typical form, above described, has the cells large and raised on prominent verrucæ. The two principal variations from this type are as follows:

Var. Dowii Verrill.

Similar in mode of branching to the preceding form but somewhat more flabelliform and regular, branchlets rather smaller. Cells flat, or scarcely raised, when contracted often eight-rayed. Spicula much like those of the typical form. Color deep red.

San Salvador,—Capt. J. M. Dow; Pearl Islands,—F. H. Bradley.

Var. pallida Verrill.

Corallum more or less flabelliform, branching dichotomously, branchlets round, sometimes as large as the main stem, usually smaller. Cells a little raised, forming low verrucæ. In fresh specimens, the cells are often surmounted by a small conical mass of convergent spicula, from the bases of the tentacles. Color dull grayish white, or yellowish. In life, "stem white or light drab; polyps bright yellow," —F. H. B.

Spicula of the cœnenchyma pale pink or colorless, transparent; polyp-spicula orange red. Longer spindles rather long and slender, acute, covered with distantly scattered, unequal, prominent, rough warts. Some of the largest are stouter, but acute, and often curved or irregular in outline. Stouter spindles very irregular in form and size, often blunt, very rough and thorny, warts not crowded.* Clubs slender, small end acute, enlarging regularly toward the large end, which is crowded with warts of small size.

The longer spindles measure ·216^{mm} by ·090, ·204 by ·084, ·204 by ·060, ·180 by ·060; stouter spindles ·132 by ·084, ·132 by ·060, ·120 by ·072; clubs ·162 by ·048; heads ·102 by ·072; crosses ·192 by ·132; polyp-spindles ·252 by ·042, ·240 by ·042, ·240 by ·036, ·204 by ·042, ·204 by ·030.

Pearl Islands,—F. H. Bradley.

This form resembles, in its branches and cells, *var. Dowii*, but differs in its color and somewhat in the spicula, which are less thickly warted and usually not quite so stout.

Psammogorgia teres Verrill, sp. nov.

Plate V, figure 18. Plate VII, figure 1.

Corallum dichotomous, large, flabelliform, with rather large, round branches, which are often curved. The base is expanded, often giving rise to more than one trunk. The stem forks within half an inch from the base, where it is large and round. The main branches again fork irregularly, and also give off numerous branches and branchlets at distances of half an inch or less, in an irregularly subpinnate and often secund manner. These are all round and thick, and bend outward at the axils with a broad curve, and then turn upward, but most of them are more or less crooked throughout, and not unfrequently coalesce. The terminal branchlets are considerably smaller than the main branches, and usually taper slightly to the blunt ends. Cells large, distant, scattered over the whole surface, flat or very little raised. Cœnenchyma thin, with a finely granulated surface, bright red. Axis dull yellowish, woody in appearance; thick, opaque, and soft in the branchlets. Height 10 inches; breadth 8 inches; diameter of trunk ·40; of main branches ·18 to ·22; of branchlets ·12 to ·15. Spicula bright red, varied in size and form. The greater part are rather large, short, stout spindles, covered with numerous, very prominent, rough warts, arranged on each end in two or three irregular whorls; ends scarcely acute. Others are longer and more slender,

---

* These principally form the external layer, but are mingled with a few clubs and other forms. In this genus there is no very distinct superficial layer of smaller club-shaped spicula, such as is found in *Eunicea, Plexaura*, and *Plexaurella*. Hence I place the genus in this family with some doubt. It is, apparently, allied to *Astrogorgia* and may possibly belong to the Primnoidæ, near *Muricea*.

with acute ends, but equally rough. Some head-like spicula are about as long as broad, sometimes nearly spherical, crowdedly covered with large, thorny warts, those about the middle largest. There are also short, stout spindles, crowdedly covered with warts on the whole surface. Club-shaped spicula occasionally occur, having the larger end but little expanded, covered with large, prominent, thorny warts; these with the two preceding forms chiefly compose the external layer. Cross-spicula, with four or six roughly warted branches, frequently occur. Besides these, there are many small spicula of various forms, but all are covered with rough warts, and most of them are short and stout. Polyp-spindles are long, slender, acute, usually curved, covered with small, sharp warts.

The longer spindles measure ·192^{mm} by ·084^{mm}, ·174 by ·078, ·168 by ·090, ·168 by ·048, ·144 by ·066, ·132 by ·072; stouter spindles ·156 by ·096, ·132 by ·090, ·132 by ·078, ·120 by ·096; warty head-spicula ·168 by ·096, ·144 by ·120, ·144 by ·090, ·108 by ·096; clubs ·132 by ·072, ·120 by ·060; crosses ·144 by ·096, ·120 by ·084; polyp-spindles ·264 by ·054, ·227 by ·048, ·204 by ·036, ·198 by ·048.

Pearl Islands, in 6 to 8 fathoms, rare,—F. H. Bradley.

Resembles somewhat *var. Dowii* of the preceding species, but is much larger, with stouter branches and branchlets, and larger and more distant cells. The surface is smoother and the cells are usually not at all raised. The color is also brighter red. The spicula are quite different.

Psammogorgia fucosa Verrill.

Amer. Journal Science, xlviii. p. 427, Nov., 1869.
Gorgonia fucosa Val., Voyage Vénus, Pl. 15 bis.
Plexaura fucosa Val.; Edw. and H., Corall., i, p. 154, (*non* Verrill).

Mazatlan.—Voyage of the Venus. A large species allied to *P. teres.*—Reprint.

Psammogorgia gracilis Verrill, sp. nov.

Plate V, figure 19. Plate VI, figure 10.

Corallum slender, flabelliform, the branchlets subparallel and elongated. The stem, in the only specimen seen, is slender, and at the height of about an inch subdivides into four main branches, one of which then passes onward, like a continuation of the stem, undivided for nearly 1·5 inches, when it gives off branchlets pinnately on each side, at distances of from ·10 to ·40. Two of the other main branches subdivide near their origin into several long, slender, ascending branches and branchlets, some of which fork near their ends. The branchlets are all about equal in size, varying in length from less than

1 inch to 2·5, with a diameter of about ·07; they are round, slender, and scarcely taper. The cells form low, swollen verrucae, which are closely crowded over the whole surface. Cœnenchyma moderately thick. Axis slender and wood-yellow, opaque even at the ends. Color light red. Height 5 inches; breadth 4; diameter of stem ·10.

Spicula bright red; club-shaped spicula numerous, with the small end very acute. The larger spindles are rather slender, ends very acute, warts prominent, not crowded, forming five or six irregular whorls on each end, which become very small near the points. Shorter spindles very rough, with obtuse ends. Clubs very numerous, about as long as the spindles, but much broader, the large end covered with numerous, large, prominent, rough warts and spines, which diminish toward the small end, which tapers to a sharp point. Polyp-spindles pale yellow, long and slender, covered with small, nearly smooth warts.

The longer spindles measure ·240^{mm} by ·060, ·228 by ·060, ·228 by ·048, ·222 by ·072, ·168 by ·036; stouter spindles ·168 by ·072, ·144 by ·084, ·102 by ·066; clubs ·252 by ·084, ·216 by ·072, ·210 by ·084, ·192 by ·084, ·168 by ·060; polyp-spindles ·150 by ·018, ·144 by ·036, ·132 by ·030, ·114 by ·036.

Pearl Islands, very rare,—F. H. Bradley.

This species is remarkably distinct from the preceding three in its mode of branching, its long and quite slender branchlets, and especially in its very peculiar spicula. It differs widely from all other Gorgonians of the coast, known to me, in the form and abundance of the singular club-shaped spicula.

Family, PRIMNOIDÆ.

Primnoaces Val.; Edw. and Haime, Corall., vol. i, p. 138.
Primnoadæ, Acanthogorgiadæ and *Muriceidæ* Gray, Ann. and Mag. Nat. Hist., 1859, p. 442.
Primnoaceæ Kölliker, Icones Histiol., p. 135, 1865.
Plexauridæ (*pars*) and *Primnoaceæ* Verrill, Revis. Polyps, E. Coast U. S., p. 8, 1864.

Corallum usually branched, sometimes simple. Axis horn-like or more or less calcareous, especially at base. Cells prominent, covered with large scales or spicula. Cœnenchyma with large scales or spicula, the outer ones conspicuous at the surface. Longitudinal ducts many and equal on all sides, or few and symmetrically arranged.

Muricea Lamouroux (restricted).

Muricea (*pars*) Lam'x, Expos. meth., p. 509, 1821; Blainville, Man. d'Actinologie, p. 509; Ehrenberg, Corallenthiere, p. 134; Dana, Zoöph., p. 673; Edw. and Haime, Corall., vol. i, p. 142, 1857, etc.
Muricea Kölliker, Icones Histiologicæ, ii, p. 135, 1865; Verrill, American Jour. Science, vol. xlv, p. 411, 1868.

Corallum variously branched, usually dichotomous or arborescent. Axis horny, rarely becoming calcareous at the base in large specimens. Cœnenchyma composed of large, one-sided, very warty, and often curved spindles, mingled with many smaller ones of various sizes, the exterior being formed mainly of the large ones, which become imbricated on the surface of the verrucæ and usually project from the surface. The cells are prominent in various degrees, and either tubular or bilabiate with the lower side projecting. Polyps retractile, the tentacles stiffened at base with long, warty spindles.

Dr. Kölliker has very judiciously restricted this genus by the removal of *Paramuricea* and *Echinogorgia*, two well defined and natural genera. As now limited *Muricea* is a well characterized genus, which is widely distributed in the tropical seas, but apparently more fully represented on the American coasts than elsewhere. In the West Indies and on the Atlantic coasts there are at least five species, while on the Pacific side eighteen have already been discovered. The species from the East Indies, China, etc., which I have seen, are smaller and less typical than the American forms.

The species of *Echinogorgia* are mainly from the East Indies. The *Paramuriceæ* are found on the European coasts, in the Mediterranean, and one species, at least, in the West Indies and at Florida (*P. clathrata* (Dana sp.). The genus, *Thesea* Duch. and Mich., is a rare West Indian form. *Bebryce* Phil. is from the Mediterranean. *Anthogorgia* and *Astrogorgia* Verrill, as yet represented only by one species each, are from Hong Kong, while the genus, *Heterogorgia* V., is known only from Panama Bay. *Acanthogorgia* Gray, seems allied to *Muricea*, and especially to *Heterogorgia*. It has several species: *A. coccinea* V.,[*] from Hong Kong; *A. Atlantica* and *A. Grayi* Johns., from Madeira; *A. hirsuta* Gray, locality doubtful; and *A. aspera* Pourtales,[†] off Havana, in 270 fathoms. *Blepharogorgia Schrammi* Duch. and Mich., from Guadaloupe, is referred to the same genus by Pourtales, but it appears to agree better with *Paramuricea*. The genus, *Lcis* Duch. and Mich., is also allied to *Muricea* and has two West Indian species.

A.— *Verrucæ tubular; cells not bilabiate, lower border not prolonged.*

Muricea acervata Verrill.

Proceedings Boston Soc. Nat. History, vol. x, p. 327, Apr., 1866.

Plate VII, figure 5. Plate VIII, figure 1.

Corallum arborescently branched, dichotomous, rather stout and rigid. The trunk divides very near the base into two or three main

[*] Now *Echinomuricea coccinea* V., Am. Jour. Sci., xlvii, p 285.—Reprint.
[†] Bulletin Museum of Comparative Zoölogy, No. 6, p. 113, 1867.

branches, which part again at one or two inches from their origin; the secondary branches often subdividing irregularly two or three times, but many remaining simple and two or three inches long. All the branches are thick and rigid, and of nearly the same size with the primary branches, mostly smallest at their origin, enlarging toward the tips, which are bluntly rounded and often slight clavate. All the branches bend outward at base, often nearly at a right angle, and then curve upward with a broad curve and become sub-parallel. Cells eight-rayed at the summit of large, elevated, rounded verrucæ, the rays separated by narrow but very distinct sunken grooves, which extend over the summits and somewhat down the sides of the verrucæ in contraction. Verrucæ unequal, larger and smaller ones intermingled, rather elevated, about as high as broad, somewhat crowded, but uniformly arranged, mostly standing nearly at right angles to the branch, their surface covered with closely imbricated, slightly rough, and rather regular fusiform spicula. Cœnenchyma rather thick, covered with spicula similar to those of the verrucæ. Axis black, compressed somewhat at the axils, rigid and brittle at the ends. Color deep brown. Height of largest specimen about 8 inches; breadth 5; diameter of branches ·30 to ·35; of verrucæ ·07; length of verrucæ ·10.

Spicula yellowish brown and reddish brown. Longer spindles long, moderately stout, usually acute at each end, but sometimes with one end blunt, often somewhat bent, covered closely with small spinules, which on most parts are small, sharp, and conical, but on one side they are usually more closely crowded, and take the form of low, rough, lacerate warts. Stouter spindles usually stout-fusiform and rapidly tapering to each end, covered on one side with small, crowded, rough warts, on the other with conical spinules; these like the others, are frequently bent or irregular, and often one end is truncate or obtuse. Small spicula of these two forms are numerous, some having conical, often lobate spinules, others rough warts, not so crowded as in the larger ones. Other small spicula have the form of rough, warty heads, with lobate warts; others are quite small and irregular spicula with large, subdivided warts; some become club-shaped and rough, others more slender, with scattered spinules.

The longer spindles measure 2·00^{mm} by ·400, 1·90 by ·365, 1·44 by ·243, 1·37 by ·200, 1·29 by ·213, 1·20 by ·150, 1·14 by ·228, 1·06 by ·187; the stouter ones 1·35 by ·325, ·912 by ·248, ·436 by ·243; the small irregular spicula ·187 by ·060; heads ·137 by ·121; clubs ·187 by ·105, ·152 by ·090.

Panama, very rare,—F. H. Bradley.

The large, rounded, unequal, eight-rayed verrucæ are sufficient to distinguish this from all other known species. Two specimens only were obtained.

Muricea tubigera Verrill, sp. nov.

Plate VII, figure 7. Plate VIII, figure 2.

Corallum stout and rigid, dichotomously branched, with greatly elongated, squarrose verrucæ. The trunk divides at about an inch from the base into two main branches, which fork at about an inch from their origin. The secondary branches usually fork again at distances varying from two to five inches, and the tertiary branches are often again divided. The terminal branches are from 1·5 to 2·5 inches long and nearly as large as the main branches (·4 inch), obtusely rounded, and sometimes a little enlarged or clavate at the ends. The branches are but little divergent and form acute angles. The cœnenchyma is only moderately thick, but is crowdedly covered with very long, rather slender verrucæ, which stand nearly at right angles to the surface and give the branches a thick appearance. The verrucæ are enlarged or clavate at their summits, which are rounded and conspicuously eight-rayed in contraction; their sides covered with closely imbricated, long, rather slender and sharp spicula, which project but little from the surface. At the tips of the branches the verrucæ are smaller and densely crowded. Axis horn-like, light wood-brown at base, black and somewhat compressed in the branches. Color light greenish brown when dried.

Height of the largest specimen 8 inches; breadth 4·5; diameter of main branches, including verrucæ, ·50; of branchlets ·40 to ·45; length of verrucæ ·15 to ·20; diameter ·05; their summits ·08.

The spicula are yellowish white, and similar to those of the preceding species, but longer, more slender, sharper at the ends, and usually with less crowded warts and spinules. The spindles of the cells are not larger than those of the cœnenchyma, but often stouter; the latter are mostly very slender and acute, often larger and blunter on one end than the other, or somewhat club-shaped, the spinules being more crowded on the larger end and mostly truncate, while on the small end, which is long, slender and acute, they are sharp, conical, and distantly scattered.

The longer spindles of the cells measure 2·28^{mm} by ·324, 1·36 by ·182, 1·32 by ·152, 1·29 by ·137, ·851 by ·091, ·608 by ·061; the stouter ones 1·36 by ·228, ·988 by ·187, ·699 by ·121; the small irregular ones ·213 by ·071, ·187 by ·106, ·121 by ·061; heads ·076 by ·076; the longer spindles of the cœnenchyma measure 2·37 by ·325, 1·80 by

·175, 1·57 by ·200, 1·57 by ·175, 1·52 by ·197, 1·29 by ·167, 1·14 by ·121, 1·09 by ·136, ·942 by ·106.

Pearl Islands and Panama, very rare,—F. H. Bradley.

This species is very distinct from the preceding by its very long, slender, and smaller verrucæ, its longer and sharper spicula, and its thicker branches. The latter character and the closely crowded cells separate it widely from *M. hispida* and *M. horrida*.

Muricea hispida Verrill.

Proceedings Boston Society of Natural History, vol. x, p. 328, 1866.

Plate VII, figure 4. Plate VIII, figure 3.

Corallum dichotomous, sparingly branched, somewhat flabelliform. The main branches arise close to the base and bend outward and upward with a wide curve, before becoming perpendicular and subparallel. The secondary branches arise from the outward curvature of the primary ones, and quickly become of the same size. The branches are slender, though the long verrucæ give them a rather thick appearance, and gradually enlarge to the tips. The cœnenchyma is thin and but little developed. The cells are rather large and regular, at the summit of very long, rather large, tubular verrucæ, which are narrow at base and enlarged to the summit, or subclavate in form, the sides being covered with long, sharp spicula, which project considerably at the summits. Axis very slender, round and black at base, amber-color and translucent in the branchlets. Color, when dry, umber-brown.

Height of the largest specimen 4 inches; diameter of branches, excluding verrucæ, ·12; length of verrucæ ·16; diameter at summit ·07.

Spicula yellowish white, mostly relatively large, very long, slender, sharp spindles, often curved or crooked, covered on one side with small, very sharp, conical spinules, on the other with small, very closely crowded, rough warts; ends usually very acute. Stouter spindles are numerous, which are frequently irregular in form, often bent, sometimes enlarged, branched, or forked, near one end; one or both ends often obtuse or truncate. The small spicula are mostly regular warty spindles, acute at each end, but often bent in the middle, and are relatively less abundant than in most species.

The longer spindles measure 2·60^{mm} by ·300, 2·30 by ·275, 2·07 by ·250, 2·05 by ·300, 2·00 by ·300, 1·70 by ·175, 1·67 by ·225, 1·65 by ·200, 1·57 by ·225; the stouter spindles 2·00 by ·375, 1·75 by ·375, 1·65 by ·300, 1·39 by ·350; the majority of the small spindles about

·425 by ·100, ·400 by ·125, ·375 by ·100, and ·425 by ·062; the spinules of the larger spindles are about ·025 long.

Panama, very rare,—F. H. Bradley.

The spicula of this species resemble most those of *M. tubigera*, but while the branches are much smaller, the spicula are absolutely much larger. They are also rougher, with larger spinules, and the small spicula are much less abundant and more regular in form. Its thin cœnenchyma, and long, clavate, tubular cells, with slender projecting spicula, will at once separate it from all other species, except, perhaps, *M. horrida* Mob.

Muricea horrida Mobius.

Neue Gorgoniden des Naturhist. Mus. Hamburg, p. 11. Tab. III, fig. 3–8, 1861; Kölliker, Icones Histiolog., p. 135, 1865.

"*M. arborescens, ramosissima, ramis teretibus, verrucis polypiferis cylindratis, obtusis. Cœnenchyma spiculis fusiformibus, verrucosis, fulvis suffultum.*"

This species, as described and figured by Mobius, forms an openly and loosely branched corallum, with slender divergent branches, covered with loosely arranged, tubular, and somewhat clavate verrucæ, which are obtuse or truncate and eight-rayed at summit, the sides and upper margin with a few slightly projecting points of long and large spicula. The cœnenchyma is thin and the verrucæ are about equal in length to the diameter of the branchlets and smaller branches. The long spindles are stout fusiform, with distantly arranged, rough, unequal warts. The two figured would measure 1·45^{mm} by ·30^{mm}, and 1·07 by ·23.

Peru (Hamburg Museum).

Muricea squarrosa Verrill, sp. nov.

Plate VI, figure 13. Plate VIII, figure 4.

Corallum dichotomous, the branches subdividing two or three times, branching nearly in a plane. The trunk usually divides close to the base into two or more main branches, each of which usually forks again within half an inch. Some of the central secondary branches rise nearly perpendicularly and do not subdivide for one or two inches, or even more, but the outer ones often fork two or three times more, at distances of about half an inch. The terminal branches and branchlets are from one to four inches long, round, subparallel in large specimens, tapering but little, usually obtuse at the ends, and nearly as large as the main branches. The branches usually spread at a large angle at their origin, and bend upward in a broad curve, the outer ones often forming right angles at their origin. The prominent verrucæ are regularly arranged on all sides, and pretty close together, though scarcely crowded, and usually stand nearly at right angles to the branches, but often incline obliquely upward at a wide angle, and never become imbricated. They are moderately large, usually somewhat higher than broad, nearly equal, round, tubular, truncate, the terminal opening looking obliquely upward and outward, the surface covered with many large fusiform spicula, the ends of which project strongly at the summit in the form of small sharp spines, which are often more numerous and larger on the lower margin, causing the cells to approach the characters of those of the second section of the genus. Cœnenchyma moderately thick, filled with large spindles at the surface. Color deep yellowish brown, varying to light brownish yellow and to deep umber brown.

Height of largest specimens 8 inches; breadth 6; diameter of largest branches, including verrucæ ·30 to ·35; of branchlets ·24 to ·28; length of verrucæ ·08 to ·10, often less; diameter ·06 to ·07.

The spicula are light yellowish and brownish, mostly large, stout, warty spindles, many of them irregular, bent or lobed. The longer spindles are large, rather stout, tapering gradually to each end, or frequently with one end irregular, truncate or obtuse, the surface crowdedly covered with small, rounded, rough warts, except upon one side where the warts are usually replaced by small, sharp, conical spinules. The stouter spindles are larger and thick, mostly irregular, bent, lobed, or with one end truncate, but agreeing in the character of the surface with the longer ones. The small spindles are mostly slender, acute at each end, regularly covered with truncate or rounded warts, sometimes with sharp spinules on one side.

The longer spindles measure $1·80^{mm}$ by $·425^{mm}$, 1·80 by ·375, 1·75 by ·375, 1·70 by ·350, 1·70 by ·300, 1·65 by ·225, 1·62 by ·375, 1·57 by ·250, 1·25 by ·250, 1·42 by ·200, 1·12 by ·200, 1·07 by ·175; the stouter ones 1·70 by ·440, 1·57 by ·500, 1·50 by ·500, 1·42 by ·425, 1·37 by ·450, 1·25 by ·400, 1·12 by ·300, ·850 by ·225; the small spindles ·500 by ·100, ·375 by ·075, ·300 by ·062, ·225 by ·062.

Panama and Pearl Islands, in pools at extreme low-water mark, not common,—F. H. Bradley.

This species is easily distinguished by its few, moderately thick branches, evenly covered by the squarrose, tubular verrucæ, which are usually considerably higher than broad. The spicula somewhat resemble those of *M. acervata* and *M. echinata*, but can readily be distinguished from either.

B.—*Verrucæ more or less prominent; cells bilabiate, or opening upward, with the lower lip more or less prolonged.*

1.—*Verrucæ large, elevated, spreading, neither appressed nor imbricated, or but slightly so.*

Muricea crassa Verrill, sp. nov.

Plate VII, figure 10. Plate VIII, figure 5.

Corallum very large, dichotomous, branching nearly in a plane, the branches thick, clavate, covered with large, prominent, coarse verrucæ, which are rough with very large, thick, blunt spicula.

Three or four large main branches usually arise from a thick, swollen base. These fork at distances of two or three inches, many of the secondary branches being three or four times dichotomous; while others are subpinnate, the branchlets usually alternating on opposite sides and from one to two inches apart; others give off branchlets only on the outside. The branches and branchlets are all thick, often crooked, and bend outward at first, in a broad curve, and then upward. Toward the base some of the branches are occasionally coalescent. The terminal branchlets are from one and a half to four inches long, smaller at base than the branches, but enlarging toward the obtusely rounded end, where they are much enlarged and often clavate, frequently having a diameter of half an inch or more. The crowded verrucæ stand at nearly right angles to the surface of the branchlets and are very large, prominent, rough with large, stout, coarse spicula, which are mostly rather blunt at the ends, forming therefore coarse but not sharp spinules at the summit, a cluster of which are a little prolonged, so as to form a short lower lip, which is usually a little incurved in contraction, so as to conceal the cell, which opens upward and inward. The large verrucæ of the branchlets are usually broad at base, somewhat conical, higher than broad, strongly echinate at summit; those of the main branches and trunk are distantly scattered, rounded, low, scarcely as high as broad.

Cænenchyma moderately thick, coarse, with very large, irregular, blunt spicula, conspicuous at the surface. Axis horn-like, light wood brown at base; round, black, strongly striated in the larger branches, with the axils scarcely compressed; soft, thick, rigid and brittle when dry, and dark brown in the terminal branchlets. Color dark brown, yellowish brown at base.

Height 20 inches; breadth 18; diameter of main branches ·50 to ·90; of terminal branchlets ·30 at base, ·50 or ·60 near the tips; height of verrucæ ·15 to ·20; diameter ·10.

The spicula are reddish brown, mostly very large, thick, coarse, unequal, and irregular, with the ends obtuse or truncate, and the surface rough with minute crowded warts. In the verrucæ the spicula are mostly very stout spindles, oval, oblong, or clavate, in nearly all cases irregular, but generally with one end largest and truncate, obtuse, or divided into two forks or lobes. Their most common size is about half a millimeter in diameter and two long, but there are many much larger ones, and a few quite regular and slender spindles of smaller size. Those of the cœnenchyma are mostly very large, thick, oblong, irregular spicula, obtuse, truncate, or irregular at the ends, mostly bent or distorted and often lobed, most of the larger ones about one-third as broad as long.

The stout spicula of the cells measure 3·20^{mm} by ·875^{mm}, 3·12 by ·600, 2·25 by ·875, 2·12 by ·575, 2·00 by ·575, 2·00 by ·500, 1·75 by ·675, 1·75 by ·375, 1·70 by ·800, 1·45 by ·575, 1·40 by ·875, 1·37 by ·300, 1·25 by ·575, 1·07 by ·325, ·875 by ·450. Those of the cœnenchyma 4·00 by 1·25, 4·00 by 1·20, 3·25 by 1·00, 2·87 by 1·25, 2·75 by 1·25, 2·75 by ·875, 2·25 by ·950, 2·25 by ·800, 1·00 by ·450; the most slender spindles 1·75 by ·225, 1·00 by ·200; the smaller ones ·650 by ·125, ·525 by ·125, ·450 by ·125 ·275 by 150.

Pearl Islands,—F. H. Bradley.

This species is very different from all others in its great size, very large, coarse, rough verrucæ, and the remarkably large, thick, irregular spicula.

Muricea echinata Val.

Muricea echinata Valenciennes, Comptes-rendus. 1855 (no description); Edw. and Haime, Corall., vol. i, p. 143, 1857; Verrill, Bulletin Museum Comp. Zoöl., p. 36; Proc. Bost. Soc. Nat. Hist., vol. x, p. 328, 1866.

Plate VIII, figure 6.

Corallum irregularly dichotomous or subpinnate, branching nearly in a plane, with clavate branchlets and elongated echinate verrucæ, with the lower lip prolonged and the cells opening upward and inward.

The trunk usually divides, close to the base, into two or three main branches, most of which subdivide several times at distances of one third or half an inch, the central ones usually dichotomous and the outer ones often subpinnate, the branches spreading at first at a wide angle and then curving upward. The terminal branches and branchlets are mostly from one to four inches long, enlarging toward the end, often distinctly clavate, the tips enlarged and obtusely rounded. The verrucæ are mostly slender, clavate, very prominent, especially on the terminal branchlets, not crowded, spreading outward and upward at a wide angle, not imbricated, covered with large, stout spindles, with sharp ends, some of which form the prolonged lower lip and project from the upper part of the verrucæ, in the form of sharp rough spinules. The cells are small and open inward and upward, in contraction nearly concealed by the incurved lower lip, filled with small convergent yellow spicula, from the bases of the tentacles. The cœnenchyma is thin, covered with large spindles. Color deep reddish brown; cells yellow inside. In life "deep red, polyps bright yellow."

Height of largest specimens 6 or 8 inches; breadth about the same; diameter of the main branches, including verrucæ, ·30; of the branchlets at origin ·25; near the ends ·37; length of the longest verrucæ on the terminal branchlets ·15 to ·18; diameter ·05 of an inch.

Dwarf specimens occur only two or three inches high, with the largest branches about ·25 in diameter, and the verrucæ ·10 of an inch long. These grow in shallow water, in rocky pools, etc.

The spicula are reddish and yellowish brown, mostly rather large, rough, acute spindles, of which the larger ones are often bent, irregular, lobed, or with one end truncate. The longer spindles, when perfect, usually have the ends quite acute; some are moderately stout, others quite slender, covered on one side with small but very sharp spinules, on other parts with small, crowded, rough, rounded or truncate warts. When the spindles are bent the spinules are usually on the concave side. The stouter spindles are quite irregular and variable in size and form, but are usually rather thick, often crooked, and with one or both ends blunt or truncate, and very closely covered with warts and spinules. The medium sized spindles are quite regular, slender, and very acute, warted like the larger ones. The smallest are nearly white, regular, some acute and others blunt, covered with prominent very rough warts, which are not crowded.

The longer spindles measure 1·95^{mm} by ·450^{mm}, 1·75 by ·425, 1·75 by ·250, 1·62 by ·275, 1·52 by ·225, 1·50 by ·375, 1·45 by ·350, 1·45 by ·275, 1·45 by ·175; the stouter ones 2·00 by ·750, 1·62 by ·750, 1·60 by ·575, 1·55 by ·450, 1·45 by ·450, 1·35 by ·500, 1·10 by ·475, 1·00 by ·625, ·600 by ·250; the medium sized spindles 1·35 by ·250, 1·27 by ·225, 1·15 by ·150, 1·00 by ·425, ·900 by ·125; the small spicula ·650 by ·125, ·350 by ·100, ·325 by ·100.

Panama, in rocky pools at low-water mark, common,—F. H. Bradley, C. F. Davis, J. H. Sternbergh; Pearl Islands,—F. H. Bradley.

Var. flabellum.

Branches much more numerous and crowded, several principal ones starting nearly together close to the base, and giving off numerous short, crooked branchlets, mostly on the outer side, which are often at distances of less than a quarter of an inch apart. Terminal branchlets one or two inches long, ·25 in diameter, often tapering. Verrucæ very slender, prominent, the lower lip much prolonged, acute, the surface and summit rough with the sharp ends of the spicula. Cells small, opening upward, often filled with a cluster of bright yellow spicula from the bases of the tentacles. Color deep brown.

Pearl Islands,—F. H. Bradley.

This species somewhat resembles the two following in color and external appearance. From the first it differs greatly in mode of growth, and somewhat in the spicula; from the second (*M. austera*) in its much more slender, longer, and spreading verrucæ, and very decidedly in its spicula.

Muricea fruticosa Verrill, sp. nov.

Plate VII, figure 2.

Corallum large, very branching, cæspitose, fruticose, with rather small, somewhat clavate branchlets, and prominent, spreading, spinose verrucæ.

The trunk is very stout and short, arising from a large irregular base, and usually divides at once into several large, unequal main branches, which rapidly divide and subdivide in an irregular manner, the branches and branchlets usually not more than one quarter or half inch apart. Sometimes several large main branches can be traced for some distance, giving off numerous small branches from all sides, but more frequently the subdivision is so rapid that the main branches are very soon lost among the crowded and crooked branches. The small branches near the ends often divide in an irregularly dichotomous manner, and sometimes coalesce; they are very numerous, nearly equal in size, and usually much curved and crooked, spreading at their origin with a broad curve. The terminal branchlets are short, mostly ·5 to 1·5 inches long, often curved, of moderate size, narrowed at base, enlarging to the obtusely rounded end. Verrucæ close together, but not imbricated, spreading outward and upward, quite prominent, conical, about as high as broad toward the outer ends of the branchlets, where they are more developed than below, and furnished with an acute prolonged lower lip, the surface covered with long, stout spindles, some of which are about as long as the verrucæ. Cells small, situated on the upper side of the verrucæ, near the end, the aperture filled with the yellow polyp-spicula, from the bases of the tentacles. On the surface of the larger branches the verrucæ are low, rounded, and without a prolonged lower lip; on the trunk and main branches they are distant, small, and but little prominent.

Cœnenchyma thin, its surface composed of very conspicuous, stout spindles, often larger than those of the verrucæ. Color of the branchlets and verrucæ deep reddish brown, branchlets yellowish brown, trunk and main branches yellow, tinged with brown. Axis horn-like, yellowish wood-brown at the base and in the larger branches, darker reddish brown and translucent in the smaller ones, light amber-yellow, translucent, and slender, in the branchlets.

The largest specimen is 15 inches high, greatest breadth, across the upper surface of the clump, 22 inches; least diameter 16; diameter of trunk 1·4; of main branches ·75 to 1 inch; of branchlets at origin ·12 to ·17; near the ends, including verrucæ, ·20 to ·25; length of longest verrucæ ·08 to ·10; diameter ·05 of an inch. Another specimen is 15 inches high, and the same in breadth.

The spicula vary in color from brownish yellow and yellowish white to deep reddish brown. The larger ones are mostly stout, relatively large, blunt, and frequently irregular or crooked spindles. The longer spindles are rather thick in the middle portion, tapering somewhat abruptly to the ends, which are not usually very acute; one side covered with small, very sharp spinules, the other parts with crowded rough warts. The stouter spicula are thick and massive, usually blunt or even truncate at one or both ends, but sometimes tapering to blunt points, often crooked; some of the smaller ones entirely lose their spindle-shape, even becoming triangular; others have the large end forked; while some are quite irregular, compressed, sometimes as broad as long, one side divided into large, sharp, lacerate teeth or spines. The medium sized spindles are more regular, quite stout in the middle, usually tapering to acute points, one side covered with quite large and very sharp spinules, the other with closely crowded rough warts. Other still smaller spicula are quite slender, regular, very warty spindles, light yellow in color. The smallest are very small, snow-white, very warty spindles, some very slender, others relatively short.

The longer spindles measure 2·90^{mm} by ·650^{mm}, 2·50 by ·500, 1·75 by ·350, 1·57 by ·325, 1·55 by ·350, 1·55 by ·300, 1·55 by ·225, 1·50 by ·425, 1·45 by ·350, 1·40 by ·250, 1·27 by ·300, 1·20 by ·250; the stout spicula 2·37 by ·650, 2·25 by ·625, 2·10 by ·675, 2·00 by ·575, 1·75 by ·525, 1·70 by ·525, 1·62 by ·550, 1·62 by ·500, 1·50 by ·475, 1·35 by ·575, 1·07 by ·375, ·725 by ·300; the medium sized spindles 1·07 by ·250, 1·07 by ·225; 1·00 by ·275, 1·00 by ·250, 1·00 by ·200, ·900 by

·200, ·875 by ·200, ·825 by ·200, ·700 by ·150; the smaller spindles ·575 by ·175, ·575 by ·100, ·550 by ·100, ·500 by ·100, ·475 by ·100 ·450 by ·075, ·425 by ·100; the smallest white spindles ·135 by ·075, ·325 by ·062, ·175 by ·075, 1·75 by ·062; some of the small triangular ones ·450 by ·425; the irregular prickly spicula ·400 by ·325. The polyp-spindles measure ·375 by ·100, ·325 by ·075, ·275 by ·075, ·225 by ·100, ·200 by ·075, ·200 by ·062.

Pearl Islands, brought from 6 to 8 fathoms below low-water mark by divers,—F. H. Bradley.

Var. miser.

Corallum dwarfed, forming small, thickly branched, rounded, cæspitose clumps, from two or six inches in diameter and about the same in height, the subdivision taking place rapidly from close to the base. Branches and branchlets small and slender, the latter a little enlarged toward the ends, and from ·5 to 2 inches long. Verrucæ as in the typical form, but smaller, nearly obsolete on the larger branches. Color of branchlets deep brown, of branches and often the bases of branchlets very light yellow. Diameter of branchlets ·10 to ·15; length of longest verrucæ ·04 to ·06 of an inch. The spicula are similar to those of the typical form, but smaller.

Pearl Islands, in rocky pools at extreme low-water mark,—F. H. Bradley; Corinto,—J. A. McNiel.

This species is more nearly allied to *M. echinata* than to any other. Its cæspitose growth and far more numerous and smaller branches will usually separate it readily. The verrucæ are smaller and shorter, and the spicula are different, though quite similar in general appearance. They are mostly stouter and blunter than the corresponding forms in *M. echinata*, while the large, stout spindles of the cœnenchyma are decidedly larger, even in smaller specimens. The medium sized spindles are also decidedly stouter and less acute.

Muricea austera Verrill, sp. nov.

Plate VIII, figure 7.

Corallum large, dichotomous, fruticose, sometimes cæspitose, with rather thick, obtuse branchlets, covered with close, scarcely appressed, sub-conical verrucæ, having an acute lower lip.

In the largest specimen, several trunks arise from a broad base, four or five inches in diameter. These quickly fork, and the branches in their turn rapidly divide, being, in some cases, five or six times dichotomous, producing a rather coarse cæspitose clump, though some of the main branches and their divisions have a tendency to arrange themselves in a single plane,—a feature that is more characteristic of the smaller specimens. The branches and branchlets usually arise from ·5 to 1·5 inches apart, spreading in a wide curve at first, or even nearly at right angles, and then becoming sub-parallel. The branches occasionally coalesce sparingly. The terminal branchlets are ·5 to 2 inches long, as large as or larger than the smaller branches, and mostly increase in size from their origin to the end, which is well rounded. The verrucæ are prominent, sub-conical, with an acute lower lip, near together, but yet scarcely crowded, and not imbricated, usually forming an angle of about 45° with the surface, closely covered by rough, stout, rather short spindles, tapering to the ends, which scarcely project above the surface, except slightly at the summit of the verrucæ. Cells opening on the upper side of the verrucæ, filled when fresh with a cluster of light yellow polyp-spindles. Cœnenchyma moderately thick, firm, with a hard rough surface, covered with stout, mostly obtuse, rough spicula, some of which are much larger than those of the verrucæ. Axis wood-brown and not calcareous at base; black in the branches and usually a little compressed, especially at the axils; yellowish brown, coarse, and rigid in the branchlets. Color uniform reddish or yellowish brown.

Height of largest specimen, from Panama, 9 inches; breadth 15 by 13; diameter of main branches ·40; of secondary ·30; of branchlets at base ·20 to ·25; at summit, including verrucæ, ·25 to ·35; length of verrucæ ·05 to ·10; diameter about ·05. Another sub-flabelliform specimen from Pearl Islands is 9 inches high and 10 broad, with the branches and verrucæ as in the other. One from Cape St. Lucas is 8 inches high and 6 broad; the branchlets near the ends mostly ·35, rarely ·40, in diameter; the longest verrucæ ·12 of an inch in length.

The largest spicula are all rather short and stout, mostly oblong or oval in outline, with obtuse or truncate ends, only a portion of them being short spindles. The longer spicula are mostly oblong, with obtuse ends, or stout fusiform, tapering somewhat to one or both ends, which are blunt; one side covered with large, conical spinules, the others with rather large, close set, rough warts. The stouter spicula differ but little from the longer ones, except in being shorter and thicker, generally oblong or oval, and truncate at the ends. They are often irregular, or lobed at one or both ends. The small spindles are rather stout, tapering but little, blunt at the ends, and covered with large, prominent, rough warts, about their own diameter apart. Small, irregular, very warty or spiny spicula occur, which are nearly as long as broad; also irregular star-shaped spicula, and nearly round warty heads. The polyp-spicula are mostly small, rather slender, oblong spindles, with blunt ends, closely covered with small rough warts.

The single specimen from Cape St. Lucas has spicula which average somewhat larger, but agree well in form and appearance with those of the Panama specimens.

The longer spicula measure 1·45^{mm} by ·400^{mm}, 1·22 by ·400, 1·17 by ·375, 1·15 by ·375, 1·15 by ·325, 1·12 by ·375, 1·12 by ·300, 1·07 by ·300, 1·05 by ·350, 1·02 by ·325, ·850 by ·275; the stouter ones 1·47 by ·500, 1·02 by ·400, 1·00 by ·375, ·975 by ·500, ·950 by ·425, ·900 by ·450, ·750 by ·300, ·700 by ·375, ·675 by ·325, ·650 by ·350, ·625 by ·300; the small spindles ·425 by ·100, ·375 by ·100, ·350 by ·125; the small irregular, thorny spicula ·275 by ·175, ·225 by ·150, ·175 by ·100; the stars ·200 by ·200, ·200 by ·150, ·175 by ·175; the heads ·175 by ·150, ·175 by ·100; the polyp-spindles ·500 by ·100, ·450 by ·112, ·450 by ·075, ·425 by ·125, ·400 by ·137, ·400 by ·100, ·375 by ·100, ·350 by ·087, ·325 by ·075, ·300 by ·100, ·250 by ·075, ·225 by ·062. The longer spicula from the Cape St. Lucas example measure 1·67 by ·550, 1·50 by ·500, 1·50 by ·425, 1·50 by ·375, 1·25 by ·300, 1·12 by ·325; the stouter ones 1·60 by ·550, 1·40 by ·575, 1·30 by ·500, 1·27 by ·450, 1·25 by ·500, ·875 by ·450.

Pearl Islands, rare, brought with *M. crassa* and *M. fruticosa* from 6 to 8 fathoms by divers,—F. H. Bradley; Panama, at extreme low-water, on reef, very rare,—F. H. Bradley; Cape St. Lucas,—J. Xantus, from Smithsonian Institution; La Paz,—J. S. Pedersen.

This species resembles in color and general appearance *M. echinata* and *M. fruticosa*, but is quite distinct from both in its short, stout, blunt spicula. From the latter it differs, also, in its much stouter and less numerous branches and larger verrucæ; from the former in its shorter, broader, and more conical verrucæ and firmer texture.

Muricea retusa Verrill, sp. nov.

Plate VIII, figure 8.

Corallum dark purplish, dichotomous, sparingly branched, branches rather thick, with large sub-conical verrucæ, which are not crowded.

The trunk forks near the base and, in the only specimen seen, each main branch subdivides again at the distance of about an inch. One of the secondary branches again forks at two inches from its origin, the others remain simple and about two inches long. The branches spread widely at first and are about equal in size throughout, the terminal branches being a little enlarged toward the end. The verrucæ are rather large, stout, subconical, nearly as broad as high, not crowded, standing at an angle of about 45° on the upper part of the branches and at a greater angle below, their surface covered with short, thick, rather obtuse spindles, with their sides elevated and very conspicuous at the surface, but the ends not projecting. The lower lip of the verrucæ is rather obtuse and not much prolonged. The cœnenchyma is thick, covered with stout, irregular, blunt spicula, some of them considerably larger than those of the verrucæ. Color deep purplish brown.

Height 3 inches; breadth 2·5; diameter of branches ·30; length of verrucæ ·08 to ·12; breadth ·06 to ·08.

The spicula are mostly deep red or purple, varying toward yellowish, and consist mostly of short, stout, usually irregular, blunt spindles, or oblong spicula, three or four times as long as broad; and very short and thick, irregular, massive spicula, often more than half as broad as long. The longer spicula are partly stout, blunt spindles, often irregular or bent, and closely covered with rough warts, with stout conical spinules on one side; these come mostly from the verrucæ. Others, coming from the cœnenchyma, are oblong or irregularly formed, one end often dilated, frequently truncate. The stouter spicula are very massive and irregular, usually oblong, and truncate at both ends, often with one end dilated, frequently lobed, crowdedly warted, except on the spinulose sides. Others are irregularly triangular and flattened, one edge spinulose, the sides warted. All the stouter irregular spicula appear to come from the cœnenchyma. The smaller spindles from the verrucæ are pretty regular, stout fusiform, or even somewhat oval in outline, the ends not very acute.

The longer spicula measure 1·47^{mm} by ·500^{mm}, 1·40 by ·350, 1·27 by ·450, 1·10 by ·300, 1·05 by ·325, 1·00 by ·300, ·925 by ·250, ·900 by ·225, ·875 by ·325; the stouter ones 1·20 by ·550, 1·02 by ·600, 1·02 by ·500, 1·00 by ·550, 1·00 by ·475, ·950 by ·500, ·925 by ·450, ·750 by ·525, ·700 by ·450, ·625 by ·425; the triangular flattened ones 1·15 by ·575, ·775 by ·400, ·625 by ·375; heads ·275 by ·275; the small oval spindles ·750 by ·300, ·625 by ·225, ·600 by ·225, ·475 by ·225, ·450 by ·250, ·450 by ·175, ·250 by ·150.

Pearl Islands, attached to the base of a large specimen of *M. fruticosa*, from 6 to 8 fathoms,—F. H. Bradley.

This species is closely allied to *M. austera*. Its spicula are still shorter, thicker, and more irregular, approaching, in this respect, those of *M. crassa*, though much smaller. The verrucæ are also larger than those of *M. austera* and less rough. The peculiar rich color will probably prove to be a good specific character, since the color in the species of this genus appears to be remarkably constant, although quite variable in some genera of Gorgonidæ.

Muricea formosa Verrill, sp nov.

Plate VIII, figure 15.

Corallum white, dichotomous, the branches moderately stout, divergent, with elongated squarrose verrucæ.

The single specimen in the collection forks at about half an inch from the base; one branch divides again within half an inch; the other forks at two inches, each division again subdividing irregularly. The branchlets diverge at first with a wide angle, often even 90°, and then curve upward; they are short, somewhat conical, obtuse at the end. The verrucæ are elongated, somewhat conical, with the acute lower lip projecting beyond the upper, and spiny with the projecting ends of elongated, sharp spicules. Cells placed on the upper side and near the end of the verrucæ, surmounted by a cluster of white polyp-spindles when the polyps are contracted. Cœnenchyma rather thin, the surface covered with rather short and stout, nearly regular spindles. Axis wood-brown at base, brownish black in the branches. Color pure white throughout.

In life, "the color, both of branches and polyps, is pure white; polyps very inconspicuous, sessile, with eight short, pinnate tentacles," —F. H. B.

Height 4 inches; breadth 3; length of branchlets ·5 to 1·5; diameter, including verrucæ, ·30 to ·35; length of verrucæ ·08 to ·12; diameter ·04 to ·06.

The spicula are clear white, of moderate size, comparatively smooth; the larger are mostly rather elongated spindles from the verrucæ, with one end usually quite sharp; and short, stout, blunt spindles and irregular spicula from the cœnenchyma. The longer spindles from the verrucæ sometimes taper regularly to both ends, which are acute; others have one end short, the other tapering abruptly, truncate, or even forked; the outer surface is covered with very small, crowded warts, the inner surface with very small, low spinules, which gives them a rather smooth appearance when moderately enlarged. The stout spicula, mostly from the cœnenchyma, are in large part short, stout spindles, often regularly elliptical in outline, with the ends regularly tapering and blunt; some are irregular spindles, one end often much the largest and blunt or rounded, the other somewhat acute; others are of various shapes, sometimes sub-triangular, often bent. All are covered with very small warts and spinules, like the longer ones. The polyp-spindles are mostly small, short spindles, very unequally and roughly warted; others are more slender and very small spindles; others are longer, slender, not very acute spindles, with more distant warts.

The longer spindles measure 1·35ᵐᵐ by ·325ᵐᵐ, 1·25 by ·175, 1·22 by ·250, 1·22 by ·175, 1·17 by ·275, 1·15 by ·175. 1·12 by ·275, 1·07 by ·200, 1·05 by ·250, 1·00 by ·250, ·950 by ·250, ·950 by ·225, ·950 by ·150, ·925 by ·250, ·925 by ·225, ·900 by ·200, ·875 by ·225, ·850 by ·225, ·750 by ·175, ·725 by ·225, ·725 by ·175, ·725 by ·150, ·600 by ·100; the stout spindles 1·45 by ·450, 1·32 by ·375, 1·17 by ·400, 1·15 by ·300, 1·12 by ·275, 1·10 by ·425, 1·05 by ·325, ·975 by ·300, ·925 by ·350, ·900 by ·350, ·850 by ·300, ·850 by ·275, ·800 by ·225, ·775 by ·275, ·775 by ·225, ·750 by ·300, ·750 by ·250, ·700 by ·250, ·675 by ·300, ·650 by ·200, ·425 by ·250; the irregular stout spicula ·950 by ·450, ·925 by ·350, ·800 by ·300, ·775 by ·375, ·725 by ·350, ·700 by ·300, ·650 by ·300, ·600 by ·325, ·525 by ·275, ·425 by ·275, ·400 by ·250, ·350 by ·225; the polyp-spindles ·450 by ·100, ·425 by ·100, ·400 by ·100, ·375 by ·125, ·350 by ·112, ·350 by ·062, ·325 by ·112, ·325 by ·087, ·300 by ·100, ·300 by ·075, ·300 by ·050, ·275 by ·062, ·225 by ·062, ·175 by ·075.

Zorritos, Peru, dredged in 3 fathoms,—F. H. Bradley.

This species resembles *M. albida* in color and size of branches, but has not the appressed verrucæ, with a flattened lower lip, of that species, and the spicula of the verrucæ are much longer, sharper, and more projecting, while all the spicula are much less roughly warted. It somewhat resembles *M. squarrosa* in size and mode of branching and in the divaricate verrucæ, but differs in the elongated lower lip and much stouter spindles of the verrucæ, as well as in color. It also bears some resemblance to the whitish variety of *M. tubigera*, but has smaller branches, shorter verrucæ, with a well-marked lower lip, and much shorter and stouter spicula.

The Zorritos specimen is infested by a small parasitic worm, which forms numerous tubes in the cœnenchyma and surface of the axis. When living "from each tube are protruded a pair of long, slender, flexible tentacles, zoned with black and white, and a long, worm-like process, mammillated on both sides, and showing a dark line (intestine?) in the centre."

These worms are about a quarter of an inch long and quite slender, with small bundles of setæ along the sides, the posterior extremity tapering. In alcohol the tentacles are relatively large, with large dark brown spots, arranged in pairs along the whole length, producing the "zoned" appearance. Each worm has two holes at the surface of the cœnenchyma, which are close together and have a slightly raised border. From one of the holes the tentacles are protruded; from the other, the posterior end of the body. The lower part of the tube, bent into a U-shaped form, is more or less deeply excavated in the substance of the axis.

2.— *Verrucœ scarcely prominent. Cells opening outward, with the lower lip little developed.*

Muricea robusta Verrill.

Muricea robusta Verrill, Bulletin Museum of Comp. Zoöl., p. 36, 1864; (*pars*) Proc. Boston Soc. Nat. Hist., vol. x, p. 329, 1866.

Plate VII, figure 3.   Plate VIII, figure 9.

Corallum brown, irregularly dichotomous, with few, stout, mostly crooked branches, pretty closely covered by the rather large, unequal cells, which have the border but little elevated.

When young it rises as a simple, clavate, often crooked stem to the height of 2 or 3 inches, attaining a diameter of ·35 to ·40 near the summit, which is bluntly rounded. Larger specimens usually divide within 1·5 inches from the base, the main branches again forking within an inch of their origin, and the resulting branches are irregularly once or twice dichotomous. The branchlets are irregular, crooked, arising from ·5 to 2 inches apart, spreading at their origin in a broad curve, stout and rigid, of nearly uniform size throughout, the ends obtusely rounded. Verrucæ upon the branches and trunk inconspicuous, consisting of a slightly elevated margin around the rather large and conspicuous cells, which are crowded over the whole surface and open outward. Toward the ends of the branchlets the verrucæ become more prominent by reason of the greater development of the lower border of the cells, which forms a concave, semi-circular, or crescent-shaped lower lip, with a somewhat thickened and obtuse edge, the surface scabrous and granulous with small rough spicula. Cœnenchyma thick, and granulous with small spicula. Axis in the branches black and scarcely compressed at the axils, brown and rigid in the branchlets. Color dull yellowish brown.

Height of largest specimen 8·5 inches; breadth 4; diameter of trunk ·40; of branchlets ·35; of largest verrucæ ·06; length of lower lip, when longest, ·04.

Spicula orange-brown and light yellow, quite small for the genus, but very rough, the larger ones consisting in great part of stout, irregular, thorny clubs. The longer spindles are rather slender, irregular, the sides closely covered with very rough unequal warts, one end often lacerately divided into large, unequal, sharp spinules. The stouter spicula are in part short, stout, very roughly warted spindles; with more numerous and usually large, stout, irregular, very rough clubs. The latter are bluntly pointed at the small end, the sides covered with crowded rough warts, the large end lacerately divided into large, unequal and irregular, sharp spinules. Among the smaller spicula are many short, irregular spindles, roughly warted on one side, and bearing large, elongated, sharp, oblique spinules on the other; also more regular short warty spindles and warty heads; others are quite slender and very roughly warted spindles, often lacerate at one end. The polyp-spicula are deep brown.

The longer spindles measure $.825^{mm}$ by $.175^{mm}$, $.825$ by $.162$, $.775$ by $.175$, $.750$ by $.250$, $.700$ by $.150$, $.675$ by $.125$, $.625$ by $.175$, $.625$ by $.125$, $.550$ by $.175$, $.525$ by $.125$; the stouter spindles $.625$ by $.375$, $.625$ by $.250$, $.475$ by $.200$; the stout clubs $.575$ by $.200$, $.575$ by $.175$, $.550$ by $.200$, $.525$ by $.200$, $.450$ by $.250$, $.450$ by $.175$; the longer spinules of the clubs are about $.100$ to $.125$ in length; the irregular lacerate spicula $.475$ by $.325$, $.225$ by $.200$; the smaller stout spindles $.325$ by $.150$, $.275$ by $.125$, $.250$ by $.137$; the warty heads $.225$ by $.175$, $.200$ by $.150$; small slender spindles $.450$ by $.125$, $.400$ by $.112$, $.375$ by $.100$.

Acapulco, Mexico,—A. Agassiz.

This species resembles *M. purpurea* and *M. albida* in its stout branches and mode of subdivision, but differs from both these and all others in its nearly obsolete verrucæ. Its spicula are very different in form and size from those of *M. albida*.

3.— *Verrucæ curved upward at the apex, generally more or less appressed and usually imbricated.*

a.— *Cœnenchyma thick; branches stout. obtuse, dichotomous.*

Muricea albida Verrill.

Muricea robusta (pars) Verrill, Proc. Boston Soc. Nat. History, vol. x, p 329, 1866.
Muricea albida Verrill, American Journal Science, xlv. p. 412, May, 1868.

Plate VII, figure 9. Plate VIII, figure 10.

Corallum white, dichotomous, branching nearly in a plane, with stout, rather long branches, thick cœnenchyma, and large, close, somewhat appressed verrucæ.

When young this species usually grows to the height of two or three inches as a simple, straight, clavate stem, generally quite slender at the base and gradually enlarging to near the summit, where the diameter, including verrucæ, is $.20$ to $.35$ inch, the end obtusely rounded. The first branch usually arises from one side, about 1 or 1·5 inches from the base, and soon becomes about as long and large as the original stem. Each of the two main branches usually forks again at distances of ·5 to 1 inch, their divisions mostly remaining unequal, some of them remaining long simple branchlets, others irregularly two or three times dichotomous, the branches all spreading in one plane. The larger specimens are usually irregularly and sparingly branched, the branches being seldom more than three times dichotomous, the distance between the divisions being two or three inches. Sometimes the secondary branches arise only from the upper side of the outer branches, and are then sub-parallel and erect. In other specimens the branches all rise directly, spreading but little even at base. More commonly the branches spread outward at their origin in a broad curve, or even nearly at right angles, and then bent upward and are usually more or less crooked and slightly enlarged toward the tips, though sometimes of uniform size or even slightly tapering. The verrucæ are rather large and prominent, crowded, usually appressed and loosely imbricated, yet on some of the branches they are often erect, spreading sometimes even at right angles. The upper side is rudimentary, the verrucæ consisting almost entirely of the broad, elongated, more or less flattened and incurved lower lip. The cells are large, occupying nearly the whole of the upper side of the verrucæ, when fresh surmounted by a large cluster of white polyp-spicula from the bases of the tentacles. The surface is somewhat rough with rather small imbricated spicula, many of which project a little at the summit. The cœnenchyma is thick and compact, covered with stout, thick spicula. The axis is a little compressed at the axils; clear black in the larger branches; brown, slender, and rigid in the branchlets. Color uniform yellowish white. In life, "the color, both of branches and polyps, is pure white,"—F. H. B.

Height of the largest specimen 11 inches; breadth 5; diameter of trunk ·37; of branchlets ·30 to ·40; length of verrucæ ·08 to ·10; breadth ·06 to ·08. Another specimen is 6·5 inches high; 4 broad; diameter of trunk ·45; of branchlets at base ·38 to ·40; near tips ·45 to ·48; length of longest verrucæ ·12. A third specimen is 5·5 inches high; 8 inches broad; diameter of branchlets ·30 to ·37.

The spicula are white, larger than in the other species of this subsection and more regular. The larger ones are mostly rather blunt oblong spindles, covered with small, very rough, crowded warts on the convex outer side, and with large, prominent, sharp spinules on the inner surface, which is often straight or concave. The longer spindles are only moderately stout, one end usually larger than the other and more or less obtuse, the other end generally acute, the surface rough with unequal warts and spinules. The stouter spindles are short and thick, frequently irregular and crooked, both ends usually tapering to blunt points, one being often quite obtuse, the surface densely covered with small rough warts. Some stout spicula are club-shaped, with the large end divided into two or three blunt, warty lobes. The medium sized spindles are very strongly warty with large, unequal, rough warts, which are not crowded; most of them are quite slender and acute, others stouter and blunter.

The longer spindles measure $1 \cdot 42^{mm}$ by $\cdot 325^{mm}$, $1 \cdot 37$ by $\cdot 350$, $1 \cdot 37$ by $\cdot 325$, $1 \cdot 37$ by $\cdot 275$, $1 \cdot 32$ by $\cdot 300$, $1 \cdot 25$ by $\cdot 300$, $1 \cdot 20$ by $\cdot 275$, $1 \cdot 12$ by $\cdot 275$, $1 \cdot 12$ by $\cdot 225$, $1 \cdot 04$ by $\cdot 275$, $1 \cdot 02$ by $\cdot 225$, $\cdot 950$ by $\cdot 225$, $\cdot 875$ by $\cdot 175$, $\cdot 825$ by $\cdot 200$, $\cdot 825$ by $\cdot 175$; the stouter spindles $1 \cdot 50$ by $\cdot 500$, $1 \cdot 37$ by $\cdot 350$, $1 \cdot 32$ by $\cdot 350$, $1 \cdot 17$ by $\cdot 475$, $1 \cdot 17$ by $\cdot 425$, $1 \cdot 17$ by $\cdot 350$, $1 \cdot 12$ by $\cdot 300$, $\cdot 925$ by $\cdot 300$, $\cdot 875$ by $\cdot 325$, $\cdot 800$ by $\cdot 350$, $\cdot 700$ by $\cdot 300$, $\cdot 700$ by $\cdot 250$, $\cdot 575$ by $\cdot 300$, $\cdot 500$ by $\cdot 250$; the stout clubs $1 \cdot 25$ by $\cdot 500$, $\cdot 825$ by $\cdot 325$, $\cdot 325$ by $\cdot 250$; the smaller spindles $\cdot 950$ by $\cdot 150$, $\cdot 900$ by $\cdot 250$, $\cdot 725$ by $\cdot 150$, $\cdot 725$ by $\cdot 125$, $\cdot 675$ by $\cdot 150$, $\cdot 650$ by $\cdot 100$, $\cdot 525$ by $\cdot 100$, $\cdot 525$ by $\cdot 075$, $\cdot 425$ by $\cdot 100$.

Panama, in rocky pools at low-water mark,—A. Agassiz, J. H. Sternbergh, F. H. Bradley; Pearl Islands, common,—F. H. Bradley.

This species is very distinct from the others of this sub-section, in its white color and the much larger and more regular spicula. Its color and peculiar verrucæ will also readily separate it from all other species which resemble it in size and mode of branching.

Muricea hebes Verrill.

Muricea hebes (*pars*) Verrill, Bulletin Museum Comp. Zoöl., p. 36, 1864; Proc. Boston Soc. Nat. Hist., vol, x, p. 328, 1866.

Plate VII, figure 8. Plate VIII, figure 11.

Corallum yellowish brown, small, sparingly dichotomous, forming low clumps of few branches, which are short, moderately stout, and clavate.

The base is flat and expanded, often giving rise to several stems, which mostly fork close to the base, each branch dividing again at from ·5 to 1 inch from its origin. Some of these branches again fork, but many remain simple and are 1 to 2·5 inches long. When young the stems are often erect, simple, clavate, and 1 or 2 inches high. The branchlets are as large as or larger than the branches before division. They are usually curved, sometimes of uniform size throughout, but generally enlarge toward the blunt tips, so as to be decidedly clavate, and vary in length from half an inch to two inches. The verrucæ are often unequal, rather small, crowded, loosely imbricated, mostly somewhat appressed; the upper lip very short or wanting; the lower one prolonged, flattened, and incurved, the lower surface rough and spinulose with the sharp projecting points of the small spicula, which are numerous and imbricated. The cells are situated on the upper and inner surface of the verrucæ and open upward, but are nearly concealed by the incurved lower lip. The cœnenchyma is thick and rather firm, showing but little between the crowded verrucæ of the branchlets. Color dull reddish brown or yellowish brown, varying in shade. In life "stem and polyps deep orange,"—F. H. Bradley.

Height of largest specimen 3 inches; breadth 3·75; diameter of smaller branches and base of branchlets ·23 to ·25; of branchlets near tips ·30 to ·32; length of verrucæ ·06 to ·10; breadth ·05. Another specimen is 2·5 inches high; 3·5 broad; with the brachlets ·25 to ·30 in greatest diameter. Most specimens are considerably smaller, the branchlets often not more than ·20 in diameter, with the verrucæ also considerably smaller.

The spicula are light yellowish brown and yellowish white in color, and relatively small, the larger ones consisting of both longer and stouter warty spindles, and irregular, flattened, rough spicula, often as broad as long, and usually with one edge lacerately divided. The longer spindles are mostly rather stout, often irregular, with a very roughly warted surface, and sharp prominent spinules on one side; the ends usually acute, one often blunter than the other. The stouter spindles are short, thick, often oblong or oval, both ends usually blunt, one often smaller than the other, the surface roughly warted. The irregular flattened spicula of the cœnenchyma are numerous and relatively large, very roughly warted, and with one edge deeply divided into irregular, lacerate teeth or spindles, which are usually sharp. The forms vary exceedingly, some being somewhat oval, quadrangular, triangular, or head-like, but the majority are quite irregular. The small spicula are mostly either quite slender, or short and thick warty spindles.

The longer spindles measure ·875^{mm} by ·275^{mm}, ·775 by ·200, ·775 by ·150, ·750 by ·175, ·750 by ·125, ·725 by ·225, ·725 by ·175, ·700 by ·225, ·675 by ·200, ·650 by ·137, ·625 by ·150, ·600 by ·150, ·600 by ·125, ·575 by ·100, ·550 by ·125, ·450 by ·100; the stouter spindles ·775 by

·350, ·775 by ·300, ·750 by ·350, ·750 by ·325, ·725 by ·300, ·725 by ·275, ·700 by ·275, ·675 by ·325, ·650 by ·300, ·625 by ·325, ·625 by ·300, ·625 by ·225, ·600 by ·325, ·600 by ·250, ·600 by ·225, ·575 by ·325, ·575 by ·275, ·550 by ·275, ·500 by ·200, ·450 by ·225, ·425 by ·300, ·400 by ·225; the irregular flattened spicula ·700 by ·325, ·625 by ·475, ·625 by ·275, ·575 by ·400, ·550 by ·450, ·525 by ·400, ·525 by ·375, ·475 by ·375, ·450 by ·325, ·425 by ·425; the heads ·425 by ·300, ·250 by ·200; the small spindles ·425 by ·150, ·400 by ·100, ·400 by ·087, ·375 by ·150, ·300 by ·125. Some spindles from the verrucæ are included among the preceding measurements of larger spindles, others measure ·825 by ·250, ·800 by ·200, ·775 by ·162, ·625 by ·200, ·625 by ·175.

Panama and Pearl Islands, common in rocky pools near low-water mark,—F. H. Bradley; Acapulco,—A. Agassiz; Corinto,—J. A. McNiel.

This species is liable to be confounded with the young of *M. austera* and *M. albida*, and perhaps other species; from the latter it differs in color and in having smaller verrucæ; from the former in its less projecting, more appressed and smaller verrucæ, and lower growth, as well as lighter color; and from both it differs widely in its much smaller and very differently shaped spicula, which more nearly resemble those of *M. robusta* and *M. purpurea*. From the last it may be at once distinguished by its color and less appressed verrucæ, which are much rougher, owing to the projecting points of the more acute spicula; from the former it differs in its well developed verrucæ, smaller cells opening upward, lower growth, and less robust branches.

Muricea purpurea Verrill.

Muricea hebes (pars) Verrill, Bulletin Museum Comp. Zoöl., p. 36, 1864.
Muricea purpurea Verrill, American Jour. Science, vol. xlv, p. 412, May, 1868.

Plate VII, figure 6. Plate VIII, figure 12.

Corallum sparingly dichotomous, with stout, obtuse, rigid, mostly curved branches, usually arranged nearly in one plane, closely covered by small, appressed, granulous verrucæ.

When young it often rises to the height of 2 to 4 inches as an upright, simple, clavate stem, ·25 to ·32 inch in diameter. Other specimens are two or three times dichotomous before they become two inches high. The larger specimens, when well developed, usually consist of several trunks arising near together from a broad, expanded base, forming open clumps of stout, crooked branches, which are sparingly divided, the branchlets upon each main stem generally spreading nearly in one plane. The trunk often forks within half an inch from the base, but at other times at two or three inches. The main branches are about as large as the trunk and divide again at ·5 to 3 inches from their origin. Some of the secondary branches remain simple, but most of them divide again in an irregularly dichotomous manner, the branches being from ·5 to 2 inches apart. The branches almost always diverge greatly at first, sometimes even almost at right angles, and then bend upward with a broad curve. The branchlets are mostly crooked, or variously curved, divergent, about as large as the branches, sometimes slightly tapering, but usually uniform in size or a little clavate, obtusely rounded at the end, varying in length from ·5 to 2 inches. In two specimens some of the main branches are broad and somewhat flattened, diameter ·65 by ·30. The largest specimens consist of a single stem, which divides at the height of two inches, the first branch remaining simple and about three inches long, the main stem divides again within half an inch, and each of the nearly equal main branches forks at about half an inch from its origin, and their subdivisions are again dichotomous at ·5 to 1·5. Some of the resulting branches remain simple, but most of them are once and a few twice dichotomous, at distances of 1 to 2·5 inches. The branchlets are all curved or crooked, 1 to 2·5 inches long, ·35 in diameter, mostly a little clavate, very obtuse and, like the branches, are situated nearly in one plane. The verrucæ are rather small, short, crowded, usually appressed and somewhat imbricated, the upper lip obsolete, the lower one well developed, oval, obtusely pointed, the tip often incurved. On the trunk and lower part of branches the lower lip is usually less developed, not appressed, often obliquely truncated, the cells opening upward and outward. The surface of the verrucæ is strongly granulous with the very small and short, warty spicula, but not spinulose. Cœnenchyma thick, firm, granulous. Axis yellowish brown at base; brownish black in the branches and compressed at the axils; yellowish brown, coarse, rigid, and brittle in the branchlets. Color uniform reddish purple, the surface when dry covered with a film of dull yellowish.

The largest single specimen is 9 inches high; 7 broad; diameter of trunk ·40; of branchlets ·28 to ·35; length of largest verrucæ ·06 to ·07; breadth at base ·05 to ·06. One of the clumps is 6 inches high; breadth 9 by 5·5. In some dwarf specimens the diameter of the branchlets is only ·20 to ·25. In some specimens the largest verrucæ become ·10 of an inch long, and ·06 or ·07 broad.

The spicula are small and bright reddish purple, sometimes tinged with yellowish. The larger ones are mostly short and stout spindles, stout thorny clubs, and short irregular spicula, lacerately spinulose on one side. The larger spindles are usually somewhat oblong, blunt at both ends, often irregular, closely covered with larger, very rough warts, except on the inside, which bears rather large, prominent, sharp spinules. The clubs are very stout and rough, often one-sided or irregular, the small end not very acute, covered with crowded rough warts, the larger end much dilated, lacerately divided into many long, sharp, often very slender, unequal spinules. The irregular spicula are very short and thick, often nearly as broad as long, sometimes oval, very rough with large, crowded, prominent, lacerate warts, one side lacerately divided into long, very sharp spinules. Very rough warty heads occasionally occur, similar to the last. The small spindles are mostly rather stout, blunt at the ends, and covered with very prominent, not crowded, somewhat rough warts. The polyp-spindles are mostly slender, acute, yellowish brown spindles, covered with small but prominent warts.

The larger spindles measure ·625^{mm} by ·225^{mm}, ·600 by ·200, ·575 by ·275, ·575 by ·200, ·550 by ·300, ·550 by ·250, ·550 by ·200, ·550 by ·175, ·500 by ·225, ·500 by ·150, ·475 by ·200, ·450 by ·200, ·425 by ·175, ·425 by ·150, ·400 by ·150, ·375 by ·150, ·350 by ·175; the stout clubs ·575 by ·300, ·550 by ·300, ·525 by ·250, ·500 by ·250, ·500 by ·200, ·475 by ·250, ·475 by ·200, ·450 by ·225, ·450 by ·200, ·425 by ·225, ·425 by ·200, ·425 by ·175, ·400 by ·225, ·400 by ·200, ·400 by ·175, ·325 by ·200, ·325 by ·150; the irregular stout spicula ·575 by ·325, ·575 by ·250, ·550 by ·275, ·525 by ·300, ·500 by ·250, ·450 by ·175, ·400 by ·300, ·400 by ·200, ·375 by ·225, ·350 by ·175, ·325 by ·225, ·325 by ·200; the heads ·325 by ·225, ·300 by ·275; the small spindles ·300 by ·112, ·262 by ·100, ·250 by ·125, ·250 by ·100, ·225 by ·112, ·200 by ·100; the polyp-spindles ·262 by ·037, ·250 by ·050, ·225 by ·062, ·225 by ·050, ·175 by ·050.

Pearl Islands and Panama, in rocky pools at low-water mark, common,—F. H. Bradley; Panama,—J. H. Sternbergh, A. Agassiz; Acapulco,—A. Agassiz; Corinto,—J. A. McNiel.

This species differs from most others in color and in the small granulous verrucæ. *M. retusa*, which has a somewhat similar but darker color, has much larger, spreading verrucæ and very different larger spicula. In some respects it is allied to *M. hebes*, which it considerably resembles, except in color, when young. Young specimens of these two species were formerly confounded by me,—a mistake that might readily have been avoided by an examination of the spicula, which are very different. The spicula of this species are remarkable for their relatively small size, roughness, and stout forms, among which the thorny clubs are, perhaps, the most characteristic.

Muricea clavata (*Gonigoria clavata* Gray)* appears to be closely allied to this species, and may prove identical upon actual comparison. The specimen described and figured is evidently young, consisting of a simple clavate stem, as in the young of many other species of *Muricea*. Its locality is unknown and the description is not sufficiently detailed to determine whether it be identical with this or not.

b.—*Cœnenchyma rather thin; branchlets slender.*

Muricea appressa Verrill.

Gorgonia plantaginea Val., Voyage de la Vénus, Zoöph., Pl. 15, 1846,† (*non* Lamarck).
Muricea appressa Verrill, Bulletin Museum Comp. Zoöl., p. 37, Jan., 1864; Proc. Boston Soc. Nat. Hist., vol. x, p. 329, 1866.
Eunicea Tubogensis Duch. and Mich., Supl. Corall. des Antilles, p. 17, Tab. 3, fig. 5 and 6 (after May, 1864), in Mem. Reale Accad. Sci., Torino, xxiii, p. 111, 1866.

Plate VIII, figure 13.

Corallum deep brown, sometimes yellowish white, flabelliform, much subdivided, with small, closely appressed verrucæ.

When young the corallum is quite slender; the small trunk divides within a quarter or half an inch from the base into two or three main branches, each of which usually forks again within about a quarter inch, and the resulting branches subdivide irregularly in a dichotomous or sub-pinnate manner, so that specimens 2·5 inches high often have more than twenty branchlets, all of which are quite slender and nearly equal in diameter. The large specimens are usually very numerously branched, all the branches standing nearly in one plane, the principal branches mostly sub-pinnate, often secund. The branchlets usually arise at ·25 to ·50 of an inch apart, and, after curving outward a little at base, rise nearly parallel with the branch from which they originate; they are usually quite slender, flexible, mostly 1 to 6 inches long, varying considerably in diameter in different specimens. The verrucæ are quite small, crowded, closely imbricated, with the lower lip much elongated and incurved, so as to conceal the cells, usually closely appressed, but not invariably so; their surface is scabrous, covered with small, short, and very rough spicula, the ends but slightly projecting. Cœnenchyma thin, very little exposed, except on the base and main branches, covered with small rough spicula and slender spindles. Axis black at base and in the larger branches, finely striated longitudinally and usually compressed, especially at the axils,

---

* Proceedings of the Zoölogical Society of London, 1851; Annals and Magazine of Natural History, vol. 3, page 422, 1859.

† The figure represents a coarse, poorly grown specimen. Spicula from the original type agree with those of our typical form,—Reprint.

light brown, slender, setiform, and flexible in the branchlets. Color, except in the light variety, uniform deep brown. In life, "the stem is dull red, polyps brownish yellow,"—F. H. B.

The largest specimens are often 18 inches across; a medium sized one measures in height 8 inches; breadth 10; diameter of trunk ·25; of main branches ·20; of branchlets ·10 to ·12. A stouter branched specimen is 10 inches high; 10 broad; diameter of trunk ·50; of main branches ·25 to ·35; of branchlets ·12 to ·18; length of verrucæ ·06; breadth ·03. In some specimens many of the branchlets do not exceed ·08 in diameter. A specimen from Zorritos is 15 inches high; 8 broad; diameter of branchlets ·12 to ·18; many of the simple terminal branchlets are 6 to 9 inches in length, some tapering very slightly to the end, others of nearly uniform size throughout their length.

The spicula are small, yellowish brown and deep reddish brown. The larger ones are mostly very rough spindles; very thorny, stout clubs; very slender, warty spindles; and stout, irregular, lacerate spicula. The larger spindles are mostly rather stout, somewhat irregular, covered on the outside with very rough, unequal warts, on the inside with large, sharp, lacerate spindles. The clubs are short and stout, often one-sided, the small end acute and warty, the other end much enlarged, lacerately divided into large, prominent, rough spinules. The irregular spicula are of various forms, often flattened, with one edge deeply divided into large, unequal, lacerate spinules. The slender spindles are of various lengths, some being very long and slender, with acute ends, covered on all sides with small, well separated warts.

The larger spindles measure ·925^{mm} by ·125^{mm}, ·900 by ·150, ·750 by ·175, ·700 by ·125, ·575 by ·175, ·575 by ·150, ·550 by ·200, ·525 by ·187, ·525 by ·175, ·525 by ·162, ·500 by ·200, ·500 by ·175, ·500 by ·150, ·475 by ·125, ·450 by ·150, ·450 by ·125, ·425 by ·150, ·425 by ·125, ·400 by ·125, ·350 by ·125, ·275 by ·175; the slender spindles ·800 by ·100, ·725 by ·075, ·700 by ·125, ·700 by ·100, ·625 by ·075, ·575 by ·075, ·525 by ·100, ·525 by ·087, ·525 by ·075, ·500 by ·112, ·500 by ·100, ·475 by ·075, ·425 by ·087, ·425 by ·075, ·350 by ·062; the clubs ·600 by ·225, ·550 by ·200, ·525 by ·225, ·500 by ·275, ·450 by ·200, ·450 by ·175, ·450 by ·150, ·400 by ·150, ·375 by ·175, ·375 by ·150, ·375 by ·125, ·350 by ·137, ·325 by ·175, ·275 by ·125; the irregular spicula ·500 by ·325, ·475 by ·275, ·450 by ·250, ·450 by ·200, ·425 by ·175, ·400 by ·175, ·400 by ·125, ·250 by ·125, ·225 by ·150, ·150 by ·150.

Zorritos, Peru, dredged in 3 to 5 fathoms, F. H. Bradley; Pearl Islands, in pools at extreme low-water mark, F. H. Bradley; Panama,—J. H. Sternbergh, F. H. Bradley; Corinto, Nicaragua,—J. A. McNiel; La Paz,—J. Pedersen.

Var. flavescens.

Corallum agreeing in the mode of branching and in size and form of branchlets and verrucæ, with the typical specimens, but yellowish or whitish in color. In life, "stem and polyps pure white, polyps ·12 of an inch long, ·03 in diameter, nearly transparent; tentacles eight, very short, appearing as mammillæ on the edge of the disk,"—F. H. B.

The height of a specimen from Zorritos is 8 inches; breadth 11; diameter of branchlets ·10 to ·15. Another one is 12 inches high; 10 broad; diameter of branchlets mostly about ·12; length of branchlets mostly 2 to 5 inches.

The spicula are white and agree very well with those of the typical form, but the larger spindles and clubs, in the specimens examined, average somewhat larger and are, perhaps, a little rougher.

The larger spicula measure ·825^{mm} by ·200^{mm}, ·750 by ·200. ·750 by ·175, ·725 by ·125, ·625 by ·150, ·575 by ·150, ·475 by ·200; the clubs ·650 by ·212, ·625 by ·225, ·575 by ·200, ·500 by ·225, ·500 by ·200.

Zorritos, Peru, dredged in 3 to 5 fathoms; and Pearl Islands, at extreme low-water mark,—F. H. Bradley; Corinto,—J. A. McNiel.

This species can scarcely be confounded with any other, unless with the following, from which it differs in its more numerous, shorter, and less slender branchlets, larger, stouter, and more incurved verrucæ, and especially in the character of the spicula.

The specimen figured by Duchassaing and Michelotti[*] is evidently the young of this species. The projecting points of the spicula, represented in their magnified figure, should have been a sufficient indication of its generic affinities.

Muricea tenella Verrill, sp. nov.

Plate VI, figure 12. Plate VIII, figure 14.

Corallum whitish, dichotomous, with long and very slender branchlets, and prominent, slender, acute verrucæ, covered with long, slender spindles.

The typical specimens from Panama are small and slender. The trunk divides within half an inch from the base into two or three nearly equal branches, each of which forks again within a quarter inch. The secondary branches afterward subdivide at distances of ·25 to ·80 of

---

[*] Although the exact date when their memoir was published is unknown to me, it certainly was subsequent to the publication of this species in the Bulletin of the Mus. Comp. Zoöl., which is sufficiently evident from the foot-note on page 7, dated "Turin, ce 17 mai, 1864."

an inch, the branchlets mostly arising from their outer side in a somewhat secund manner. They curve outward a little and then rise subparallel to the branches, and some of them again subdivide. The terminal ones are from ·5 to 2 inches long, very slender and flexible, of nearly uniform size throughout.

A large specimen from Zorritos consists of seven large, compressed, divergent branches, arising together from close to the base. These rapidly divide into many long, slender branches, which form an acute angle with the larger branch, and arise at distances of ·25 to 1 inch apart, becoming more distant outward. The secondary branches divide in the same manner, and likewise many of the resulting branchlets. In this manner the branches form a broad, rounded, fan-shaped corallum, with long, very slender, flexible, terminal branchlets, some of which are 5 or 6 inches long, but most of them 2 or 3 inches. The verrucæ are very small, but usually quite prominent, with an elongated, slender, sharp, lower lip, which is often but little incurved at tip, and composed of long, slender, acute spindles, which project at the tip.

In the Panama specimens the verrucæ are not crowded and scarcely imbricated or appressed, but in the large specimens from Zorritos they are smaller, crowded, more or less imbricated, with a shorter and less acute lower lip. The cœnenchyma is thin, covered with small, slender, rough spindles. Axis black and somewhat compressed in the larger branches, strongly compressed in the large specimens; brown and setiform in the branchlets. Color, of dry specimens, grayish white; in alcohol dark gray, polyps brown. In life, "stem white, polyps dark brown." In the Zorritos specimen, during life, "the stem is pure white, polyps light brown, body of polyps transparent. The eight tentacles appear as mere thickenings of the edge of the disk, often giving it a somewhat angular form,"—F. H. B.

The largest Panama specimens measure 3·5 high by 3 broad; and 4 inches high by 3·5 broad; diameter of branchlets, including verrucæ, ·10 to ·12; length of verrucæ ·05 to ·06; diameter ·02 or ·03. The largest specimen from Zorritos is 17 inches high; 18 broad; diameter of largest branches at base ·30 to ·40; of branchlets ·07 to ·10.

The spicula are white, the larger ones consisting of remarkably long, slender, and acute warty spindles, which are often bent; of somewhat stouter and shorter, roughly warted and spinulose spindles; with a few very rough, often lobed, irregular spicula, and rather long, thorny clubs. The characteristic, very slender, acute spindles are covered with very small, scattered warts.

The larger spindles measure ·875^{mm} by ·150^{mm}, ·825 by ·150, ·775 by ·150, ·750 by ·150, ·700 by ·150, ·700 by ·125, ·675 by ·125, ·550 by ·137; the slender spindles 1·12 by ·112, 1·12 by ·087, 1·10 by ·100, ·900 by ·087, ·875 by ·100, ·775 by ·100 ·775 by ·062, ·750 by ·100, ·750 by ·075, ·700 by ·075, ·650 by ·087, ·625 by ·075, ·575 by ·075, ·375 by ·050; the clubs ·575 by ·112, ·450 by ·137; the irregular spicula ·400 by ·175, ·375 by ·250, ·325 by ·200, ·300 by ·150.

Zorritos, Peru, dredged in 3 to 5 fathoms,—F. H. Bradley; Panama and Pearl Islands, in rocky pools at extreme low-water mark, very rare,—F. H. Bradley; Corinto,—J. A. McNiel.

This species is remarkably distinct from all others known by reason of its very slender branches; long, slender, and acute verrucæ; and its extremely slender and sharp spindles.

It resembles most the slender specimens of *M. appressa*, var. *flavescens*, in external characters. The spicula are most like those of *M. aspera*, but are much smaller and more slender.

Muricea aspera Verrill, sp. nov.

Corallum yellowish white, flabelliform, with somewhat slender branches, which are subpinnate.

Only two specimens of this species were obtained, both of which are imperfect at base, and may be only branches from a much larger specimen. Each specimen is once dichotomous and both main branches are subpinnate, giving off branchlets at distances of ·25 to ·50 of an inch, which spread outward at a wide angle, often nearly at right angles. Some of these again divide in the same manner. The terminal branchlets are rather slender and mostly from 1 to 1·5 inches long, narrowed at base and usually enlarged a little toward the end. The verrucæ are prominent, loosely imbricated, usually slightly appressed, but sometimes not at all so, usually with an elongated, acute lower lip, formed of long slender spicula, which project slightly at the end. The upper lip is rudimentary or entirely wanting. On the larger branches the lower lip is often but little developed, and the large cells open outward. The cœnenchyma is thin, covered with long spindles, some of them quite stout. Axis black in the larger branches; yellowish brown, slender, and brittle in the branchlets.

Height of largest specimen 5·5 inches; breadth 4; diameter of branchlets ·10 to ·16; length of longest verrucæ ·10; diameter ·05.

The spicula are white and consist mostly of long, very slender spindles, most of which are very acute; and larger and stouter, but quite long spindles. The larger spindles are mostly somewhat irregular or crooked, sometimes forked at one end, usually acute at each end, but sometimes blunt or truncate at one or both, densely covered with rough, unequal warts. The slender spindles are very long, slender, acute at both ends, often bent, the surface covered with small, distant warts.

The larger spindles measure 2·00^{mm} by ·325^{mm}, 1·65 by ·350, 1·57 by ·200, 1·52 by ·250, 1·37 by ·200, 1·35 by ·300, 1·32 by ·250, 1·20 by ·200, 1·17 by ·275, 1·17 by ·250, 1·17 by ·200, 1·10 by ·200, 1·05 by ·250, 1·02 by ·225, 1·02 by ·200, ·800 by ·150; the slender spindles 1·37 by ·125, 1·32 by ·125, 1·25 by ·112, 1·25 by ·125, 1·12 by ·150, 1·07 by ·125, 1·05 by ·100, ·100 by ·100, ·925 by ·150, ·900 by ·087, ·875 by ·100, ·875 by ·087, ·825 by ·100.

Panama, at extreme low water, very rare,—F. H. Bradley.

This species bears little resemblance to any other, except the two preceding, from both of which it differs in having much longer and larger spicula. Its branches are much shorter and stouter than those of *M. tenella*, and the verrucae are very different from those of *M. appressa*.

Remarks on the subdivisions of the Genus, Muricea.

In addition to the 18 species of *Muricea* described in the preceding pages, there are at least 12 other species now known, of which all except four are in the Museum of Yale College.*

All those species which I have examined may be naturally grouped in three divisions, which do not appear, however, to be of more than subgeneric value, even if entitled to that rank. But in view of the manifest tendency among recent authors to multiply generic divisions, I have thought it proper to recognize these groups and give them names.

Group 1, *Eumuricea*. This division corresponds with section A, page 419. It includes those species with tubular verrucae, without a prolonged lower lip, and usually 8-rayed at summit in contraction. The spindles both of the cœnenchyma and verrucae are long and usually sharp pointed. The 5 species described above are all that are known to me. Typical species, *M. acerrata* V.

---

* The species not in this collection are *M. vatricosa* (Val.) Köll.; *M. humosa* (Esp.) Köll.; *M. tuberculata* (Esp.) Köll.; *M. sulphurea* Ehr. Also *M. elongata* Lamx. (*non* Dana), which is believed to be an *Acis*, from W. Indies.

Group 2, *Muricea* (typical). This group corresponds to section B, p. 425. It embraces those species in which the verrucæ are bilabiate, or have a prolonged lower lip. The spindles of the cœnenchyma and verrucæ are similar and usually stout, but sometimes slender and pointed.* In addition to the 13 species described above, it includes *M. muricata* V. (*M. spicifera* Lx.); *M. lima* E. and H.; *M. pendula* Verrill; *M. laxa* Verrill; and *M. elegans* Duch. and M., from the Atlantic coast of America; and probably *M. vatricosa* Köll., Archipel. Bizagos, Africa; and *M. sulphurea* Ehr., locality unknown.

Group 3, *Muricella*. This division includes those species which have a rather thin cœnenchyma, filled with long spindles; with low, subconical verrucæ, arising from between the large spicula and usually standing at right angles to the surface, and covered with much smaller and shorter spindles. The species are *M. flexuosa* V., Hong Kong; *M. nitida* V., Ebon I.; probably *M. humosa* Köll., and *M. tuberculata* Köll., from unknown localities; and one or two undescribed species, which I have seen, from the E. Indies.

This group approaches the genus, *Acis* D. and Mich., but the latter differs in having scale-like spicula covering the verrucæ.

Echinogorgia aurantiaca Verrill, (Leptogorgia, 1st Ed., see p. 413).

Callao, Peru.—Edwards and Haime. A species allied to *E. sasappo* of the East Indies.—Reprint.

Heterogorgia Verrill.

American Journal of Science, xlv, p. 413, May, 1868.

Corallum dichotomous, with a horn-like axis. Cœnenchyma rather thin, with a smoothish or finely granulous surface, filled with quite small spicula, which are not conspicuous at the surface, and consist of various forms of roughly warted, short spindles, heads, doubleheads, double-stars, crosses, with many irregularly shaped, small, rough spicula. Verrucæ rounded, somewhat prominent, smoothish below, armed at summit with long, sharp, often crooked spindles, which project from the surface around the cell in the form of sharp, divergent spinules. The name alludes to the remarkable diversity in the sizes and forms of the spicula.

---

* *M. robusta*, *M. purpurea*, and *M. hebes* V. depart considerably from the more typical species of this group, in having smaller, short, stout, very rough and irregular spicula. *Gonigoria clavata* Gray (see page 444) appears to belong to the same group, and in case a subgeneric name be desirable for these species *Gonigoria* may be used.

Heterogorgia verrucosa Verrill, loc. cit., p. 414.

Plate VI, figure 11. Plate VIII, figure 16.

Corallum grayish or yellowish white, low, dichotomous, with clavate branchlets and large, rounded, echinate verrucæ.

Young specimens sometimes grow to the height of two inches before dividing, and are then clavate and obtusely rounded at summit. Other specimens, however, divide dichotomously within half an inch from the base; the main branches again divide at a distance of ·5 to 1·5 inches. In some cases part of the secondary branches are also sparingly dichotomous. The branchlets bend outward at base with a broad curve and are mostly irregularly curved and crooked, like the branches, and usually clavate and obtuse at the end, though sometimes of uniform size. The verrucæ are large, rounded, prominent, not crowded, standing at right angles with the surface of the branches, slightly eight-rayed at the summit and armed with numerous long, very sharp, rough, spindle-shaped spicula, which project from the surface in the form of short, divergent spinules. The sides of the verrucæ and the cœnenchyma are nearly smooth, showing under a strong lens a finely granulous surface composed of small rough spicula. Cells small, sometimes surmounted by a conical cluster of very slender, white polyp-spindles. The cœnenchyma is rather thin and firm, composed of small rough spicula. Axis dull yellowish brown, wood-like in appearance. Color pale yellowish gray when dry, a little darker in alcohol. In life, "stem dull yellowish brown, polyps gamboge-yellow,"—F. H. B.

Height of largest specimens 3 inches; breadth 1·5; diameter of largest branches ·25; of branchlets near tips ·20; length of branchlets 1 to 2; height of verrucæ ·04 to ·06; diameter ·05 to ·07.

The spicula consist chiefly of large, more or less elongated, roughly warted spindles from the verrucæ; much smaller, very rough spindles and heads from the surface of the verrucæ and cœnenchyma; and very slender, small, smoother spindles from the polyps. The largest spindles are elongated; some of them are slender and tapering to one or both ends; others quite stout but equally long; all are covered with large, rough, well separated warts, and one side with short, sharp spinules; they are frequently irregular, often obtuse at one end, and not very acute at either. With these are many shorter and stouter spindles, which show a regular series of forms between the longest spindles and short, thick, oval or oblong spicula, which are not thrice longer than broad, the surface crowdedly covered with rough warts, the inner side with large spinules, the ends often blunt or obtuse, one of them sometimes forked. The small spicula of the cœnenchyma are of various forms of small, very roughly warted spindles, heads, double-heads, double-stars, crosses, and various irregular and compound forms. The polyp-spindles are slightly and distantly warted, quite slender and acute; most of them are straight and pretty regular; some are much curved and very acute at both ends; others are slender club-shaped, more strongly warted at the larger end.

The longer spindles measure 1·50^{mm} by ·300^{mm}, 1·50 by ·275, 1·35 by ·300, 1·27 by ·275, 1·22 by ·225, 1·15 by ·275, 1·12 by ·250, 1·10 by ·250, 1·10 by ·225, 1·07 by ·250, 1·07 by ·225, 1·05 by ·250, 1·02 by ·225, 1·00 by ·225, ·975 by ·225, ·950 by ·225, ·925 by ·150, ·900 by ·225, ·875 by ·150, ·825 by ·175, ·800 by ·200, ·775 by ·175, ·750 by ·175, ·750 by ·125, ·675 by ·150, ·625 by ·125, ·575 by ·125, ·500 by ·125; the stouter spindles 1·55 by ·375, 1·25 by ·350, 1·22 by ·300, 1·20 by ·375, 1·20 by ·300, 1·15 by ·325, 1·15 by ·300, 1·12 by ·300, 1·05 by ·325, ·900 by ·250, ·850 by ·225, ·850 by ·200, ·825 by ·275, ·775 by ·250, ·725 by ·300, ·725 by ·275, ·700 by ·250, ·700 by ·200, ·450 by ·150; the stout irregular spicula 1·05 by ·325, 1·00 by ·400, ·975 by ·450, ·925 by ·275, ·925 by ·325, ·900 by ·375, ·650 by ·275, ·625 by ·275; the stout spicula with one end forked 1·15 long by ·675 across the forks, 1·00 by ·475, ·925 by ·450, ·675 by ·325; the small spindles from the cœnenchyma ·350 by ·100, ·325 by ·087, ·300 by ·125, ·275 by ·150, ·275 by ·125, ·275 by ·100, ·250 by ·100, ·212 by ·150; double-heads ·162 by ·112, ·162 by ·100, ·150 by ·112; the heads ·300 by ·200, ·212 by ·125, ·200 by ·175, ·150 by ·100, ·125 by ·100, ·125 by ·087, ·125 by ·075; the double-stars ·137 by ·075, ·125 by ·100, ·100 by ·075; the crosses ·300 by ·175, ·225 by ·100, ·200 by ·112, ·175 by ·150, ·175 by ·100, ·162 by ·100, ·150 by ·100; the straight polyp-spindles ·425 by ·075, ·400 by ·075, ·375 by ·075, ·375 by ·062, ·350 by ·075, ·350 by ·050, ·325 by ·075, ·275 by ·062, ·250 by ·037; the curved polyp-spindles ·475 by ·050, ·450 by ·062, ·300 by ·037; the polyp-clubs ·425 by ·083, ·425 by ·075, ·400 by ·075, ·375 by ·075, ·350 by ·062.

Pearl Islands, in rocky pools at extreme low-water, on the reef, very rare,—F. H. Bradley.

Heterogorgia tortuosa Verrill, loc. cit., p. 414.

Corallum pale yellowish, subflabelliform, with more numerous branches and more slender, crooked branchlets, covered with small scattered verrucæ.

In the largest specimens the trunk divides irregularly, close to the base, into several branches, some of which are very irregularly four or five times dichotomous; the branchlets diverge frequently at right angles and are mostly very crooked, usually tapering somewhat to the obtuse tips, 1 to 3·5 inches long. One small specimen is simple for 1·5 inches from the base and then gives off subpinnately from each side seven crooked branchlets, which are mostly alternate on the opposite sides and from ·3 to ·5 of an inch apart; the lower ones diverge nearly at right angles and some of them branch near the end, or at ·75 to 1·25 of an inch from their bases.

The verrucæ are rather small, low, rounded or subconical, distantly scattered, opening outward, armed at the summit with a few small, slender, projecting spinules, their sides, like the cœnenchyma, having a very finely granulous surface, appearing smooth to the naked eye. Cœnenchyma rather thin, firm, filled with very small rough spicula. Axis dull brownish yellow, wood-like in appearance, its surface strongly furrowed longitudinally, giving it a corrugated or irregularly fibrous appearance.

Color a uniform dull yellowish or buff. Height of largest specimen 5·5 inches; breadth 5; diameter of largest branches ·20; of terminal branchlets ·10 to ·15; height of verrucæ ·03 to ·04; diameter ·04 to ·05.

The spicula are white, much smaller than in the preceding species. The larger ones consist of more or less stout, very roughly warted spindles, which are often irregular and usually acute; and of long, slender, very sharp spindles, with very small, distant warts or spinules. The small spicula of the cœnenchyma are of various forms of crosses, heads, double-heads, clubs, short spindles, etc., all of which are very roughly warted. The larger rough spindles measure ·375^{mm} by ·125^{mm}, ·350 by ·100, ·325 by ·125, ·325 by ·112, ·325 by ·100, ·312 by ·075, ·300 by ·112, ·300 by ·100, ·300 by ·087, ·300 by ·075, ·300 by ·062, ·275 by ·125, ·275 by ·112, ·275 by ·087, ·275 by ·062, ·250 by ·112, ·250 by ·100; the long, sharp, curved spindles ·575 by ·075, ·575 by ·050, ·550 by ·087, ·450 by ·075, ·400 by ·062, ·375 by ·050, ·325 by ·050; the small crosses ·175 by ·125, ·125 by ·087, ·100 by ·075, ·075 by ·062; the heads ·100 by ·075, ·087 by ·075, ·062 by ·062; the double-heads ·125 by ·075, ·100 by ·075, ·087 by ·075, ·087 by ·062, ·062 by ·050; the clubs ·125 by ·087, ·125 by ·075, ·087 by ·062; the small spindles ·125 by ·075, ·112 by ·062, ·100 by ·050, ·100 by ·037.

Pearl Islands, in rocky pools at extreme low-water mark,—F. H. Bradley.

This appears to be quite distinct from the last in its smaller and more numerous branches, smaller and less prominent verrucæ, and much smaller spicula. Possibly a large series of specimens might show intermediate forms, but none occur in this collection.

Primnoa Lamouroux.

Primnoa Lamx., Polypiers flexibles, p. 440, 1816; Dana, Zoöph., p. 676; Edw. and Haime, Corall., vol. i, p. 139; Kölliker, Icones Histiol., p. 135.

Axis more or less calcareous, especially at the base, which is usually quite stony. Verrucæ usually in whorls, very prominent, covered with scale-like, imbricated spicula. Cœnenchyma also covered by smaller scale-like spicula. Type, *P. reseda* Pallas sp. (*P. lepadifera* Lamx.).

Primnoa compressa Verrill.

Proceedings Essex Inst., vol. iv, p. 189, 1865.

This species is, as yet, known only by its axis. It is much branched, flabelliform. The smaller branches arise alternately from each side of the main branches, forming acute angles with them. Branches and branchlets strongly compressed, delicately striated, hard and stony, dark brown near the base, yellowish white and setaceous in the branchlets.

Height 24 inches; diameter of largest branches ·25.

Aleutian Islands,—Capt. Gibson.

Family, BRIAREIDÆ Gray.

Briaracées (section) Edw. and Haime, Coralliaires, vol. i, p. 188, 1857.
Briareidæ (family) Gray, Annals and Mag. Nat. Hist., vol. 4, p. 443, 1859.
Briaraceæ (family) Verrill, Memoirs Boston Society Nat. Hist., 1, p. 10, 1863.
Briaridæ (family) Verrill, Proceedings Essex Institute, vol. iv, p 148, 1865.
Briareaceæ (sub-family) Kölliker, Icones Histiol., p. 141, 1865.

Corallum arborescently branched, lobed, or encrusting foreign substances. Axis composed of calcareous spicula, which are not consolidated. Cœnenchyma well developed, filled with small, rough spicula, of various forms. Surface granulous. Cells scattered.

The typical genera of this family are *Briareum, Paragorgia, Titanideum*, and allied forms. These are usually arborescently branched, or rise in irregular lobes, with a well marked spiculose axis. To these typical genera Dr. Kölliker has added *Sympodium* and *Erythropodium*, which are normally encrusting or parasitic species, with a thinner cœnenchyma and apparently without a distinct axis, and may, perhaps, be best compared with the spreading basal portion of *Briareum*.

The position of the following genus seems doubtful, and though agreeing best, in the structure of its spicula, with this family, it may belong to the *Alcyonacea*, near *Rhizozenia*, which Dr. Kölliker refers to the *Cornularidæ*.

Callipodium Verrill, gen. nov.

Corallum encrusting stones and shells, with a firm, more or less thickened, finely granulous cœnenchyma, which may spread either in broad expansions or narrow stolons. Polyps rather large, at the summit of round-topped verrucæ, which are more or less elevated above the surface of the cœnenchyma and either distantly scattered or closely crowded together; in the latter case often united laterally nearly to their summits. Polyps wholly contractile, and also capable of involving the summits of the verrucæ, which, in contraction, are usually distinctly eight-rayed.

Spicula short, of moderate size, brightly colored, very abundant in the cœnenchyma and verrucæ, of various forms and sizes, mostly with very roughly warted prominences, the largest about ·30^{mm} long. The most abundant forms have 3, 4, 5, 6, or 8 irregular projections, covered at the ends with rough spinulose warts. Some are short, stout, blunt spindles, about twice as long as broad, with distant, prominent, rough warts. Some approach the forms of double-clubs, double-heads, heads, and crosses. Others are of various irregular forms, with distant rough warts. Type *C. Pacificum* V.

This genus in some characters resembles *Erythopodium* Kölliker, in others *Rhizozenia* Ehr., or at least *R. rosea* Dana (*Evagora* Phil.) as characterized by Dr. Kölliker, which may not belong to the same genus with *R. Thalassantha*, the original type of the genus. The polyps of *Rhizozenia* are said to be non-contractile; the texture of the cœnenchyma is quite different; and the spicula (in *R. rosea*) are much smaller. *Erythropodium* is described as having a membranous base, with scarcely prominent verrucæ, and the spicula are much smaller and differently shaped.

Having had no opportunity to examine typical specimens of either of those genera I have found it difficult to decide to which the present genus is most nearly allied. In the texture of the cœnenchyma, and especially in the structure of the spicula, it appears to be more nearly allied to the *Briareidæ* than to the *Cornularidæ*, and I am therefore inclined to regard it as an encrusting genus of the former family, since even the typical species of the genus *Briareum* is sometimes found growing in broad encrusting sheets on stones, or parasitically covering the dead axis of many species of *Gorgonidæ*.

Callipodium Pacificum Verrill.

Sympodium Pacifica Verrill, Proc. Boston Soc. Nat. Hist., vol. x, p. 329, 1866.
Erythropodium Pacificum Verrill, Amer. Jour. Sci., vol. xlv, p. 415, May, 1868.

Plate V, figure 22. Plate IX, figure 1.

Corallum red, encrusting, spreading over the surface of stones and shells, either as broad, rather thin sheets, which are usually irregular and often interrupted, or in the form of stolon-like expansions, which may be broad, or quite narrow, and are often reticulated, as in the specimen figured.

Verrucæ irregularly and usually distantly scattered, sometimes a little crowded, on the stolons often arranged in a single series, quite large, usually very prominent and more or less conical, with a rounded, eight-rayed summit; sometimes, when fully contracted, having the form of low rounded warts. Cœnenchyma rather thin, firm, very spiculose, its surface, like that of the verrucæ, strongly granulose with the small rough spicula.

Color, when dry, bright red; in alcohol a deep, clear red. When living, "dull brick-red to purplish red. Polyps, when fully closed, mere pimples on the surface, when expanding they show first a low rounded cone, marked with pointed groups of red spicula, between which now come forth the nearly transparent polyps, which have eight small, acute, pinnate tentacles, swollen at base, surrounding the mouth of the opaque, pinkish white stomach. Height from attachment to summit of tentacles ·20 inch; diameter ·05,"—F. H. B. According to Mr. Bradley's outline sketch of the expanded polyps, the tentacles are very acute, and the pinnæ, which are confined to the outer half, are long and slender.

The largest specimens in the collection almost completely cover portions 3 inches by 1·5 on the surface of the stones; thickness of cœnenchyma, when dry, ·02 to ·03; height of verrucæ above the surface ·04 to ·10, average about ·06; diameter ·05 to ·08, average about ·07. The breadth of the stolons in the reticulated specimens varies from ·05 to ·25, the narrow parts being extremely thin.

The spicula are bright red, very roughly but distantly warted, and very diversified in size and form. The larger ones are partly short, stout, blunt spindles, with few (often not more than twelve) large, distant, rough warts; partly of three, four, five, and six-pronged star-spicula, each branch or prong terminated by one or several rough warts; partly of very roughly warted heads; and of various irregular, very rough forms. The small spicula agree in their forms, to a considerable extent, with the large ones, but in addition to the spindles, heads, and

3 to 6 pronged stars and crosses, there are also double-heads, clubs, double-clubs, and various irregular forms.

The larger spindles measure $\cdot 212^{mm}$ by $\cdot 125^{mm}$, $\cdot 200$ by $\cdot 100$, $\cdot 175$ by $\cdot 125$, $\cdot 175$ by $\cdot 112$, $\cdot 175$ by $\cdot 100$, $\cdot 162$ by $\cdot 125$, $\cdot 150$ by $\cdot 112$, $\cdot 150$ by $\cdot 100$, $\cdot 125$ by $\cdot 087$; the three-pronged spicula $\cdot 200$ by $\cdot 150$, $\cdot 175$ by $\cdot 162$, $\cdot 150$ by $\cdot 150$, $\cdot 150$ by $\cdot 125$, $\cdot 125$ by $\cdot 125$, $\cdot 125$ by $\cdot 100$; the four-armed crosses $\cdot 212$ by $\cdot 175$, $\cdot 175$ by $\cdot 162$, $\cdot 137$ by $\cdot 112$, $\cdot 125$ by $\cdot 125$; the five-rayed stars $\cdot 162$ by $\cdot 150$, $\cdot 125$ by $\cdot 087$, $\cdot 112$ by $\cdot 100$; the six-pronged spicula $\cdot 162$ by $\cdot 112$, $\cdot 150$ by $\cdot 125$; the irregular spicula $\cdot 175$ by $\cdot 137$, $\cdot 162$ by $\cdot 125$, $\cdot 150$ by $\cdot 125$, $\cdot 125$ by $\cdot 112$. Among the small spicula some of the smaller spindles measure $\cdot 100$ by $\cdot 062$, $\cdot 075$ by $\cdot 050$; heads $\cdot 100$ by $\cdot 075$, $\cdot 075$ by $\cdot 075$; double-heads $\cdot 062$ by $\cdot 032$, $\cdot 050$ by $\cdot 037$; clubs $\cdot 125$ by $\cdot 075$, $\cdot 075$ by $\cdot 050$; double-clubs $\cdot 100$ by $\cdot 050$, $\cdot 087$ by $\cdot 037$.

Panama and Pearl Islands, at low-water mark; and Zorritos, Peru, from half-tide downward, on the under side of projecting stones and on shells,—F. H. Bradley; La Paz,—J. Pedersen.

Callipodium aureum Verrill, sp. nov.

Plate V, figure 23.

Corallum yellow, encrusting, consisting of crowded, elongated, tubular corallites, united nearly to their summits, thus forming a corymbose cluster, with an uneven surface.

The verrucæ in the central parts, where most crowded, project but slightly above the surface and are rather large, rounded, and distinctly eight-rayed in contraction. Some of the lateral verrucæ project about $\cdot 10$ inch. Cœnenchyma thickened, very spiculose, its surface and that of the verrucæ granulous. Color, in alcohol, bright orange-yellow.

Height $\cdot 5$ of an inch; breadth 1; diameter of verrucæ about $\cdot 08$.

Spicula bright golden yellow, similar in form to those of the preceding species, but larger, and with longer and more slender branches or rays in the star-shaped forms. The larger spindles are mostly rather stout, blunt, with distant, very prominent, large warts, which are spinulose at summit; they are often irregular or lobed, and some are rather slender. The star-shaped spicula have mostly three or four, sometimes five or six, rays or branches, which are mostly unequal and irregular, but usually considerably elongated and often slender, smooth at base, but covered at the ends with a cluster of rough warts or spinules. Irregular, roughly warted clubs and double clubs, nearly as large as the spindles, also occur sparingly. Irregularly formed spicula of various shapes, but with very prominent warts, are frequent.

The small spicula have all the forms seen among the larger ones, and in addition there are warty heads, double-heads, and other forms. The polyp-spindles are slender and slightly warted.

The larger spindles measure ·275^{mm} by ·075^{mm}, ·250 by ·112, ·225 by ·150, ·225 by ·125, ·225 by ·112, ·225 by ·100, ·225 by ·087, ·225 by ·075, ·212 by ·125, ·212 by ·087, ·212 by ·075, ·200 by ·125, ·200 by ·112, ·200 by ·075, ·187 by ·087, ·187 by ·075, ·175 by ·087, ·162 by ·100, ·162 by ·087, ·150 by ·100; the irregular warty spicula ·275 by ·137, ·225 by ·100, ·200 by ·162, ·200 by ·125, ·187 by ·125, ·175 by ·112; the three-branched spicula ·212 by ·112, ·200 by ·125, ·200 by ·100, ·187 by ·150, ·187 by ·137, ·175 by ·150, ·162 by ·112, ·150 by ·150, ·125 by ·125; the four-branched stars or crosses ·225 by ·187, ·187 by ·125, ·175 by ·162, ·137 by ·137; the six-branched spicula ·175 by ·125; the clubs ·187 by ·087, ·175 by ·100, ·162 by ·100. The small spindles ·125 by ·087, ·100 by ·075, ·100 by ·062; the clubs ·100 by ·037; the heads ·125 by ·087, ·112 by ·087, ·087 by ·087, ·075 by ·075.

Panama,—F. H. Bradley. There is also a specimen from Panama in the Museum of Comparative Zoölogy.

Suborder, ALCYONACEA Verrill.

Alcyonides (family) Edw. and Haime, Coralliaires, vol. i, p. 102, 1857.
Sarcophyta (suborder) (*pars*) Gray, Ann. and Mag. Nat. Hist., 4, p. 443, 1859.
Alcyonidæ (suborder) Verrill, Mem. Boston Soc. Nat. Hist., i, p. 3, 1863.
Alcyonacea (suborder) Verrill, Proceedings Essex Inst., iv, p. 148, 1865.
Alcyonidæ (family) Köll., Icones Histiolog., p. 131, 1865.

Polyps usually elongated, the body-cavity tapering below. Cœnenchyma, when present, fleshy, usually with slender, rather simple spicula. No distinct axis.

Family, ALCYONIDÆ.

Halcyonina (*pars*) (family) Ehrenberg, Corall. des rothen Meeres, p. 56, 1834.
Alcyoninæ (*pars*) (subfamily) Dana, Zoöphytes, p. 599, 1846.
Alcyoninæ (*pars*) (subfamily) Edw. and Haime, Coralliaires, vol. i, p. 113, 1857; Kölliker, Icones Histiolog., p. 132, 1865.
Alcyoniadæ (*pars*) (family) Gray, Annals and Mag. Nat. Hist., vol. 3, p. 443, 1859.
Alcyoninæ (family) Verrill, Mem. Boston Soc. Nat. Hist., i, p. 3, 1863.
Alcyonidæ (family) Verrill, Proc. Essex Inst., iv, p. 148, 1865.

Corallum fleshy, attached by the abundant cœnenchyma, usually branched. Polyps much elongated, usually highly contractile, spicula mostly long and rather simple.

Alcyonium rubiforme Dana.

Lobularia rubiformis Ehr., Corall. des rothen Meeres, p. 58, 1834.
Alcyonium rubiforme Dana, Zoöphytes, p. 625, 1846; Verrill, Mem. Boston Soc. Nat. Hist., i, p. 4, 1863; Verrill, Proceedings Essex Inst., iv, p. 190, 1865.

Corallum red, with a short trunk, which divides into numerous, large, rounded lobes, or short, obtuse branchlets. The lobes, in contraction, are often subglobular, covered with numerous small polyps. Cœnenchyma, between the retracted polyps, even and granulous. Polyps in expansion much exsert; tentacles long, lanceolate, acute, with rather long lateral lobes. Color, in alcohol, brick red, not diaphanous.

Arctic Ocean, north of Behring's Straits, in 35 fathoms,—Capt. John Rodgers; West Coast of Behring's Straits, in the Laminarian zone,—Dr. Wm. Stimpson (North Pacific Exploring Expedition); Banks of Newfoundland,—Coll. Essex Institute; Northern Seas of Europe,—Ehrenberg.

Specimens apparently identical with this species were recently obtained by me at Eastport, Me., in 10 fathoms.

The northern species of Alcyonidæ require careful revision. This species is evidently closely allied to *A. carneum* Ag., occurring on the coast of New England, from Cape Cod to the Gulf of St. Lawrence.

Alcyonium (?) Bradleyi Verrill, sp. nov.

. Corallum, in the only specimen observed, rising as an elongated, subconical, simple stalk, with a rounded summit, and a somewhat spreading base. Whole surface covered with numerous, scattered, small polyps, which are very exsert in expansion.

Height, while living, 1 inch; diameter ·25 to ·33; polyps ·05 to ·25 long, in expansion; diameter ·02 to ·03 of an inch.

"Whole surface and bodies of polyps yellowish white; tips of polyps dark crimson, surmounted by eight· yellowish white, semi-oval, tentacular lobes. Whole group flexible, without a solid axis."

Panama Bay, dredged in 3 to 4 fathoms, on loose shells,—F. H. Bradley.

The specimen from which the description and drawings were made by Mr. Bradley has not been found among his collections. Therefore the generic characters cannot be ascertained at present with certainty.

Order, ACTINARIA Verrill.

Actinaria (pars) Dana, including *Actinidæ* (family), *Zoanthidæ* (family), and *Antipathacea* (tribe), Zoöphytes, 1846; Gosse, Actinologia Britannica, p. 6, 1860.

Zoanthaires (pars) Edw. and Haime, including *Actinaires* and *Antipathaires* (suborders), Corall., i, p. 224, 1857; Verrill, Mem. Boston Soc Nat. Hist., i, p. 14, 1863.

Actinaria (order) Verrill, Proceedings Essex Inst., iv, p. 147, Feb.—April, 1865; ditto, vol. v, p. 315, 1868.

(?) *Actinoids*, "*Actinaria* Edw." (order) A. and Mrs. E. C. Agassiz, Sea-side Studies in Natural History, p. 7 and 152, after May, 1865. (No characters given or limits assigned perhaps not intended to include *Antipathacea*).

Body fleshy, or coriaceous, composed of from six, or ten, to several hundred spheromeres, which are usually in multiples of six, united only by the outer wall of the body, so as to leave, between adjacent spheromeres, interambulacral spaces in which the new spheromeres originate during growth. Basal or abactinal region well developed, specialized, either free or attached, sometimes capable of secreting a horn-like support (*Antipathes*), or a thin corneus pelicle (*Adamsia, Cancrisocia*). No coral or solid calcareous deposits in the wall or radiating lamellæ. Ambulacral chambers open from the summit to the base. Tentacles usually simple, hollow, tubular, or conical, mostly in multiples of six; sometimes only six or ten.

Although the Actinians are evidently numerous, both in species and individuals, upon the tropical portion of the Pacific coast of America, it is remarkable that but one species has hitherto been described from the entire region between Paita, Peru, and San Francisco, Cal. In the collections of Mr. Bradley there are large numbers of *Actiniæ*, but in most cases it would be almost useless to attempt descriptions of these animals from preserved specimens alone. Consequently I have omitted most of the species which are unaccompanied by notes or drawings made from the specimens while living.

Many of the *Actiniæ* from Peru and Chili have been well figured and described by Lesson* and by Drayton,† while those of the northern coast (Sitcha) have been briefly described by Brandt,‡ whose unsatisfactory diagnoses refer almost exclusively to the colors, which

---

* Histoire naturelle des Zoöphytes recueillis dans le Voyage autour du monde de la Corvette de sa majesté, la Coquille, 1822—1825. Captaine Duperrey. Par R.-P. Lesson, Paris, 1832.

† United States Exploring Expedition, during the years 1838—1842, under the Command of Charles Wilkes, U. S. N. Vol. vii, Zoöphytes. By J. D. Dana. Actinidæ by Mr. Joseph Drayton. Philadelphia, 1846.

‡ Prodromus descriptiones animalium a Mertensio in orbis terrarum circumnavigatione observatorum. J. F. Brandt, 1835.

are notoriously variable in this group, and especially so in some northern genera, like *Urticina* and *Bunodes*.

Suborder, ACTINACEA Verrill.

Actinina (family) Ehrenberg, Corall. des rothen Meeres, 1834.
Actinidæ (family) Dana, Zoöphytes, p. 122, 1846.
Actiniaires (pars) (suborder) Edw. and Haime, Corall., i, p. 224, 1857.
Astræacea (pars) (tribe) Gosse, Actinologia Britannica, p. 7, 1860.
Actininæ (subfamily) Duch. and Mich., Corall. des Antilles, 37, 1860, from Mem. Reale Accademia delle Scienze, Turin; ditto, (pars) (family) Supplément aux Corall., 1864, from Mem. Reale Accad., xxiii, 1866.
Actinaria (pars) (suborder) Verrill, Mem. Boston Soc., Nat. Hist., i, p. 14, 1863.
Actinacea (suborder) Verrill, Proc. Essex Inst., iv, p. 148, 1865; ditto, vol. v, p. 317, 1868.

Polyps free and simple, rarely compound, with a well developed and muscular base, which is used both as an organ of locomotion and adhesion. Tentacles varying in number from 10 to several hundred, and quite varied in size and structure; sometimes branched.

The ambulacral spaces usually bear some other organs, such as branchiæ, tubercles, suckers, colored spherules, and special pores.

Family, THALASSIANTHIDÆ Verrill.

Proceedings Essex Inst., iv, p. 148, 1865.

Body more or less cylindrical in expansion, usually broad. The disk bears various ambulacral organs in the form of simple or compound tubercles, or arborescent and variously lobed branchiform organs, in addition to, or replacing, the simple tentacles. Several of these disk-appendages usually arise from each ambulacral chamber, and when true tentacles are present, they may be outside or inside of them, or on both sides. Base a flat locomotive disk.

This family is almost confined to the tropical seas. It includes four well marked subfamilies.

1. *Phyllactinæ* Edw. and Haime. Disk bears both simple tentacles and lobed tubercles, or compound branchiform appendages.

2. *Thalassianthinæ* (pars) Edw. and Haime. Disk bears large, compound tentacles or branchiform organs, all of one form, without simple tentacles.

3. *Heterodactylinæ* Verrill. Disk bears large, compound, branchiform organs of two kinds. No simple tentacles. Includes *Heterodactyla* Ehr. and *Sarcophianthus* Less.

4. *Discostominæ* Verrill (non *Discosomæ* D. and M.). The disk bears small, tentacle-like papillæ, or small, sparingly lobed tubercles,

several of which originate from each radiating chamber or ambulacral space, and are therefore arranged in simple radiating lines, or in radiating groups when more than one series arise from the same chamber. These false tentacles increase in size from the centre to the margin of the disk. The disk is usually broad and widely expanded, but generally capable of complete contraction.

This subfamily includes the true genus, *Discosoma* Leuck. (? *Ricordea* D. and M.), excluding many forms wrongly referred to it by various authors;* *Homactis* and *Stephanactis* Verrill;† and apparently *Echinactis* E. and H., *Corynactis* Allman, *Aureliania* Gosse, and *Capnea* Forbes. But most of the descriptions and figures of these genera are insufficient to determine with certainty whether the "tentacles" originate each from a distinct chamber or not. For the three genera last mentioned Gosse has formed the family, *Capneadæ*, but he does not refer to this character, and regards all the disk-tubercles as true tentacles.

Subfamily, PHYLLACTINÆ Edw. and Haime.

Metridium (genus) Ehrenberg, 1834, (*non* Oken); Dana, Zoöph., p. 150, 1846.
Phyllactinæ (subfamily) Edw. and Haime, Corall., i, p. 291, 1857; Verrill (*pars*), Mem. Boston Soc. Nat. Hist., i, p. 15, 1863.

Column usually rather low and broad, its surface generally bearing verrucæ or suckers, sometimes nearly smooth. Disk broad, the tentacles placed considerably within its margin. The branchiform appendages either form a circle just within the margin and outside of the tentacles, *Oulactis;* are mingled with the tentacles, *Rhodactis;* or cover the buccal area within the circle of tentacles, *Actinotryx;* or are placed both within and outside of the circle of tentacles, *Amphiactis* V.‡ These organs differ greatly in number, size, and form in the different genera, as well as in position.

The genus, *Aulactinia*, which I formerly referred to this subfamily, on account of the lobed, sub-marginal, branchiform papillæ, appears to belong rather with the *Bunodinæ*. The same is true of *Oulactis granulifera* (Les. sp.) E. and H., and *Anthopleura Krebsii* D. and M. It was on account of these and other similar forms that the group was formerly made a subfamily of *Actinidæ* by me, but in that family the branchiform appendages are really lateral organs, originating from or below the margin.

---

* *Discosomus* was used among Reptiles by Oken in 1816, and *Discosoma* among Arachnida in 1830 by Perty. Ehrenberg has proposed to substitute the name *Discostoma*, for Luckart's genus.
† Proceedings Essex Institute, vol. vi.   ‡ Proc. Essex Institute, vol. vi.

Oulactis Edw. and Haime.

Metridium (pars) Dana, Zoöph., p. 150, 1846, (*non* Oken).
Oulactis E. and H., Corall., vol. i, p. 292, 1857; pars, Duch. and Mich., Corall. des Antilles, p. 46, 1860.

Column covered with verruciform suckers. Disk broad; simple tentacles placed at some distance from the margin; outside of them a circle of numerous, large, frondescent, branchiform organs.

Oulactis concinnata Edw. and Haime.

Metridium concinnatum Drayton, in Dana, Zoöph., p. 152, Pl. 5, fig. 40 and 41, 1846.
Oulactis concinnata E. and H., Corall., vol. i, p. 292, 1857.

Column low, broad, dilated above and below. Disk very broad, strongly radiate, margin undulated, sides covered with large tuberculiform suckers, to which pebbles and fragments of shells adhere. Tentacles half an inch long, stout, subulate, sub-triangular, the lower side slightly concave. Branchiform organs nearly ·5 of an inch long, 1 to 1·5 lines broad, frondescently laciniate.

Column ochreous olive, with olive-green suckers; three branchiæ of a white color alternate with a brown one; simple tentacles similar to column, but paler, faintly striped with pale purple; disk purple. Another variety has the column green, with ochreous suckers. Diameter at middle, in expansion, 2 inches; at disk 3.

San Lorenzo, near Callao, Peru, buried to its tentacles in sand,—U. S. Exploring Expedition.

Lophactis Verrill, gen. nov.

Column elevated; its walls firm, sub-coriaceous, in contraction rough with deep corrugations and wrinkles, not verrucose, and without apparent suckers in the preserved specimens. Simple tentacles large, placed at a considerable distance from the margin. Branchiæ few in number (12), arranged in a circle between the margin and the tentacles, large and broad, laterally compressed, the upper edge of each bearing a series of finely subdivided papillæ, which consequently form radiating rows of secondary branchiæ. The large branchiform organs are united together on the side nearly to their summits by a thin membrane, which forms a naked area between the branchiæ and tentacles, and they are also united on the outside by adherence to the marginal fold, so that, when contracted, there are deep chambers or cavities between them.

This genus is closely allied to *Phyllactis*, but the latter has more numerous branchiæ, which are quite different in structure, and are longer and much more exsert, and connected together only on the inside by a membrane that does not reach the summit.

Lophactis ornata Verrill, sp. nov.

This curious species is known only from one specimen, which is well preserved in alcohol, with the disk and tentacles expanded.

The column is higher than broad, though evidently much contracted; the surface has a finely papillose, or deeply and closely wrinkled appearance, and appears to be covered with a dark-colored, thin, inseparable, epidermal layer; its substance is firm and tough, somewhat leathery.

The disk is broad; mouth with numerous marginal folds; buccal disk small, surrounded by a circle of 96 simple tentacles, which are rather long, enlarged somewhat at the end, which is marked with about ten sulcations. They are apparently arranged in four or five circles. The 12 branchiæ are large, with a broad membrane uniting them together on the inside and separating them from the tentacles; their summits are arched, bearing along the crest a narrow, closely convoluted frill, having its edge finely divided into a fringe-like structure; below the crest there is a transversely thickened portion; the lower part is thinner, with strong, longitudinal, muscular folds. These organs, therefore, are probably capable of being considerably extended during life. Height, of specimen in alcohol, 1·5 inches; diameter of disk 1; length of tentacles ·3; of branchiæ from base ·5; along crest ·4.

Pearl Islands,—F. H. Bradley.

Asteractis Verrill, gen. nov.

Column versatile in form; walls firm and sub-coriaceous. Disk broad, capable of involution, bearing, near the mouth, a circle of numerous simple tentacles, and outside of these a corresponding number of radiating rows of small, sessile, somewhat lobed and subdivided tubercles or papillæ, increasing in size to the margin, which is crenulate or dentate with the last tubercles of each series.

This genus is somewhat allied to *Oulactis* but differs in having branchiform organs, consisting of rows of sessile papillæ on the disk, instead of distinct, prominent, frondescent appendages, rising from its surface. The column differs, moreover, in lacking verruciform suckers.

To this genus probably belong *Actinia flosculifera* Les. (*Oulactis flosculifera*[*] Duch. and Mich.) and *Oulactis formosa*[†] D. and M. from

---

[*] Coralliaires des Antilles, p. 46, Pl. vii, figures 7, 11, 1860.
[†] Loc. cit., p. 47, Pl. vii, fig. 4, 5.

the West Indies. But the figures and descriptions of the branchial appendages are too indefinite to make this certain, while both species are said to have lateral pores, which I have not been able to see in the following species, when contracted, though they may exist.

Asteractis Bradleyi Verrill, sp. nov.

Column whitish, sometimes low and broad, expanding from about the middle to the margin of the broadly expanded disk; at other times vase-shaped, contracted near the base, cylindrical above, the disk partly contracted; at other times cylindrical, the portion of the disk exterior to the tentacles involved, but the tentacles still protruding. Surface in contraction strongly wrinkled transversely, less so longitudinally, near the margin with papilliform interspaces.

The tentacles are 48 in number, in three rows; the 12 primary ones about ·5 of an inch long; the 12 secondary about ·3; the 24 smallest ones about ·25. All the tentacles are slender and pointed, the larger ones spotted with white. The small branchial papillæ form 48 radiating series, the 12 rows corresponding to the primary tentacles extend from the margin to their bases; the 12 corresponding to the secondary ones extend about half way to their bases; the 24 small ones extend only about quarter way to the bases of the small tentacles. The inner part of each row is formed of very small, scarcely distinct, slightly prominent, crowded papillæ; farther outward they become larger, more prominent, and slightly lobed; the outer ones are considerably larger, crowded, divided into five or six, slightly rounded lobes, the outermost one forming the dentate margin of the disk.

Color of the column, in life, white; largest tentacles delicate pink, bearing four or five, eye-like spots of white, and fading out to white at the tips; secondary tentacles pale pink, with similar, but commonly more numerous, white spots; smallest ones white.

Height, in expansion, ·5 to ·7; diameter of disk ·3 to 1 inch; of column in middle ·3 to ·5; diameter of buccal disk, inside of tentacles, in full expansion, ·5. The same specimen, in alcohol, is about ·5 high; ·5 broad at base; with the partly contracted disk ·35 broad.

Panama Reef, on rocks above half tide,—F. H. Bradley.

This species appears to be rare, as only one specimen is in the collection, which is accompanied by notes and drawings made from it while living. In the drawings there are twelve conspicuous, dark spots, about midway between the tentacles and margin, and corresponding with the primary tentacles. These are not referred to in the notes and nothing corresponding to them can be seen upon the specimen. Whether they be mere color spots, disk pores, or tubercles, is uncertain. When fully expanded the column showed longitudinal lines.

According to Mr. Bradley's notes it is a hardy species, feeds well, and bears rough handling.

Family, ACTINIDÆ.

Actinina (pars) Ehrenberg, including *Actinia* (genus) and *Cribrina* (genus), Corall. rothen Meeres, p. 31, 1834.

Actinia (genus) Dana, Zoöphytes, p. 122, 1846.

Actinina (subfamily) Edw. and Haime, excluding "*Actinines pivotantes*," Corall., i, p. 230, 1857.

Actininæ (pars) (subfamily) Duch. and Mich., Corall. Antilles, 1860.

Actinidæ (family) Verrill, Mem. Boston Soc. Nat. Hist., i, p. 15, 1863; Proceedings Essex Inst., iv, p. 148, 1865; ditto, vol. v, p. 320, 1868.

Body more or less cylindrical in expansion, with a distinct, flat, muscular, basal disk. Tentacles round, simple, surrounding the buccal disk in few or many cycles, sometimes obsolete. Walls perforate or imperforate. Ambulacral appendages on the sides of the body various.

This extensive family may be divided into several sub-families, which are, however, not always well defined.

1. *Bunodinæ.* Column bears tubercles or verruciform suckers, which are imperforate, or rarely perforate, but do not emit acontia.

2. *Sagartinæ.* Column perforated with special pores, for the emission of acontia. Surface smooth, or with inconspicuous contractile suckers.

3. *Phellinæ.* Column elongated, covered to near the margin with a persistent epidermal layer or tunic. Lateral pores and acontia few, or entirely wanting.

4. *Actininæ.* Column smooth, fleshy, destitute both of verrucæ or suckers and special pores. No acontia. Margin with or without colored spherules. Includes *Actinidæ* and *Antheadæ* Gosse.

Subfamily, BUNODINÆ.

Actinines verruqueuses (section) Edw. and Haime, Corall., i, p. 263, 1857.

Bunodidæ (family) Gosse, Ann. and Mag Nat. Hist., 3d ser., i, p. 417, 1858; Actinologia Britannica, p 185, 1860.

Bunodidæ (subfamily) Verrill, Mem. Boston Soc. Nat. Hist., i, p. 15, 1863.

Cereæ (family) Duch. and Mich., Suplem. Corall. Antilles, Mem. Reale Accad., Torin, xxiii, p. 124, 1864–6.

Bunodinæ (subfamily) Verrill, Proc. Essex Inst., vi, 1868.

The column is usually rather low and broad. The verrucæ of the sides may be simple rounded tubercles or elongated papillæ, without perforations; prominent suckers with a concave surface and thickened border; perforated verrucæ, ejecting water in contracting; or, near the margin of the disk, lobed or sparingly branched papillæ. The margin may be a smooth thickened rim, crenulate or dentate by the uppermost tubercles, or it may bear colored spherules. The disk is usually broad. The tentacles large and not very numerous, usually completely contractile.

Bunodes Gosse.

Cribrina (pars) Ehr., Corall. rothen Meeres, p. 40, 1834.
Bunodes Gosse, Trans. Linn. Soc., xxi, p. 274, 1855; Actinologia Britannica, p. 189, 1860; Verrill, Mem. Boston Soc., i, p. 15, 1864.
Cereus (pars) Edw. and Haime (*non* Oken), Corall., i, p. 263, 1857.
Anthopleura (pars) Duch. and M., Supl. Corall. Antilles, in Mem. Reale Accad., Turin, xxiii, p. 125, 1864-6.

Corallum more or less elevated, texture firm, surface covered with conspicuous verruciform suckers, concave above, or low rounded tubercles, which are arranged in vertical lines along each ambulacral chamber, the uppermost one in each row largest and projecting at the margin, so as to form a somewhat dentate or tuberculate border. The suckers usually, if not always, have the power of adhering firmly to foreign substances. They generally decrease in numbers and size from the margin downward, often becoming obsolete below. Tentacles rather large, not numerous, very contractile, usually separated from the margin by a narrow but distinct naked area or "fosse."

Bunodes cruentata Gosse.

Actinia cruentata Drayton (Couthouy, MS.), U. S. Expl. Exp., Zoöphytes, p. 138, Pl. 3, fig. 23, 1846.
Cereus cruentatus Edw. and H., Corall., i, p. 268, 1857.
Bunodes cruentata Gosse, Actin. Britannica, p. 194, 1860.

Column with small sucker-tubercles arranged in vertical rows, conspicuous near the margin, smaller toward the base. Tentacles about 48 in number, long, subulate. In expansion the mouth has four lobes. Color faint purplish red, with numerous vertical lines of darker red, deepening to crimson near the disk; suckers rose-white, yellowish when expanded; tentacles intense blood-red; disk brownish purple, alternating with radiating pale ochreous lines.

Orange Bay, Terra del Fuego, buried to tentacles in sand,—J. P. Couthouy, U. S. Expl. Exp.

Bunodes papillosa Verrill.

Actinia papillosa Lesson, Voyage Coquille, Zoöphytes, p. 78, Pl. iii, fig. 2, 1832, (*non* Ehrenberg, 1834

Cereus papillosus Edw. and H., Corall., i, p. 267, 1857.

Column low and broad, covered throughout with numerous, crowded, conspicuous verrucæ, closely arranged in vertical rows. Tentacles very numerous, rather short, in three series. Mouth (as figured) with six lobes, in expansion. Color bright green, the verrucæ lighter, each surrounded by a circle of bright red; tentacles bright red, with lighter tips, disk flesh-colored.

Talacahuano, Chili, to Lima, Peru, on submerged rocks; very common near Quiriquine,—Lesson.

Bunodes pluvia Verrill.

Actinia pluvia Drayton, op. cit., p. 144, Pl. 4, fig. 30, 1846.

Cereus pluvia E. and H., Corall. i, p. 267, 1857.

Column broad, 2·5 inches in diameter at middle, expanding above and below to 3·25. Surface closely covered throughout with small, rounded tubercles or papillæ, upper margin not tuberculate. Tentacles numerous, somewhat crowded, in three series, ·5 inch long, stout (over a line thick at base), subulate. Disk strongly marked with radiating lines, mouth prominent. Color very variable; sometimes bright orange throughout, with the tentacles a little darker and the disk paler. Some have dull red tentacles; others pale red, with the mouth very deep red. In others the column is dark brownish green, with the papillæ bright orange, tipped with white beads or dots.

The orange variety, when disturbed, "ejected water from all its tentacles to a distance of 2 or 3 feet."

San Lorenzo I, Peru, on rocks,—J. P. Couthouy, U. S. Expl. Exp.

This species may prove to be identical with the preceding, but this cannot be determined from the original figures and descriptions.

Bunodes ocellata Verrill.

Actinia ocellata Lesson, op. cit., p. 79, Pl. iii, fig. 5, 1832.

Cereus ? ocellatus Edw. and H., Corall., i, p. 268, 1857.

Column covered with small verrucæ, regularly arranged in vertical rows, and scarcely crowded. Tentacles numerous, short, subequal, slender, crowded. Column brownish; the verrucæ bright red; tentacles brownish red with light tips; disk lighter, brownish near the mouth, which is red within.

Paita, Peru, in crevices among rocks, rare,—Lesson.

This species and the two preceding, appear to be true Bunodes, so far as can be judged from the figures and descriptions, but yet on re-examination they may be found to belong to other allied genera.

Urticina Ehrenberg (emended).

Urticina (subdivision of *Actinia*) Ehr., Corall. rothen Meeres, p. 33. 1834.

Rhodactinia Agassiz, Comptes-rendus, xxv, p. 677, 1847, (without description); Verrill, Mem. Boston Soc. Nat. Hist., i, p. 18, 1864.

Bunodes (*pars*) Gosse, Trans. Linn. Soc, xxi, p. 274, 1855.

Cereus (*pars*) Edw. and Haime, Corall., i, p. 263. 1857, (*non* Oken).

Tealia Gosse, Ann. and Mag. Nat. Hist., 3d series, i. p. 417, 1858; Actin Brit., p. 205.

Column low and broad, in expansion usually broader than high, margin with a more or less distinct fold or "parapet." Surface covered with irregularly and distantly scattered verruciform suckers, which are often small and inconspicuous, but capable of strong adhesion. Margin of the disk slightly dentate or tuberculate, or not at all so. Tentacles large and stout, retractile. Type *U. crassicornis* Ehr.

Urticina crassicornis Ehr.

Actinia crassicornis Müller, Prod. Zoöl. Danica, p. 231, 1776; Johnston, British Zoöphytes, i, p. 226, Pl. 40; Van Beneden, Faune Litt. de Belgique, Polypes, p. 191.

Actinia spectabilis Fabr., Fauna Groenl., p. 351, 1788.

? *Actinia coriacea* Cuvier, Tabl. élém., p. 653, 1797; Règne Animal, tom. iv, ed. i, p. 51. 1817; Rapp, Polypen im Allg., p. 51, Taf. i, fig. 3 and 4, 1829; Johnston, Br. Zoöphytes, i, p. 224, Pl. 39, 1847.

? *Actinia Holsatica* Müller, Zoöl. Danica, iv, p. 23, Pl. 139, 1806.

Isacmœa (*Urticina*) *crassicornis* Ehrenberg, Coral. rothen Meeres, p. 33, 1834.

? *Isacmœa* (*Urticina*) *papillosa* Ehr., op. cit., p. 33, (perhaps = *U. digitata*)

? *Cribrina coriacea* Ehr, op. cit, p. 40.

? *Actinia bimaculata* Grube, Actinien, p. 4, fig. 4, 1840.

Rhodactinia Davisii Agassiz. Comptes-rendus, xxxv, p. 677, 1847; Verrill, Mem. Boston Soc. Nat. Hist., i, p. 18, 1864.

Actinia obtruncata and *A. carneola* Stimpson, Invert. of Grand Menan, p. 7, 1853.

Bunodes crassicornis Gosse, Trans. Linn. Soc., xxi, p. 274, 1855.

Actinia? felina Edw. and H., Corall., i, p. 242, 1857.

? *Cereus coriaceus* Edw. and Haime, Corall., i, p. 264, Pl. C 1. fig. 4, 1857.

Tealia crassicornis Gosse, Ann. and Mag. Nat. Hist., ser. 3, i, p. 417, 1858; Actinologia Britannica, p 209, Pl. iv, fig. 1, 1860.

? *Bolocera eques* and *Stomphia Churchiæ* Gosse, Actin. Brit., p. 222 and 351, Pl. viii, fig. 5, ix, fig. 6.

? *Actinia elegantissima* Brandt, Prodromus descr. Anim. a Mertensio, p. 13. 1835; Edw. and H., Corall., i, p. 289.

? *Actinia Laurentii* Brandt, op. cit., p. 13 ; Edw. and H., Corall.. i, p. 289

Column large, low, usually broader than high in full expansion, the surface bearing small, distant suckers, which are capable of becoming verrucose and attaching foreign substances, or of becoming low, rounded, slightly prominent papulae, or they may be entirely contracted to the level of the general surface, which then appears nearly smooth, but often longitudinally and transversely striated. Tentacles large and stout, numerous, usually banded. Mouth large, with strongly marked lobes, the stomach often everted.

Color very variable; column usually some shade of red or green, or variously mottled and striped with these colors; often bright red and uniform flesh color. Tentacles usually banded with alternating rings of white and some shade of red or pink; sometimes uniform red or flesh-color. Disk usually lighter than the column, frequently pale reddish, or greenish, or mottled; usually, if not always, with radiating stripes of brighter red or crimson, which extend from near the mouth to and among the bases of the tentacles, two of these stripes going to each tentacle and embracing its base on each side. Small white spots often occur in front of the inner tentacles. The angles of the mouth are usually bright red. Large specimens are often 4 to 6 inches in diameter; tentacles 1 to 1·5 inches long; ·20 to ·25 in diameter at base.

Occurs commonly on all the northern coasts of Europe, from France* northward; Iceland; Greenland; Arctic America, southward to Cape Cod. On the Pacific coast in the Arctic Ocean north of Behring's Straits, in 30 fathoms, and in Behring's Straits,—North Pacific Expl. Exp.; Sitcha,—Brandt; Puget Sound,—Dr. C. B. Kennerly.

The numerous specimens obtained by the North Pacific Exploring Expedition do not appreciably differ from those of the north Atlantic coasts, preserved in the same manner. Nor is there anything in Brandt's descriptions to indicate a specific difference.

A. elegantissima Brandt, is said to have the body pustulous, greenish red or spotted. Tentacles moderate, dilated, and white in the middle, purple at the end. From Sitcha.

A. Laurentii Br., has the body red, blotched irregularly with green and brown. Tentacles vermilion red. Behring's Straits.

Evactis Verrill, gen. nov.

The column bears vertical rows of verruciform suckers or tubercles, and is perforated by numerous openings from which water is ejected when the body suddenly contracts. The inner tentacles are smaller and shorter than the outer ones; mouth with four prominent lobes. Type *Actinia artemisia* Drayton.

---

* The southern European form (*U. coriacea*) is more verrucose and may be distinct from the true *U. crassicornis* of the north.

This genus is allied to *Anthopleura* Duch. and Mich., but the latter is represented as having equal tentacles, and the uppermost tubercles are subdivided and sub-tentaculiform. It resembles *Bunodes*, but in the latter the walls are imperforate and the inner tentacles are largest.

Evactis artemisia Verrill.

Actinia artemisia Drayton, op. cit., p. 149, Pl. 4, fig. 38, 1846.
Cereus artemisia Edw. and Haime. Corall., i, p. 268, 1857.

Column low, broad, subcylindrical, often dilated in the middle, and covered with regular vertical lines of prominent, rounded tubercles, which are obsolete below, the upper ones larger and forming a row around the margin of the disk. Tentacles in three series, stout, subulate, the inner ones ·5 inch, the outer ones 1 inch in length. Disk radiated; mouth with four prominent lobes.

Column yellowish green; the tubercles dark sap-green, the green line extending to the base, though the tubercles are obsolete below. The colors of the tentacles are various and shaded like those of the prism. Disk greenish, darker toward the tentacles; the mouth flesh-colored. Diameter, in expansion, 2·25 inches

Discovery Harbor, Puget Sound, abundant,—U. S. Expl. Expedition; Puget Sound,—Dr. C. B. Kennerly.

"This species occurs buried to the tentacles in sand, and also attached to pebbles or shells two or three inches below the surface. On contracting, water spurts from various small lateral orifices, as from a watering-pot,"—C. Pickering.

Evactis ? xanthogrammica Verrill.

Actinia xanthogrammica Brandt, Prod. descrip. anim., p. 12, 1835; Edw. and H., op. cit., p. 289.
Bunodes xanthogrammica Gosse, Actin. Brit., p. 194, 1860.

"Body sub-verrucose, yellowish green. Tentacles numerous, elongated, fusiform, flattened below, copper-green, with small, transverse, yellow spots."

Sitcha Island,—Brandt.

This species may prove identical with the preceding, and in that case would have priority. There are no certain indications of its generic affinities, and I have placed it here mainly on account of its general resemblance to *E. artemisia*.

Cladactis Verrill, gen. nov.

Column firm in texture, low, broad, crowdedly covered with elevated, sub-tentaculiform tubercles or papillæ, which have round, inflated tips, those on the sides simple or two or three lobed; those at the margin of the disk elongated, pedunculated, the end divided into 2 to 6 rounded lobes. Tentacles numerous, rather long, the inner ones largest. Disk broad, with a naked area or "fosse" between the tentacles and the margin.

Cladactis grandis Verrill, sp. nov.

A large species with the entire surface of the column covered with close vertical rows of crowded, elongated papillæ, which are smaller below, but larger and more complex near and at the margin. The uppermost sub-marginal ones are elevated, with a distinct peduncle, the outer portion divided into about six, rounded, inflated lobes in the larger ones, two to four in the smaller ones. The papillæ become nearly sessile below, but many of them have two or three rounded lobes. The tentacles are moderately large, rather stout, very numerous (528 in a large one), in many rows, forming seven or eight cycles, apparently but little contractile, separated from the margin of the disk by a broad shallow fosse. Buccal disk broad, radiated. The mouth is large, elongated, with strong gonidial folds, and numerous lobes along the sides.

General color greenish-brown or olive; "twelve rows of light colored tubercles, with three or more rows of smaller dark ones between each pair of rows of larger ones; disk dark greenish brown; tentacles of nearly uniform greenish brown." In alcohol the specimens are grayish blue, with dull blue tentacles. Some of the larger specimens, when preserved in alcohol, are about 3 inches in diameter and 2 high; length of inner tentacles 1 inch.

Paita; and Zorritos, Peru; Pearl Islands; and Panama, on stones below half-tide mark,—F. H. Bradley. Rio Brito, near San Juan del Sur, Nicaragua,—B. Silliman.

This species appears to be the most abundant Actinian of the Panamian Fauna in the littoral zone. It occurs under the wharf of the Panama Railroad Co. at Panama. It appears to have limited powers of contraction, since most of the specimens preserved in alcohol have the tentacles more or less extended and the disk exposed. In some cases, however, the disk is so involved as to conceal the tentacles. Mr. Bradley states that it is "very sensitive."

It appears to be allied to some of the species referred to *Cystiactis* by Edw. and Haime, but the latter group appears to include representatives of more than one genus. There is, moreover, nothing in their descriptions to indicate that either of their species have compound tubercles, which is one of the most prominent characters of the present genus, when mature. In young specimens, however, the marginal tubercles are only 2 or 3-lobed, while those of the sides are simple rounded tubercles, and scarcely crowded.

There are no openings apparant in the sides of the body.* In this respect the genus differs from the typical species of *Anthopleura* (*A. Krebsii*), as well as in the character of the lateral tubercles. *A. grandifera* D. and M. appears to belong to this genus, however, since it is said to be imperforate and tuberculated.

Cystiactis Edw. and Haime, op. cit., p. 276.

"Body entirely covered by subtentaculiform tubercles, or having the aspect of large, very salient pustules."

Cystiactis Eydouxi Edw. and Haime, op. cit., p. 276, 1857.

"Tentacles short, moderately numerous, longitudinally striated by contraction; the external ones smaller than the internal. Body covered with large vesicles of very unequal size, very close, and irregularly arranged. Specimens preserved in alcohol have a uniform brown color."

Coasts of Chili,—Eydoux (Mus. Paris).

The single character upon which the genus, *Cystiactis*, is based is too indefinite, or too imperfectly defined, to be of much importance in identifying genera. Specimens from Brazil, that appear to be identical with *C. Gaudichaudi* E. and H., appear, however, to be generically distinct. The same is true of *Cystiactis Eugenia* D. and M.,† from St. Thomas. But, so far as the description shows, *C. Eydouxi* may not differ from *Cladactis*, since it is not stated whether the marginal tubercles be simple or compound. Should they prove identical, *Cystiactis* may, therefore, be restricted to *C. Gaudichaudi* and similar species.

Anthopleura Duch. and Mich.

Anthopleura D. and M., Corall. des Antilles, p. 40, 1860; ditto (*pars*), Supl. Corall. des Antilles, p. 32, 1864–6.

Column subcylindrical, somewhat elevated, bearing adhesive, verruciform suckers with concave tops, which are arranged in longitudinal rows, and diminish in size and frequency toward the base. Margin surrounded by a circle of elongated papillæ, corresponding to the rows of suckers, and more or less lobed or incised, with small per-

---

* *C. cavernata* (*Bunodes cavernata* V.) from S. Carolina, has the wall perforated by small, inconspicuous pores, from which water may be ejected.

† Supplément Corall. des Antilles, in Mem. Reale Accad., Turin, xxiii, p. 129, Pl. vi, fig. 1, 1866.

forations on the lower side, from which water may be ejected. Similar perforations occur in the sides below the margin. Tentacles elongated, subequal, rather numerous, separated from the margin by a narrow but distinct fosse. Type, *A. Krebsii* D. and M., 1860.

This genus was originally based upon a single species, with the characters given above. Subsequently two other species were added by the same authors, having quite different structures, and the generic characters were modified accordingly. As defined in the later work the genus does not differ materially from *Bunodes*, and in fact one of the species referred to it, *A. pallida*, appears to be a true *Bunodes*, having imperforate walls and simple tubercles. The other species, *A. granulifera*, has imperforate walls, non-adhesive tubercles, those around the margin being compound. This probably belongs to our genus, *Cladactis*. It seems necessary, therefore, to restrict the genus to its original limits, including only those species with perforated walls, adhesive suckers, and compound sub-marginal papillæ. As thus limited it is allied to *Aulactinia** nobis, and to *Evactis*. The latter differs, however, in having the outer tentacles largest, and the margin surrounded by simple tubercles; the former has more complex sub-marginal appendages and appears to be imperforate, but when better known may prove to be identical.

Anthopleura Dowii Verrill, sp. nov.

Actinia Dowii Bradley, MS.

Column cylindrical, but little elevated, with vertical rows of rather distant, large, adherent, verruciform suckers, which have concave summits; the upper ones largest, becoming more distant and much smaller below, nearly obsolete near the base. Surface between the suckers smooth in expansion, when contracted covered with elevated, reticulated wrinkles. Corresponding to each row of suckers there is a prominent, inflated, submarginal tubercle; these are mostly divided into 2 to 6, slight, rounded lobes, each one perforated on the lower side by several small pores, through which water may be ejected, but no openings through the walls below could be detected in preserved specimens. Margin of the disk separated from the tentacles by a narrow fosse. Tentacles rather slender, elongated, subulate, arranged in three rows, in the larger specimens 108 or more, in smaller ones often only 48. Disk broad, with radiating striations, mouth small, with numerous folds; stomach often everted.

---

* Memoirs Boston Soc. Nat. History, i, p. 20, 1864.

Color quite variable; "column often flesh-colored; disk very variable, from uniform olive-brown to variegated with greenish and yellowish, sometimes all greenish white, in other specimens with six bands of pale yellow alternating with dark lines about the mouth, the rest of the disk being greenish brown; tentacles very inconstant in color, varying from dark brown, yellow, orange, and pink, to purple and dark greenish brown, sometimes plain, often with 1 to 5 light yellow, small, irregular spots, the inner surface commonly darker colored."— F. H. B.

The larger specimens, preserved in alcohol, are about 1·5 inches high, and 1 in diameter.

Pearl Islands; and Panama, under the wharf of the Railroad Co., below half-tide mark,—F. H. Bradley; Realejo,—F. H. Bradley; Acajutla, San Salvador, on buoy,—Capt. J. M. Dow.

This species appears to be tolerably common. In alcohol most of the specimens have the tentacles expanded, often with the stomach everted, others have the disk entirely involved. Mr. Bradley states that it bears rough handling well.

The following observations apply to an Acajutla specimen, which has not been found in the collection with its corresponding number, but which probably belongs to the same species with that described above.

"Base broad, 1 inch in diameter; body stout, with lines of small light drab pustules running down from the small tentaculiform lobes on the edge of the disk; disk 1·5 inches broad, dark brown, with whitish stripes radiating from the small yellowish red mouth; tentacles moderately stout, in three rows (16 : 48 : 48), outer two rows ·05 inch from edge of disk, inner ones ·06 farther inward, base light drab, tips dark red, sometimes marked near the tips with small white spots on the inner side,"—F. H. B.

A species somewhat resembling this in general appearance, as preserved in alcohol, but evidently distinct, is in the collection from the Pearl Islands. This has very exsert, adhesive suckers, with concave tops, on the middle of the body, but becoming smaller and sessile above and below. Sub-marginal tubercles small and simple. Tentacles long and slender, in moderate number. In contraction the body is oval, 1·5 inches long; 1 in diameter. It may be a *Bunodes*.

Phymactis Edw. and Haime.

Actinia (*pars*) Drayton, op. cit., p. 125, 1848.
Phymactis Edw. and H., Corall., i, p. 274, 1857.

Column rather low and broad, covered with prominent verrucæ.

Margin surrounded by a circle of bright colored spherules, or eye-tubercles. Tentacles rather large and numerous. Mouth large and prominent with many lateral folds.

Phymactis clematis Edwards and H., op. cit., p. 275.

Actinia clematis Drayton, op. cit., p. 130, Pl. I, fig. 4 and 5, 1846.

Column low, usually much broader than high, base and disk broader; the disk broadest, dilated, and thrown into four or five lobes or folds by the undulations of the margin. Pustules or verrucæ of the walls large, numerous, crowded. Marginal tubercles or spherules large, rounded, 1·5 lines broad, yellow or red. Naked portion of disk less than half the whole diameter. Tentacles short and numerous, rather stout, in about five series.

Color quite variable; "in one variety the body with the disk and tentacles, is of a deep rich green color; the centre of the disk a little paler, the marginal tubercles a bright yellow, and the under part of the foot yellow. In another the body is a deep crimson, with the tubercles of the lateral surface deep green, and the marginal tubercles vermilion; the tentacles dark lake, and the central part of the disk a paler lake; under surface of the base a bright orange, approaching vermilion,"—J. Drayton.

Diameter at middle 2·5 inches; diameter of disk 4; height of column about 2; length of tentacles ·5 to ·75.

Valparaiso, Chili,—U. S. Expl. Exp.

In the work of Edwards and Haime the locality is erroneously given as "Côtes du Brésil."

Phymactis florida Edw. and H., op. cit., p. 274.

Actinia florida Drayton, op. cit., p. 131, Pl. 2, fig. 6, 7, 8.

Column low, about as broad as high, somewhat dilated at base and summit; margin of base undulate, of disk somewhat plicate, usually in five folds; surface crowdedly covered with verrucæ. Tentacles "short, about ·5 inch, nearly equal, subulate, stout, crowded, in 5 imperfect series." Disk strongly radiated, the tentacles occupying a breadth of ·5 to ·75 of an inch.

Color variable; "one variety has a royal smalt-color, with the papillæ of the surface a fine ultramarine, the disk a paler blue, and the marginal tubercles pearly white. Another is verdigris-green, with the papillæ of the same color, and the marginal tubercles yellow. Another apparently of the same color, though a little higher (near 3 inches), has the papillæ of the lateral surface of a sap-green color on a reddish ground, with the tentacles a dull purple, the disk between the tentacles and the mouth light grayish green, the mouth flesh-color, and the under surface of the base scarlet,"—J. Drayton.

Height 2 to 2·5 inches; diameter at middle 2·25; diameter of disk 3. San Lorenzo I., off Callao, Peru,—U. S. Expl. Exp.

This species may, quite possibly, prove to be only a variation of the preceding one, depending on locality, state of expansion, etc. It appears to differ principally in having shorter and more numerous tentacles and a less dilated disk.

Subfamily, SAGARTINÆ Verrill.

Actinines perforées (section) Edw. and Haime, Corall., i, p. 278, 1857.
Sagartiadæ (family) Gosse, 1858; Actinologia Britannica, p. 9, 1860.
Sagartidæ (subfamily) Verrill, Mem. Boston Soc. Nat. History, i, p, 21, 1864.
Sagartinæ (subfamily) V., Proc. Essex Inst., vol. v, p. 322, 1868; ditto, vol. vi, 1869.

Column very changeable in form, usually capable of great extension into long, cylindrical, or pillar-like forms, or of contracting into a low, flattened, conical shape. Surface in full expansion mostly smooth, not verrucose, often with retractile suckers, which are not conspicuous except while in use; in contraction the surface is usually covered with close transverse or reticulate wrinkles. Walls perforated by special openings (*cinclidæ*) through which thread-like, stinging organs (*acontia*) are ejected when the animal is irritated, sometimes in great profusion, in other cases very sparingly and reluctantly. Margin simple or nearly so, usually without special appendages (*Nemactis* is an exception). Tentacles usually numerous, generally slender and elongated, highly contractile.

Species can usually be recognized as members of this subfamily by the smooth, thin walls, usually showing the internal lamellæ, and by their perforations and the existence of acontia. But the latter characters are frequently overlooked, even in living specimens, and are generally difficult to detect in specimens contracted in alcohol, except in a few genera where the borders of the pores are raised (*Adamsia*). Most of the species referred by Edwards and Haime to *Paractis*, and described as lacking perforations and all appendages of the walls, are really *Sagartians* in which the perforations have been formerly overlooked. Therefore I have here referred several similar species of simple Actinians to this group, although the lateral pores and acontia have not actually been observed.

Metridium Oken.

Actinia (*pars*) Linnæus, Lamark, Cuvier, Dana, etc.
Metridium Oken, Lehrbuch der Naturg., iii, p. 349, 1815, (*non Metridium* Ehrenberg, Dana, Gosse, etc., = *Oulactis*).
Actinoloba (*p rs*) Blainville, Dict. des Sci. Nat., 1830; ditto, Manuel d'Actinologie, p. 322, 1834; Gosse, Actinologia Brit., p. 11, 1860.
Cribrina (*pars*) Ehrenberg, op. cit., p. 40, 1834.
Metridium Edw. and H., Corall., i, p. 252, 1857; Verrill, Mem. Boston Soc. Nat. Hist., i, p. 21, 1864.

Column very changeable, in full expansion usually tall, pillar-like, expanding toward the disk, or lower and nearly as broad as high; in contraction forming a low cone; surface nearly smooth, with abundant mucus; integument firm, thickened when old, forming at some distance below the margin a thick smooth fold, above which the wall is thinner and translucent. Disk broad, frilled, or thrown into lobes or broad undulated folds, toward the margin. Tentacles very numerous, the inner ones larger, more or less scattered on the disk, the outer ones becoming gradually smaller and more crowded, those at the margin very small and crowded. Walls perforated by scattered openings, not very apparent except when fully expanded. Acontia abundant, but not often emitted except when greatly irritated.

Metridium fimbriatum Verrill.

Proceedings Essex Inst., vol. iv, p. 151, 1865.

Base broadly expanded. Column very changeable, either low and broad, or greatly elongated, the fold or "parapet" nearly an inch below the margin. Tentacles very numerous, encroaching so much upon the disk as to leave only a narrow central area around the mouth, short, very slender, filiform, pointed. Edge of disk thrown into numerous deep frills.

Color of column variable; often translucent pale orange, punctate with dark brown; or light umber-brown; tentacles a lighter tint of the same, white within; mouth deep orange, or light yellowish brown, surrounded by a broad band or halo of purplish.

Harbor of San Francisco, Cal., adhering to the bottom of floating piles, etc., Oct., 1855,—Dr. Wm. Stimpson; Puget Sound,—Dr. C. B. Kennerly.

This species is closely allied to *M. marginatum* of the New England Coast, and *M. dianthus* of Europe. From the former it appears to differ chiefly in having longer and more slender tentacles, with the "parapet" farther from the margin of the disk.

It is possible that the three will eventually be found to belong to one very variable and widely diffused species, but until direct and careful comparisons of numerous living specimens of each can be made, this question cannot be positively settled.

Metridium reticulatum Edw. and Haime, op. cit., p. 255.

Actinia reticulata Couthouy, in Dana, Zoöph., p. 144, Pl. 4, fig. 31, 1846.
Actinoloba reticulata Gosse, Actin. Brit., p. 24, 1860.

"Exterior smooth and reticulately corrugate, subcylindrical, 1·5 inches high, 2·5 thick, with the disk very much dilated (3·5 broad), and margin somewhat five-lobed, not tuberculate; tentacles very numerous, quite short (3 lines), not turgid and covering the greater part of the disk, the inner a little the largest; mouth somewhat prominent, 6 to 8 lines long."

The column is "covered with a sort of raised network, produced by the corrugations of the external envelope." The disk "is broadly dilated, and the five lobes, or folds, are never effaced so as to leave the disk circular." Tentacles "short, subulate, and disposed in 9 or 10, close, alternate series, the inner ones longest, decreasing to marginal ones, which are mere papillæ."

Column "fulvous orange, sometimes olive-brown, with an indistinct zone of black surrounding the superior margin; tentacles olivaceous; disk between tentacles and mouth bright ochreous, with strong radiating lines, crossed by others of a pale olive-green; mouth velvet purplish-black."

"This Actinia is remarkable for the opacity of all its parts; the colors are all soft and rich, but even in the young they lack that transparency usually met with in these zoöphytes."

Orange Harbor, Terra del Fuego, attached to stones and shells,—J. P. Couthouy, U. S. Expl. Exp.

The specimens of this species preserved in alcohol strongly resemble those of *M. marginatum* and other species of this genus, to which we believe it really belongs, notwithstanding the wrinkled epidermal (or mucous) layer, an appearance which may have been due, in part at least, to imperfect expansion of the column.

The following species, of which the genus is not determinable from the description, may belong here.

(?) **Actinia Mertensii** Brandt, Prod. descr. anim., p. 13, 1835; Edw. and Haime, Corall., i, p. 289.

"Body brown, mingled with black. Tentacles moderate, white. Disk pale brown, with white lines." Coast of Chili,—Mertens.

Cereus Oken.

Cereus Oken, Lehrbuch der Naturg., iii, p. 349, 1815, (type, *C. bellis*).
Actinocereus Blainv., Dict. Sci. Nat., lx, p. 194, 1830.
Cribrina (*pars*) Ehr., Corall., rothen Meeres, p. 40, 1834.
Sagartia (*pars*) Gosse, Trans. Linn. Soc., xxi, p. 274, 1855; (*Scyphyia*) Actinologia Brit., p. 25, (123), 1860.
Cereus (*pars*) Edw. and Haime, Corall., i, p. 263, (269), 1857.
Cereus Verrill, Bulletin Mus. Comp. Zoöl., p. 58, 1864; Mem. Boston Soc. Nat. Hist., p. 24, 1864.

Column very changeable in form, capable of becoming tall, pillar-like, or contracting to a low, depressed cone; no submarginal fold; upper part with small, inconspicuous, contractile suckers; walls nearly smooth, pierced by scattered, inconspicuous pores or cinclidæ. Disk broadly expanded, wider than the column, sometimes undulated at the margin. Tentacles numerous, more or less scattered on the disk, usually rather stout, the inner ones considerably largest; the outer ones quite small. Type, *C. bellis*.

Oken, in constituting this genus, stated that the walls are perforated, and named *C. bellis* as a typical species, therefore it seems not only proper, but necessary, to restrict the name to the group which contains that species. Edwards and Haime have erroneously extended the genus so as to include all the imperforate, verrucose species, belonging to *Urticina* and *Bunodes*, as well as *C. bellis* and allied species.

Cereus Fuegiensis Verrill.

Actinia Fuegiensis Couthouy, op. cit., p. 145, Pl. 4, fig. 32, 1846.
Discosoma? Fuegiensis Edw. and Haime, Corall., i, 257, Pl. C2, fig. 2, (from Dana. Zoöph.), 1857.
Sagartia Fuegiensis Gosse, Actin. Brit., p. 38, 1860.

"Subcylindrical, 2 inches in diameter, exterior smooth, upper and lower extremities sparingly dilated, margin of base slightly undulate; tentacles throughout remotely scattered, turgid, 3 lines long; mouth small, circular, 5-cleft; form of animal when contracted very much depressed, convex."

The tentacles are scattered over a large part of the disk, about 1 to 1·5 lines apart, nearly in five series, and have "the form of a grain of wheat." The inner ones are considerably largest.

Disk bright orange; column darker orange, with transverse parallel lines or markings of dark brown; tentacles grass-green; mouth pale orange.

Orange Harbor, Terra del Fuego, on rocks,—J. P. Couthouy, U. S. Expl. Exp.

This species is referred to *Cereus* mainly on account of its general resemblance to *C. bellis*, but as neither lateral pores nor acontia have been observed, it may belong properly in some other genus.

The original specimens I have not been able to find in the Smithsonian collections.

Calliactis Verrill, gen. nov.

Adamsia (pars) Edw. and H., Corall., i, p. 278, 1857, (*non* Forbes).

Column very changeable in form, in full expansion elevated, sub-cylindrical, with a broadly expanded base, in contraction forming a broad, low, flattened cone, or convex disk. Surface nearly smooth in expansion, except near the base, where there are one or more transverse rows of conspicuous lateral pores or cinclidæ, which have thickened, permanently raised borders. Basal margin, below the pores, thin and expanded, usually with additional internal lamellæ intercalated between the larger ones that extend to the disk, all of which are usually visible through the thin but firm walls. Tentacles numerous, slender, subulate, highly contractile. Acontia highly developed, emitted freely from the cinclidæ. Type, *C. decorata* (*Actinia decorata* Drayton).

This genus appears to be abundant in the tropical seas, the species generally living upon univalve shells inhabited by hermit crabs. The colors are usually brilliant and varied. It is allied to *Adamsia*, which has similar basal cinclidæ, but the latter has a low growth, spreading to a great extent laterally, and the tentacles are short and imperfectly retractile, while the base has the power of forming a tough pelicle to extend the aperture of the shell; its base also extends around the aperture in two broad lateral lobes, which unite where they come in contact, giving the body an annular form. To this genus belong several undescribed species from the Pacific Islands, with the following, and perhaps other, described species.

C. decorata (Drayton sp.), Pl. 3, fig. 24. Houden I., in lagoon.
C. tricolor (Lesueur sp.). West Indies.
C. bicolor (Les. sp.). West Indies.
C. Egletes (*Adamsia Egletes* D. and M.), Supl., Pl. vi, fig. 17. St. Thomas, W. I.
C. fusca (Quoy and Gaim., Astrolabe, p. 145, Pl. 11, fig. 8 and 9). Amboinia.
C. ? polypus (Forskal sp.). Red Sea.

Calliactis variegata Verrill, sp. nov.

Base broadly expanded, adhering to shells, the edge thin and spreading. Column broad, moderately elevated in expansion, when contracted forming a low cone, usually rounded at summit. Surface in alcoholic specimens closely wrinkled transversely and minutely corrugated on the upper parts, or sometimes cancellated, or covered with reticulated wrinkles with elevated interspaces, smoother near the edge of base, where it is radiated with conspicuous dark lines of unequal length, corresponding to internal chambers, and alternating with narrower light lines, corresponding to the lamellæ; the edge crenulated. Cinclidæ at about ·25 or ·30 inch from the edge of the base, forming a circle of about 24, rather distant, conspicuous, perforated verrucæ, often with another more or less complete circle a short distance below, in which the cinclidæ correspond in position with the upper ones, but appear to be smaller. Acontia pink, long, and fine, protruded freely both from the mouth and cinclidæ. Tentacles slender, of moderate length, " arranged in four series (24–24–96).''

Column "marked at base with light purplish brown spaces, separated by 97 olive-brown lines, extending ·25 to ·50 inch from edge of base; above these a row of 24 white perforated spots" (cinclidæ); rest of column "mainly olive-brown, striped with six longitudinal bands of dark pink, which are sometimes divided so as to form six pairs of bands. Mouth small, when open pinkish yellow, surrounded by a white space marked with dark radiating lines; followed by a circle of dark brown, marked with 12 narrow white rays; then follows a circle of dark brown, marked with 24, minute, white spots; then a narrow space with 12, nearly equal, alternating dark and white bands, opposite to which the tentacles are mainly of corresponding tint; sometimes all the tentacles have white tips, the rest light brown; sometimes all are surrounded with alternating dark and light bands.

The largest specimens are about 2 inches broad.

Panama Bay, dredged in 2 to 6 fathoms, attached to large shells occupied by hermit-crabs,—F. H. Bradley.

This species is closely allied to *C. decorata* Drayton, sp., with which it agrees, to a considerable extent, in its pattern of coloration.

Sagartia Gosse.

Cribrina (*pars*) Ehr , Corall., rothen Meeres, p. 40, 1834.
Sagartia (*pars*) Gosse, Trans. Linn. Soc , xxi, p. 274, 1855; Actin. Brit., p. 25 and 122, 1860.
Paractis (*pars*) Edw. and Haime, Corall., i, p. 248, 1857.

Column very changeable in form, usually elevated and pillar-like in full expansion. Base and disk only moderately enlarged. Walls smooth or nearly so, often with small retractile suckers on the upper part. Cinclidæ not elevated, inconspicuous when closed, scattered over the surface. Acontia usually abundant. Tentacles rather numerous, near the margin, long and slender; one in the line with the longer diameter of the mouth is often capable of great elongation.

It seems necessary to restrict this genus to the group considered typical by Gosse,* with which the "rather less typical group," to which he gives the subgeneric name, *Thoe*, and some other forms, may also be united.

Sagartia impatiens Gosse.

Actinia impatiens (Couthouy MS.) Drayton, op. cit., p. 135, Pl. 3, fig. 13, 1846.
Paractis impatiens Edw. and H., Corall., i, p. 248, 1857.
Sagartia impatiens Gosse, Actin. Brit., p. 38, 1860.

Column "nearly cylindrical, 1 to 1·5 inches in diameter and height, sometimes very much elongated and writhing. Sides smooth, but somewhat corrugate-striate, and above, color delicately tessellated. Base sparingly dilated. Tentacles subequal, an inch long, stout, subulate, in 2 series. Mouth prominent, with 8 lobes within.

The body has nearly a flesh-color, except near the summit, where it is finely chequered with green; the tentacles and disk are deep crimson; the mouth has a small opening and a pale yellow color."

Orange Harbor, Terra del Fuego, in tide-pools among the crevices of rocks,—U. S. Expl. Exp.

Sagartia lineolata Verrill.

Actinia lineolata (Couthouy MS.) Drayton, op. cit. p. 137, Pl. 3, fig 22, 1846.
Paractis lineolata Edw. and H., Corall., i, p. 248, 1857.

Column, as observed in imperfect expansion, forming a low, depressed, rounded cone, in contraction nearly flat; sides smooth, vertically lined with brown. Tentacles 24, in 2 series, 6 to 8 lines long, rather stout. Disk small, radiated with whitish lines. Mouth small, not prominent, circular, retaining its circular form even in contraction; its margin with convex folds corresponding with the tentacles.

Column pale ochre, on which are disposed a number of longitudinal lines of an amber-color, arranged regularly, "a broader one alternating with two narrower, so as to leave between each of the broader lines three ochreous ones of the same width." Near the base the colors are fainter, giving the appearance of an indistinct zone. Tentacles pale flesh-color. Disk purplish brown, with flesh-colored lines extending from the base of the tentacles nearly to the centre. Diameter from ·5 to 1·5 inches, rarely more than ·5.

Forge Cove, near Orange Harbor, Terra del Fuego, on small stones just below low-water mark,—J. P. Couthouy, U. S. Expl. Exp.

---

* Actinologia Britannica, p. 122.

This species is said to be very active, frequently changing its position, and keeping its tentacles actively in motion. The young were observed in several instances to be ejected from the mouth.

Sagartia crispata Verrill, sp. nov.

Actinia crispata Bradley, MS.

Base broadly expanded. Column, as observed, in expansion subcylindrical and rather low, but little higher than broad. Edge of disk deeply undulated or frilled. Tentacles numerous, very small, in about two rows, close to the edge, the outer row smallest. Acontia numerous and fine, emitted freely. Column light brown above, below marked with dark olive-brown lines and numerous white blotches on a light brown ground-color; inner tentacles dark brown, tipped with yellow, brown, and white; outer row light brown, with white tips. Diameter of base 1 inch; of column ·5; height of column 1 inch.

Panama Bay, dredged in 4 to 6 fathoms, on a large murex (*Phyllonotus*),—F. H. Bradley.

Sagartia carcinophila Verrill, sp. nov.

Base expanded; column elongated, pillar-like, or subcylindrical, in full expansion; capable of contracting to a slightly convex disk. Tentacles in two or three rows at the edge of disk (not seen in full expansion), rather short and blunt.

Column "olive-brown, marked with 24 white longitudinal lines, alternating at the base with a pair of short white lines in each interspace; tentacles same color with the body, but slightly lighter, marked near the tip with two oval spots of dark greenish brown."

Diameter ·5 of an inch; height about 1 inch.

Panama Bay, dredged in 3 or 4 fathoms, adhering to the carapax of a Hepatus-like crab (*Hepatella amica* Smith),—F. H. Bradley.

Sagartia Panamensis Verrill, sp. nov.

Column very extensible, expanding to edge of disk, flesh-colored, translucent, showing the internal lamellæ. Disk rather broad, ·75 of an inch in diameter. Tentacles at the edge of the disk, marked with alternate bands of dark brown and white.

Panama, east reef, on rocks above half-tide,—F. H. Bradley.

Sagartia Bradleyi Verrill, sp. nov.

Column rather short, ·35 of an inch in diameter. Tentacles as long as the diameter of the disk, placed on its edge, in about three rows of nearly equal length; the inner row of 12, a little longer.

Column greenish brown; tentacles greenish brown, the outer ones lighter. In other specimens, supposed to be of the same species, the column is "flesh-color to olive, base of tentacles, especially outer ones, often colored white or pale yellow, occasionally with irregular, small, transverse, white or straw-colored spots on the brown tentacles."

Panama, south reef, near half-tide mark among stones,—F. H. Bradley.

The specimens in alcohol are broader than high; the tentacles obtuse, not retracted; the column with strong longitudinal sulcations.

Sagartia nivea Verrill.

<blockquote>

Actinia nivea Lesson, Voyage Coquille, p. 81, Pl. iii, fig. 8, 1832, Plates, 1826, (non S. nivea Gosse = S. Gossei Verrill).

Actinia ? nivea Edw. and H., Corall., i, p. 247, 1857.

</blockquote>

Very changeable in form, often subconical, subcylindrical, or vase-shaped, or the upper portion of the column may be withdrawn into the lower by an infolding of the walls near the summit;* surface very smooth, very soft to the touch, marked with longitudinal sulcations. Mouth small, roundish oblong, with a semicircular fold at each end. Tentacles very numerous, crowded at the margin, rather long, fine and slender. Color bluish white, often more or less mottled with light brownish.

Height 1 to 1·25 inches, in expansion; diameter ·5 to ·75; length of tentacles ·25 to ·40.

Paita, Peru, very common, found by thousands fixed upon the piles of the wharf in front of the city,—Lesson; Callao, Peru, in vast numbers, in the interstices among *Discinæ*, *Balani*, etc., adhering to the bottom of an old vessel,—F. H. Bradley.

Several thousand specimens were obtained by Mr. Bradley, and are in excellent preservation, many of them with the tentacles expanded. These appear to belong to Lesson's species, but this cannot be positively affirmed. Most of these are small, but some, even in partial contraction, are 1½ to 2 inches long; ·5 to ·75 in diameter; the tentacles ·5 of an inch long, when least contracted. The surface is smooth, or finely wrinkled transversely, the integument thin but firm, often showing the internal lamellæ. The tentacles are very numerous, crowded, long and slender. Color of column white; tentacles in alternating clusters of whitish and dull bluish, in the alcoholic specimens.

---

* I have also observed this habit in *S. modesta* V., from Long Island Sound, and in other species.

As the name, *nivea*, is preoccupied by this species, I propose for the *Sagartia nivea* Gosse, of Great Britain, the name, *Sagartia Gossei*, in honor of its discoverer.

Sagartia Lessonii Verrill.

Actinia bicolor Lesson, op. cit. p. 78, Pl. iii, fig. 3, 1832, Plates, 1826, (*non A. bicolor* Lesueur, 1817).
Actinia (?) *bicolor* Edw. and H., Corall., i, p. 246, 1857.

Column vase-shaped, higher than broad, contracted above the base and then gradually enlarging to the disk, surface smooth, mouth small, with a slightly thickened border; disk radiated. Tentacles in two series, crowded at the margin, moderately long, slender, nearly equal. Color of column snow-white; of tentacles emerald-green.

Height in expansion about 1·25; diameter of column ·75; across expanded tentacles 1·10; length of tentacles ·35 to ·40 of an inch.

Near Paita, Peru, very common,—Lesson.

This species appears to be closely allied to the preceding and may prove to be identical when reëxamined.

Sagartia (?) Peruviana Verrill.

Actinia Peruviana Lesson, op. cit., p. 75, Pl. ii, fig. 3, 1832, Plates, 1826.
Actinia ? Peruviana Edw. and H., Corall., i, p. 246, 1857.

Column sub-cylindrical, enlarging from the base to the summit; surface smooth, sulcated near the base. Disk flat, dilated, mouth large, oblong, with swollen lips. Tentacles in two series, of moderate length, subequal, round and somewhat swollen at base, attenuated toward the end, which is acute.

Color of column bright light green, the folds between the sulcations near the base brownish; mouth flesh-color; disk clear pale green, with regular, fine, radiating lines of brown; tentacles rosy white.

Height in expansion 1·75; diameter at base 1·10; at summit 1·40; length of tentacles ·60 to ·70 of an inch.

Paita, Peru, in crevices of rocks and buried in sand, common,—Lesson.

Sagartia (?) nymphæa Verrill.

Actinia nymphæa Drayton, op. cit., p. 146, Pl. 4, fig. 33, 1846.
Puractis (?) *nymphæa* Edw. and H., Corall., i, p. 252, 1857.

Column smooth, dilated above and below, margin of base crenate, sides with corresponding vertical lines. Tentacles stout, in 3 series, slender, mouth a little prominent, and a sixth of an inch long. In contraction the form is a low truncated cone. Column whitish, marked with vertical, pale ochreous lines, 1·5 lines apart; disk pale purplish; tentacles yellow.

Height ·68 of an inch; breadth of disk and base 1; length of tentacles ·16 to ·20.

Valparaiso, Chili,—U. S. Expl. Expedition.

Sagartia (?) rubus Verrill.

Actinia rubus Drayton, op. cit., p. 147, Pl. 4, fig. 34, 1846.
Paract's rubus Edw. and H., Corall., i, p. 249, 1857.

Column small, smooth, dilated above and below, base crenated, sides with interrupted vertical lines. Tentacles short, in 2 series, mouth a little prominent, about a sixth of an inch long. Color of column ash-brown, vertically marked with slate-colored, dotted lines; tentacles white; disk rich purple; mouth the same, except that the opening is whitish.

Height ·75 of an inch; diameter at base and disk 1; length of tentacles about ·20.

Valparaiso, Chili,—U. S. Expl. Exp.

This species is very near the last, if not identical, which is quite probable. The principal differences are in color and, apparently, in the number and length of the tentacles, which appear to be longer and fewer in this form.

Several other undescribed species of *Sagartia* are known to occur on different parts of the coast. One species from Panama is remarkable for the thinness and transparency of its walls when preserved in alcohol. It grows to a considerable size, some of the preserved specimens being 1·5 inches high and 1 in diameter.

Other species were collected at the Gulf of Georgia and well figured by Mr. A. Agassiz, several years ago.

Nemactis Edw. and Halme, op. cit., p. 282, 1857.

Actinia (pars) Dana, Zoöphytes, 1846.

Margin of the disk, outside of the bases of the tentacles, surrounded by a single circle of bright colored, rounded tubercles. Acontia long and slender, protruded from the mouth, and *perhaps* from lateral pores.

The authors of this genus give as one of its characters " pores situated near the border of the disk,"—a character which may possibly exist, but of which there is no proof. In Drayton's figures acontia are represented as protruding from the mouth, which, if carelessly observed, might appear to be figured as coming from the sides, but in the description of *A. primula* we find it stated that " the threads passing from its mouth are the spermatic cords, which are often protruded in a relaxed or exhausted state of the animal."

Nemactis primula Edw. and Haime loc. cit.
Actinia primula Drayton, op. cit., p. 134, Pl. 2, fig. 12 to 15, 1846.

Small, scarcely an inch high and broad, slightly dilated above and below. Tentacles short, 2 or 3 lines long, slender, arranged in 3 series. Mouth somewhat prominent, ·33 of an inch long. Column with vertical colored lines, which are often interrupted.

One variety has a flesh-colored column, with many dark orange, parallel vertical lines; tentacles white at base, tips orange; disk yellowish brown; mouth pale flesh-color; tubercles and margin of disk green. Another is pink at base, bright green above, with vertical dotted lines of carmine; disk carmine; tentacles bright yellow; marginal tubercles dull green. In another the outer tentacles are white, the rest red; disk and mouth light blue; tubercles white. A fourth variety is white, clouded with pink and green, dotted with crimson; outer tentacles white, the rest brilliant carmine; disk pale lake; marginal tubercles green.

Shores of San Lorenzo I., in tide pools,—U. S. Expl. Expedition.

Nemactis Draytonii Edw. and Haime, op. cit., p. 282.
Actinia primula (pars) Drayton, op. cit., p. 135, Pl. 2, fig. 16, 1846.

Form and general appearance as in the preceding, "with prominent green tubercles but no distinct tentacles." Column pale bluish, with vertical brown lines. Disk bluish white, with brown radii; mouth reddish.

San Lorenzo,—U. S. Expl. Expedition.

Nemactis (?) Chilensis Verrill.
Actinia Chilensis Lesson, Voyage Coquille, p. 76, Pl. 2, fig. 5, 1832.
Dysactis Chilensis Edw. and H., op. cit., p. 262, 1857.

Column, as figured, subconical, decreasing in size from the base upward, marked with vertical sulcations. Disk of moderate size, radiated. Mouth rather large, oblong. Tentacles of moderate length, slender, subulate, arranged in one row around the margin, about 50 in number. Fourteen very long, slender, filiform, snow-white organs, apparently acontia, are represented as emerging from the margin outside of the true tentacles. No marginal tubercles are figured.

Color of column light green, with vertical lines of dark green; disk pinkish with darker radii; tentacles orange, tinged with crimson.

Height nearly 1 inch; diameter 1·25; length of tentacles ·35 to ·50; of filiform organs 1·5.

Bay of Talcahuano, Province of Concepcion, Chili, in crevices of rocks where the waves break with force, at the entrance; also upon the shores of Quiriquine Island,—Lesson.

The position of this species is still uncertain. The filiform organs, represented in the figure, were regarded as an outer series of longer tentacles by Edw. and Haime. They have, however, much greater resemblance to acontia in length and slenderness, as well as in color and irregular number. The general appearance is that of a Sagartian, but as no marginal tubercles are described or figured, it may not belong to *Nemactis*, but in the state of expansion represented the tubercles might be concealed from view.

Sub-family, PHELLINÆ Verrill.

Proceedings Essex Inst., v, p. 324, 1868.

Column elongated, covered with a thickened, persistent, epidermal deposit, except that near the margin, and sometimes close to the base, the surface is naked and may be retracted within the thickened portion. Acontia very few and seldom emitted,—perhaps entirely wanting in some species.

Phellia Gosse.

Annals and Mag. Nat. Hist., ser. 3, vol. ii, p. 193, 1859; Actin. Britannica, p. 134, 1860; Verrill, Proc. Essex Inst., v, p. 325, 1868.

Column mostly covered with a persistent epidermal deposit to which particles of mud, sand, and dirt of various kinds often firmly adhere; upper portion, near the margin, naked, smooth. Margin simple, not tuberculate. Tentacles marginal, in moderate numbers, the outer ones usually considerably shortest. Acontia observed only in one or two species, few, sparingly emitted from the mouth, and from pores near the base.

Phellia inornata Verrill, sp. nov.

Base small, not dilated. Column when contracted obpyriform, when expanded obconic, the surface covered with adherent grains of sand. Disk small, wider than base. Tentacles small, arranged in one row at the margin. Color dirty white throughout.

Height ·5 inch; diameter of base ·06; of disk ·12 of an inch.

Panama and Pearl Islands, on loose shells in 4 or 5 fathoms,—F. H. Bradley.

Phellia ? rubens Verrill, sp. nov.

Column small, subcylindrical, "mostly covered with slime." Tentacles numerous, slender, in one row, "raised on a thin expansion, which forms a wall about ·12 of an inch high around the linear mouth, length equal to two-thirds the diameter of the disk.

Column dull red; tentacles bright scarlet. Height ·50 to ·75; diameter ·25 of an inch.

Zorritos, Peru, attached to a Chama in 4 fathoms,—F. H. Bradley.

The specimens of this species have not been found in the collection and its generic characters are doubtful.

Phellia Panamensis Verrill, sp. nov.

A large species, with the column much elongated, subcylindrical, or enlarging upward, capable of great extension or of contracting into the form of a tall cone by involving the summit; surface entirely covered, except on a narrow band below the margin, with a thick and firm mud-colored epidermis, which is thrown into fine, close, irregular wrinkles, the intervening spaces appearing like small, irregular papillæ. Naked space below the margin smoothish in full expansion, more or less corrugated and with papilliform wrinkles in partial contraction. Tentacles about 96 in number, the 12 inner ones large and stout, much larger than the others, which decrease gradually in size to the outer ones, which are quite small and crowded at the margin. In dissecting a large specimen, it was found that the 12 septa corresponding to the 12 large inner tentacles, are much larger than the others, with the inner edges strongly thickened and muscular, and bear the large convoluted ovaries throughout nearly their whole length, while the intervening small septa are very narrow, not thickened, and bear no sexual organs. Color in life unknown. In alcohol the column is mud-colored, except near the margin, where it is white. Height of the largest specimen, partly contracted in alcohol, 3 inches; diameter 1. Another specimen is 3 inches high and ·5 in diameter.

Panama,—F. H. Bradley.

This large and fine species is known only from alcoholic specimens, most of which have the disk and tentacles expanded.

Phellia arctica Verrill.

Proc. Essex Inst., vol. v, p. 328, 1868.

Arctic Ocean, north of Behring's Straits, in 30 fathoms,—North Pacific Expl. Expedition.

This species grows to a pretty large size, and is remarkable for having, in the only specimen seen, peculiar ova-like bodies imbedded in the surface of the column.

Subfamily, ACTININÆ Verrill.

Actiniadæ (family) Gosse, Annals and Mag. Nat. Hist, vol. i, p. 416, 1858.
Actiniadæ and *Antheadæ* (families) Gosse, Actin. Brit., p. 171 and 148, 1860.
Actininæ and *Antheinæ* (subfamilies) Verrill, Proc. Essex Inst., v, p. 321 and 322, 1868.

Column smooth, or nearly so, sometimes sulcated vertically. Wall imperforate and destitute of verrucæ and suckers. No acontia. Margin with or without colored tubercles. Tentacles usually numerous, long, mostly contractile, sometimes non-retractile.

The existence of numerous forms combining the characters of *Actinia* and *Anthea* (*Anemonia*) appears to require the union of these seemingly very diverse genera into one subfamily.

Owing to the difficulty in ascertaining the existence of acontia and lateral pores in preserved specimens, some species referred to the *Sagartinæ* may belong here, while some of the species referred here may belong to *Sagartia*.

Paractis Edw. and Haime, op. cit., p. 248, (restricted).

Column smooth, imperforate. Tentacles retractile; no marginal tubercles.

This genus was established for numerous species supposed to have these characters, but as most of them were known only by figures and descriptions, many species were wrongly placed in it. Thus of 19 species referred to the genus, some of them doubtfully however, by Edwards and Haime, at least 12 appear to be Sagartians, and most of the others are of doubtful affinities.

Whether a genus having the characters assigned to this really exists, may, therefore, be reasonably doubted. But as species occur which apparently agree with the diagnosis and cannot well be referred elsewhere, it may be best to place them provisionally in this genus, until better known.

Paractis (?) nobilis Verrill, sp. nov.

Column changeable in form, subcylindrical or somewhat elongated and pillar-like in expansion, capable of contracting to the form of a low cone. Surface, in preserved specimens, smoothish in expansion, when partly contracted the lower part of the column is covered with close, deep, transverse wrinkles, becoming more irregular and reticulated above, the upper part with about 48 vertical raised folds or wrinkles, which by contraction are bent in a zigzag manner. Margin with a distinct fold, crenated by the vertical folds. Tentacles of moderate size, about 48 in number.

Height about 1 inch, when partially contracted in alcohol; diameter ·5 to 1 inch.

Panama,—F. H. Bradley.

The following description, which is unaccompanied by numbered specimens, probably refers to this species. "Body large, 1·5 inches in diameter; the column fluted, with 48 vertical sulcations, corresponding to lobes of the base and disk. Base 2 inches in diameter. Disk broad, with wrinkled flutings corresponding with the tentacles; mouth small. Tentacles 48, in two series of 24 each, slender, 1·5 inches long. Color of column red; tentacles olive-brown, with a light streak up the inner side; mouth surrounded by 24 rays of alternating greenish and reddish brown, running to the tentacles. Grows to a large size. Specimens were seen 3 inches across the disk, others were reported as large as 5 inches."

Panama, on northeast reef, at three-quarters tide,—F. H. Bradley.

Epiactis Verrill, gen. nov.

Integument firm. Column subcylindrical, capable of involving the summit and contracting into a hemispherical form, with a distinct sub-marginal fold or "parapet," separated from the tentacles by a narrow fosse; surface smoothish, in contraction reticulately wrinkled. Near the base it is surrounded by a circular wrinkle or depression, upon which there are borne a variable number of young, of various sizes, appearing as if originating from surface buds, but possibly produced from ova attached in this place to the skin. These young may be removed without rupture of the integument, although they adhere quite firmly and leave a depression in the surface of the skin, but there are no apparent lateral openings in the wall. Tentacles numerous, about 50, in preserved specimens short and thick, arranged in several rows.

Epiactis prolifera Verrill, sp. nov.

Base dilated, crenulate. Column in contraction hemispherical or subconical, broader than high; surface with fine reticulated wrinkles above, near the base transversely wrinkled, the uppermost of these wrinkles more marked and bearing, in all except very small specimens, a circle of young of various sizes, which vary in number from very few up to 30 or 40. When most numerous they are closely crowded, somewhat in two rows. Parapet well marked, its edge rises into slight ridges between vertical wrinkles. Tentacles in alcoholic specimens short, stout, obtusely rounded at the end, about 50 in number in the larger specimens, and apparently arranged in several rows and somewhat scattered on the disk. Color of column, in alcohol, yellowish brown; the lateral buds or young, white.

Height of the largest specimens, in contraction, ·4 inch; diameter of base ·5; length of tentacles ·1; diameter of lateral buds or young ·01 to ·08 of an inch.

Puget Sound,—Dr. C. B. Kennerly.

The young borne upon the sides give this Actinian a very singular appearance, and are very remarkable, since nothing of the kind has, apparently, been previously observed. Whether they should be regarded as buds, or as ova temporarily attached and developed in this position, I am unable to determine from the preserved specimens, but in either case they appear to remain attached for a considerable time and probably derive nutriment from the parent. The smallest observed have already 6 small tentacles and a slightly prominent mouth; the greater number have 12 tentacles and a small protuberant mouth; the largest ones are nearly all entirely contracted, but appear to have 24 tentacles, and show the internal radiating lamellæ through the walls. In contraction these young are nearly hemispherical. Specimens less than ·25 of an inch in diameter have no young upon the sides.

Anactis picta Ehr., Corall. rothen Meeres, p. 45, 1834.

Actinia picta Lesson, op. cit., p. 80, Pl. 3, fig. 6, 1830.

Column depressed, as broad as high; surface smooth, green, showing close vertical lines of darker green; a well marked fold or "parapet" at some distance from the tentacles, the intervening space, in the figure, appearing like a part of the disk. "Tentacles short, reddish brown; upon the flat buccal disk is a reddish zone, covered with ovals of orpiment-yellow, placed side by side, and touching by their base, or only separated on the sides by a small reddish brown ray."

The figure shows the appearance when not fully expanded. The buccal disk is contracted and apparently concealed by the partially retracted tentacles; outside of the tentacles (?) there is a broad flat area, bordered outwardly by the rounded parapet, and having a light orange ground-color, with 18 radiating bands of light blue, increasing in width outwardly, each one bordered on both sides by a row of small black spots, and with a circle of similar small spots connecting them together at the outer ends, just within the parapet.

Diameter about 1 inch; height a little less.

Paita, Peru, not common,—Lesson.

The true characters and the position of this species are very doubtful. It may belong to the *Sagartinæ*, near *Nemactis Draytonii*, or it may be allied to *Asteractis*, the figure and description not being accurate enough to determine. The name, *Anactis*, was given under the impression that it has no tentacles, and in fact it is not certain whether the lines in the central part of the figure are intended to represent tentacles or lines on the disk.

Sub-order, ZOANTHACEA Verrill.

Proceedings Essex Inst., vol. iv, p. 147, 1865; ditto, vol. v, p. 316, 1868.

Polyps mostly compound, increasing by budding, permanently attached by the base, which is generally small, and by stolon-like or membranous expansions from which the buds arise, in compound species. Walls but slightly muscular, the summit capable of involution with the tentacles.

In all the species of this suborder, which have been dissected, peculiar flattened organs, having a curved or crescent-shaped form and a transversely striated surface, are found attached to the principal radiating lamellæ, near the base of the stomach. These were first described and figured by Lesueur, who called them "arenated organs" and supposed them to have the functions of a liver. Dana described them more fully and supposed that they might be branchial organs. The latter view seems most probable, when we consider the character of the outer integument in these animals, which is always thick and firm and often indurated by adhering grains of sand, thus preventing it from acting as an effectual organ of respiration, as it does in most *Actinidæ*. Nor is this want supplied by large tentacles, or by branching tentaculiform organs seen in many *Actinians*. Therefore there appears to be a necessity for some special branchial organs, but careful examinations of living or fresh specimens can alone determine positively whether the "arenated organs" are of this nature.

This group appears to include three families: *Zoanthidæ*, in which the buds arise from basal stolons or membranes; *Bergidæ*, in which the stolons arise from the sides above the base; and *Orinidæ*, which remain simple and have tubular openings upon the disk, through which thread-like organs (acontia?) are said to be emitted. Perhaps the simple forms referred to *Isaura* or *Hughea* may be admitted as a fourth family when more fully studied, but at present no sufficient characters can be given, since all *Zoanthidæ* must, at first, be simple.

The genus *Sphenopus*, referred to this group by Gray, is a free form and appears to be more closely allied to *Edwardsia*.

Family, ZOANTHIDÆ Dana.

Zoanthina (family) Ehr., Corall., des rothen Meeres. p. 45. 1834.
Zoanthinæ (subfamily) Edw. and H., Corall., i, p. 298, 1857; (*pars*) Duch. and Mich., op. cit., p. 49, 1860.
Zoanthidæ (family) Dana. Zoöph., p. 417, 1846; Gosse, Actin. Brit., p. 295, 1860; Verrill, Mem. Boston Soc. Nat. Hist., i, p. 34; Proc. Essex Inst., v, p. 316, 1868.

Polyps attached by the base, usually compound, the buds arising either from basal stolons or broad expansions. Integument either smooth and naked, or thickened with imbedded and firmly adherent grains of sand.

In the number and arrangement of the internal lamellæ and tentacles, this family, and perhaps, also, the entire suborder, departs from the ordinary rule among *Actinaria* and *Madreporaria*. The tentacles seldom appear to present regular cycles in multiples of six. They are ordinarily arranged in two alternating circles, each having the same number, which is often an odd number, the entire number being, therefore, an even number, and the new tentacles appear to be introduced in pairs at one side and symmetrically to a median plane passing through the odd tentacles and the longer axis of the mouth and stomach.

Mammillifera Lesueur.

Journal Phil. Academy, vol. i, p. 178, 1817; Ehr., op. cit., p. 36; Duch. and Mich., Corall., des Antilles p. 51, 1860.
Palythoa (*pars*) Dana, Zoöph., p. 422, 1846; Edw. and Haime, Corall., i, p. 301, 1857.

Compound, increasing by buds that arise from broad, membranous, basal expansions, which at times may become in some parts narrow and more or less linear, covering broad surfaces of stones, etc. Polyps rather low, subcylindrical, or subcampanulate with a narrow base, in contraction forming rounded verrucæ, or low mammiform prominences. Tissues throughout fleshy and smooth, covered with mucus, but not agglutinating sand.

By the smooth soft tissue of the polyps and basal membranes, this genus is more nearly allied to typical *Zoanthus*, than to *Palythoa* (*Corticifera*), which has its integuments thickened by a layer of sand. From *Zoanthus* it differs mainly in having smaller, shorter, or more sessile polyps, and in the tendency to form continuous basal membranes, instead of linear stolons, but the latter character is not invariable even in the same species. The tentacles are usually shorter and less numerous.

Mammillifera Danæ Verrill.

Zoantha Danai LeConte, Proc. Philad. Acad. Nat. Science, v, p. 320, 1851.
Zoanthus (Mammillifera) Danæ Verrill, Proc. Boston Soc. Nat. Hist., x, p. 329, 1866.

The original description is as follows: "pallide purpurascens, tentaculis brevissimis, crassitie non longioribus, disco viridi, extrorsum purpurascente, ore parvo purpureo-marginato, tentaculis externis basi pallidis. Diam. disci ·25 unc."

"Remarkable for the shortness of the tentacula, which, when fully extended, are scarcely longer than the diameter of their base. The disk is radiately rugose, brilliant green, margined both internally and externally with purple. The root is broad, the animals closely associated, capable of extending 1·25 inches."

The specimens referred to this species form broad patches, covering the surface of rocks, the basal expansion being mostly continuous, but occasionally, in some parts, taking the form of broad irregular stolons, rarely linear for a short distance. The basal membrane and surfaces of the polyps are smooth and soft, without any adhering sand. The polyps in preserved specimens are closely arranged, but usually not so crowded as to be in contact, and vary in height from ·2 to ·5 of an inch; diameter of mature polyps is usually about ·2 of an inch. Column sub-cylindrical, with a rounded top when contracted, or low and mammiliform. Tentacles, in specimens dissected, 46 to 54 in number, in two regular rows, very short, thick, and obtuse, in the largest specimens in two alternating rows of 27 each. Inside of the bases of the inner tentacles, but alternating with them, are 27, small, oblong, tubercles, which are, therefore, opposite the outer tentacles. Disk strongly radiated.

In the interior the lamellæ are arranged bilaterally, 21 broad ones bearing the peculiar "arcuated organs" (branchiæ?) below the stomach; in the spaces between each pair of these there is usually one narrow lamella, but in two adjacent spaces on one side there are three intervening lamellæ, and in two other spaces, placed symmetrically in respect to the median plane, there are two small lamellæ. This arrangement is, therefore, nearly the same as in *M. auricula*, as figured by Lesueur.* It would appear, therefore, that the lamellæ and tentacles increase by pairs, introduced one on each side of the median plane passing through the longer axis of the mouth and stomach, as observed in *Arachnactis* by Mr. A. Agassiz.†

---

* Journal Philadelphia Academy, i. Pl. viii, fig. 3.
† Journal Boston Soc. Natural History, vol. vii, p. 525, 1863.

The branchiform organs are dark greenish, broad, short, strongly arched.

Panama,—LeConte; Pearl Islands,—F. H. Bradley.

Mammillifera nitida Verrill.

Polyps close together on a broad basal membrane, rather tall, sub-cylindrical, with a smooth soft surface; height, of preserved specimens, ·30 to ·40; diameter ·12 to ·15 of an inch. Tentacles, in the specimen dissected, 54, rather long, slender, pointed. Color, in alcohol, dark greenish.

Acajutla, San Salvador,—F. H. Bradley.

The slenderness and length of the tentacles will distinguish this species from the preceding.

Mammillifera conferta Verrill, sp. nov.

Polyps so closely crowded upon the basal membrane that they are usually in contact and pressed into polygonal forms. Column in contraction, low, rounded, mammilliform, about as broad as high. Surface smooth, showing the internal lamellæ through the walls. Tentacles, in the specimens dissected, about 54, very short, like small, rounded papillæ, arranged in two regular series. Color, in alcohol, nearly white. Height, in contraction, ·08 to ·12; diameter ·10 to ·12 of an inch.

San Salvador,—Capt. J. M. Dow; Acapulco,—A. Agassiz.

This species covers the surface of shells, etc., with its crowded polyps, which are usually so close together as to entirely conceal the basal membrane.

Epizoanthus Gray (sens. mod.). (GEMMARIA, 1st Ed.).

Gemmaria Duch. and M., Corall. des Antilles, p. 55, 1860 (*non* McCrady).
Palythoa (pars) Edw. and H., Corall., i, p. 301, 1857.
Epizoanthus and *Gemmaria* Gray, Proc. Zoöl. Soc. London, 1867, p. 237.

Polyps arising from a broad, thin, basal membrane, sometimes covering dead shells occupied by hermit-crabs. Column more or less elevated; surface indurated by a layer of firmly adherent grains of sand.

Epizoanthus elongatus Verrill. (GEMMARIA ELONGATA, 1st Ed.).

Basal membrane thin, encrusting rocks. Polyps very unequal in size and height, mostly elongated, not crowded, separated usually by distances less than the diameter of base. Column tall, sub-cylindrical, often constricted somewhat at base, transversely wrinkled, the surface covered throughout by a nearly uniform layer of small grains of sand. Tentacles, in specimens dissected, numerous, about 46, in two rows, elongated, small, slender, acute, each one having a small tubercle outside of its base.

Color, in alcohol, dark yellowish brown beneath the sandy layer, which is composed of differently colored grains. In a specimen dissected there were 42 internal lamellæ, of which 15 bore convoluted cords on the lower half.

Height of the larger polyps ·30 to ·40; diameter ·10 to ·12 of an inch.

Zorritos, Peru; and Pearl Islands,—F. H. Bradley.

Epizoanthus humilis Verrill, sp. nov. (GEMMARIA HUMILIS, 1st Ed.).

Basal membrane continuous, thin, but firm. Polyps very unequal in size, closely arranged, usually in contact at base, low, in contraction forming rounded verrucæ, which are often broader than high. Surface covered with a thin layer of fine sand, at the top of the contracted polyps showing about 12, distinct, radiating sulcations. Color light yellowish brown, when preserved in alcohol. Height of largest polyps, contracted in alcohol, ·06 to ·08; diameter ·08 to ·10 of an inch.

Panama,—F. H. Bradley.

Epizoanthus crassus Verrill. sp. nov. (GEMMARIA CRASSA, 1st Ed.).

Polyps large, elongated, subcylindrical; surface, in contraction, strongly wrinkled transversely, and covered with a thick layer of fine sand; summit with about 20 strong sulcations, which radiate from the centre of the involved summit. Integument thick and firm. Tentacles about 66, acute, moderately long, with a small papilliform tubercle, or secondary tentacle, in front of the base, and a larger, tentaculiform tubercle outside the base of each, the latter bearing sand on its outer surface.

Height of contracted polyps 1·25; diameter ·25 of an inch.

Acajutla, San Salvador,—F. H. Bradley.

The specimen dissected had a very large cavity below the stomach, with 66, narrow, radiating lamellæ, which suddenly become broad near the base, meeting at the centre and nearly filling the cavity. The ovaries were attached to the broad portion, and the parts filled with enlarged eggs rose upward into the cavity, the eggs being arranged in single series.

The marginal processes outside each of the tentacles were larger than the true tentacles, broad, laterally compressed, rounded at tips, the outer edge covered with sand; below their bases the sand grains were aggregated in masses, as if attached to small papillæ. The papillæ in front of the bases of the tentacles were nearly half as long as the tentacles and similar in form.

Sub-order, ANTIPATHACEA.

Antipathina (family) Ehr., op. cit., p. 154, 1834.
Antipathacea (tribe) Dana, Zoöph., p. 574, 1846.
Antipatharia (suborder) Edw. and H., Corall., i, p 311, 1857.
Antipathacea (suborder) Verrill, Proc. Essex Inst., iv, p. 147, 1865.

Polyps short, arising by budding from a common basal membrane, which secretes an internal horn-like axis, or support, from its internal surface, similar to the axis of *Gorgonidæ*. Tentacles few and simple, 6 to 24 in number.

This suborder appears to include but two families: *Antipathidæ* in which the polyps have 6 tentacles; and *Gerardida*, in which they have 24. The living polyps have been observed, however, in but few species, and when better known it may become necessary to establish other families.

Family, ANTIPATHIDÆ Dana, Zoöph., p. 574.

Polyps with 6 tentacles. Axis simple or variously branched; usually black, with the surface more or less spinulose, sometimes smooth, not sulcated.

Antipathes Pallas (restricted).

Elenchus Zoöphytorum, p. 205, 1766; Edw. and H, Corall., i, p. 314, 1857.

Axis much branched and subdivided; the branchlets not coalescent. Surface of the branchlets spinulose.

This genus, which is here adopted as restricted by Edwards and Haime, is not yet satisfactorily circumscribed, since generic characters derived only from the mode of growth and branching are always unsatisfactory in classifying compound Zoöphytes. It is probable that when more of the species shall have been examined in the living state, or when the microscopic structure of the preserved specimens shall have been more fully investigated, it will become necessary to remodel the genera of this family.

Antipathes Panamensis Verrill, sp. nov.

Corallum arborescently and densely branched and finely subdivided; the small branches mostly bipinnate and tripinnate. The trunk is quite stout and subdivides in an irregularly arborescent manner into many secondary branches, which divide in the same way. The resulting small branches arise in large numbers along the sides of the larger branches, at distances of ·08 to ·20 of an inch, many of them remaining small, simple or sparingly divided branchlets, but mostly subdividing in a pinnate, bipinnate, or even tripinnate manner. The final branchlets are ·08 or ·10 of an inch apart, small, slender, rather short, rarely more than ·15 long without branches, scarcely ·02 in diameter. Their surface is densely covered with small, sharp spinules, which are directed obliquely outward and toward the tips of the branchlets.

Color of the trunk and main branches dull brownish black; branchlets very dark brown.

Height 13 inches; breadth 10; diameter of trunk ·50; of main branches ·15 to ·25 of an inch.

Pearl Islands, brought from 6 to 8 fathoms by pearl divers,—F. H. Bradley.

Order MADREPORARIA Verrill, from Edw. and Haime (restricted).

Madrepora (genus) (*pars*) Linnæus; Pallas; Ellis; Esper, etc.
Polypiers lamelliferes (*pars*) Lamarck. 1816; Lamouroux, 1821.
Zoanthaires pierreux Blainville, 1830.
Actinaria (suborder) (*pars*) Dana, Zoöphytes, 1846; Gosse, Actin. Brit., 1860.
Madreporaria (*pars*) (suborder of *Zoantharia*) Edw. and Haime, Corall., vol. ii, p. 4, 1857, (includes *Milleporidæ* and other Hydroids); Verrill, Mem. Boston Soc. Nat. Hist., vol. i, p. 14, 1864, (excludes Hydroid *Tabulata*).
Actinaria (order) (*pars*) Agassiz, Contributions to Nat. Hist. U. S., vol. i, p. 151, 1857; vol. iii. p. 60, 1860, (includes both *Actinaria* and *Madreporaria*, excluding *Tabulata* and *Rugosa*).
Madreporaria (order) Verrill, Proceedings Essex Inst., vol. iv, p. 145, Feb., 1865; and vol. v, p. 18, May, 1866; A. and Mrs. E. C. Agassiz, Sea-side Studies, after May, 1865.

Polyps simple, or compound by budding and self-division, the basal region imperfectly developed and serving only for attachment; never locomotive. Tentacles and spheromeres usually in multiples of six, the tentacles simple, tubular, generally covered with stinging organs (lasso-cells), which are grouped in clusters on the surface. The lower part of the outer wall and usually the radiating walls of the internal chambers, or the connective tissue in these chambers, secrete carbonate of lime and thus form stony corals, consisting essentially of a more or less circular cell, with radiating internal septa, which correspond in number and position with the tentacles.

Suborder, MADREPORACEA Dana (restricted).

Madreporacea (tribe) (*pars*) Dana, Zoöphytes, p. 428, 1846.
Madreporaria perforata Edw. and Haime, Corall., iii, p. 89, 1857.
Madreporaria (suborder) Verrill, Mem. Bost. Soc., i, p. 14, 1864.
Madreporacea (suborder) Proc. Essex Inst., iv, p. 147, 1865; ditto, v, p. 19, 1866.

Tentacles mostly long, in limited numbers, often but 12, marginal, the disk small, the tentacles therefore concentrated near the mouth, upper part of the polyps elongated, cylindrical, much exsert above the cells when expanded, but capable of contracting into them; growth chiefly vertical. Coral porous, chiefly mural and septal; sometimes simple, but generally compound by budding, rarely by fissiparity.

Family, MADREPORIDÆ Dana.

Zoöphytes, U. S. Exploring Expedition, p. 431, 1846.
Madreporidæ (*pars*) and *Poritidæ* (*pars*) Edw. and H., Corall., iii. p. 89 and 207, 1860.

Corals always compound, increasing by budding, consisting of small, elongated, tubular corallites, which have very deep, open cells, and are united by an abundant, porous cœnenchyma. The corallites are usually of two sorts in each species: in *Montipora* differing on the opposite sides of foliaceous species; in *Madrepora* the terminal one on each branch differing from the lateral. Within the cells are six or twelve radiating septa, often rudimentary, but usually continuous. Polyps small, tubular, exsert, with twelve tentacles.

This family, as limited by Prof. Dana, appears to be a very natural one, and includes but two genera: *Madrepora* and *Montipora*. These have been widely separated by Edwards and Haime, who refer the former as a subfamily, *Madreporinæ*, to their large family *Madreporidæ*, which includes also *Eupsammidæ* and *Turbinaridæ*, both of which ought to rank as families. *Montipora* they unite with *Psammocora* into a subfamily, *Montiporinæ*, which is referred to *Poritidæ*.

But the *Poritidæ* are destitute of the abundant cœnenchyma and deep cells, characteristic of *Madrepora* and *Montipora*. The resemblance between certain species of these two genera, both in appearance and structure, is very close, the chief difference being that in *Madrepora* there is usually a terminal, or leading polyp at the end of each branch, which is not the case in *Montipora*. In each genus there are branching, foliaceous, encrusting, and massive species. The resemblance in the living polyps, as observed by Dana, is equally close.

The great genus, *Madrepora*, so abundant in species and individuals in the West Indies and on the Atlantic coast of Central America, and especially in the central Pacific, East Indies, Indian Ocean, and Red Sea, appears to be entirely wanting on the west coast of America, and the genus *Montipora*, which is abundant in the Indo-Pacific region, but entirely wanting in the Atlantic, is represented only by one species.

Montipora Blainville (emended).

Montipora and *Porites* (pars) Blainv., Dict. des sci. naturelle, t. lx, 1830; Manuel d'actinol., p. 388, 1834.
Montipora Quoy and Gaimard, Voy. Astrolabe, Zoöph., p. 247, 1833.
Manopora Dana, Zoöph., p. 489, 1846.
Alveopora (Edw. and H'ime), Polyp. foss. des terr. pal., p. 146, 1851, (non Blainville).
Montipora Edw. and H., Corall., iii, p. 267, 1860.

Corallum various in form, glomerate-massive, encrusting, foliaceous, lobate, or branching. Corallites small, scattered over the surface, either immersed, or with irregular, somewhat raised, lacerate, or spinulose borders. Cœnenchyma abundant, porous or spongy, usually echinulate at the surface, and often rising into papilliform processes, ridges, or crests between the cells; usually very different on the two surfaces. Cells small, widely separated, deep, without columella or pali. Septa little developed, either six or twelve, often trabicular, the secondary, when present, smaller than the primary ones. Polyps with twelve short tentacles.

Montipora fragosa Verrill, sp. nov.

Corallum sub-ramose or lobate, forming irregular conglomerate masses, which become elevated, and at the summit divide into small unequal, somewhat acute, very papillose branches, or into large, expanded, flat-topped lobes, which are scarcely papillose above. The papillæ on the branches and outer sides of the lobes are very slender and elongated, unequal, roughly spinulose, and directed obliquely upward. The cells are distinctly scattered among the papillæ, small (about ·02 inch), very inconspicuous, with six distinct septa. Toward the summits of the lobes the papillæ are appressed to the surface and become indistinct. On the broad summits of the nearly flat lobes there are no papillæ and the surface is nearly even, having a very open, porous, or spongy structure, with few indistinct, immersed cells. On the smaller lobes and depressed parts of the larger ones the surface rises into small rounded lobules, or large rounded varrucæ, with an openly spinulose, lacerate surface. Color of the unbleached coral brownish yellow, in some parts pinkish. Height 3·4 inches; breadth at top 4; diameter of branches ·25 to ·75; of larger lobes 1·75; length of free branches ·50 to ·80; length of longest papillæ ·10; diameter ·01 to ·02 of an inch.

"California,"—Maj. Wm. Rich. Probably from the Gulf of California.

This curious coral is known only by one specimen, which is, perhaps, in some respects abnormal. It is possible that the broad flat tops of the lobes are produced by the shallowness of the water in which it grew, or by some other disturbing cause. Therefore the structure upon the branching part, which does not rise so high, is probably more characteristic. It was collected by Maj. Rich and received with *Allopora Californica* V. and several *Gorgonidæ*. The latter are from La Paz, Gulf of California, which is very likely the locality of this species.

Family, PORITIDÆ Dana.

Dana, Zoöphytes, p. 549, 1846.
Poritidæ (*pars*) (*Poritinæ*) Edw. and Haime, Corall., III, p. 173, 1860.

Polyps elongated, crowded, secreting from their lower parts continuous and very porous corals, with shallow cells, from which in expansion the polyps are much exsert, with slender, flexible bodies and 12 to 24 tentacles, rarely more. Corallum massive, glomerate, encrusting, lobate, or branched, consisting of crowded corallites, united completely together by their very porous and often indistinct walls. Cells superficial or shallow, with porous septa, often represented only by series of small spinules or trabiculæ; transverse septa very rudimentary. Budding generally sub-marginal or interstitial.

Porites Lamarck (restricted).

Porites (*pars*) Lamarck, Hist. des anim. sans vert., t. II, p. 267, 1816; 2nd edit., ii, p. 432.
Madrepora (subgenus *Porites*) (*pars*) Ehrenberg, Corall. roth. Meeres, p. 115, 1834.
Porites Dana, Zoöphytes, p. 550, 1846; Edw. and Haime, Corall., III, p. 173, 1860.
Porites and *Neoporites* Duch. and Mich., Supl. Corall. des Antilles, 1864–6.

Corallum glomerate, lobed or dichotomously branched, very porous, with a rudimentary basal epitheca. Cells shallow, crowded, usually distinctly polygonal; walls thin and imperfect, or very porous; septa generally 12, sometimes 12 to 20, rarely 24, slightly developed, trabicular, or very porous, the edge consisting of small granules or papillæ. A circle of 5, 6 or more small papillæ, or paliform teeth, often scarcely distinct from the septal papillæ, surround a small, central papilliform columella, which is sometimes wanting or scarcely distinct. Polyps small, exsert, with twelve tentacles.

Neoporites, a subdivision of this genus proposed by Duchassaing and Michelotti does not seem to be well founded. The characters assigned appear to be of little importance and are not always constant in the same species, while intermediate species frequently occur.

It was based on the massive mode of growth and rudimentary pali, but in the following massive species the pali are well developed.

Porites Californica Verrill, sp. nov.

Corallum encrusting, glomerate, irregularly lobed, or sub-ramose; the lobes or branches coarse, short, rounded at top, often compressed, or confluent into wide irregular lobes, usually ·50 to ·75 of an inch thick. Cells rather large, mostly separated by very porous walls of moderate thickness, distinctly excavate, but not deep. Septa thin, rough, sparingly spinosely granulated on the sides. Columella rudimentary, spongy, often wanting, surrounded by a circle of five or six, small, prominent pali.

Height 3 to 5 inches; diameter 6 to 8 or more; length of lobes or branches ·5 to 1·5; thickness ·50 to ·75; diameter of polyp-cells ·04 of an inch.

Gulf of California near La Paz, living in 4 or 5 fathoms, from divers, and worn specimens common on the beach,—Capt. J. Pedersen.

Porites porosa Verrill, sp. nov.

Corallum encrusting, irregularly lobed and branched, much as in the preceding; lobes often rounded at top. Polyp-cells rather small and shallow, crowded, separated by thin, fragile, very porous, roughly spinulose and lacerate walls. Septa little developed, thin, narrow, the edge roughly spinulose or lacerate, the sides with small spinule-like granulations. Pali five to seven, slender, prominent, roughly spinulose at top. Columella small, porous, little developed, often wanting. Occasionally a larger cell with 24 septa and 12 pali occurs. Color of the unbleached coral dark yellowish brown.

Height 3 to 4 inches; diameter about the same; thickness of the lobes ·5 to 1 inch; diameter of cells ·03 to ·04 of an inch.

Gulf of California, near La Paz, with the last,—Capt. J. Pedersen.

Resembles the preceding, but is easily distinguished by the unusually porous texture, very thin walls and septa, and crowded cells.

Porites excavata Verrill, sp. nov.

Corallum encrusting, becoming thick, glomerate, massive, and forming irregular hemispheres. Texture rather light and finely porous, but firm. Polyp-cells rather large, polygonal or rounded, well defined, deep and excavate, separated by rather firm, regular, moderately thick, elevated walls, which are thickly covered with coarse, rough granules. Septa very distinct, narrow at summit, wide below, extending to the columella, varying in number from 10 to 24, commonly 15 to 18, the edge lacerate, the sides roughly granulous. Pali 5 to 12, small but prominent, roughly spinulose or granulous. Columella little developed, trabicular, frequently wanting. Color of unbleached coral dull brownish yellow.

Diameter 8 inches; height 4; diameter of cells ·05 to ·06 of an inch. Pearl Islands, 4 to 6 fathoms, by divers, two specimens,—F. H. Bradley.

The large, deep, regular cells readily distinguish this species from the others here described. There is no very closely allied Atlantic species. The increased number of septa is a very remarkable character.

Porites Panamensis Verrill.

Proceedings Boston Soc. Nat. Hist., vol. x, p. 329, 1866.

Corallum encrusting, usually forming broad, rather thin, somewhat convex, irregular, uneven masses; sometimes completely surrounding small pebbles and thus becoming sub-globular. Polyp-cells small, crowded, a little excavate, rather shallow, but very distinct, separated by rather thin, roughly granulous, porous, but firm, walls. Septa mostly 12, well developed, narrowed and somewhat thickened outwardly, the sides very thickly covered with coarse, rough, lacerate granules, the edge also rough and lacerate. Pali small and rather stout, roughly lacerately granulous. Columella small, inconspicuous, often wanting. Color of unbleached coral dark ash-brown.

Polyps when expanded exsert, with twelve equal, cylindrical, light brown tentacles, not swollen at the tips, which are white,—F. H. B.

Diameter of the larger masses 4 to 6 inches; thickness ·5 to 1·5; diameter of polyp-cells about ·03 of an inch.

Panama and Pearl Islands, in rocky pools and in patches over the bottom just below low-water mark,—F. H. Bradley.

Easily distinguished by the small cells and very rough walls and septa.

Porites nodulosa Verrill, sp. nov.

Corallum much subdivided into small, short, crowded, and frequently coalescent branches, which are rounded and usually not much longer than thick, and form low, crowded clumps. Cells moderately large, shallow, but clearly defined, separated by thin, roughly lacerate and porous walls. Septa usually twelve, roughly lacerate and spinulose, the sides covered with sharp, rough granules.

Pali 5 or 6, short and stout, roughly spinulose. Columella little developed, spongy or trabicular. Diameter of the larger clumps 3 to 4 inches; height about 2; diameter of branches mostly ·25 to ·35; diameter of polyp-cells about ·04 or ·05 of an inch.

La Paz, not uncommon on the beach, but mostly badly worn,— Capt. J. Pedersen.

Family, EUPSAMMIDÆ Edw. and Haime.

Caryophyllidæ (pars) Dana, Zoöphytes, p. 364, 1846.
Eupsammidæ (family) Edw. and Haime, Annals des Sci. Nat., ser. 3, x, p. 65, 1848.
Eupsamminæ (subfamily) Edw. and Haime, Corall., iii, p. 90, 1860.
Eupsammidæ (family) Verrill, Proc. Essex Inst., v, p. 28, 1866.

Corallum simple or compound, massive or variously branched. Compound species increase by lateral, basal, and sometimes interstitial budding; but the genera *Lobopsammia* and *Heteropsammia* by fissiparity. Most genera are without distinct cœnenchyma; but in the genera, *Astropsammia* and *Pachypsammia** the cœnenchyma is well developed and spongy. Corallites generally elongated, cylindrical, or somewhat turbinate, and usually with deep cells. Walls porous, especially near the summit, generally covered by vertical rows of granular nodules, so united as to leave irregular openings and pores between them, often producing a vermiculate structure; sometimes forming distinct costæ; sometimes nearly even and solid toward the base.

Septa well developed, lamellar, generally forming four or five cycles, those of the first largest, usually with entire edges; those of the last cycle are often more developed than those of the preceding cycle and curved toward and united to them, or united together in pairs in front of them. In some genera those of the penultimate cycle are also curved toward the preceding, and sometimes even those of the tertiary cycle are curved toward those of the secondary. Owing to these peculiarities of arrangement, the septa never radiate in a regular manner from the center, as in most other families, but usually have an elegant star-like and symmetrical arrangement. Internal transverse plates or dissepiments between the septa are either wanting or distant and imperfect, rarely well developed; in *Astropsammia* all are often at one level in the different interseptal spaces, thus completely shutting off the space below. Columella always present, usually well developed and spongy, or having a cancellate structure.

---

* *Pachypsammia valida* Verrill, from Hong Kong. Procedings Essex Institute, vol. v, p. 30, 1866. By error printed "*Pachysammia*."

Polyps elongated, when expanded exsert, rising above the coral, but capable of retracting into the cells. Tentacles as numerous as the septa, elongated. Colors of living polyps generally bright, often red or orange.

Dendrophyllia Blainville.

Caryophyllia (*pars*) Lamarck, Syst. anim. sans vert., p. 370, 1801; Hist. anim. sans vert., ii, p. 228, 1816; 2d edit.. ii. p. 344

Lithodendron (*pars*) Schweigger. Handb. der naturg.

Dendrophyllia Blainville, Dict. des sci. nat., lx, p. 320. 1830; Man. d'actinologie, 1834; Dana, Zoöphytes, p. 386; Edw. and Haime, Corallinires, iii, p. 112.

Oculina (*pars*) Ehrenberg. Coral. des rothen Meeres. p. 78. 1834.

Corallum compound, low and corymbose or cæspitose, or high and arborescently branched; budding lateral or sub-basal. Corallites rather large, cylindrical, more or less elongated. Walls subcostate near the cells, covered with rough vermiculate grains in rows, with irregular spaces between, which become more irregular and often curved or variously bent below.

Polyp-cells subcircular, deep; septa scarcely projecting above the margin, rather thin, forming four complete cycles. Columella usually pretty well developed, often convex.

Dendrophyllia surcularis Verrill.

Proceedings Boston Soc. Nat. Hist., xii, p. 393, 1869.

Corallum low, rounded above, consisting of a large number of divergent, elongated, cylindrical corallites, varying greatly in size and length, and all united together into a thick base, which, on the sides, is seen to be made up of numerous, short and thick, closely branched trunks, partially united together laterally; the buds arise from all parts of the sides, and from the common basal tissue between the corallites of the upper surface; many of the longer corallites also bud on the sides and near the summit. The largest corallites are ·6 to ·8 of an inch in diameter, and project 1 to 1·4 above the base. Walls thin, very porous, covered externally with fine, subequal, scabrous costæ. Polyp-cells subcircular, very deep and open, often nearly as deep as broad, the septa not projecting above the margin. Septa in four complete cycles, often with narrow rudimentary septa of the fifth cycle. Primary and secondary septa nearly equal, narrow, thin, the lower part perpendicular, the upper part narrowed rapidly to the edge of the cell; those of the third cycle similar but smaller; those of the fourth much narrower, except far within the cell, where they join the columella; those of the fifth very narrow and thin.

None of the septa unite together within, so far as can be seen from the surface, but those of the fourth and fifth cycles are slightly bent. Columella well developed, with a regular convex surface, composed of a fine, spongy tissue. Color of the unbleached coral nearly black.

Height 3 inches; breadth 5·25.

Pearl Islands, Bay of Panama, brought from six to eight fathoms by divers,—F. H. Bradley.

Dendrophyllia tenuilamellosa Verrill.

Cœnopsammia tenuilamellosa Edw. and Haime, Annals des Sci. Nat., vol. x, p. 110, Pl. I, fig. 11, 1848; Coralliairos, vol. iii, p. 128, 1860.

Corallum forming low, rounded, convex clumps, consisting of an aggregation of unequal cylindrical corallites, which are all united together at base in a solid mass, and sometimes partially united laterally. Polyp-cells deep, circular or nearly so, with thin margin. Septa thin, in four cycles, with rudiments of the fifth in some of the larger corallites; primaries a little broader than secondaries, but similar in form, narrowed toward the summit, nearly or quite reaching the columella below, the edge nearly entire, the sides smoothish, with lines of small granules. Septa of the third cycle very narrow; those of the fourth very thin and narrow, the edge divided into slender spinules, they curve toward and join those of the third about midway between the wall and columella; those of the fifth cycle, when present, are very small and rudimentary. Columella well developed, a little prominent, occupying about a third of the breadth of the cell, composed of convoluted and cortorted porous plates. Transverse plates between the septa few and distant. Walls thin, porous, with somewhat regular, unequal, rounded costæ, which are roughly granulous and separated by deep irregularly pitted grooves. Tissue of the basal mass very openly porous and irregularly ribbed and pitted. Color of the unbleached coral dark brown, or blackish.

Height of larger specimens 2 to 2·5 inches; diameter 2 to 5; height of larger corallites ·25 to ·50; diameter ·35 to ·40; depth ·25 to ·30.

Panama and Pearl Islands, at and just below low-water mark and in tide-pools,—F. H. Bradley; La Paz,—J. Pedersen; Acapulco,—A. Agassiz.

This is very closely allied to *D. surcularis*, but is a much smaller species. The polyp-cells appear to be never more than half as large. The septa, though about as numerous, are not so well developed.

Astropsammia Verrill.

Proceedings Boston Society of Nat. History, xii, p. 392, 1869.

Corallum massive, consisting of Astræa-like corallites, united quite to their summits by an abundant, very porous cœnenchyma. Walls scarcely distinct from the cœnenchyma, very porous. Septa in four cycles, with some members of a fifth, those of the fourth uniting to those of the third. Columella usually well developed, composed of loose, convoluted and twisted lamellæ and trabiculæ. Cells at times shallow, the interseptal spaces cut off below by thin transverse septa, which often coincide in all the chambers. Budding chiefly marginal and interstitial.

This genus is very remarkable for its abundant cœnenchyma, which is almost exceptional in the family, *Eupsammidæ*.

Astropsammia Pedersenii Verrill, loc. cit.

Corallum massive, convex above, covered with large, unequal, round cells, which scarcely rise above the surface, unequally separated by an abundant, very openly and coarsely porous cœnenchyma, which sometimes equals in thickness the diameter of the cells. Walls indistinct; septa not projecting, rather thin, in the large cells four fully developed cycles, with the rudimentary ones of the fifth in about half the systems. The primary and secondary septa are nearly equal, and with those of the third join the columella; those of the fourth cycle unite to those of the third about half way to the columella. Columella large in the adult corallites, composed mostly of coarsely convoluted lamellæ and spinose projections from the edges of the septa. Transverse septa thin and distant, often closing up the chambers near the surface.

A young specimen about one inch in diameter has sixteen cells, the largest of which are ·3 in diameter and very deep, with a rudimentary columella. One cell appears to have divided by fissiparity.

Diameter of largest specimen 3·5 inches; height 2; diameter of largest cells ·40 to ·50; of smallest ·15 to ·25; distance between cells ·15 to ·30.

La Paz, Gulf of California,—Capt. J. Pedersen.

This species was named in honor of Capt. James Pedersen, whose extensive collections, made in the Gulf of California, have contributed so much to our knowledge of the marine animals of that region, and who has discovered many new and very remarkable species.

Rhizopsammia Verrill, gen. nov.

Corallum compound, low, encrusting, extending by stolon-like expansions of the base, from which buds arise. Corallites cylindrical, or nearly so, connected by thin creeping extensions of the base, which have the same porous texture as the wall. Polyp-cells subcircular or elliptical. Septa thin, crowded, a little projecting, arranged in four or five cycles, those of the last cycle well developed, uniting to those of the preceding cycle, which rise up in the form of prominent paliform lobes, beyond which the central region of the cell is deep. Columella very porous, its surface papillose. Walls very porous, destitute of epitheca, with scarcely distinct costæ, but with series of rough granules.

This genus among Madreporacea corresponds to *Astrangia* among the Oculinacea, in its mode of growth. The paliform lobes are also peculiar.

Rhizopsammia pulchra Verrill, sp. nov.

Corallum composed of clusters of corallites irregularly grouped on the surface of a stone. Corallites united only by the thin basal expansions, mostly placed at distances about equal to their own diameters, low, but variable in height, base as broad as summit, or broader. Walls thin, very porous, subcostate, the ridges nearly equal, with two or three rows of sharp rough granules, the grooves between deep, but narrow, with small, interrupted, deep pits or pores. Polyp-cells subcircular or elliptical, deep at center. Septa well developed, in four complete cycles with some of a fifth, thin, crowded. The primaries and secondaries nearly equal, slightly projecting above the margin, rounded at top, inner edge perpendicular, roughly denticulate, the sides roughly granulous; those of the third cycle thickened outwardly, and united by spongy tissue with the adjacent ones; septa of the fourth cycle thin, bending toward and soon uniting to those of the third, which beyond the point of union rise abruptly in the form of prominent paliform lobes, beyond which the inner edge is nearly perpendicular to the columella, and rudely denticulate, the sides roughly granulous. Columella, moderately developed, papillose at surface. Color of the unbleached coral reddish.

Height of larger corallites ·15 to ·20; diameter ·15 to ·25; depth of cells ·10 to ·13 of an inch.

Pearl Islands, at extreme low-water,—F. H. Bradley.

Upon the same small stone, there were, with this species, specimens of *Ulangia Bradleyi*, *Astrangia dentata*, *A. pulchella*, and a new species of *Paracyathus*.

Balanophyllia Wood.

Descriptive Catalogue of the Zoöphytes from Crag, in Ann. and Mag. Nat. Hist. xiii, p. 11, 1844; Edw. and Haime. Ann. des sci nat., x, p. 83; Corall., iii. p. 99, 1860.

Corallum simple, usually attached by a rather broad base. Walls quite porous, costate, sometimes with an epitheca. Septa thin, in four or five cycles, those of the last cycles well developed, uniting together in pairs in front of the preceding, which are interrupted. Columella well developed, spongy, not prominent.

Some species referred by authors to this genus have a narrow base, others become free at maturity.

Balanophyllia elegans Verrill.

Bulletin of the Museum of Comp. Zoölogy. No. 3, p. 44, Jan., 1864.

Plate 10, figure 3.

Corallum low, subcylindrical, with a broad, expanded base, often somewhat enlarged toward the summit. Wall nearly compact at base, quite porous above, sometimes with an imperfect epitheca reaching above the middle, often naked, strongly costate, the costæ thick, rounded, nearly equal, roughly spinulose granulous, separated by irregular, narrow, interrupted grooves, with many deep pits and pores. Polyp-cell broad elliptical or circular, rather shallow. Septa unequally projecting, those of the two first cycles considerably elevated; four complete cycles, those of the fifth usually developed in half the systems and sometimes in all, in some large specimens a few very small septa belonging to the sixth are visible. Primary septa decidedly broader than secondary, and higher, thickened outwardly, the edge rounded, nearly reaching the columella, at the summit porous, roughly serrulate, and confluent with the adjoining septa of the fourth cycle, the sides granulous; secondaries similar, but narrower and less projecting, the inner edge more deeply divided into slender spinose teeth; those of the third cycle quite narrow, about half as broad as secondaries, not reaching the point of union of those of the later cycles, and therefore leaving an enclosed space of some size in front, the edge deeply divided into rough teeth; those composed of the inner portions of the third and fourth cycles united are broad, reaching the columella, the edge lacerately divided into rough, prominent spinules; they are united to the primaries and secondaries outwardly and curving toward each other unite in front of the tertiaries, about midway between the margin and columella; free outer portion of the septa of the fourth cycle very narrow, little prominent, interrupted by a space before the point of union of the thin curved septa of the fifth cycle. Columella rather small, oblong, papillose at surface. Color of the living polyp bright orange-red, or flame-red.

Height ·20 to ·40; diameter of larger ones ·30 to ·42; depth of cup ·10 to ·15 of an inch.

Puget Sound,—C. B. Kennerly; Mendocino and Crescent City, Cal.,—A. Agassiz; Monterey,—R. E. C. Stearns; W. H. Dall.

Mr. Stearns found this beautiful species adhering to the under side of large stones at extreme low-water mark at Monterey, and observed *Trivia Californica* living parasitically upon it, the color of the living *Trivia* agreeing very closely with the bright orange-red of the polyp.

Suborder, OCULINACEA Verrill.

Caryophyllaceæ (*pars*) and *Madreporaceæ* (*pars*) Dana, Zoöphytes.
Ocellinæ (*pars*) and *Milleporina* (*pars*) Ehrenberg, Corall. roth Meeres.

Corallum simple or compound, encrusting or branched, of firm texture with imperforate, solid walls and septa. Cells generally small, tubular. Polyps when expanded rising above the cell, or long exsert, the mouth protruding, the tentacles 10 to 48, sometimes more, elongated, the tips usually, if not always, swollen or capitate, their surface covered with small wart-like clusters of urticating cells.

In this group the compound species increase by basal and lateral budding, and there is a strong tendency to form hard, compact corals, the coenenchyma being, when present, very compact; the walls are often thickened, or the cells may be partially filled up and obliterated, as in *Oculinidæ*, some *Stylasteridæ*, etc. The transverse plates within the cells are usually few and distant, and may be entirely wanting; in some cases they are coincident in all the interseptal spaces, so as to form continuous transverse plates or septa, as in *Pocilliporidæ*. The septa of the first and second cycles, at least, have the edge entire or nearly so, often all the septa are entire. The exterior of the walls is generally more or less costate, sometimes finely granulous or spinulose, but never strongly spinose.

It is obvious that in Astræacea, as hitherto constituted, there are included two distinct types of corals, characterized especially by the peculiarities of the expanded polyps. In the division here established the polyps, so far as known, are much exsert in expansion and the tentacles are swollen at the tips, but in the typical Astræacea, such as *Astræa* (*Favia*), *Mæandrina*, *Mussa*, the polyps are not exsert and they have more numerous tentacles, which taper to the end; their corals increase by fissiparity or disk-budding, the septa are serrate or echinate, and the interseptal spaces are much subdivided by small oblique plates.

Hence I have taken the *Oculinidæ*, *Stylasteridæ*, and *Stylophoridæ*, kept distinct from the *Astræidæ* by Edwards and Haime, together with certain families of their *Astræidæ*, which possess the same type of polyps, as representatives of a distinct suborder, intermediate in many respects between Astræacea and Madreporacea, the polyps being exsert, as in the latter, the corals compact and imperforate, as in the former. To this suborder it seems necessary to refer the *Pocilliporidæ*, which have corals in many respects similar to those of *Stylophoridæ* and some *Oculinidæ*, although transversely septate or tabulated, as in other widely different groups, and have exsert polyps nearly identical with those of *Stylophora* and similar genera, with 12 or 24 long tentacles, swollen at the tips.

Whether the *Caryophyllidæ* should be referred to this suborder or to Astræacea is somewhat uncertain, since the polyps of but few of the genera have been examined. It is not improbable that the family, as now constituted, includes genera belonging to both suborders, having little in common, except the negative character of lacking transverse septa,—an embryological feature that is evidently of but little importance. The genus *Caryophyllia*, like its allies, *Paracyathus*, etc., appears to have soft parts with the same general structure as *Oculina*, *Astrangia*, *Cladocora*, etc., but *Flabellum* appears to agree better with some Astræacea, like *Euphyllia*, etc. Therefore since the typical genera seem to belong here, we have placed the *Caryophyllidæ* in this suborder, as the lowest family. There are also certain other genera, generally referred to Astræacea, which seem to have greater affinities with the present division, though the soft parts are too imperfectly known to afford positive evidence; such are the genera, *Cyphastrea*, *Galaxea*, *Stylina*, etc.

Prof. Dana's second family of Caryophyllaceæ, the *Caryophyllidæ*, included many of the genera of this group, together with *Dendrophyllia* and other representatives of the Madreporacea, and also *Stylina* and *Galaxea* (*Anthophyllum*); but *Pocillipora*, *Seriatopora*, and *Stylophora* (*Sideropora*) were referred by him to Madreporacea. In his system the porous structure of the coral in Madreporacea was not regarded as of so much importance as by most later writers.

The following are the principal families included in this suborder:

Stylasteridæ. Corallum branched, with very compact, mostly smooth, often colored cœnenchyma. Cells small, much filled up below. Septa equal, 12 to 24 (sometimes only 5 or 6), often united together by their thickened inner edges so as to partially close up the cell. Costæ nearly obsolete.

Oculinidæ. Corallum encrusting or branched, with compact cœnenchyma, smooth, or slightly costate near the cells. Cells of moderate size or large, more or less filled up below. Septa 12 to 48 or more, in several unequal cycles, the edge of the principal ones entire.

Pocilliporidæ. Corallum branched or lobed, with the cœnenchyma compact at surface and mostly spinulose. Cells small, divided by transverse septa below, partially filled up. Septa 12 to 24 (rarely 36), often rudimentary, especially in young cells.

Stylophoridæ. Corallum massive, encrusting, or branched, with the cœnenchyma compact near surface and mostly spinulose. Cells small, not filled up, or but slightly so, with few irregular, transverse interseptal divisions. Septa 10 or 12 to 24.

? *Stylinidæ.* Corallum massive, astræiform. Cells of moderate size or small. Septa with entire edges.

Astrangidæ. Corallum solitary, or cæspitose, encrusting, or lobed, with little or no cœnenchyma; buds basal, or arising from stolons, or lateral. Cells of moderate size, not filled up below, with few, distant, irregular, transverse divisions. Septa numerous, in several unequal cycles, those of the first and second usually with entire edges. Includes *Astrangiæ* and *Cladocorinæ*.

Caryophyllidæ. Corallum solitary, attached or free when adult. Cells often large, increasing upward, open from the base. Septa numerous, in several unequal cycles, their edges entire.

On the west coast of America representative of but four of these families are known: *Stylasteridæ, Pocilliporidæ, Astrangidæ,* and *Caryophyllidæ.*

The *Oculinidæ* are abundant in the Atlantic, Mediterranean, and Indo-Pacific faunæ. The *Stylophoridæ* are most abundant in the Indo-Pacific, but have a few representatives in the Caribbean fauna. The *Stylinidæ* are mostly fossils of the Cretaceous and Tertiary formations of Europe, but a few species still live in the Atlantic.

Family, STYLASTERIDÆ Pourtales.

Stylasteraceæ (subfamily of *Oculinidæ*) Edw. and Haime, Corall., ii, p. 126, 1857.
Stylasteridæ Pourtales, Bulletin Mus. Comp. Zoöl., No. 7, p. 125, 1868.

The corals included in this family most frequently form delicate, arborescently branched corals, often flabelliform, and sometimes with coalescent branches, in other species the coral is irregularly lobed or encrusting. The cœnenchyma is abundant and very compact, with a smoothish or finely granulous surface, often with peculiar swellings or vesicles, which sometimes have a radiated structure and may, perhaps, indicate the position of a second form of polyps; in other cases (as in *Allopora*) there are also minute pores or openings with a raised border scattered between the ordinary cells, which appear to represent a second more rudimentary form of polyps. Therefore it is probable that in this family the polyps are dimorphous, as in *Pennatulacea* and some *Alcyonacea*, and in many Hydroids, but the soft parts have not yet been described. The polyp-cells are small, generally filled up below by a solid deposit, sometimes also partially filled up and more or less obliterated by the thickening of the septa and the union of their inner edges, thus separating the interseptal chambers from the central part of the cell, and in some genera, like *Distichipora* and *Errina*, nearly or quite obliterating some of the chambers. The septa are mostly narrow, equal or nearly so, in one to three cycles, in some instances only four to six, most frequently twelve, the third cycle, when present, rudimentary. Columella generally styliform, sometimes wanting.

This family, as now constituted, includes the following genera:— *Axohelia* E. and H.; *Cryptohelia* E. and H.; *Endohelia* E. and H.; *Cyclopora* Verrill; *Stylaster* Gray; *Allopora* Ehr.; *Distichipora* Lamarck; *Errina* Gray.

In the works of Edwards and Haime the genus *Distichipora* was placed, with other still doubtful forms, in the "incerta sedes" at the end of the list of genera. In the final work* it is placed in an appendix and doubt is expressed whether it may not belong to the Alcyonaria, rather than to the Madreporaria, while *Errina* is entirely omitted. The writer first explained the structure of these genera and referred them to their true position near *Stylaster*, in the Bulletin of the Museum of Comparative Zoölogy, No. 3, p. 46, 1864. Mr. Pourtales, who has recently discovered and described several new and very interesting members of this group, fully confirmed this conclusion in later numbers of the Bulletin.† He has also suggested that the group should form a distinct family,—an opinion in which we fully concur.

Many of the species of this family seem to be confined to great depths, where they form a considerable portion of the coral fauna, and yet there are, also, shallow-water species both in the Atlantic and Pacific. When deeper dredgings shall have been made on the west coast of America, additional genera and species may be expected, but at present two species of the genus *Allopora* are the only known representatives of the family on the whole coast.

---

* Corallinaires, vol. iii, p. 450, 1860.
† No. 6, pp. 116, 117, 1867; No. 7, p. 136, 1868.

Allopora Ehrenberg.

Allopora Ehr., Corall. rothen Meeres, p. 147, 1834; (*pars*) Dana, Zoöph., p. 697; Edw. and Haime, Corall., ii, p. 131.

Corallum encrusting, irregularly lobed, or branching. Cœnenchyma abundant, compact, the surface finely granulous, with more or less numerous, scattered ampullæ or vesicles. Cells small, irregularly arranged, scattered. Septa narrow, not exsert, usually five to ten larger, equal, thickened ones, which generally unite by their inner edges below, so as to enclose the intervening small chambers, within which may usually be seen rudimentary septa of the last cycle, in the form of small ascending points or papillæ. Columella conical or rounded, finely spinulose or hirsute.

Allopora Californica Verrill.

Proceedings Essex Institute, vol. iii, p. 37, 1866, (*non* Pourtales).

Plate 10, figure 8.

Corallum encrusting at base, rising into thick, irregularly lobed or palmate branches, three inches or more high, some of which are two inches broad and nearly half an inch thick; some are nearly round and rapidly tapering, of about the same thickness as the others. Many of the branches have an annelid tube, with two apertures side by side, in the center, and appear to be due to the encrusting habit of the coral, which covers the tubes with a thickness of from an eighth to a fourth of an inch, and in this way may rise into false branches. The worm tubes themselves are quite thin, forming a delicate separable lining for the tubes formed by the coral. Some of the branches subdivide into two or three parts near the end, which spread nearly at right angles. Cells very small, about ·02 of an inch, quite irregularly scattered over the whole surface; distance between them equal to two or three times the diameter, or from ·04 to ·07 of an inch. Cœnenchyma compact, with a minutely granulous surface, appearing smooth to the unaided eye, but having a few minute papillæ or minute vesicular ampullæ, some of which are open at top, forming small pores scattered between the cells. In a longitudinal section the cells are seen to be filled up below, and between them there are irregularly scattered, minute, rounded cavities, caused by the superficial papillæ or vesicles. Septa represented commonly by six thick triangular processes which converge toward the center of the cells, leaving only narrow, radiating spaces between them; in other cells the number varies from five to eight. The septa project slightly above the common surface, and do not reach more than half way to the center of the cell, uniting together by their thickened inner edges, down within the cell, and separating the very small interseptal spaces from the central opening; within each interseptal space there can generally be seen a minute rudimentary septa in the form of an ascending, prominent point. Cells deep in the central portion, nearly filled up below by a round, conical, minutely hirsute, whitish columella. The cells are stellate, with very slightly raised borders, somewhat unequal in size, and many are distorted; two are often seen together and more or less confluent, as if they had been formed by fissiparity or disk budding; others evidently originate by interstitial budding, while some very small rudimentary cells are intermediate between the ordinary form and the ampullæ with central openings, indicating that those are made by rudimentary or dimorphous forms of polyps. Color light minium-red.

Height 7 inches; breadth 5·50; diameter of cells ·02 to ·03, the central cavity about ·01 of an inch.

California,—Maj. Wm. Rich, U. S. A.

Probably from the Gulf of California in deep water.

The basal portion is dead and encrusted with various species of Bryozoa, Serpulæ, etc. It was collected by Major Rich during the Mexican war.

Allopora venusta Verrill, sp. nov.

Allopora Ca'ifornica Pourtales, Bulletin M. C. Z., p. 136, 1868, (*non* Verrill). no description.

Plate 10, figure 9.

Corallum encrusting and expanded at base, rising up in stout lobes or branches, two inches or more high, some of the branches broad and somewhat palmate or digitate, the terminal branchlets mostly round and about ·12 to ·15 of an inch thick, obtusely rounded at tips. Some of the branches contain worm tubes similar to those in the preceding species, with two openings side by side, and apparently of the same nature with those found in *Muricea formosa* of Zorritos, (p. 435), but other branches are quite solid. Cœnenchyma compact, having a minutely granulous surface, with a few minute, scattered vesicles and pores. Cells small, about ·03 of an inch, regular, circular, with the border sharp and distinctly raised above the general surface; some newly formed cells may be seen scattered among the others, but consisting only of a slight pit in the cœnenchyma, sometimes very superficial, circular, and rounded at bottom, in other cases a little more advanced, showing the outlines of the septa and columella. The cells are irregularly scattered over the whole surface, mostly at distances varying from ·02 to ·10 of an inch. The principal septa vary from 6 to 10, but are mostly 7 or 8, quite narrow at top, but much thickened, broader and united well together below, so as to form a cup-shaped aperture to the cell, around and above the small deep central pit, and entirely separating the very small interseptal spaces, in which the minute, round, projecting points of the small septa may be easily distinguished. Central cavity broader in its upper part than in the preceding species, but with the central pit smaller, nearly filled by the small, round, conical columella. Color light red, the branches often yellowish at tips.

Neah Bay, Washington Territory,—Collection Museum of Comparative Zoölogy.

Although this species resembles the preceding in color and mode of growth, it is quite distinct in the form and structure of the cells. In this they are raised, circular, regular, and cup-shaped, while in the preceding they are stellate, often irregular, not cup-shaped, with larger and fewer septa, the border is scarcely raised, and the columella is larger.

Family, POCILLIPORIDÆ Verrill.

Synopsis Polyps and Corals of N. Pacif. Expl. Exp., Part iv, p. 56, in Proceedings (Communications) of Essex Institute, vol. vi. p. 90, 1869.
Favositinæ (*pars*) Dana, Zoöph., p. 514, 1846.
Pocilloporinæ (subfamily of *Favositidæ*) Edw. and Haime, Corall., iii, p. 301, 1860.

Corallum with an encrusting base at first, from which arise clusters of lobes or branches, which grow by interstitially budding at the ends. Cœnenchyma abundant and very compact on the sides of the branches and base, but almost entirely wanting among the crowded terminal cells. Cells small, angular or circular, often filled up below with a solid deposit; the transverse plates generally extend entirely across the cells below. Septa 6 to 24, generally twelve, often rudimentary.

The descriptions and drawings of the polyps of *Pocillipora* by Mr. Bradley, show conclusively that the genus is a true madreporian, as we have already mentioned in other articles.[*] It seems also to be most closely allied to *Oculina* and *Stylophora*, both in the structure of the polyps and coral. Its affinities with the numerous extinct genera having the same tabulate structure is a subject requiring a great amount of careful investigation. From the *Favositidæ*, as a whole, it differs in having an abundant cœnenchyma. Favosites differs also in having perforate walls, and doubtless ought to be separated, at least

---

[*] On the Affinities of the Tabulate Corals, in Proceedings of the American Association for Advancement of Science, 1867, p. 148. See also Proc. Essex Inst., vi, p. 90, 1869.

as a distinct family, which has, perhaps, closer relations with *Madreporacea*. The genus *Seriatopora*, has been united with certain genera of fossil corals to constitute a distinct family, *Seriatoporidæ*, but it would appear to be more in accordance with their true affinities to unite *Seriatopora* and the allied genera with the *Pocilliporidæ*. The living polyps are unknown, however, and might show other relations. The *Thecidæ* E. and H., and especially *Columnaria*, are evidently very closely allied to *Pocillipora* and, ought, perhaps, to be united in the same family.

The association by Edwards and Haime, and others, of the *Milleporidæ* with *Pocilliporidæ* and allied forms, under the name, *Tabulata*, was particularly unfortunate, since they have no relations whatever, and indeed there is no resemblance except in the fact that in certain genera of both groups there are transverse septa,—an artificial character of comparatively little importance, which also occurs in the *Astræidæ* (*Cœlastræa*) and sometimes even in the *Eupsammidæ* (*Astræopsammia*). Prof. Agassiz has shown that *Millepora* belongs to the *Hydroidea*, and holding the opinion that *Pocillipora* and other tabulated corals were allied to *Millepora* he consequently united all the *Tabulata* of Edwards and Haime to the *Hydroidea*, thus removing them from the class of polyps. This view is no longer tenable, since the genus *Pocillipora* has animals identical in structure with the most typical genera of true polyps. Even were the animals of *Pocillipora* unknown, the examination of such species as *P. elongata* Dana, *P. plicata* Dana, *P. stellata* Verrill, and others, in which there are twelve well developed septa, having the same essential characters as those of *Oculinidæ* and *Stylophoridæ*, would be sufficient to convince us that the genus could not possibly belong to the *Hydroidea*, unless that group is to be so modified as to lose the principal characters by which it is separated from the class of polyps. The absence of radiating lamellæ, such as would be required to secrete the radiating septa of *Pocillipora*, *Columnaria*, and some *Favositidæ* is one of the principal class characters by which Acalephs are separated from Polyps, and is a constant feature of acalephs; the presence of such lamellæ is equally constant and characteristic of true polyps.

Pocillipora Lamarck.

Pocillopora (*pars*) Lamarck, Hist. anim. sans vert, ii, p. 273 ; 2nd ed., ii, p. 144.
Pocillopora Dana, Zoöphytes, p. 523; Edw. and Haime, Corall., iii, p. 301.

The coralla consist of clusters of branches or lobes, varying in the different species from very slender, much divided branchlets to stout, round, and obtuse, or very broad and convoluted lobes or fronds, which arise from a more or less compact encrusting base. Branches often covered with verrucæ or rudimentary branchlets, composed of a few or many cells. At the ends of the branches the cells are closely crowded, angular, closely united by their walls, without intervening cœnenchyma, but on the sides of the branches they are more or less distantly separated by the compact cœnenchyma, which is sharply granulous or spinulose at the surface. Cells small, often deep, circular where not crowded, often filled below the surface by a solid deposit, but always with transverse septa in the lower parts, which are abundant and regular. Septa narrow, generally 12, of which 6 are larger and alternate with six that are very small or rudimentary; sometimes 24. The septa are often partially or wholly rudimentary or abortive, especially in the crowded cells at the end of the branches, but in many cases two opposite ones are larger than the rest and join the columella, or there may be one larger one. The columella, when present, is small, solid, a little prominent, but is often wanting. The transverse plates have a concentric structure and are often seen incomplete, with an opening through the middle. Occasionally a cell is divided by fissiparity, but the new ones mostly appear in the angles between adjacent cells.

This genus is very abundant throughout the tropical parts of the Pacific and Indian Oceans and the Red Sea. At the Hawaiian Islands several large species of *Pocillipora* constitute an important part of the coral-reefs. In the Atlantic ocean the genus is unknown, but a fossil species occurs in the Miocene of the West Indies.

Pocillipora capitata Verrill.

Pocillipora capitata Verrill, Bulletin Mus. Comp. Zoöl., p. 60, 1864; Proc. Essex Inst., vi, p. 99, 1869.

Coralla composed of clusters of large, irregular, usually stout branches, often an inch or more in diameter, arising from a massive or encrusting base. The branches are covered, except at the ends, with more or less elongated, rising, subacute or bluntly rounded verrucæ. The branchlets are usually spreading, often rounded or clavate at the end, where the verrucæ become obsolete. Surface covered with small, rough, scattered spinules, those around the edge of the cells more prominent. Cells rather small, circular and deep on the side of the branches, and mostly separated by spaces at least as broad as the diameter of the cells, sometimes more crowded; on the ends of the branches and verrucæ, the cells are angular and separated only by thin walls. Septa twelve, usually very narrow or rudimentary, the lower part generally more developed than the upper; sometimes one is broader and joins the very small columella, which is, however, generally wanting.

The largest specimens seen are more than a foot in diameter; the branches ·5 to 1 inch; verrucæ ·30 of an inch long; ·10 to ·20 in diameter; cells ·03 to ·04 in diameter.

Acapulco,—A. Agassiz; Socorro Islands,—J. Xantus; Pearl Islands, —F. H. Bradley; La Paz,—J. Pedersen.

Pocillipora capitata, var. porosa Verrill.

Pocillipora capitata, var. porosa Verrill, Proc. Essex Inst., vi, p. 99, 1869.

Coralla forming large rounded clumps, 10 to 15 inches in diameter, with more or less elongated, divergent or crowded, angular, and often flattened branches, which are usually ·25 to ·35 of an inch in thickness; ·50 to ·75 in breadth; and 1 to 3 long, often truncate or digitately lobed at the end. Verrucæ variable, mostly ascending, often large and prominent, generally elongated, roundish, tapering to the subacute end, the upper ones often appressed, obsolete on the summits of the branches, where the cells are closely crowded. Cells large and deep, the lateral ones mostly crowded, the intervening spaces generally less than their diameters, often not half as much. Septa 12 or 24, distinct, nearly equal, narrow, slightly exsert and acute at summit. Surface of the cœnenchyma, between the cells, finely spinulose, the spinose grains often crowded, but frequently forming only a single row. The cells are but little closed up in the interior by solid deposits and the texture of the coral is, therefore, quite porous. In one large specimen the branches on one side are of the normal size and form, while on the other they become more slender and much subdivided at the ends into small, obtuse, lobe-like or digitate branchlets. The cells on this part are smaller and more distant.

The larger specimens are about 10 inches high and 12 broad; the larger branches ·50 to 1 inch in width; ·25 to ·35 in thickness; cells ·04 to ·05 of an inch in diameter.

Near La Paz, brought up by divers,—J. Pedersen.

The Museum of Yale College possesses four large and several small specimens of this form.

Pocillipora capitata, var. robusta Verrill, nov.

Coralla forming large, more or less hemispherical, close clumps of stout, angular, mostly flattened, obtuse, dichotomous branches, which usually fork at distances of from 1·5 to 4 inches, in large specimens.

The branches are covered laterally with numerous, rather large, prominent, elongated, mostly acute, ascending verrucæ, which are pretty evenly scattered over the surface and seldom crowded, rarely obtuse or rounded at the end, usually containing a dozen or more polyp-cells. The verrucæ become obsolete at the tips of the branches, which are mostly blunt or truncate and filled with closely crowded, angular polyp-cells. The cells on the sides of the branches and verrucæ are rather small, mostly separated by distances about equal to their diameter. Septa commonly six, very distinct but narrow, often twelve. Columella either a small papilla or rudimentary and scarcely distinct. Cœnenchyma between the cells compact and covered with minute rough granules. In a transverse section the cells are found to be much filled up below, and the coral quite compact; the transverse dissepiments are rather distant, the spaces between usually exceeding the diameter of the cells. Height of the largest specimens 15 to 18 inches; length of undivided branches 2 to 4; breadth ·50 to 1·50; thickness ·35 to ·75; length of average verrucæ ·30 to ·40; their diameter ·20 to ·30; diameter of cells ·02 to ·03 of an inch.

Young specimens attached to shells of *Margaritophora fimbriata* Dunker, have a few short rising branches in the middle, with a broad, thin, encrusting base. The marginal cells are obliquely appressed to the surface of the shell, their outer edges being flattened and extending, with the septa, which are here conspicuous and like elevated costæ, considerably beyond the proper edge of the cells, exactly as in *Astrangia* and the young of *Oculina*. The new cells at the edge are also produced by marginal budding, as in the genera named. A study of these marginal cells confirms the affinities of this family with the Oculinacea.

Gulf of California, south of La Paz, 3 to 6 fathoms, brought up by divers,—J. Pedersen.

The Museum of Yale College has received upwards of twenty specimens of this form, most of them of large size and quite constant in character. But some of the smaller specimens are evidently dwarfed by unfavorable conditions of growth and have very irregular branches, sometimes much divided, and the verrucæ nearly obsolete in some parts. The following form, however, seems worthy of a distinct varietal name.

Pocillipora capitata, var. pumila Verrill.

The coralla consist of elongated clumps of short, mostly obtuse and much divided, crowded branches, arising from the upper side of large, horizontal often forked, branch-like base. These clumps seem to have originated from large detached branches, which have been broken from specimens of the preceding form and, having fallen to the bottom, have served as bases for the numerous rising branchlets, which probably arose from the original verrucæ by excessive enlargement and gradual alteration to the form of branches, the largest of which subdivide and develop verrucæ like those of the parent form. Cells and cœnenchyma as in the preceding variety.

Length of the clumps 6 to 12 inches; breadth 3 to 5; height 2 to 4; length of branches ·50 to 2; their diameter ·25 to ·50.

Gulf of California, with the preceding,—J. Pedersen.

About a dozen specimens of this variety have been received.

In general appearance it is very different from the normal form.

Pocillipora lacera Verrill.
Proc. Essex Institute. vol. vi, p. 100, 1869.

Coralla consisting of more or less irregular or rounded clumps of long, irregular, often crooked, rough, and much subdivided branches. The branchlets are short and lacerately or digitately divided and lobed at the ends, the subdivisions small, variously shaped, often slender, but generally more or less compressed and obtuse at the tips, often having the appearance of elongated verrucæ, while the lateral branchlets pass gradually into the verrucæ, which are few, irregular, and distantly scattered on the larger branches. Lateral cells rather large, round, rather distant, often shallow; septa mostly 12, narrow, usually subequal, sometimes one is larger, often all are rudimentary or wanting. Columella rudimentary or wholly abortive. Cœnenchyma abundant between the cells, firm, the surface finely and evenly spinulose.

The larger specimens are 6 to 8 inches in diameter and height; the large branches ·30 to ·50 in diameter; and 2 to 6 long; the terminal branchlets mostly ·10 to ·30 long; ·10 to ·15 in diameter; the cells ·03 to ·04 of an inch in diameter.

In life, according to Mr. Bradley, the polyps are small, exsert, with twelve equal cylindrical tentacles, which are swollen at the tips; they are about equal in length to the diameter of the body, and they are arranged in a single circle around the margin, but six are held horizontally and six upright in expansion. The color of the polyps is dark brown, greenish brown, or dark green; tentacles dark brown, the tips white.

"In arrangement and form of tentacles this species closely resembles the accompanying *Porites* (*P. Panamensis*), which also has twelve cylindrical, light brown tentacles, with white tips, but the tips are not perceptibly swollen, and they are *not* held alternately upright and horizontally, as in *Pocillipora*."—F. H. B.

Pearl Islands, Panama, and Acajutla,—F. H. Bradley. "In more sheltered situations near the head of Panama Bay, this coral covers considerable surfaces, but farther out it seems to be confined to sheltered spots, and occurs in scattered clumps."—F. H. B.

This species forms loose open clumps of rather slender and irregular branches, quite unlike those of the preceding species in appearance.

Family, ASTRANGIDÆ Verrill.

Cladocoraceæ and *Astrangiaceæ* Edw. and Haime, Corall., ii, pp. 587 and 606.

The coralla in this group consist of encrusting, creeping, or more or less fasciculated clusters of rather small, cylindrical, or somewhat turbinated corallites, which have rather deep, cup-shaped, mostly circular calicles. The buds arise chiefly from the lateral walls, either from near the top, on the sides, at the base, or even on basal stolon-like extensions. In young specimens and at the margins of encrusting species the calicles are often appressed to the surfaces to which they adhere, and buds arise, also, from within the extending outer margins of the calicles.

The septa form from three to five or more, unequal cycles, the primaries and secondaries often with subentire summits, the others denticulate or deeply incised. The columella is variously developed, often papillose. The transverse dissepiments are few and distant. Cœnenchyma wanting or but slightly developed.

The polyps are quite exsert, with slender, tapering tentacles, which are swollen at the tips, and covered with minute scattered verrucæ, composed chiefly of nettling organs.

This family includes two groups distinguished by Edwards and Haime : *Cladocoraceæ*, in which the budding is lateral and the corals consist of more or less cæspitose clumps of tubular corallites; and *Astrangiaceæ*, in which the budding is mostly basal, or from creeping stolons, producing low encrusting corals.

But these two modes of growth pass by almost insensible gradations into each other. Thus there are species of *Cladocora* in which the budding is partially at or near the base, as it is in all the species while young, and there are certain species of *Astrangia* which bud at the same time from basal expansions, from within the margin of the outer calicles, and laterally from the walls near the summit (*A. Danæ* and *A. astræiformis*); while other species bud both from stolons and laterally, and have more elongated tubular corallites (*A. Haimei*, etc.). It is, therefore, impossible to make any marked distinction between these two groups of genera. It is not improbable that in adopting them as subfamilies, I have given to the mode of growth even more importance than it merits.

Sub-family, ASTRANGINÆ Verrill.

Astreinæ reptantes Edw. and Haime, Ann. des Sciences nat., 3ᵉ ser., xii, p. 175, 1849.
Astrangiaceæ Edw. and Haime, Coralliaires, ii, p. 606, 1857.

Coralla encrusting or creeping, formed of low corallites, which multiply chiefly by basal budding.

Astrangia Edw. and Haime.

Astrangia Milne-Edwards and Jules Haime, Comptes-rendus de l'Acad. des Sci, xxvii, p. 496, 1848; Ann. des Sci. nat., xii, p., 180, 1849; Coralliaires. ii, p. 613, 1857; Verrill, Revision of Polyps of Eastern Coast United States, in Memoires Boston Soc. Nat. Hist., i, p. 39, 1864.

Coralla encrusting, consisting of rather small, short, more or less turbinate corallites, which arise by budding, either from basal expansions of the wall of the parents, from the sides, or from within the obliquely extended margins of those in the outermost row, and thus form clusters, spreading over rocks, shells, etc., or in some cases thin aggregate masses, sometimes rising in the middle into irregular lobes or short branches. The calicles are circular, except when crowded or appressed, moderately deep, with a papillose columella. Septa more or less unequal, in three or four cycles, the primaries and secondaries most prominent, all with strongly granulated sides and denticulated edges, the lowest teeth larger and more or less paliform,*

---

* The following species has the basal teeth of the septa developed into well-marked, prominent pali. As it was figured, by mistake, upon the plate with the Panama species, I add a bri f description:

Astrangia palifera Verrill, sp. nov. Plate ix, figure 2.

Corallites low, cylindrical, scattered over the surface to which they adhere, usually at distances twice as great as their diameter, or even more, and connected by narrow and thin, stolon-like expansions of the bases. Calicles circular, shallow. Columella small, with about six to ten prominent papillæ. Septa twenty-four to thirty, not crowded, separated by spaces greater than their thickness, subequal, the primaries a little broader, thicker, and more prominent than the secondaries, which also somewhat exceed the tertiaries; all with finely granulated sides and rather broadly rounded, finely denticu'ated, and very slightly ex-ert summits; inner edge perpendicular, separated by a deep notch from the paliform tooth, of which there is usually but one to each septa. The paliform teeth are comparatively large, prominent, obtuse, those of the primaries largest and nearest the center the others smaller and a little farther from the in the typical species, and blending gradually with the papillæ of the columella. Transverse dissepiments few and distant. Walls naked and costate toward the summit, often covered toward the base with an imperfect epitheca and various encrustations. The polyps in expansion are sub-pellucid, and rise considerably above the calicles; the tentacles are long, slender, and covered with small white verrucæ, with a knob at the end.

This genus is widely distributed, but appears to be most abundant on the American coasts, where its numerous species range on the Atlantic side from Cape Cod to Patagonia and on the Pacific side from the Gulf of California to Peru, and perhaps farther. Three species, at least, are found in the West Indies; two on the Atlantic coast of the United States; one or more at Rio Janeiro; and one in the Straits of Magellan. One large species is found on the Atlantic coasts of Spain and Portugal; and one on the British coast. From the Indo-Pacific fauna none have been described except *A. palifera*, though others probably exist there. Two or more species are also found in the tertiary strata along the Atlantic coast of the United States.* Two species: *A. Edwardsii* Verrill (*A. Danæ* E. and H.) and *A. Michelini* E. and H., are from unknown localities, but may be identical with some of the species already referred to from the Atlantic coast of South America.

Astrangia Haimei Verrill.

Astrangia Haimei Verrill, Proc. Boston Soc. Natural History, x, p. 330, April, 1866.

Plate IX, figures 6, 6ª.

Coralla encrusting, consisting of prominent cylindrical or turbinate corallites, sometimes rising more than half an inch above the surface of the basal expansion, which connects them together, and becoming slightly turbinate and divergent when highest.

The corallites are distant from each other from ·04 to ·25 of an inch. The basal mural expansion is very thin, compact, and slightly granulated, having a smooth appearance, and usually without apparent striations. Septa from thirty to forty-eight, very narrow and thin, with the inner edges nearly perpendicular, forming a deep cup, narrow at the bottom; they are all, except those of the last cycle, which

center, according to their age, thus forming an irregular circle. Wall compact, glossy, with slight, nearly equal, finely granulated costæ.

Height of corallites ·06 to ·10 of an inch; diameter ·10 to ·13; distance between them ·15 to ·30.

Ceylon, adhering to dead corals.—Museum of Yale College.

* Both of these fossil species belong to the subgenus, *Cœnangia*,—see page 530.

are more narrow, of nearly the same width, giving an even appearance to the cavity of the cup; they project slightly above the wall, about ·01 of an inch, in the form of narrow points, alternately larger and smaller; the inner edges are thin, evenly and sharply dentate, the sides strongly granulated, but not crowded together, the spaces between them being equal to their thickness, or even wider. The columella is small, consisting of numerous even papillæ, graduating into the teeth at the base of the septa. Walls thin, granulated exteriorly, with low, even costæ on the upper part, which mostly disappear toward the base.

Diameter of cups ·10 to ·18 of an inch; depth ·06 to ·10; height of corallites usually about ·10 to ·25, sometimes ·40 to ·55 of an inch.

Panama and Pearl Islands on the reefs, at low-water in pools; Zorritos, Peru; Acajutla; Realejo; La Union, San Salvador, common,—F. H. Bradley.

The following description, found among Mr. Bradley's notes, is believed to apply to this species, for though no numbered specimen was found corresponding to it, there is no other species in the Zorritos collection to which it would apply: "Tentacles 30 or more, in two unequal rows; those of the outer row deep pink, with whitish tips; those of the inner row greenish, with whitish tips. Those of the outer row are about one-fourth as long as the diameter of the polyp, and twice as long as the inner ones. Disk nearly transparent, greenish, with eight very deep pink lines radiating from the sides of the elongated mouth."

Astrangia pulchella Verrill, op. cit., p. 331.

Coralla encrusting, consisting of patches of small, low, cylindrical corallites, scattered at distances varying from less than their diameter to more than a quarter inch, and connected together by a thin, calcareous, basal expansion, much like that of the preceding species, but smoother and with only minute granulations. Calicles shallow, conical, with a narrow center, their whole inner surface crowdedly papillose, the papillæ of the columella being confused with the teeth of the septa, and very small. Septa twenty-four, projecting very slightly above the wall, or not at all, narrow at the top but broad within, all nearly equal, the edges evenly toothed, and the sides very strongly and roughly granulated, so that the granules of adjacent septa often touch, giving them a crowded appearance. Costæ scarcely apparent, even at the summit. Diameter of the cups ·08 to ·10 of an inch; depth ·03; height ·05, sometimes more.

Panama and Pearl Islands, with the last, common,—F. H. Bradley.

Astrangia concinna Verrill, op. cit., p. 331.

Plate IX, figure 5.

The coralla consist of clusters of broad, low, cylindrical corallites, which are distant about their own diameter and connected by stolons or a thin basal expansion. Calicles not so deep as wide, cup-shaped, with a narrow papillose columella, forming the bottom. Septa from thirty-six to fifty, subequal, the primaries often a little broader, and those of the last cycle narrower than the rest. All are rounded at the top, and finely toothed, but at the middle the inner edge becomes more nearly perpendicular and has longer teeth, resembling pali, which blend with the papillæ of the columella, which are fine and numerous. The tops of the septa are thin and project slightly above the wall, the primaries most so. Their sides are not so strongly granulated as in the preceding species, and they appear thinner and less crowded. Exterior granulated, slightly costate near the summit, often encrusted with Bryozoa, etc., to near the top.

Diameter of cups ·18 to ·22; height ·10 to ·15 of an inch.

Panama and Pearl Islands, not common,—F. H. Bradley.

Resembles the last, but has much larger cells and more numerous septa, which are not so strongly granulated.

Astrangia dentata Verrill, op. cit., p. 332.

Coralla forming clusters, encrusting rocks, similar to the last, with cups of about the same size, but deeper and less open. Septa from thirty-six to forty-eight, very unequal according to their cycles, the primaries being comparatively broad and rounded above, while those of the last cycles are very narrow; they are not crowded, being separated by spaces equal to their thickness; they project unequally, the primaries about ·02 of an inch, the others slightly. All the septa are strongly and irregularly toothed, the principal ones especially so; the teeth on the upper part are rough and lacerate, those on the inner part prominent, paliform, merging into those of the columella; the sides are rudely granulous. Columella rather small, concave, forming the narrow bottom of the deep cells, covered by numerous, small, crowded, rough papillæ.

Walls thin, with subequal, low, thick, granulous costæ, which often extend on the surface of the basal expansion, and usually encrusted nearly to the edge of the cups with sponge, etc. Color of the unbleached coral dark brown.

Height of corallites ·20 to ·30; diameter ·15 to ·20; depth about ·05; some of the patches are two or three inches across.

Panama and Pearl Islands, at low-water mark in rocky pools, and in 6 to 8 fathoms on base of *Muricea*,—F. H. Bradley ; Acajutla, San Salvador,—F. H. Bradley ; Acapulco,—A. Agassiz ; La Paz,—J. Pedersen.

This species resembles the preceding more than any other species, but may easily be distinguished by the deeper calicles and more unequal septa, which are more strongly toothed.

Astrangia costata Verril. op. cit., p. 332.

Coralla consisting of from one to four, turbinate, rather high corallites, surrounded by a very thin mural expansion, usually encrusting dead shells. Cup circular, narrow and deep. Septa twenty-four to thirty, the primaries wide, about one-fourth the diameter of cup, rounded and subentire at the top, perpendicular and toothed within ; the others similar, but successively narrower, with sharp teeth throughout. The septa project very unequally, giving a notched appearance to the margin of the cups. Walls very thin, with subequal, elevated costæ, which extend to the base and on the basal expansion. The columella is very small, with few papillæ. The septa within the cell are thin and not crowded, the spaces between them being greater than their thickness, giving them a loose appearance. Diameter of the cups ·08 to ·10 of an inch ; height ·10 to ·15.

Panama, on dead shells, in 6 to 8 fathoms,—F. H. Bradley.

This is very distinct from all the others and approaches *Phyllangia*.

Astrangia Pedersenii Verrill, sp. nov.

Coralla composed of clusters of sub-turbinate corallites, connected by thin stolon-like extensions, often arranged in linear series radiating from the center of the cluster, the outer ones oblique. Corallites not crowded, the largest seldom more than a quarter of an inch high. Calicles cup-shaped, narrow and deep at center, with a thin edge and quite open interseptal spaces, which are about twice as broad as the septa. Columella very narrow, papillose. Septa thin, unequal, about 36 in the largest calicles; the primaries are about twice as wide as the tertiaries, thin, a little exsert, the summit rounded and sharply denticulate, the inner edge nearly perpendicular, with small, prominent, paliform teeth toward the base; secondaries similar but a little narrower and less exert; those of the third and fourth cycles very thin and narrow, very slightly exsert, the edge sloping from the narrow summit and sharply denticulate. Walls covered with about 36, low, nearly equal, rather distant, granulous costæ, often encrusted with nullipore, etc.

Some of the clusters are 2 inches across; the corallites ·05 to ·25 apart; ·10 to ·25 high; ·10 to ·15 in diameter; depth of cup ·06 to ·10; primaries about ·03 broad; ·02 exsert.

La Paz, on base of *Eugorgia nobilis*, in 4 to 6 fathoms,—J. Pedersen; Guaymas, on dead shells,—Dr. E. Palmer (Chicago Acad. Sci.).

This species resembles *A. Haimei* more than any of the other species, owing to its deep open calicles, but is readily distinguished by its decidedly costate exterior; by the broader and more exsert primary septa; and especially by the fewer and quite unequal septa and wide interseptal chambers.

Subgenus, Cœnangia Verrill.

Corallites united together laterally, forming small, Astræa-like, encrusting masses, sometimes rising into lobes in the middle. Calicles angular and crowded. Septa without distinct paliform teeth at base, those of the last cycles curved towards and usually united to those of the preceding cycles. Columella small or moderate, scarcely papillose, composed of contorted processes originating from the septa. Budding takes place mostly in the angles between the corallites, both around the margin and in the central parts.

Besides the following species this group includes *A. bella* and *A. Marylandica* (Conrad sp.), from the later tertiaries of the eastern coast of the United States. *A. Danæ* Ag. from the Virginian fauna, and *A. astræiformis* E. and H., from the Carolinian fauna, are intermediate between this sub-genus and the typical species, in mode of growth.

Astrangia (Cœnangia) conferta Verrill, sp. nov.

Coralla encrusting, forming Astræa-like crusts with an uneven surface, two or three inches broad and about a third of an inch thick in the middle, consisting of crowded prismatic corallites, intimately united together throughout their whole length. Calicles deep, narrow at bottom, angular, often oblique and expanded on one side, the adjacent ones separated only by a thin, sharp wall; interseptal spaces rather wide, double the thickness of the septa. Columella small, composed of rough, irregular, oblique, transverse, and more or less contorted lamellæ, arising from the inner edges of the septa, the upper surface more or less roughened with small granules, but not papillose. Septa subequal, in three cycles, usually 24 in the largest cells, all of them thin, very narrow at the top, the edge sloping to the columella or somewhat concave, sharply and roughly denticulate throughout, without distinct paliform teeth at base, the sides with few, very scattered, small, rough granules; primaries a little broader and more exsert than the others; tertiaries curved toward and mostly united to the secondaries, about midway between the margin and center. Summit of the walls between the calicles thin, rough with the projecting ends of the septa. The young corallites arise chiefly by budding between the angles of the older cells, both in the central parts and around the margin, where the calicles are oblique and strongly appressed to the surface.

The larger specimens are about three inches across; thickness varying from ·15 to ·30 of an inch; diameter of the largest calicles about ·20; depth ·08 to ·12.

Gulf of California,—J. Pedersen; Guaymas on dead shells of *Strombus gracilior*, etc,—Dr. E. Palmer (Chicago Acad. Science).

This species is more nearly allied to *A. Marylandica* and *A. bella* than to any known living species. The former differs, however, in having but 12 distinct septa and very wide interseptal chambers; the walls are thicker; the septa have smaller lateral granules and more regular teeth; and the columella is less developed. The mode of growth and union of the corallites is the same. *A. bella* has the same number of septa (24), but those of the different cycles are quite unequal. It also has considerable resemblance to *A. Danæ* and *A. astræiformis* of the Atlantic coast of the United States, but these have papillose columellæ and usually 36 septa, which are closer together, not so strongly granulous, and more evenly toothed, while the calicles are more circular and the corallites are generally free laterally, to some extent, and mostly rise above the intervening surface of the cœnenchyma.

The close relations of this species to the fossil and recent species of the temperate coasts on the Atlantic side, together with the occurrence of certain shells that are apparently identical in the two regions, but found neither in the arctic nor in the tropical regions (*Petricola pholadiformis*, etc.), is very suggestive of a former connection, perhaps in early tertiary times, between the two oceans, through the temperate parts of North America.

Phyllangia Edw. and Haime.

Phyllangia Milne-Edwards and J. Haime, Comptes-rendus de l'Acad. des Sci., xxvii, p. 497, 1848; Ann. des Sci. nat., 3ᵉ sér., xii, p. 181, 1849; Coralliaires, ii, p. 616, 1857.

Coralla encrusting, consisting of clusters of moderately large, turbinate corallites, which arise by budding from a thin, spreading expansion of the basal part of the wall of the parent corallites. The calicles are nearly circular unless crowded,—though often appressed while young,—and deep at the center. Columella often rudimentary, when most developed composed of rough, irregular, twisted and contorted processes, arising from the inner portion of the septa and uniting at the center, with a ragged upper surface. Septa very unequal, forming three or four cycles, the fifth sometimes imperfectly developed in some of the systems; the primaries and secondaries much the broadest and most exsert, with the summits broad and entire, or but slightly denticulated; within, toward the base, thin and usually narrowed and then expanded again into a slightly marked paliform lobe, the sides strongly granulated; tertiaries narrow at summit and slightly exsert, the edge strongly denticulated; those of the fourth and fifth cycles narrow and thin, with denticulated edges, those of the fourth often joining the tertiaries Walls and basal expansion naked. Costæ usually well developed. The transverse dissepiments are few and simple.

This genus differs from *Astrangia* chiefly in the deeper calicles, rudimentary and contorted columella, and in the very exsert, subentire primary and secondary septa.

Phyllangia dispersa Verrill.

Phyllangia dispersa Verrill, Bulletin Museum of Comp. Zoölogy, i. p. 47, 1864; Proceedings Boston Soc., vol. x, p. 332, 1866.

Plate IX, figures 3, 3ª.

Corallites cylindrical or turbinate, very unequal, varying in height from ·10 to ·40, and in diameter from ·20 to ·30 of an inch, and either close together or scattered at distances of ·30 to ·50 of an inch, but connected together by a continuous expansion from the enlarged basal portion of the walls. This is generally rather thin, though sometimes forming crusts two or three inches broad, the surface is granulous and the costæ of the walls extend over it in the vicinity of the corallites, gradually fading out as they recede. The walls are compact, finely granulous, covered with low, rounded, unequal costæ, those corresponding to the principal septa often becoming cristiform and denticulate toward the summit. Calicles deep at center, with conspicuous, deep interseptal chambers, giving an open appearance. Septa very unequal; the primaries are broad, much exsert (about ·10 of an inch), somewhat recurved outwardly, the inner edge usually perpendicular or overarching, the end broadly rounded, sometimes arcuate, entire or minutely denticulate, thin at the inner edge, thickened outwardly; the inner edge usually recedes toward the base, which often rises into a slight, denticulated paliform lobe, before joining the columella processes; the secondaries are similar, in adult corallites, but are considerably narrower and only rise about two thirds as high above the margin of the wall; the tertiaries are strongly denticulate and very thin, narrow in their upper part, and project but slightly above the wall, but the basal portion is broad and usually joins the columella, or unites with the secondaries before reaching it; those of the fourth cycle, and of the fifth when present, are very thin and narrow, scarcely exsert, exteriorly usually united laterally to those of the principal cycles, with the inner edges sometimes united to the tertiaries. All the septa have their sides covered with sharp granulations. Columella often rudimentary, while in other corallites of the same cluster it is pretty well developed, though occupying a small area (usually less than a fourth of the diameter of the calicle), it is composed of coarse, rough, contorted processes, originating from the inner edges of the septa, with irregular openings and a rough uneven surface.

Panama and Pearl Islands, on rocks in pools at low-water mark, and on the base of *Muricea* in 6 fathoms,—F. H. Bradley; Panama,— A. Agasisz; Gulf of Nicoya,—J. A. McNiel.

Ulangia Edw. and Haime.

Oulangia Milne-Edwards and J. Haime, Comptes-rendus de l'Acad. des Sci., xxvii, p. 497, 1848; Annales des Sci. nat., 3e ser., xii, p. 182, 1849.
Ula gia Edw. and H., Coralliaires, vol. ii, p. 617, 1857.

Coralla, so far as observed, simple, consisting of solitary corallites distantly scattered over dead shells, stones, etc., without any apparent connection, or entirely isolated. The corallites are low, broad, subcircular, and unusually large for the family. The calicles are moderately deep, or shallow, with a broad bottom occupied by a well-developed papillose columella. Septa numerous, usually in five complete cycles, unequal, all with sharply granulous sides, with the inner portion divided into numerous small prominent teeth, which blend with the papillae of the columella. The primary and secondary septa are much broader and more elevated in their outer part, with broadly rounded summits, which are usually subentire, but sometimes incised; the other septa are all strongly denticulate at summit; those of the last cycle very narrow and thin. The wall is covered at base with an imperfect epitheca and usually much encrusted with Bryozoa, Nullipora, etc.; above this it is naked and more or less costate. The transverse dissepiments are few and oblique, close to the base.

This genus is like a gigantic *Astrangia*, except that the corallites are, apparently, always quite separate, and the principal septa are usually more nearly entire at the summit. *Phyllangia* has a smaller columella, which is not papillose, and the septa are fewer, narrow, and very exsert, with nearly entire edges, while the calicles are narrow and deep.

The following and *U. Stokesiana* Edw. and Haime, from the Philippines, are the only species known.

Ulangia Bradleyi Verrill.

Ulangia Bradleyi Verrill, Proceedings Boston Soc. of Natural History, x, p. 333, 1866.

Plate IX, figure 10.

Corallites low, broad, subcircular or elliptical, with the base as broad as the margin, generally quite isolated, sometimes two or more are placed 1·5 to 3 inches apart, which were, possibly, once connected by a thin, or entirely soft, basal expansion, that has since disappeared. Calicle generally quite shallow, sometimes moderately deep and cup-shaped. Columella well developed, but not large, usually occupying less than a quarter of the breadth of the calicle, its surface crowdedly covered with small prominent, spinulose papillæ, which blend insensibly with the similar, rough, papilliform teeth, arising from the inner edges of the septa; the surface of the columella is usually concave. Septa in five complete cycles; those of the fifth are mostly quite narrow, thin, lacerately toothed; all others have the outer part suddenly rising and more or less exsert, according to their cycles, the inner portion thin, gradually sloping inward and sometimes, in large specimens, almost horizontal, most of them extending inward to the columella, but many of those of the fourth cycle joining those of the third before reaching the columella; all have the sides covered with small, sharp, spine-like granules, and the inner portion with the edge divided into prominent, rough, papilliform teeth; the primaries are a little thicker than the rest, and broader throughout, the outer portion rising almost perpendicularly from the inner, broadly rounded or subtruncate at summit, considerably exsert, the edge subentire or minutely denticulate, rarely deeply incised; the secondaries are similar to the primaries, but a little thinner and narrower, with the outer portion somewhat less exsert and the edge more frequently toothed; the tertiaries are considerably narrower than the secondaries, with the outer portion narrow and less distinct from the inner, only slightly exsert, and deeply divided into sharp, or rough, lacerate and blunt teeth; those of the fourth cycle are similar to those of the third, but a little narrower and less exsert, with the edges still more rough and lacerated. The wall is thin, usually covered nearly and sometimes quite to the summit with an epitheca, which is thickly encrusted below, but usually has a distinct, thin upper edge, above this the wall is usually feebly costate, the costæ and outer edges of septa roughly granulous or denticulate. In a vertical section the septa are roughly granulous, and perforated near the inner margin with irregular, rounded openings; the dissepiments are few and confined to the basal portion, irregular, and quite oblique. In a transverse section near the base the interseptal chambers are divided by two or three of the oblique dissepiments.

One of the largest specimens is ·63 of an inch broad; ·25 high to edge of cup; the primary septa ·06 exsert; the cup ·12 deep; the columella ·10 broad. Another specimen is ·56 broad; ·34 high, to margin; the cup ·26 deep; the primary septa ·05 exsert. An elliptical one is ·50 by ·40 in diameter; ·30 high; the primary septa ·06 exsert; the cup ·15 deep; the columella about ·10 broad. The largest specimen is ·85 broad at base; while the calicle is but ·65 broad and ·20 deep.

Panama, in rocky pools at low-water mark, and Pearl Islands on the bases of *Gorgoniæ* and on *Spondyli* in 6 to 8 fathoms,—F. H. Bradley.

Family, CARYOPHYLLIDÆ Verrill.

Turbinolidæ (*pars*) Edwards and Haime, Annales des Sci. nat., 3ᵉ ser., ix, p. 211, 1848; Coralliaires, ii, p. 7, 1857.
Cyathinæ Edw. and Haime, Annales des Sci. nat., ix, p. 285, 1848.
Caryophyllinæ Edw. and Haime, Coralliaires, ii, p. 9, 1857.

Coralla always simple at maturity.* Calicles cup-shaped, mostly circular or elliptical. Septa rather numerous, in several unequal cycles, with the edges entire or nearly so, except at the inner edge, which is sometimes divided into paliform teeth. One or more cycles of pali in front of the septa. Interseptal chambers open from the bottom. Transverse dissepiments rudimentary or wanting.

The *Turbinolidæ* of Edwards and Haime, united chiefly by the negative character of lacking dissepiments, do not appear to constitute a homogeneous group. Some of the genera, like *Flabellum*, *Rhizotrochus*, *Placotrochus*, etc., seem to be most nearly allied to

---

* According to Mrs. Thyme (Annals and Mag. Natural History, iii. p. 449, 1869), *Caryophyllia Smithii* undergoes repeatedly, while still young, complete fissiparity, the resulting portions becoming entirely free and circular. This remarkable observation needs confirmation, however.

the simple *Eusmilidæ* (*Trochosmiliaceæ* E. and H.). The soft parts of *Flabellum*, so far as known, agree more closely with those of the *Eusmilidæ* than with those of *Caryophyllia* and *Paracyathus*, while in this respect the latter genera agree very closely with the *Astrangidæ*, to some of which, indeed, they are evidently closely allied. *Syndepas* Lyman, and *Phyllangia* E. and H., so closely resemble some of the *Caryophyllidæ* that, did they not form basal stolons, they might readily be taken for members of that family. The corallites of some of the *Oculinidæ* (*Lophohelia* etc.), also closely resemble some of the *Turbinolidæ*. I have, therefore, thought it best for the present to divide the group into two families, corresponding to the subfamilies of Edwards and Haime, although, when the living polyps shall have been carefully studied in all the recent genera, it may be found that the families are not correctly limited.

The genera of which the relations are most in doubt, are the typical *Turbinolinæ* of Edwards and Haime (*Turbinolia*, *Sphenotrochus*, *Discotrochus*, *Desmophyllum*, etc.). It is possible that these belong with *Caryophyllidæ* to the *Oculinacea*, while the *Flabellinæ* may alone belong to the *Astræacea* near *Eusmilidæ*. This cannot be determined satisfactorily until the living polyps of some of these genera have been thoroughly studied.

Paracyathus Edw. and Haime.

Paracyathus Edwards and Haime, Ann. des Sci. nat., 3 sér., ix, p. 318, 1848; Coralliaires, ii, p. 52, 1857.

Corallum cylindrical or turbinate, attached by a broad, expanded base. Wall naked, costulate. Calicle cup-shaped. Septa numerous, in four or five cycles, unequal, the summits rounded and little exsert. Columella concave, composed of prominent, elongated, papilliform processes, connected with the internal edges of the septa. Pali numerous, in several series at unequal distances from the center, those of the primary cycle farthest inward; they arise from the inner edges of the septa of all the cycles except the last, or next to the last,* and are similar to the processes of the columella.

---

* According to Edwards and Haime they exist before the septa of all the cycles, except the *next to the last*, and those are larger which belong to the younger cycles. But in the three following, and many other species, they exist before all the septa except those of the *last* cycle, and those in front of the primaries are largest. Even in the figure of *P. Stokesii* by Edwards and Haime, pali are wanting only in front of the last cycle of septa.

Paracyathus caltha Verrill.

Paracyathus Caltha Verrill, Proc. Boston Soc. Nat. History, xii, p. 394, 1869.

Plate IX, figures 9, 9^a.

Corallum turbinate, with an expanding base; pedicle about onehalf the width of the summit. Costæ corresponding to all the septa, prominent near the margin of the cup and dentate; below represented only by lines of granules. Calicle cup-shaped, elliptical with flattened sides, the ratio of the axes as 100 : 140; the summit of the longer axis is somewhat lower than that of the shorter. Septa in five regular cycles; those of the first and second subequal, rather broad and stout, thickened uniformly, rounded at the summits, projecting about ·02 of an inch, finely granulated on the sides. The other septa are equidistant and diminish regularly in width and height, the last being thin and narrow. Columella formed by numerous stout, styliform processes, rounded at tip, not crowded. The pali are similar in size, but more prominent and flattened, increasing in height as the septa diminish, their inner edges denticulate. They are present before all the septa except those of the fifth cycle.

Height of largest specimen ·50 of an inch; diameter ·45 by ·32; depth of cup ·20 of an inch.

Monterey, California,—J. Xantus, (Museums of Smithsonian Institution and Yale College).

Paracyathus Stearnsii Verrill, op. cit., p 393.

Corallum with an expanded base, above which it is somewhat constricted, and then expands rapidly to the edge of the broad, shallow cup, which is broad-oval in form, the edge bent into slight lobes or undulations. Exterior of the wall with very numerous, prominent, subequal, scabrous costæ, which extend from the summit to the outer edge of the base; on the basal portion three or five smaller ones often alternate with one more prominent; toward the summit some of them have a tendency to rise into crests; all are covered with several series of small, sharp granulations, similar to those on the sides of the septa. Five complete cycles of septa, with some small ones in some of the systems belonging to the sixth cycle, so that the whole number is about one hundred and twenty. The primary and secondary septa are considerably broader than the others, broadly rounded and somewhat exsert at summit, narrowed toward the base and divided into two or three unequal, broad, stout, paliform teeth, which are rough and lacerately spinulose at summit, and covered on the sides with coarse, rough granulations. The septa of the two succeeding cycles are successively narrower, thinner, and less exsert, with similar but smaller, rough, paliform teeth. The septa of the fifth cycle are narrow and destitute of pali. Columella small, papillose, the papillæ numerous, slender, prominent, lacerately spinulose at summit.

Height ·60; diameter of narrowest part ·38 by ·50; diameter of cup ·50 by ·72 ; depth of cup ·25 of an inch.

Monterey, California,—Robert E. C. Stearns. One specimen.

Paracyathus humilis Verrill, sp. nov.

Corallum small, cylindrical, about as wide at base as summit. Wall thin, feebly costate, except near the margin of the cup, where the costæ become thinner, more elevated, and granulous. Calicle rather shallow, with a sunken center. Columella small, composed of rather open, contorted processes, with an irregular, papillose surface. Septa in four cycles; the primaries and secondaries subequal, with the inner edge perpendicular and the summits broadly rounded and considerably exsert; those of the third and fourth cycles much thinner and narrower, and very little exsert; all the septa have their sides strongly and roughly granulated. Pali prominent and rather slender, subequal, a few of them divided into two parts, most of them with irregular sides from which are developed small rough lobes, projecting in various directions. There are no pali in front of the septa of the fourth cycle.

Height of the largest specimen ·20; breadth ·22; depth of calicle ·07; the primary septa are ·06 broad and project ·05; diameter of the columella ·06 of an inch.

Pearl Islands,—F. H. Bradley.

Bathycyathus Edw. and Haime.

Bathycyathus M. Edw. and J. Haime, Ann. des Sci. naturelles, 3ᵉ sér., ix, p. 294, 1848; Corallinires, ii, p. 22, 1857.

Corallum simple, elongated, attached by a broad base. Costæ fine, close, and simple. Calicle elliptical, very deep. Columella slightly developed, composed of irregular processes. Septa well developed, in five cycles (in the known species); those of the last cycle more developed than those of the preceding one, towards which they closely approach exteriorly; primaries and secondaries about equal. Pali narrow and elevated, in a single circle around the columella.

Two species of this genus, besides the following, are known: *B. Indicus* Edw. and H. is from the Island of Juan Fernandez, at the depth of 80 fathoms; *B. Sowerbyi* Edw. and H. is from the upper Cretaceous green-sand, Wiltshire, England.

Bathycyathus Chilensis Edw. and Haime.

Annales des Sci. nat., 3e sér., ix, p. 294. Pl. 9, fig. 5, 1848; Coralliaires, ii, p. 23, 1857.

Corallum with the calicle subelliptical; the ratio of the axes as 100 : 166; the summits of the small axis a little reëntrant and more elevated than those of the large axis, which are rounded. Columella oblong, reduced. Septa very close, very little thickened externally and becoming very thin within, with the faces covered with numerous, very fine 'grains, disposed in series parallel to the edge. Pali very thin, covered with extremely prominent grains, with the internal edge a little flexuous.—(Edw. and Haime).

Height, $\cdot 40^{mm}$; larger axis of the calicle, $\cdot 25$; smaller, $\cdot 15$; depth of fossette, $\cdot 13$.

Coast of Chili,—Gay.

Family, TURBINOLIDÆ Edw. and Haime (restricted).

Turbinolinæ Edw. and Haime, Ann. des Sci. nat., ix, p. 235; Coralliaries, ii, p. 95, 1857.

The genera referred to this group are distinguised by the entire absence of pali, and generally by the very open appearance of the chambers between the septa. It includes two groups, or sub-families, already referred to on page 536: the *Turbinolinæ*, in which there is no epitheca and the calicles are generally circular; and *Flabellinæ*, in which the wall is complete'y covered by a pelicle-like epitheca, and in which the calicles are usually elliptical.

Desmophyllum Ehrenberg.

Desmophyllum Ehrenburg, Corall. des rothen Meeres, p. 75, 1834; Edw. and Haime; Ann. des Sci. nat., ix, p. 252, 1848; Coralliaires, ii, p. 76, 1857.

Corallum simple, elevated, attached by an encrusting base. Wall naked, usually smooth below and costate or crested near the summit. Calicle very deep at center, without a columella. Septa broad, much exsert, generally curved outward.

This genus includes several living species from the West Indies; Mediterranean; Atlantic coasts of Europe; Japan; and the following from South America. It also occurs in the Miocene of southern Europe.

Desmophyllum Cumingii Edw. and Haime.

Desmophyllum Cumingii Edw. and Haime, Ann. des Sci. nat., 3e sér., ix. p. 254, Pl. 7, fig. 11, 1848; Coralliaries, ii, p 77, 1857.

This species differs from *D. cristagalli* in this that it is much less elongated, and fixed by a large and scarcely curved base. Ratio of the axes as 100 : 157. The septa are proportionally less projecting, and one can distinguish on their sides lines of fine and very scattered grains, parallel to the superior edge; the fosette of the calicle is still more narrow.

Height, 40 millim.; longer axis of the calicle, 26; smaller axis, 19; the primary septa project 5.—(Edw. and Haime).

Pacific coast of South America,—H. Cuming.

This species I have not seen, and therefore reproduce the description given by Edwards and Haime.

As it was collected by Mr. Hugh Cuming, it probably belongs to the Panamian fauna.

Suborder, FUNGACEA Verrill.

Fungidæ (family) Edw. and Haime, Corall., iii. p. 1; + *Merulinaceæ* (tribe) op. cit., ii, p. 627; + *Echinoporinæ* (subfamily) op. cit., p. 621; + *Siderastræa*, and some other genera referred to *Astræidæ*.

Fungacea Verrill. Proceedings Essex Institute, iv. p. 146, 1865; American Journal of Science, vol. xl, p. 128, 1865.

Polyps short and broad, not exsert, either simple, or becoming compound by marginal budding, rarely by fissiparity; in compound species the individual polyps are usually not clearly separated by definite walls, the septa of adjacent cells blending. Tentacles various in number and form, usually short and lobe-like, or bilobed, often rudimentary or wanting. Coralla generally broad and low, in comp und species usually foliaceous or encrusting, the growth chiefly centrifugal, the septal system composing the chief part of the coral. Walls imperfectly developed, often rudimentary or wanting, when present usually forming the basal or attached portion. Interseptal chambers generally open from top to bottom, though mostly partially interrupted by transverse bars or trabiculæ, which unite adjacent septa; but sometimes crossed by well formed dissepiments, as in *Pavonia* and *Siderastræa*.

Family, FUNGIDÆ Dana (restricted).

Fungidæ (pars) Dana, Zoöphytes U. S. Expl. Exp., p. 283, 1846.
Funginæ (subfamily) Edw. and Haime, Ann. des Sci. nat., 3e ser., xv, p. 75, 1851; Coralliaires, iii, p. 4, 1860.
Fungidæ Verrill, Proc. Essex Inst., iv, p. 146, 1865.

Coralla simple or compound, free or attached, low and broad, the compound forms often foliaceous. Walls basal, little developed, often strongly costate, perforated by irregular openings, destitute of epitheca. Septa dentate, low, widely spreading, in simple species very numerous, in compound ones often but few. Interseptal chambers crossed by transverse trabiculae. Costae echinulate, often spinose.

In some compound genera the polyps are of two or more kinds, the lateral or secondary ones often very imperfectly developed, but the central, primary polyp, even in these, has the essential structure of the typical forms.

Fungia Lamarck.

Fungia (pars) Lamarck, Syst. des animaux sans vert., p. 369 1801; Hist. Anim. sans vert., ii, p. 236, 1816; 2nd ed., p. 369, 1836; Ehrenberg, Corall. des rothen Meeres, p. 48, 1834.

Fungia Dana, Zoophytes U. S. Expl. Exp., p. 287, 1846; Edw. and Haime, Ann. des Sci. nat., 3e sér, xv, p. 76, 1851; Coralliaries, iii, p. 5, 1860.

Corallum simple, circular or nearly so, while young turbinate and attached by a narrow base; the outer margin growing outward rapidly and becoming horizontal or revolute, the pedicle breaks off and the coral afterward remains free, resting upon the flat or concave basal surface, formed by the wall, which in life is completely covered by a lime-secreting membrane, by which the scar of adherence is soon obliterated. Wall more or less perforated by irregular openings, especially near the margin, covered with radiating costae, which are denticulate or even spinose. Septa very numerous, unequal; the principal ones high and thickened near the central fosette, those of the later cycles broadest near the margin, becoming thin and uniting together toward their inner edges, usually with a more or less marked tentacular tooth at the points where they become narrower. Central fosette small. Columella little developed, trabicular.

This genus is represented by many large and fine species, several of them becoming more than a foot in diameter, in the Indo-Pacific fauna. These species abound in the shallow lagoons of the Feejee and Society Islands, Kingsmills, Phillipines, and throughout the tropical parts of the central Pacific and Indian Oceans, extending on the coast of Africa from Zanzibar to the coral reefs of the Red Sea. In the Atlantic Ocean none have hitherto been found, unless a small undescribed species, dredged by Mr. Pourtales, of the U. S. Coast Survey, at a great depth between Florida and Cuba, really belongs to this genus.

The following is remarkable as the only species hitherto discovered on the Pacific coast of America. It appears to be very local in its habitat, having been as yet found only at one small island.

Fungia elegans Verrill.

Fungia elegans Verrill, Amer. Journal of Science. 2d ser. xlix, p. 100, Jan. 1870.

Plate X, figures 1 and 2.

Corallum, when young, regular and round, often becoming slightly oval; when adult, usually more or less angular, the edge plicated, forming six to twelve lobes. The upper surface becomes very convex in mature specimens and the lower surface deeply concave and covered with very numerous, fine, subequal, elevated costæ, which are finely dentate on the outer half, becoming nearly entire and very faint toward the center, which usually shows the scar, where it was attached when young. Septa thick and rather crowded, very unequal, the six primaries very prominent and thick at the inner end; those of succeeding cycles successively shorter and less elevated. Edges of septa unevenly crenulate, or finely dentate. Columella slightly developed, loosely spongy; median fosette small, narrow, elongated; the two septa in the direction of its longer diameter much less elevated and thinner than the rest. Trabiculæ stout, conspicuous, often coalescing into continuous transverse plates.

The smallest unattached specimens are ·90 of an inch broad by ·35 high; ordinary specimens are about 1·90 broad by 1·10 high; some of the largest 2·25 by 1·15; 2·35 by 1·20; 2·40 by 1·25; 2·55 by 1·11.

Near La Paz,—J. Pedersen.

Of this small but very interesting species Capt. Pedersen has sent more than one hundred specimens, all of which came from a single locality.

Family, AGARICIDÆ Verrill.

Fungidæ (pars) Dana, Zoöphytes U. S. Expl. Exp., p. 283, 1846.
Lophoserinæ Edw. and Haime, Comptes-rendus de l'Acad. des Sci., xxix, p. 71, 1849.
Lophoserinæ (pars) Edw. and Haime, Ann. des Sci. nat., 3ᵉ ser., xv, p. 101, 1851;
 Coralliaires, iii. p. 35, 1860.
Lophoseridæ Verrill, Proc. Essex Inst., iv. p. 146, 1865.

Coralla simple or compound. Wall, and basal disk of compound species, compact, imperforate, costate. Costæ generally nearly equal, seldom echinulate or dentate. Septa compact, usually few, low, prolonged outwardly, extending between adjacent cells. In compound species the coral is generally encrusting, or thin and foliaceous, the polyps covering one or both sides of the foliæ, and budding chiefly around the margins, from the prolonged septal systems. The cells are not separated by definite walls. In some genera, however, like *Pavonia* and *Siderastræa*, the coral forms more or less thickened plates, or even globular masses, while the interseptal chambers have transverse dissepiments, as well as trabiculæ.

Since *Lophoseris* is a late synonym of *Pavonia* it is undesirable to use it for the derivation of the family name. *Pavonidæ* is in use in ornithology.

Pavonia Lamarck.

Pavonia (pars) Lamarck, Syst. des animaux sans vert., p. 372, 1801; Hist. nat. des anim. sans vert., ii, p. 238, 1816; 2nd edit., ii, p. 376.
Pavonia Ehrenberg, Corall. des rothen Meeres, p. 104, 1834; Dana, Zoophytes U. S. Expl. Exp., p. 319, 1846.
Lophoseris Edw. and Haime, Comptes-rendus de l'Acad. des Sci., xxix, p. 72, 1849; Ann. des Sci. nat., 3ᵉ sér., xv, p. 121, 1851; Coralliaires, iii, p. 65, 1860.
Pavonia Verrill, Bulletin Mus. Comp. Zoölogy, i, p. 54, 1864; Proc. Essex Inst., v, p. 45, 1866.

Coralla compound, adherent, encrusting or foliaceous, generally with rising crests, foliæ, or lobes of various kinds; sometimes thick and massive, often thin and delicate. The foliaceous forms usually have both surfaces covered with polyps, but some of the horizontally spreading species are foliaceous near the edge, with polyps only on the upper side, the lower side being naked and finely costulate. Polyp-cells scattered, clearly defined, but not separated by distinct walls, the adjacent ones united by prolongations of the septa.

Columella tubercular, sometimes rudimentary. Septa few, generally more or less thickened. Dissepiments, in the thick species, well developed; in the thinner ones represented only by trabiculæ.

The name, *Pavonia*, was rejected by Edwards and Haime because Hubner used it among insects in 1816, but they overlooked the fact that the genus was first established in the earlier work of Lamarck, published in 1801.

This genus has nearly the same distribution as *Fungia*. It is found throughout the tropical regions of the Pacific and Indian Oceans, from the west coast of America to the east coast of Africa, and from the Hawaiian Islands, Southern Japan, Hong Kong, and the Red Sea on the north, to Australia and Zanzibar on the south. It is represented in this great area by many species. No species has yet been found in the Atlantic Ocean, where it is replaced by *Agaricia*.

Pavonia gigantea Verrill.

Pavonia gigantea Verrill, Proc. Boston Soc. Nat. Hist., xii, p. 394, 1869.

Plate IX, figure 7.

Corallum very large, thick, encrusting, near the edges often somewhat free; upper surface nearly flat or variously undulated and uneven, covered with large, distant, stellate cells, which are either irregularly scattered, or sometimes in somewhat regular rows for a short distance, and in the latter case contiguous laterally, but the rows are separated by spaces equal to once or twice the diameter of the cells, which are united by very prominent septo-costal lamellæ. In the largest cells there are usually twenty-four septa, in three regular cycles, often twelve, sometimes only eight or ten, and frequently irregular numbers, between twelve and twenty-six, but in all cases they are alternately large and small. The larger septa are very stout, much thickened at the margin, tapering to a sharp edge within, the sides and edge roughly granulous; the costal part is very prominent, thick, but less so than the marginal part, sharp-edged, and almost always continuous with one of the large septa of an adjacent cell. The alternating small septa are not more than half as wide, thin, much less prominent, slightly thickened at the margin, and extend as thin costal lamellæ between the much thicker and more prominent primary ones to adjacent cells, but they are often interrupted and variously branched. Stout trabiculæ are often visible at the surface between the costal lamellæ. Columella represented by a small central tubercle, which is often wanting, and a deeper, large, solid portion, which fills the center of the cell below, and unites with the inner edges of the septa. The endotheca consists of distinct, regular, thin, nearly horizontal, transverse septa, as in many Astræans; these are about ·03 to ·05 of an inch apart in the same interseptal chamber, as seen in a vertical section. The radiating septa are solid and continuous.

The largest specimen is nearly three feet long, two feet broad, and eight inches thick in the middle; diameter of cells mostly ·08 to ·12; distance between them, in the direction of the costal plates, generally ·10 to ·16 of an inch.

Pearl Islands,—F. H. Bradley.

It was brought from seven fathoms by Mr. Clarke, a pearl collector who gave great assistance to Mr. Bradley while making his collections.

Pavonia clivosa Verrill, op. cit., p. 395.

Plate IX, figure 8.

Corallum thick and massive, lobed, or rising into very large rounded eminences or oblong ridges, thickly covered with stellate cells, which are smaller and nearer together than in the preceding species. Cells mostly uniformly scattered, often closely crowded and contiguous on the summits of the prominences, usually separated on other parts at distances about equal to their own diameter. Septa generally from sixteen to twenty-four, alternately larger and smaller; the larger ones rather thin, only little thickened even at the margin, roughly granulous on the sides; their costal prolongations elevated and rather thin.

Smaller septa about half as wide, a little thinner and less elevated, as are also their costal prolongations. Columella a small tubercle, often prominent, sometimes flattened. Internal structure as in the preceding, but the transverse septa are nearer together.

The largest specimens are ten inches to two feet in diameter; and often a foot thick or high; some of the prominences or lobes are from four to six inches in diameter, and nearly as high; diameter of cells mostly ·05 to ·06; distance between them ordinarily ·05 to ·08.

Pearl Islands, at extreme low-water of spring tides,—F. H. Bradley.

Stephanaria Verrill.

Stephanocora Verrill, Proc. Boston Soc. Nat. History, vol. x, p. 330, 1866, (*non* Ehrenberg).
Stephenaria Verrill, Transactions Conn. Acad., i. p. 340, 1867.

Coralla compound, consisting of irregular short, lobe-like branches. Cells moderately large, with two or three cycles of septa, which are denticulate on the edge, well developed, and mostly confluent with those of adjacent cells. Walls indistinct or wanting, the divisions between the cells indicated only by small, granular points, which sometimes interrupt the septa of adjoining cells. Columella papillose. Paliform papillæ before all the principal septa, the inner ones becoming confounded with the columella.

This genus resembles *Synarœa* V. and *Psammocora* Dana, but differs from the first in the well developed septa, and many other characters, and from the last in having papilliform pali and columella.

Stephanaria stellata Verrill.

Stephanocora stellata Verrill, op. cit., p. 330, 1866.

Plate IX, figures 4, 4ª.

Coralla forming rounded clumps of short, irregularly lobed and contorted branches, which are very unequal in size and form; sometimes nearly simple and angular, with a large cell at the top; at other times, even on the same clump, having the summit very much expanded, so as to form flattened, contorted lobes, with acute summits and lateral crests, or even mæandriniform lobes. The branches are usually about an eighth of an inch distant, sometimes more, the sides covered with rather large, starlike, shallow cells, one, or several, larger than the others often terminating the branches, which appear to increase by the upward extension of one of the edges of these cells by submarginal budding. Septa twelve to twenty, often with other rudimentary ones, rather thick and strong, with sharp, spiny granulations or teeth on the sides and edges, and mostly confluent with those of adjacent cells. Color of the unbleached coral ash-gray or yellowish gray.

Height of coral 3 inches; length of living portion of branches ·25 to ·45; the diameter of the larger cells ·10 of an inch.

Panama and Pearl Islands,—F. H. Bradley; La Paz, Gulf of California,—J. Pedersen.

ADDENDA.

Since the preceding article has been in press several collections have been received from new localities, containing, in some cases, additional varieties and species, some of which are introduced here to make the article more complete, while the others will be enumerated in the geographical lists in the next article. Some of the species of the west coast have also been figured and described during the past year in foreign works. Dr. Albert Kölliker, especially, has very fully described some of the *Pennatulidæ* in his admirable work on that group.

Renilla amethystina Verrill, p. 379.

Renilla reniformis (*pars*) S. Richiardi, Monografia della famiglia dei Pennatularii, in Archivo per la Zoologia, l'Anatomia e la Fisiologia, Ser. ii, vol. i, p. 133. 1869, (*non* Pallas).

Dr. Richiardi has made a serious mistake in referring this very distinct species to the common species of the southern coast of the United States. He also refers *R. Danæ* V. and *R. peltata* V. to *R. reniformis*, both of which are very distinct from it, approaching *R. violacea* more nearly, though apparently quite distinct from that species also. It is probable that he is personally unacquainted with these species.

Leioptilum undulatum Verrill, p. 381

Pennatula undulata Richiardi, op. cit., p. 33.

Leioptilum undulatum Kölliker, Anatomisch-Systematische Beschreibung der Alcyonarien, I, Pennatuliden. (Abhandl. d. Senckenb. Naturf. Gesellschaft, Bd. vii), p. 143, Taf. X, figures 76, 77, 78. 1870.

Prof. Kölliker describes three additional specimens from Mazatlan, all of which were larger than the original specimen. They were respectively 127^{mm} long by 32^{mm} broad; 167 long, the feather 89, stock of 78; and 235^{mm} long, the feather 133, stock 102, breadth of feather 58, stock 22, greatest breadth of the pinnæ 48, height 26. The last specimen had 32 pinnæ on one side and 34 on the other.

Dr. W. Newcomb last year dredged two specimens in the Gulf of Fonseca, one of which he has sent to the Museum of Yale College. He has also loaned me a colored drawing, made from one of these specimens while living, by Mrs. Newcomb.

The specimen referred to is considerably smaller than those previously described, and is evidently quite immature. Its entire length is 66^{mm}, of which the pinnate portion, or feather, is 38, and the peduncle 28. The pinnate portion is rather oblong, very little rounded on the sides and obtusely rounded at the end. The ventral surface (dorsal according to Kölliker) of the stalk is narrow below and concealed by the pinnæ, which meet but do not overlap; the upper part is broader and not concealed, its surface is nearly smooth, light gray with streaks of brown. The dorsal surface (ventral, Kölliker), comprising about half the entire circumference, is thickly covered, except along a linear, median, naked space on the lower half, with rounded verrucæ, formed by the rudimentary polyps, or asexual zoöides; the outer verrucæ are largest, those nearer the middle becoming smaller and more crowded; the verrucæ are purplish brown, owing to numerous minute purplish spicula, the surface between is grayish white. There are 22 pinnæ on each side, with a few other rudimentary ones; the larger ones are broadly rounded, the edge thick and slightly undulated, forming nearly a half circle; they are attached by a narrow base, the polyps of the edge extending in front to the point of attachment, but the dorsal edge is naked, elevated, thin, and concave; the sides are smooth, grayish white, except near the outer border, which, like the edge and the bodies of the polyps, is purplish, owing to the minute purple spicula with which those parts are filled. The polyps are closely arranged on the thickened edge, in about three rows. The peduncle is constricted just below the feather, swollen below the middle, blunt at the end, and yellowish below, blotched with purplish brown on the upper part of the dorsal surface.

Length 2·65 inches; the feather 1·55; the peduncle 1·10; breadth of the feather ·80; of the peduncle ·40; of the stock in middle of feather ·35; breadth of largest pinnæ ·50; their height in center ·30; of posterior edge ·20; width of polyp-bearing edge ·07.

The specimen drawn by Mrs. Newcomb, was, when living, 4·55 inches long; the feather 2·85; the peduncle 1·65; greatest breadth of feather 1·40; of peduncle ·80. The feather is more oval in outline, the middle pinnæ being more extended; the peduncle is strongly constricted above, suddenly expanded below the constriction, and thence tapering to a point. The color of the peduncle, in life, was orange-yellow at the lower end, light yellow in the middle, upper part spotted with dark gray and brown; front of stalk tinged with purple; back grayish, the verrucæ dark brown; pinnæ, on the back and sides, whitish, the edge with the polyps yellowish brown.

Ptilosarcus Gurneyi Gray, p. 382.

Ptilosarcus Gurneyi Richiardi, op. cit., p. 61, Tav. IX, fig. 58; Kölliker, op. cit., p. 146.

This species has an elongated, club-shaped form, the peduncle constituting from one-third to nearly one-half the entire length. The pinnate portion is thick, rather oblong, slightly tapering both ways from the middle. The pinnæ are numerous, 50 to 54 on each side, crowded, broad, rounded, nearly semicircular, attached by a broad base, the posterior edge extending beyond the base in the form of a rounded lobe; the edge is thickened and covered by small polyps, arranged in about four rows, each polyp surrounded by prominent, spine-like spicula. Dorsal surface (ventral according to Kölliker) of the stalk with two broad bands of small, crowded, granule-like papillæ, formed by the asexual zoöides or "rudimentary polyps." The peduncle is thick, bulbous, very muscular, the surface strongly sulcated in contraction; the interior with four longitudinal canals. Axis long, slender, fusiform, tapering to the long, slender, recurved points.

A large specimen from Puget Sound, in alcohol, is 10 inches long; the feather 5·25; the peduncle 4·75; greatest breadth of feather 2; diameter of peduncle 1·25; breadth of largest pinnæ 1·50; height ·80.

Prof. Kölliker describes a specimen from Vancouver Island, belonging to the Museum of Stockholm, which has quite different proportions: whole length 283^{mm}; feather 180; peduncle 103; breadth of peduncle 20; of feather 45 to 50; of pinnæ 25; height of pinnæ 30^{mm}. This specimen had 54 pinnæ on each side.

Stylatula, page 382.

In addition to *S. gracilis* and *S. elongata*, Richiardi refers to this genus *Virgularia Finmarchica* Sars; *V. multiflora* Kner, from the Adriatic Sea; and *V. elegans* Danielsen, from Christiansand.

Leptogorgia Agassizii Verrill, p. 388.

Some of the specimens from La Paz are of large size (12 to 18 inches high and 18 to 24 broad) and form complex fronds. The more regular ones give off several lateral fronds from near the base of the primary ones; these are at first nearly at right angles to the main frond and attached to it vertically by one edge, but they soon bend around laterally and become parallel to the primary frond; other fronds often arise from the secondary ones, especially from the part where the bend occurs, and spread in the opposite direction. In some specimens all the secondary fronds, often amounting to a dozen or more, are thus united together, leaving between them large square or oblong spaces, often open both from above and below. In one specimen the fronds are numerous, more or less united together, and spreading outward in all directions, while the upper sides are proliferous and give rise to many small fronds, thus producing a large and pretty regular rosette.

These specimens have slender branchlets and small meshes. The color is bright red or purplish, mingled with yellow.

Leptogorgia pulchra, sp. nov.

Corallum reticulated, flabelliform, either simple and extending in one plane, or composed of several fan-shaped fronds arising from the sides of the primitive one nearly at right angles and then becoming parallel. The trunk usually divides close to the base into several principal branches which subdivide rapidly and soon lose themselves among the reticulated branchlets. The meshes are variable in form and size, but commonly angular with rounded corners, often squarish, frequently higher than broad. The branchlets, in the typical form, are rather thick, squarish, with prominent rounded verrucæ, arranged in about two rows on each side, and rather crowded, but in the slender form fewer and more distant, and often but slightly elevated. The cells, when open, are mostly slightly bilobed.

Color light or deep reddish or purplish and usually tinged with yellow or orange, often yellowish red or brick-color, or various shades of reddish brown.

Height of the larger specimens 8 to 15 inches, generally broader than high; diameter of the branchlets, in the best grown specimens, about ·08, in some cases the branchlets vary in the same specimen from ·05 to ·10, sometimes they are slender throughout and not more than ·05 in diameter.

The spicula are deep red and bright yellow, or orange-yellow, mingled usually in about equal numbers. The longer double-spindles are rather slender, oblong fusiform, rather obtusely pointed, with a pretty broad median space and about three well separated whorls of low crowded warts on each end, and small terminal clusters. The stouter double spindles are similar, but more oblong in form and blunter, with about two crowded whorls and a terminal cluster of warts on each end. Many small spicula have a wider median space and one whorl, with a terminal cluster close to it, on each end; minute rounded heads are frequent. The polyp-spicula are mostly bright red, but some yellow; they are mostly rather slender with few slight denticulations on one or both sides. The longer double-spindles measure ·102^{mm} by ·036^{mm}, ·096 by ·036, ·090 by ·030, ·084 by ·030; the stouter ones ·090 by ·036, ·084 by ·036, 078 by ·036; the small spicula with single whorl on each end ·054 by ·024, ·048 by ·024, ·040 by ·024.

La Paz,—6 to 8 fathoms, by divers,—J. Pedersen.

Leptogorgia pulchra, var. exilis, nov.

Corallum flabelliform, loosely reticulated, with larger, squarish or oblong meshes. Branchlets quite slender, roundish, with smaller, scattered, sometimes prominent, but more commonly scarcely raised, rounded verrucæ, which are mostly arranged alternatingly in about four rows on the branchlets, on the terminal ones often in a single row on each edge.

Color, as in the typical form, variable, but always formed by a mingling of some shade of red with bright yellow or orange spicula, in various proportions. Some of the specimens are 12 to 15 inches high and about as wide; branchlets ·04 to ·07 in diameter; meshes ·20 to ·25 wide; ·25 to ·75 high.

The spicula agree very nearly in size, form, and color with those of the typical form.

La Paz, by pearl divers,—J. Pedersen.

Several specimens of this variety are in the collection. They differ so much from the typical specimens, which are more numerous, that they might readily be mistaken for a distinct species, but one large specimen has the branches, branchlets, and verrucæ of the typical form throughout the greater part of its extent, but toward one edge they gradually diminish in size, while the verrucæ diminish at the same time in size and number, until we have the extreme form of the slender variety, forming a considerable portion of the upper end and one edge of the frond, thus proving the specific identity of the two forms. The spicula, also, even from extreme specimens of each form, show very little variation.

This species in external form has considerable resemblance to *L. media* and *L. Agassizii*. The typical form has about the same sized branchlets and meshes as the former, but has more prominent verrucæ; it is much coarser than *L. Agassizii* and has larger meshes, but some of the forms might be mistaken for a coarse variety of the latter. The spicula are, however, very different from both those species, which have spicula remarkable for their short stout forms, with bluntly rounded ends and crowded warts.

The slender variety resembles, in the size of the meshes and branchlets, *L. eximia*, but the latter has entirely different spicula, remarkable for the distant and elongated warts.

Leptogorgia tenuis, sp. nov.

Corallum flabelliform, consisting of very slender branches and branchlets, which are loosely reticulated, many of the branchlets besides the terminal ones, remaining free. The meshes are generally about a quarter of an inch wide, and vary in length from a quarter of an inch to nearly an inch. The larger branches are roundish with distant, scattered, relatively large, subconical, prominent verrucæ, which form about four irregular rows. The terminal branchlets are very slender, with the conspicuous, conical verrucæ alternating in a single row on each edge; the tips enlarged and flattened, terminated by two verrucæ. Cœnenchyma thin, firm, finely granulous. Axis blackish.

Color bright light red, uniform throughout. The spicula are light red and yellowish, and are quite regularly fusiform. The longer double-spindles are slender and very acute, with a well defined median space, bordered by large wreaths of short rough warts, beyond which there are three or four whorls of smaller warts, diminishing gradually to the ends, where they blend with the acute terminal ones. The stouter double-spindles are similar in form and structure and only a little less acute, with the warts more crowded. There are a few minute spicula, with a wide median space and a single whorl and terminal cluster of warts on each end. The polyp-spicula are light pink slender, with a few low blunt denticulations on one or both sides.

The longer double-spindles measure $\cdot 138^{mm}$ by $\cdot 042^{mm}$, $\cdot 132$ by $\cdot 042$, $\cdot 120$ by $\cdot 036$, $\cdot 108$ by $\cdot 036$; the stouter double-spindles are $\cdot 138$ by $\cdot 048$, $\cdot 126$ by $\cdot 048$, $\cdot 120$ by $\cdot 054$, $\cdot 120$ by $\cdot 048$, $\cdot 108$ by $\cdot 048$, $\cdot 090$ by $\cdot 048$.

La Paz, on base of *Eugorgia nobilis*, var. *excelsa*, in from 4 to 6 fathoms,—J. Pedersen. One specimen.

Externally this species most resembles *L. eximia*, though the branchlets are more slender and the verrucæ fewer and larger. The spicula are entirely different, being more regularly fusiform and acute, with much less prominent and more numerous warts. They resemble those of *L. Adamsii* more than those of any other species, but are larger, and stouter, and less acute. In external appearance it also resembles the slender variety (*exilis*) of the preceding species, but the spicula are much larger, more regularly fusiform, and much more acute, with comparatively few of the short blunt forms.

Leptogorgia labiata, sp. nov.

Leptogorgia ramulus, var. (page 396).

Of this form, hitherto regarded as a northern dwarfed variety of *L. ramulus*, I have more recently seen additional specimens from other localities, all of which present the same characters, both of external appearance and spicula. I am therefore led to regard it as a distinct species.

It is low and densely branched, rigid, the branchlets short, thick, squarish, generally blunt, sometimes clavate, but often obtusely pointed. The verrucæ are conspicuous, elevated, rounded, closely arranged in about four longitudinal rows, divided at the summit or on the upper side into two lateral lobes or lips, which form the borders of the oblong cells.

The color is red or brownish, generally more or less tinged with yellow, especially around the cells.

The largest specimens seen are about five inches high and four broad; the terminal branchlets ·25 to 1 in. long; about ·12 in diameter.

The spicula are somewhat larger than those of *L. ramulus*, and decidedly stouter and more rounded at the ends, with more crowded warts, which usually form a rounded terminal cluster. They are rose-red and light yellow.

Acapulco,—A. Agassiz; Cape St. Lucas,—J. Xantus; Corinto, Nic.,—J. A. McNiel; Tehuantepec, Mexico,—Dr. Sumichrast (Chicago Academy).

Leptogorgia exigua, sp. nov.

This form I have formerly regarded as a dwarf variety of *L. cuspidata*, but having recently seen numerous specimens from several widely separated localities, I am led to regard it as a peculiar species, allied to *L. cuspidata* and *L. rigida*.

Although quite variable in color and somewhat so in form, it nevertheless always has characteristic features by which it may be easily recognized. The color is really less variable, when closely examined, than it would seem to be at first sight. It is a mixture of purplish red and yellow in varying proportions, the yellow spicula being generally more or less concentrated around the cells, and often tinging the whole surface, while at other times red or purplish spicula predominate at the surface, giving this hue to the whole coral. It is a low, thickly branched, rather rigid species, the branches arising subpinnately and ascending. The branchlets are roundish, slightly tapering, generally with obtusely pointed or rounded ends. The cells are small, not prominent, often sunken, evenly scattered over the surface, except along a narrow, ill-defined naked space on each side of the branches, which sometimes shows a slight groove.

Color purplish red or brown, with or without a tinge of sulphur yellow; reddish or purplish with a circle of sulphur-yellow around the cells; or yellowish more or less mixed with purplish or reddish at the surface. Axis black.

Height 2 to 5 inches; breadth about the same; length of terminal branchlets ·25 to 1·50; diameter ·10 to ·15.

The spicula are mostly small and blunt, bright rose-red or light purplish, mixed with bright yellow. The longer double-spindles are not numerous, rather oblong, stout, blunt, with about three crowded whorls and a terminal cluster of low, rough warts. The stouter double-spindles are numerous and of various forms, mostly short and thick, obtuse or rounded at the ends, with about two crowded whorls of rough warts on each end; some have a very narrow median space; others a well defined one; many short stout spicula have but one whorl of warts each side of the median, with rounded terminal clusters; minute ones of the same kind are abundant. There are also numerous rough heads and double-heads, of various sizes. The spicula are smaller and blunter, or more rounded, than in *L. rigida* and *L. cuspidata*, and there are none of the stout acute double-spindles, that are abundant in those species.

The longer double-spindles measure ·132^{mm} by ·042, ·102 by ·042, ·096 by ·036, ·084 by ·036; the stouter double-spindles ·102 by ·048, ·096 by ·048, ·084 by ·048, ·078 by ·042, ·072 by ·048; the heads ·072 by ·060, ·072 by ·048, ·060 by ·048, ·042 by ·042; the double-heads ·060 by ·048, ·042 by ·036.

Corinto, Nic., at low water, both yellowish and purplish varieties, common,—J. A. McNiel; Gulf of Nicoya, by pearl divers, small yellowish variety,—J. A. McNiel; Tehuantepec, Mex.,—Dr. Sumichrast (Chicago Acad.); Acapulco,—A. Agassiz; Guaymas,—Dr. E. Palmer (Chicago Acad. Science).

Eugorgia nobilis, var. excelsa Verrill, page 409.

This variety forms fan-shaped fronds and grows to a very large size, some of the specimens exceeding in height those of any other species of the west coast known to me. The base is large and spreading. The trunk is thick at base, usually very short, dividing at once into a number of main branches. Sometimes several trunks arise from the same expanded base and form large parallel fronds, close together. The main branches give off, subpinnately from each side, at distances of ·5 to 2 inches, irregularly alternating secondary branches, which on the outer branches are more numerous on the upper or inner side of the branches. The secondary branches subdivide in the same manner, as do their branches and branchlets in turn, until many of them are five or six times divided. The branches and branchlets mostly start out at a wide angle and then bend abruptly upward and become sub-parallel. The terminal branchlets are often from two to six inches long without division, and usually rather slender, a little compressed, with a well-marked median groove and a very narrow median naked space. The polyp-cells are very numerous, scarcely raised, and form a broad band on each side.

The color is uniform light yellowish brown or chestnut, varying somewhat in tint in different specimens, sometimes nearly brick-red.

One of the largest specimens is 34 inches high; 28 broad; diameter of the base 6; of the trunk 1·50; of the main branches mostly ·30 to ·40; of the terminal branchlets ·05 to ·12, but mostly about ·10 of an inch.

The spicula are pale yellow and pink. The longer double-spindles are moderately slender and acute, with about three irregular whorls of well-separated, prominent warts. The stouter double-spindles are larger and much stouter, bluntly rounded at the ends, with two or three whorls and a terminal cluster of large, rough warts, which are often crowded, but sometimes well separated. The double-wheels are unusually small, mostly longer than broad, with very small terminal and larger median wheels.

The longer double-spindles measure ·108^{mm} by ·036^{mm}, ·102 by ·042, ·102 by ·036, ·102 by ·030, ·096 by ·024, ·090 by ·033; the stouter double-spindles ·090 by ·042, ·084 by ·048, ·084 by ·045, ·078 by ·045; the double-wheels ·048 by ·042, ·042 by ·042, ·042 by ·036, ·036 by ·030, ·030 by ·030.

La Paz, 6 to 8 fathoms, by divers,—J. Pedersen; La Paz,—Major Wm. Rich; Acapulco,—A. Agassiz.

Eugorgia multifida Verrill, sp. nov.

Corallum flabelliform, the branches very numerously divided in a pinnate manner, forming densely ramulous, but not reticulated fronds, two or more sometimes arising from the same base.

The trunk divides at the base into several large, irregular, divergent and crooked branches; these often give off similar large and irregular secondary branches, which like the secondary branches are closely pinnate along their whole length the pinnae or branchlets being separated by intervals of ·10 to ·15 of an inch; most of these are again pinnate and many of them bipinnate and tripinnate, in the same manner, the branches being everywhere closely crowded, and often separated by spaces not exceeding their diameter, and seldom exceeding ·15 or ·20 of an inch. The branchlets are short and variously curved, spreading abruptly at wide angles, the terminal ones varying in length from ·10 to ·50 of an inch; they are more or less angular and covered, except along a narrow, often indistinct, median space, with crowded, prominent, rounded verrucae. Main branches strongly sulcated on the sides; and partially covered with distant, scattered verrucae.

Color deep orange-brown; the borders of the cells mostly bright yellow; the main branches streaked with red and yellow, more or less blended, due to the two colors of the spicula.

The largest specimen is 22 inches high; 24 broad; diameter of the main branches ·25 to ·40; of the branchlets ·05 to ·10, mostly about ·07.

The spicula are deep red and bright yellow intermingled with some that are light purplish. They are large for the genus, and consist largely of short, stout double-wheels with much fewer double-spindles.

The longer double-spindles are quite slender, mostly acute, with a wide median space, and there are four whorls of small, separate warts on each end. The stouter double-spindles are similar, but blunter and have more crowded warts. The double-wheels are mostly about as broad as long, with a well developed median space, bordered by broad, often sharp-edged "wheels," beyond which there is a smaller terminal wheel on each end; the edges of the wheels are often rough or warty on one side.

The longer double-spindles measure $·132^{mm}$ by $·042^{mm}$, ·126 by ·030, ·108 by ·036; the stouter double-spindles measure ·132 by ·048, ·120 by ·048, ·108 by ·048, ·108 by ·042, ·102 by ·054, ·102 by ·042; the double-wheels ·066 by ·048, ·060 by ·060, ·060 by ·054, ·054 by ·054.

La Paz. in 6 to 8 fathoms, by divers, rare,—J. Pedersen; Mazatlan,—J. Dickinson; Acapulco,—A. Agassiz.

In mode of growth, this species resembles *E. aurantiaca* and *E. Damiana*, but it is more densely ramulous, with larger and more prominent verrucae than either of those species, and the double-wheels are stouter and in form quite different from those of both, and much larger than those of the latter. The color is also peculiar in the six specimens examined.

The two following descriptions are reproduced from the American Journal of Science, xlviii, pp. 427 and 428, 1869. The spicula were prepared from the original specimens and sent by Prof. A. Kölliker.

Psammogorgia fucosa Verrill, p. 417.

The spicula from the original example of this species show that it is very distinct from the species that I have hitherto referred to it (*Leptogorgia Caryi*). It appears, judging from the spicula, to be a *Psammogorgia*, allied to *P. teres*, but quite distinct. The figure represents it as 10 inches high and 9 broad, with the branches about ·15 of an inch thick, enlarged at the axils. Several stems arise from one base, as is usual in *P. arbuscula*, the largest trunk being half an inch in diameter. The branches are irregularly dichotomous, the divisions being ·5 to 2 inches apart; the final branchlets are stout, scarcely tapering, obtuse or clavate at the ends, often crooked, ·5 to 1 inch long, ·12 to ·18 of an inch in diameter. Cells small, oblong or oval, flat on the branches, slightly raised on the branchlets. Color dull reddish.

It is remarkable for the great diversity in form and color of the spicula. These are white, yellowish, light red, deep red, and amethystine intermingled. They are mostly stout, blunt, and covered with large rough warts. Among them are various forms of spindles, double-spindles, double-heads, heads, and stout warty clubs, with various irregular forms. The stout double-spindles, which are most numerous, are short and thick, mostly with obtusely rounded ends, sometimes acute, median naked space narrow, bordered by whorls of large, coarse, rough warts, beyond which there are usually one or two whorls of smaller warts and a terminal cluster, but in many cases there are none between the median whorls and the terminal cluster, in other cases the whorls become crowded and thus the forms pass into large, stout "double-heads," in which the ends are rounded and densely covered with rough warts.

Numerous spicula lack the naked median space and are densely covered with large rough warts, some of these are short and rounded, in the form of heads; others are longer, tapering at both ends, and have the form of very stout spindles; others are large at one end, with the other tapering, or club-shaped. The polyp-spicula are long, slender spindles, tapering quite regularly to both ends and covered with small warts. The large double-spindles measure ·156^{mm} by ·072, ·156 by ·066, ·150 by ·072, ·144 by ·084, ·144 by ·060; the smaller ones ·120 by ·060, ·108 by ·060, ·072 by ·048; double-heads ·132 by ·096, ·132 by ·090, ·096 by ·084; the heads ·108 by ·084, ·048 by ·048; the stout spindles ·156 by ·072, ·144 by ·072, ·120 by ·072; the clubs ·144 by ·084, ·144 by ·072, ·096 by ·048; the polyp-spicula ·156 by ·030, ·156 by ·024, ·144 by ·024, ·102 by ·024.

Mazatlan,—Voyage of the Venus.

Echinogorgia aurantiaca Verrill, pp. 413 and 450.

The spicula of this species show that it is an *Echinogorgia*, pretty nearly allied to *E. susappo*. The spicula are yellow, mostly large, broad, flattened clubs, or scale-clubs, the smaller end often acute, sometimes blunt, covered with rough warts, the large end usually terminating in one or more broad, flat, irregular, rounded scales, which are often lobed, or even subdivided into sharp, lacerate spinules. With these are many, more or less regular, four-branched crosses, with rather slender, acute, warty branches; and various forms of irregular, often branched, warty spindles and compound spicula.

The clubs and scale-clubs resemble those of *E. susappo* figured by Dr. Kölliker in his Icones Histiologicæ, Taf. xviii, figs. $9_{,1}$ and $9_{,3}$. The scale-clubs measure ·290^{mm} by ·216^{mm}, ·288 by ·204, ·288 by ·156, ·264 by ·192, ·260 by ·168, ·240 by ·156, ·216 by ·156, ·192 by ·132, ·192 by ·084, ·180 by ·084; the crosses ·240 by ·192, ·180 by ·156, ·144 by ·120, ·120 by ·096; the irregular spindles ·336 by ·072, ·288 by ·0-4, ·252 by ·084.

Callao, Peru,—Mus. Paris.

Heterogorgia papillosa Verrill, sp. nov.

Corallum dichotomous, consisting of few, elongated crooked branches, which are two or three times divided. The branches are of nearly uniform size, and bend out in a broad curve at the axils. The terminal branchlets are from one to three inches long without division, and blunt at the end; like the branchlets they are round and crooked, covered on all sides with prominent papilla-like verrucæ, which are mostly eight lobed and open at summit. The lobes of the verrucæ are supported by long slender, sharp, curved spicula, which project but little from the surface. The lower parts of the verrucæ and the surface of the cœnenchyma are smoothish, and consist mostly of quite small, rough spicula. The axis is rigid, grayish, and wood-like in appearance, the surface showing an interwoven fibrous structure; in the branchlets thick, soft, and yellowish.

Color yellowish white, throughout.

The only specimen obtained is 5 inches high; 3 broad; diameter of branches and branchlets ·10 to ·14; height of largest verrucæ ·05.

The spicula are white and smaller than in the other species of the genus. The most conspicuous are roughly warted spindles and double-spindles, varying from long slender acute forms to stout, blunt, and irregular ones. With these are many rough irregular crosses and irregularly branched spicula. The crooked spicula from the verrucæ are long and quite slender, acute, variously curved, often bow-shaped, covered with small distant warts. The polyp-spicula are smaller and straighter, with fewer warts. The larger spindles and double-spindles measure ·336^{mm} by ·096^{mm}, ·336 by ·072, ·288 by ·084, ·264 by ·108, ·264 by ·084, ·264 by ·072, ·252 by ·060, ·240 by ·096, ·240 by ·072, ·240 by ·060, ·228 by ·096, ·228 by ·072, ·222 by ·108, ·222 by ·102, ·216 by ·078, ·192 by ·072; the crosses ·144 by ·108, ·108 by ·084; the long curved spicula ·432 by ·042, ·360 by ·042, ·360 by ·036, ·336 by ·030, ·312 by ·030, ·244 by ·030.

La Paz, on shell with *Eugorgia nobilis, var. excelsa*, in 6 to 8 fathoms, one specimen,—J. Pedersen.

No. 7.— *On the Geographical Distribution of the Polyps of the West Coast of America.*

In the preceding article I have included all the species hitherto described by others from the west coast of America, as well as those examined by myself. It is certain, however, that many additional species remain to be discovered. The tropical region or Panamian province, extending from Cape Blanco, Peru, to Lower California, and including the Gulf of California, is the only portion of the coast from which even tolerably complete collections have been made, and yet in that great region only the littoral and shallow water species have been collected. Doubtless many new and interesting forms will hereafter be discovered in the deeper waters and on the submerged banks off the coast.

Concerning the polyp-fauna of the coast of Lower California, we know almost nothing. From the coast farther northward a few small collections have been brought, and the lists of species from those regions are certainly very imperfect. From the coasts of Peru and Chili a greater number of species, mostly Actinians, have been described, but many of these need reëxamination from living specimens, and many others doubtless remain undescribed. The polyps of the Araucanian and Galapagos provinces are entirely unknown. From the Fuegian region several species of Actinians were described in the

Report on the Zoöphytes of the United States Exploring Expedition, but it is probable that even there several other species will hereafter be found. It will, therefore, be useless to attempt any generalizations upon the extent and limits of the several faunae occupying these coasts, but it appears desirable to bring together the species already known from each zoölogical province.

So far as can be judged from these imperfect lists, the faunal divisions are the same for the Polyps as for the Echinoderms, and since these were discussed in a previous article in this volume (pp. 336 to 339), it is unnecessary to give their limits or extent at this time.

ARCTIC PROVINCE.

ALCYONARIA.

Primnoa compressa Verrill.
Aleutian Islands.

Alcyonium rubiforme Dana.
Behrings Straits and Arctic Ocean.

ACTINARIA.

Urticina crassicornis Ehr.
Arctic Ocean to Puget Sound.

Phellia arctica Verrill.
Arctic Ocean.

Of the four species known from this fauna two (*Alcyonium rubiforme* and *Urticina crassicornis*) are found also on the north Atlantic coasts of America and Europe. The latter also extends southward to the Oregonian fauna. The others are not known to occur south of the Aleutian Islands.

SITCHIAN PROVINCE.

ACTINARIA.

Urticina crassicornis Ehr.
Arctic Ocean to Puget Sound.

Evactis? xanthogrammica Verrill.
Sitcha.

The two species known from Sitcha afford but little evidence in regard to the character of the fauna, for the first is a species of wide distribution on all the northern coasts both of the Atlantic and Pacific, while the second is a doubtful species, which may prove identical with *E. artemisia* of the Oregonian fauna.

OREGONIAN PROVINCE.

ALCYONARIA.

Ptilosarcus Gurneyi Gray.
Vancouver I., Puget Sound and Cape Flattery (80 feet) to Monterey.

ACTINARIA.

Urticina crassicornis Ehr.
　Arctic Ocean to Puget Sound.
Eractis artemisia Verrill.
　Puget Sound.
Metridium fimbriatum Verrill.
　Puget Sound to San Francisco.

Sagartia, several sp. ined.
　Gulf of Georgia.
Epiactis prolifera Verrill.
　Puget Sound.

MADREPORARIA.

Balanophyllia elegans Verrill.
　Puget Sound to Monterey.

Allopora venusta Verrill.
　Noah Bay.

Of the seven described species in this list, three are not known to occur elsewhere. Three extend southward into the Californian province, and *U. crassicornis* extends northward to the Arctic Ocean.

CALIFORNIAN PROVINCE.

ALCYONARIA.

Ptilosarcus Gurneyi Gray.
　Vancouver Island to Monterey.
(?) *Virgularia gracilis* Gabb.
　Monterey.

Stylatula elongata Verrill.
　San Francisco to Monterey.
Leptogorgia Caryi Verrill.
　(?) Near San Francisco.

ACTINARIA.

Metridium fimbriatum Verrill.
　San Francisco to Puget Sound.

Sagartia, sp.

MADREPORARIA.

Paracyathus caltha Verrill.
　Monterey.
P. Stearnsii Verrill.
　Monterey.

Balanophyllia elegans Verrill.
　Monterey to Puget Sound.

Among the eight species described from this fauna there are three that are found also in the Oregonian. The rest have not yet been recorded from beyond the limits of the fauna.

PANAMIAN PROVINCE.

ALCYONARIA.

Renilla amethystina Verrill.
　San Salvador to Zorritos.
Leioptillum undulatum Verrill.
　Gulf of California to Gulf of Fonseca.
Stylatula gracilis Verrill.
　Cape St. Lucas to Panama.

Leptogorgia Floræ Verrill.
　Panama Bay.
L. Agassizii Verrill.
　Gulf of California to Acapulco.
L. media Verrill.
　Gulf of California to Nicaragua.

L. Adamsii Verrill.
 Nicaragua to Zorritos, Peru.
L. pulchra V., and *var. exilis* V.
 Gulf of California.
L. rutila Verrill.
 Acapulco.
L. eximia Verrill.
 Bay of Panama.
L. tenuis Verrill.
 Gulf of California.
L. stenobrochis Verrill.
 San Salvador to Zorritos.
—— *var. Englemanni* Horn.
 Mazatlan and Acapulco to Panama
L. ramulus Verrill.
 San Salvador to Zorritos.
L. labiata Verrill.
 Guaymas and Tehuantepec to Nicaragua.
L. pumila Verrill.
 Zorritos.
L. diffusa Verrill.
 Gulf of Nicoya and Panama Bay.
L. Californica Verrill.
 Margarita Bay and Cape St. Lucas.
L. alba Verrill.
 Guaymas to Panama.
L. flexilis Verrill.
 San Salvador to Panama Bay.
L. rigida Verrill.
 Gulf of California to San Salvador.
L. cuspidata Verrill.
 Cape St. Lucas to Acapulco.
L. exigua Verrill.
 Guaymas to Nicaragua and Zorritos.
Eugorgia ampla Verrill.
 Margarita Bay and Gulf of California.
—— *var. purpurascens* Verrill.
 Nicaragua to Zorritos.
E. nobilis Verrill.
 Nicaragua and Bay of Panama.
—— *var. excelsa* Verrill.
 Gulf of California and Acapulco.
E. Bradleyi Verrill.
 Gulf of Nicoya to Panama Bay.

E. Daniana Verrill.
 Gulf of Nicoya and Bay of Panama.
E. multifida Verrill.
 La Paz and Mazatlan to Acapulco.
E. aurantiaca Verrill.
 Gulf of California to Acapulco.
Phycogorgia fucata Val.
 Mazatlan.
Psammogorgia arbuscula Verrill.
 Gulf of Nicoya to Panama Bay.
—— *var. Dowii* Verrill.
 San Salvador and Pearl Islands.
—— *var. pallida* Verrill.
 Pearl Islands.
P. teres Verrill.
 Guaymas (Dr. E. Palmer) to Panama Bay.
P. fucosa Verrill.
 Mazatlan.
P. gracilis Verrill.
 Pearl Islands.
Muricea acervata Verrill.
 Panama.
M. tubigera Verrill.
 Bay of Panama.
M. hispida Verrill.
 Panama.
M. squarrosa Verrill.
 Panama Bay.
M. crassa Verrill.
 Panama Bay.
M. echinata Val.
 Bay of Panama.
—— *var. flabellum* Verrill.
 Panama Bay.
M. fruticosa Verrill.
 Bay of Panama.
—— *var. miser* Verrill.
 Nicaragua to Bay of Panama.
M. austera Verrill.
 Gulf of California to Bay of Panama.
M. retusa Verrill.
 Pearl Islands.
M. formosa Verrill.
 Zorritos.

M. robusta Verrill.
   Acapulco.
M. albida Verrill.
   Panama Bay.
M. labes Verrill.
   Acapulco to Bay of Panama.
M. purpurea Verrill.
   Acapulco to Bay of Panama.
M. appressa Verrill.
   Gulf of California to Panama and Zorritos.
—— *var. flavescens* Verrill.
   Nicaragua to Zorritos.
M. tenella Verrill.
   Nicaragua to Zorritos.

M. aspera Verrill.
   Panama.
Heterogorgia verrucosa Verrill.
   Bay of Panama.
H. tortuosa Verrill.
   Bay of Panama.
H. papillosa Verrill.
   La Paz.
Callipodium Pacificum Verrill.
   Gulf of California to Zorritos.
C. aureum Verrill.
   Panama.
Alcyonium? *Bradleyi* Verrill.
   Panama.

ACTINARIA.

Lophactis ornata Verrill.
   Panama Bay.
Asteractis Bradleyi Verrill.
   Panama.
Cladactis grandis Verrill.
   Nicaragua to Zorritos, Peru.
Anthopleura Dowii Verrill.
   San Salvador to Panama Bay.
Bunodes (?), sp.
   Pearl Islands.
Calliactis variegata Verrill.
   Panama Bay.
Sagartia crispata Verrill.
   Panama Bay.
S. carcinophila Verrill.
   Panama Bay.
S. Panamensis Verrill.
   Panama Reefs.
S. Bradleyi Verrill.
   Panama Reefs.
Sagartia, sp. ined.
   Panama.

Phellia inornata Verrill.
   Panama Bay.
P. (?) rubens Verrill.
   Zorritos.
P. Panamensis Verrill.
   Panama.
Paractis (?) nobilis Verrill.
   Panama.
Mammillifera Danæ Verrill.
   Panama Bay.
M. nitida Verrill.
   San Salvador.
M. conferta Verrill.
   Acapulco and San Salvador.
Epizoanthus elongatus Verrill.
   Panama Bay and Zorritos, (?) La Paz.
E. humilis Verrill.
   Panama.
E. crassus Verrill.
   San Salvador.
Antipathes Panamensis Verrill.
   Panama Bay.

MADREPORARIA.

Montipora fragosa Verrill.
   (?) Gulf of California.
Porites Californica Verrill.
   Guaymas and La Paz.

P. porosa Verrill.
   La Paz.
P. excavata Verrill.
   Pearl Islands, Panama Bay.

P. Panamensis Verrill.
Panama Bay.
P. nodulosa Verrill.
La Paz.
Dendrophyllia surcularis Verrill.
Pearl Islands.
D. tenuilamellosa Verrill.
Panama Bay, Acapulco, La Paz.
Astropsammia Pedersenii Verrill.
La Paz.
Rhizopsammia pulchra Verrill.
Pearl Islands.
Allopora Californica Verrill.
(?) Gulf of California.
Pocillipora capitata Verrill.
La Paz and Socorro Islands to Panama Bay.
—— *var. porosa* Verrill.
La Paz.
—— *var. robusta* Verrill.
Near La Paz.
—— *var. pumila* Verrill.
Near La Paz.
P. lacera Verrill.
Acajutla to Panama Bay.
Astrangia Haimei Verrill.
San Salvador to Panama and Zorritos.
A. pulchella Verrill.
Panama Bay.

A. concinna Verrill.
Panama Bay.
A. dentata Verrill.
La Paz to San Salvador and Panama.
A. costata Verrill.
Panama Bay.
A. Pedersenii Verrill.
Guaymas and La Paz.
A. (Cœnangia) conferta Verrill.
Gulf of California.
Phyllangia dispersa Verrill.
Gulf of Nicoya and Panama Bay.
Clangia Bradleyi Verrill.
Panama Bay.
Paracyathus humilis Verrill.
Pearl Islands.
Desmophyllum Cumingii E. and H.
South America.
Fungia elegans Verrill.
Gulf of California.
Pavonia gigantea Verrill.
Pearl Islands.
P. clivosa Verrill.
Pearl Islands.
Stephanaria stellata Verrill.
La Paz to Bay of Panama.

In this list there are 104 species, none of which have been found beyond the limits of the province. An examination of the list will show, however, that there are sufficient reasons for recognizing the three subdivisions of the fauna, already given in the case of the Echinoderms (p. 337). But the three subdivisions are not equally well known. The Actinians of the Mexican and Equadorian sub-provinces are almost wholly unknown, only one or two species having been examined from each, while from the Panamian division a considerable number are now made known, although there must be many additional ones. The shallow water Gorgonians and corals have been pretty fully collected in both the Mexican and Panamian regions, but from the Equadorian we have only the small collection obtained by Mr. Bradley at Zorritos. In the present state of our knowledge some of the species found in each of the three sub-provinces are peculiar to it, while many extend also to one of the other, and a considerable portion are found in all three, or throughout the whole extent of this great province. Future explorations will undoubtedly reduce the number of species peculiar to each subdivision, as most of the late collections have done, for there can be no doubt but that part of the apparent differences in the faunæ are due to the incompleteness of the collections. Local peculiarities of the particular places at which the various collections have been made have also undoubtedly increased the apparent differences.

As the list now stands, there are known from the Mexican subdivision 42 species; of these, 20 species are peculiar to the region; 16 are found also in the Panamian subdivision; and 6 are found in both these and the Equadorian regions, ranging to Zorritos.

From the Panamian subdivision there are 80 species known; of these, 51 are peculiar to it (including 16 of Actinaria); 16 are found also in the Mexican district; 7 are common to the Panamian and Equadorian regions; and 6 range through the three sub-provinces.

Of the Equadorian polyp-fauna we know but 17 species; of these 4 are peculiar to it; 7 are found also in the Panamian; and 6 extend through both the Panamian and Mexican regions, even to the Gulf of California.

For convenience of reference some local lists are added, which will at least serve to illustrate the most common and conspicuous species of the several localities.

List of species collected at Guaymas by Dr. E. Palmer.

The following species are in the collection of the Chicago Academy of Sciences:

Leptogorgia Agassizii V.	*Psammogorgia teres* V.
L. media V.	*Astrangia Pedersenii* V.
L. alba V.	*A. (Cœnangia) conferta* V.
L. labiata V.	*Porites Californica* V.
L. exigua V.	

List of species collected near La Paz by Capt. J. Pedersen.

Leptogorgia Agassizii V. Common.	*Eugorgia nobilis*, var. *excelsa* V. Common.
L. media V. Not common.	*E. multifida* V. Rare.
L. pulchra V. Common.	*E. aurantiaca* V. Common.
—— var. *exilis* V. Common.	*Muricea austera* V. Not common.
L. tenuis V. Very rare.	*M. appressa* V. Common.
L. rigida V. Abundant.	

Heterogorgia papillosa V. Rare.	*Astropsammia Pedersenii* V. Rare.
Callipodium Pacificum V. Rare.	*Pocillipora capitata* V. Common.
Epizoanthus elongatus V. Rare.	—— *var. porosa* V. Not common.
Porites Californica V. Not common.	—— *var. robusta* V. Common.
	—— *var. pumila* V. Common.
P. porosa V. Common.	*Astrangia dentata* V. Rare.
P. nodulosa V. Common.	*A. Pedersenii* V. Not common.
Dendrophyllia tenuilamellosa V. Rare.	*Fungia elegans* V. Rare.
	Stephanaria stellata V. Rare.

The fauna at Cape St. Lucas appears to be similar to that of La Paz. The collections made there by Mr. J. Xantus include many of the species common at La Paz, especially *Leptogorgia rigida*, *L. Agassizii* and *L. media*, in abundance. He also collected a few additional species, although his collection was much less extensive than that of Capt. Pedersen. At Acapulco considerable collections, chiefly of Gorgonians, have been made by Mr. A. Agassiz, Mr. D. B. Van Brunt, and others. The common species are mostly the same as at La Paz, and there appears to be but little difference in the faunæ of the two localities, except what may be explained by the incompleteness of the collections received. A few species (*Leptogorgia rutila* V., *L. stenobrochis*, *var. Englemanni*, *Muricea robusta*, *M. purpurea*, etc.) common at Acapulco, have not been found at La Paz.

From the coasts of San Salvador and Nicaragua I have seen several collections, made by Capt. Dow, Mr. Bradley, Mr. J. A. McNiel, and others, but none of them can be considered as at all complete, even for the Gorgonians. So far as can be judged from these collections, the faunæ of those coasts are essentially the same as that of Panama Bay.

List of species collected on the coast of Nicaragua by J. A. McNiel.

The following species were collected by Mr. McNiel on the beach at Corinto, and by the aid of divers in the Gulf of Nicoya. Those species found only at one of these places are designated either by (C.) or (N.) according to the locality. The first series from this collection is in the Peabody Academy of Science, Salem, Mass., by which Mr. McNiel was sent out:

Leptogorgia media V. (C.)	*Psammogorgia arbuscula* V. (N.)
L. Adamsii V. Large.	*Muricea fruticosa*, *var. miser* V. (C.)
L. stenobrochis V.	
L. ramulus V. (C.)	*M. hebes* V. (C.)
L. labiata V. (C.)	*M. purpurea* V. (C.)

L. diffusa V. (N.) Large.   *M. appressa* V.
L. alba V. Common.   —— *var. flavescens* V. (C.)
L. exigua V. Common.   *M. tenella* V. (C.)
Eugorgia Daniana V. (N.) Large. *Cladactis grandis* V. (C.)
E. ampla, var. purpurascens V. (C.) *Astrangia dentata* V. (N.)
E. Bradleyi V. (N.) Yellow variety. *Phyllangia dispersa* V. (N.)
E. nobilis V. (N.)

PERUVIAN PROVINCE.

ALCYONARIA.

Leptogorgia Peruana Verrill.   *Eugorgia rubens* Verrill.
   Callao.   Paita.
(?) *Muricea horrida* Mobius.   *Echinogorgia aurantiaca* Verrill.
   "Peru." Perhaps this belongs to the   Callao.
   Panamian Province.

ACTINARIA.

Oulactis concinnata E. and H.   *Sagartia nivea* Verrill.
   Callao.   Paita and Callao.
Bunodes papillosa Verrill.   *S. Lessonii* Verrill.
   Callao to Talcahuano, Chili.   Paita.
B. plucia Verrill.   *S.* (?) *Peruviana* Verrill.
   San Lorenzo Island.   Paita.
B. ocellata Verrill.   *Nemactis primula* Edw. and H.
   Paita.   San Lorenzo Island.
Phymactis florida Edw. and H.   *N. Draytonii* Edw. and H.
   San Lorenzo Island.   San Lorenzo I.
                                       Anactis picta Ehr.
                                       Paita.

Of the fifteen species in this list, only one (*Bunodes papillosa*) is known to extend its range beyond the limits of the fauna.

CHILIAN PROVINCE.

ALCYONARIA.

Leptogorgia (?) *Chilensis* Verrill.   *L.* (?) *arbuscula* Verrill.
   Algarrobo, south of Valparaiso.   I. Santa Maria.
L. (?) *platyclados* Verrill.
   I. Santa Maria.

ACTINARIA.

Bunodes papillosa Verrill.   *Phymactis clematis* Edw. and H.
   Talcahuano to Callao.   Valparaiso.
Cystiactis Eydouxi Edw. and H.   *Actinia* (?) *Mertensii* Brandt.
   Chili.   Chili.

Sagartia ? nymphaea Verrill.
Valparaiso.
S. ? rubus Verrill.
Valparaiso.

Nemactis ? Chilensis Verrill.
Bay of Talcahuano and Quiriquina Island.

MADREPORARIA.

Bathycyathus Chilensis E. and H.
Chili.

Of the eleven species known from this province, none are known elsewhere, except *Bunodes papillosa*, which is also found in the Peruvian fauna.

FUEGIAN PROVINCE.

ACTINARIA.

Bunodes cruentata Gosse.
Orange Bay.
Metridium reticulatum E. and H.
Orange Harbor.
Cereus Fuegiensis Verrill.
Orange Harbor.
Sagartia impatiens Gosse.
Orange Harbor.
Sagartia lineolata Verrill.
Forge Cove, near Orange Harbor.

MADREPORARIA.

Astrangia, sp.
Straits of Magellan.

The six species known from this fauna appear to be peculiar to it.

For want of room, the lists, giving a detailed comparison between the tropical faunæ of the Atlantic and Pacific coasts and originally intended to accompany this article, have been reserved for the next volume.

No. 8.—*Additional Observations on Echinoderms, chiefly from the Pacific coast of America.* By A. E. VERRILL.

Presented January, 1871.

ATLANTIC SPECIES.

Pteraster Danæ Verrill.
Proc Boston Soc. Nat. Hist., xii, p. 386, April, 1869.

Plate IX, figures 11, 11^a.

Upper surface moderately convex; radius of disk to that of rays as 1 : 1·18; rays broad, subtriangular, the tips recurved so as to expose the end of the ambulacral grooves on the upper side. The dorsal membrane is perforated by minute scattered pores, and numerous small, slender, acute spines project from its surface at regular intervals; these are larger on the disk and quite small on the outer part of the rays. Central opening small, somewhat rounded, surrounded by small spines. Dorsal paxillæ, as seen when the dorsal membrane is removed, elevated and rather stout, surmounted at the summit by six to ten, slender, acicular, divergent spinules, one of which is usually larger, and projects through the membrane. Rays beneath bordered on each side by about thirty, slender, transverse, spine-like ribs, which project but slightly beyond the margin, and are connected by the web-like membrane quite to their ends. Interambulacral plates thin, each usually bearing four very slender, elongated spines, many of them with small pedicellariæ near the tips; the inner one considerably shortest; all connected together by a web, which retreats between the points to a considerable extent; near the mouth there are often five spines. At each interradial corner of the mouth there are ten long, slender, pointed spines, the six middle ones about equal in length, the two outer ones on each side much smaller, the outermost considerably smaller than the preceding; just back of these, and side by side, are two long, slender, somewhat curved, acute spines, about equal in length to the longer ones of the group in front of them.

Radius of disk ·37 of an inch ; of rays ·57 ; width of rays at base ·50 ; elevation of back ·35 ; length of longest transverse ribs of the rays beneath ·15 ; of interambulacral spines ·06 to ·08 ; of the spines at mouth angles, about ·08.

This species was labeled "Rio Janeiro?" It was perhaps from dredgings made in 30 fathoms off the east coast of Patagonia,—J. D. Dana, U. S. Expl. Expedition.

There is but one specimen of this species in the collection, which has been dried from alcohol. It is more nearly allied to *P. pulvillus* Sars* than to *P. militaris*. The latter has much longer arms and only three or four spinules on the dorsal paxillæ; the former has more numerous spinules on the paxillæ, shorter and more numerous interambulacral spines, and quite different mouth-spines. The dorsal surface is also different from that of either species, as well as the proportions.

Plagionotus Africanus Verrill, sp. nov.

Test broad oblong-oval, somewhat angulated opposite the interambulacra, truncate and slightly emarginate anteriorly, obliquely truncate behind; margin rather high and abruptly rounded, especially at the anterior end; upper surface slightly convex, in one specimen depressed at the center. Ovarial openings four, large, the two anterior oblong and divergent, unequal, the others round. Anterior ambulacrum broad, slightly depressed, the plates large and nearly as high as broad, perforated by conspicuous double pores. Anterior lateral ambulacra very divergent, rather broad, narrow at first, increasing rapidly in width to the middle or beyond, the outer portion broad, oblong, obtuse at the end, which is slightly recurved. Posterior ambulacra considerably longer, little curved, but strongly divergent, usually increasing in width to the outer third, beyond which they are somewhat narrowed and curved forward. The anterior and posterior interambulacra are, therefore, relatively broader than in *P. pectoralis*, and the lateral ones narrower. Peripetalous fasciole narrow, but well defined and sunken, with a rather regular oval outline, which is only slightly angulate, or rather undulated, laterally, but beyond the middle of each anterior interambulacrum it bends downward nearly at right angles for a short distance, and then, after forming another similar angle, bends a little downward in crossing the anterior end. A slight ridge, corresponding to the angle of the fasciole, extends upward to the center, dividing the interambulacra into two unequal areas, the smaller of which is next to the anterior ambulacrum; both of these areas bear oblique rows of large tubercles, which do not extend over the dividing ridge.

In the lateral interambulacra the very large tubercles are numerous, extending to near the apex, mostly arranged in oblique, more or less curved rows; in the posterior area they are more unequal in size

---

* Oversigt af Norges Echinodermer, p. 62, Tab. 6, figs. 14–18, Tab. 7, 8, Christiania, 1861.

and less regularly arranged, forming clusters rather than rows, and extend backward beyond the fasciole, nearly to the anal area. The plastron is broad oval, emarginate behind, the sides pretty regularly curved. The subanal area is broadly cordate, with three or four conspicuous pores on each side, from each of which a well-marked groove extends to the center. The fasciole surrounding it is broad and well defined; the branches extending up near the sides of the anal area are narrower, but depressed and conspicuous. The anal area is large, nearly circular, but with a sharp angle on the upper side; more than half of its diameter is occupied by a thin central membrane, which is somewhat semicircular, rounded below, its surface toward the edge bearing minute, scattered, rounded plates, which, nearer the edge, increase in size and form two or three disconnected circles of detached plates. These are mostly rounded, or more or less oblong, though quite irregular in form and size, but the outer rows are composed of successively larger and closer plates. Those of the outermost row are considerably the largest and are mostly in contact, though still quite irregular in size and form, and mostly with rounded angles and sides; on the upper side there is a triangular group of four or five similar plates, between the outermost row and the small plates of the inner circles. The actinostome is very broad crescent shaped, with rounded corners, not at all produced, or even slightly emarginate, anteriorly; but it is strongly labiate, the lower border much thickened, prominent, and broadly rounded. The actinal area is occupied by a thin membrane, which bears comparatively few (about 25), mostly large and disconnected, irregularly shaped plates, most of which are not in contact; the larger ones are pierced by one or two pairs of small pores, and the marginal ones bear a few small miliary tubercles. The outer row contains 9 or 10 plates, which are transversely oblong and very unequal in size and form, but mostly in contact at their ends; inside of these there is an irregular row of 8, large, irregularly rounded plates, which are mostly not in contact, often leaving considerable spaces of naked membrane between. The inner portion of the membrane bears an irregular group of five or six, unequal, smaller, well separated, rounded plates.

The largest specimen is 6·50 inches long; 5·35 broad; 2·05 high; length of anterior lateral ambulacra from apex 2·35; greatest breadth ·38; length of posterior ones 2·80; breadth ·45; diameter of largest ovarial pores ·09 by ·05; average breadth of fasciole, about ·06; length of plastron 3·35; breadth 1·35; transverse diameter of anal area ·58; longitudinal diameter ·65; diameter of its largest plates ·08 to ·10; transverse diameter of mouth 1·03; longitudinal diameter ·25; its largest plates ·15 to ·25; medium sized plates ·10 to ·12. Another specimen is 5·50 inches long; 4·30 broad; 1·85 high. A small specimen, distorted above, is 4·18 inches long; 3·30 wide; 1·95 high; actinal area ·60 wide; ·23 long. In this the inner plates of the actinal area are smaller and more numerous.

Sherbro Island, west coast of Africa,—Rev. D. W. Burton.

This species is closely allied to *P. pectoralis* Ag., from Florida and the West Indies. For the sake of comparison some details, not mentioned in the published descriptions, are here added.

Plagionotus pectoralis Agassiz and Desor.

Spatangus pectoralis Lamarck, Hist. an. sans vert., iii, p. 383; Desmoulins, Echin.. p. 380.
Brissus pectoralis Agassiz. Prodromus, p. 184.
Brissus (Plagiotus) pectoralis Ag. and Des., Cat. Rais., Ann. des Sci. nat., viii, p. 13 1847; vi, Tab. 16. fig. 15.
Plagionotus pectoralis Gray. Cat. Ech. Brit. Museum. p. 50, 1855; A. Agassiz, Bulletin Mus. Comp. Zoöl. I, p. 275. 1870.
Plagionotus Desorii Gray. op. cit., p. 51.

Several West Indian specimens of this species, of various sizes, which I have had opportunities to compare with the African specimens, present the following differences.

The test is much more depressed, the margin less elevated and often comparatively acute, rising with a gradual slope on all parts, except at the posterior end. The outline is also more regularly elliptical, with rounded sides; the anterior end is more deeply emarginate, with the anterior ambulacrum more sunken. The anterior lateral and posterior ambulacral petals are longer and narrower, with the sides parallel for a great part of the length, and they are less divergent, being directed at first more anteriorly and posteriorly, but are more strongly recurved toward the outer ends; this renders the lateral interambulacra broader and the anterior and posterior ones narrower. The large tubercles are quite variable in number in *P. pectoralis*, but are often more numerous, though not usually arranged in such regular rows. In all the specimens of the latter, which I have seen, there are no large tubercles on the triangular area of the anterior interambulacra next to the anterior ambulacral zone, which bears large tubercles in *P. Africanus*. The small tubercles are smaller in the former. The peripetalous fasciole is broader in *P. pectoralis*; and the plastron is longer and more oblong, with the sides more nearly parallel. The anal area is smaller, ovate, the upper end narrowed and pointed. The mouth is not so broad transversely, but is more produced and rounded anteriorly. Both these areas are covered by numerous, small, crowded, polygonal plates.

Another specimen of *P. pectoralis* from Tampa Bay, Florida, in the Museum of Comparative Zoölogy, which I have also had an opportunity to compare with the African specimens, in company with Mr. A. Agassiz, differs considerably in form from the West Indian specimens, of similar size, and if all the specimens from that region should prove to have the same characters, it ought to be regarded as at least a marked variety. This specimen is of about the same size as the larger African specimen, and agrees nearly with it in form, though it is somewhat more depressed and the sides are less abrupt, especially anteriorly; the anterior end is even less emarginate; and the ambulacral furrow less sunken, with small erplates and more numerous pores. The ambulacral petals are not so narrow and oblong as in the West Indian specimens, though much more so than in the African. The ovarial openings are small and round; the fasciole wide; the plastron oblong; the large tubercles and the mouth and anal areas are as in the typical form, differing in the same way, therefore, in all these characters from the African specimens. The actinal membrane is covered with numerous, small, crowded, polygonal plates. The anal area is also covered with small, crowded, polygonal plates, much more numerous than in *P. Africanus*. The most constant and important differences are, therefore, found in the form of the actinal and anal areas and the character of their plates; the size and form of the ovarial openings; the width of the fasciole; and the form of the plastron.

A large specimen of *P. pectoralis* from Turk's Island, in the Museum of the Boston Society of Natural History, is 9 inches long; 6·75 wide; 2·50 high.

PACIFIC SPECIES.

OPHIUROIDEA.

Ophiothela mirabilis Verrill, (pp. 268, 376).

This species has been received from La Paz, Cape St. Lucas, Corinto, and Gulf of Fonseca, in addition to Panama and Pearl Islands. In all cases it was found clinging in large numbers to the branches of *Muricea* and *Gorgonidæ*. The genus appears to be widely distributed in the tropical parts of the Pacific Ocean, *O. Danæ* V.[*] lives upon *Melitodes virgata* V. at the Feejee Islands. A species occurs at Japan, on *Mopsella Japonica* V., and Dr. Lütken has observed one on a *Parisis* from the China Seas.

---

[*] Proceedings Boston Soc. Nat. Hist., xii, p. 391, 1869.

Hemipholis gracilis Verrill.

These Trans. p. 262 (read Jan., 1867, published March, 1867); Proc. Bost. Soc. Nat. Hist., xii, p. 391.

Hemipholis affinis Ljung., op. cit., p. 322 (read Nov., 1866, published 1867, note on fly-leaf dated May 18, 1867); Lyman, Bulletin M. C. Z., i, p. 336, 1870

"Ljungman's species from Guayaquil, appears to be identical with *H. gracilis*. Judging from the date of Prof. Lóven's note, our name has priority of actual publication."*

---

*Mr. Lyman, in the work cited, without giving any additional information objects to the remark quoted above, in the following words: "This whole matter of priority in descriptions is of no sort of interest to science, except as a matter of *registration*. Nor is it profitable to enter on the question of what constitutes *publication*. But we may say, that the partial distribution of loose sheets of an incomplete paper, though a useful and praiseworthy custom, constitutes no greater claim for *priority* than the reading of a paper before an ancient and distinguished Academy, and the speedy publication of that paper in its complete and connected form."

We believe there are very few naturalists, at the present day, who are willing to admit that anything less than the *actual printing* of descriptions or recognizable figures can give *priority* to the names of species or genera, and this without reference to the reputation or *antiquity* of the society before which a paper may be read. In case of descriptive papers, or diagnoses, as everyone knows, nothing more than the title is usually read, and many additions are often made afterwards, before or during printing. Therefore if Mr. Ljungman's paper was *printed* before March, 1867, his name should be adopted, otherwise not. On this question Mr. Lyman gives us no positive information.

We notice, however, that Mr. Lyman invariably dates certain of his own species from their first publication in the Proceedings of the Boston Society of Natural History, although they were distributed in sheets containing parts of incomplete papers, the mode of publication and distribution being precisely the same in the two cases. And if *antiquity* of the Society has anything to do with the matter, the advantage is on the side of the Connecticut Academy to the extent of some 40 years! I am not aware, however, that any member of this Academy would consider himself justified, on that account, in claiming priority of *publication* for matters contained in hundreds of communications made to the Academy during the past 80 years, but not yet printed.

The question of *priority* of names has, however, an importance far greater than Mr. Lyman's remark would imply, for every working naturalist is painfully conscious of the great amount of time and labor that he is constantly obliged to spend in unravelling the intricate synonymy of well known genera and species, most of which has been caused by the careless or willful neglect of the salutary rules of nomenclature, in which *priority of publication* is one of the most fundamental principles. And whenever a naturalist, to save his own time, selfishly neglects to ascertain the correct synonymy of the species which he describes or mentions, he is merely heaping up labor for future naturalists, whose time might be much better employed, than in correcting the imperfect work of their predecessors.

Simplicity, *accuracy*, and *permanency* of nomenclature are, therefore, of vast importance for the future development of Zoölogy and whatever contributes to this end we regard as far more worthy of careful attention, than any slight personal honor or dishonor that may be connected with the naming of species or genera, whether new or old.

Pectinura maculata Verrill, Amer. Jour. Sci., xlviii, p. 431.

Ophiarachna maculata Verrill, Proc. Boston Soc. Nat. Hist., xii, p. 388, 1869.

Dr. Lütken has adopted the name, *Pectinura* Forbes (*non* Heller) for the genus to which this large species from New Zealand belongs.

ASTERIOIDEA.

Oreaster occidentalis Verrill, (pp. 278, 374).

Pentaceros occidentalis Verrill (by error), Am. Jour. Science, xlix, p. 99, 1870. (Corrected to *Oreaster occidentalis*, p. 227).*

Of this hitherto rare species 21 specimens of various sizes have been received from La Paz. They show but little variation except that due to age or state of preservation. Some specimens are so dried as to leave the disk and rays plump and rounded above, while in others the interradial spaces are so shrunken as to make both the rays and disk angular. In some most of the upper and part of the lower marginal plates bear small obtuse spines or tubercles; in others there are few or none of these; the two smallest specimens have none, though others, scarcely larger, have quite a number. The smallest specimen has the longer radius 1 inch; the shorter ·50. This, however, has nearly the form and all the essential characters of the adult, though the spines and tubercles are less numerous.

Nidorellia armata Gray, (pp. 280, 372).

Numerous specimens of this species were received from La Paz, where it is common at the depth of a few fathoms.

The La Paz specimens present all the variations described in those from Panama. Some of the larger ones are unusually spinose, having large triangular groups of spines on the interradial regions of the upper side, and in some cases three rows of large spines on the rays.

Gymnasteria spinosa Gray.

Annals and Mag. Nat. Hist., 1840, p. 278; Synopsis of Species of Starfishes in British Museum, p. 8, 1866; Verrill, Proc. Boston Soc. Nat. Hist., xii, p. 384, 1869.

A starfish collected at La Paz by Capt. Pedersen, seems to be identical with this species, originally obtained at Panama by Mr. H. Cuming. There are three specimens in the collection.

Form pentagonal, with rather broad, tapering, somewhat depressed, triangular rays. Radii as 1 : 2·2. The skeleton consists of moderately

---

* The name, *Pentaceros*, was used for a genus of fishes by Cuvier and Val. (vol. iii, p. 30, 1828; see also Günther, Catal. Fishes of British Museum, i, p. 212) long before it was employed by Gray for this genus. For this reason *Oreaster* was substituted by Müller and Troschel.

large, rounded and polygonal plates, joined by their edges, so as to leave variously shaped spaces between, with their surface roughened by minute, granule-like prominences and covered with a thin membranous skin, which allows the roughness of the plates to show through it. The median dorsal plates on each ray are stout, rather rhomboidal, with the angles produced and rounded and the center tubercular; they bear a row of eight to twelve, stout, elevated, blunt spines, one to each plate. The sides of the rays near the base are formed by about four series of plates; in the two intermediate rows rounded; in the upper and lower ones with lateral prolongations, which articulate with the dorsal and marginal plates in such a way as to leave rather large, transverse, oblong openings between; toward the end of the rays the plates become more regular and uniform, mostly polygonal, and more closely united, except that there are still larger openings next to the marginal plates, forming a regular series. Marginal plates stout, prominent, projecting laterally, and rounded on the outer side, much broader than high, forming a single row, with the plates placed alternately a little above and below the median line, about 12 to 16 on each side of the ray, each one bearing a stout, elongated, conical spine. Plates of the lower side rounded and subpolygonal, unequal, some of them bearing a very small central tubercle, mostly closely united, so as to leave only small pores between. Each interambulacral plate bears an outer, stout, oblong, blunt spine, compressed or wedge-shaped at the tip, and an inner group of four or five slender ones, of which the lateral are very short and the two middle ones considerably longest, all connected together by a thin web. On each margin of the mouth there is a group of five to eight, rather slender, subequal, obtuse spines, connected together by a web. Near the margin of the disk and rays, above and below, there are many rather large pedicellariæ, oblong or subcylindrical in form, obtuse at the tips. The dried specimens are light red above, yellowish below.

The largest specimen is 1·50 inches from center to edge of disk; 2·75 to tip of rays; breadth of rays at base 1 to 1·25; length of largest spines ·20 to ·22; diameter at base, about ·08.

A smaller one has the radius of disk ·68 of an inch; of rays 1·50; length of dorsal and marginal spines ·10 to ·12; diameter ·05 or ·06; diameter of upper and lower plates ·05 to ·10, mostly about ·08.

Mithrodia Bradleyi Verrill, (p. 288).

From La Paz there are two dry specimens of this species. The smaller and more perfect one is 3·50 inches from the center to the tips of the rays; ·50 to the edge of the disk; length of largest spines ·15;

diameter ·06. The color is brownish orange above, reddish below. There is a median row of 6 to 8, distant, large, blunt spines on the upper side of each ray, which does not extend nearly to the end of the ray; on each side of the dorsal surface, near the margin, there is a similar row of 10 or 12, longer spines, which extend to the end of the rays and are directed obliquely upward; on each side of the ventral surface there are two rows of spines, like the last, but the row next to the interambulacral plates has 18 or 20 spines. All these spines are surrounded at base by about 6 radiating ossicles beneath the surface, each of which bears on its outer end one of the small roughly granulated papillæ, which are numerous on the dorsal surface. There are usually 6, small, slender spines on the inner edge of each interambulacral plate, of which the two middle ones are longest and the two outer very small; the single stout spine on the outer edge of each plate is about twice as long as the longest of the inner ones.

Acanthaster Ellisii Verrill.

Echinaster Ellisii Gray, Annals Nat. Hist., 1840, p. 281; Synopsis Starfishes of British Museum, p. 12, 1866.
Acanthaster solaris (*pars*) Duj. et Hupé, Hist. nat. des Zooph. Ech., p. 352, 1862.
Acanthaster Ellisii Verrill, Proc. Boston Soc. Nat. Hist., xii, p. 385, 1869.

Two specimens received from Capt. Pedersen, who collected them at La Paz, appear to belong to this rare species. The diameter of the smaller one is 1·5 inches; length of rays ·40. The spines are long (·15 inch) and quite slender. There are five madreporic plates, which are small, round, and prominent; and 13 rays. Color light red, the upper spines rose-red; those below pink with white tips; the general color of the lower surface is yellowish white.

The larger specimen is 4 inches in diameter; greater radius 2 inches; radius of disk 1·25; length of largest spines of back ·25; diameter at base ·05. It has 5 madreporic plates and 12 rays, separated below by small interradial areas. The whole surface, above and below, is covered with small granules, which also extend over the surface of the spines, nearly to the tips. The interambulacral plates bear a row of slender, elongated, blunt spines, bordering the ambulacral furrows, each plate bearing a group of three spines, of which the central is the longest; between these groups there is often a large, long, rounded, slightly tapering, obtuse pedicellaria, nearly equal in length and size to the smaller spines adjacent; on the outer part of each of these plates there is also a long and large, obtuse spine, similar to those on the interradial plates.

Echinaster tenuispina Verrill, sp. nov.

Radii about as 1 : 5·8. Rays five, rounded, long, moderately stout, tapering to the end. Spines of the dorsal surface small, but very numerous, tapering, subacute, arranged in many scarcely defined rows, of which there appear to be about 16 on the rays. The interambulacral plates bear numerous, crowded, divergent spines, of about the same size and form as those of the dorsal surface, those of the opposite sides crossing; three of these arise from each plate, in a transverse row; the middle one is considerably largest and longest, the outer one somewhat shorter and blunter, the inner one much smaller, slender and acute. The skin is smooth and glossy; in the angles between the rays beneath and along the lower side of the rays there are numerous slender transverse furrows.

Radius of disk ·60 of an inch; of rays 3·50; width of rays at base ·62; length of largest spines ·06.

Color of dried specimens deep reddish brown.

La Paz,—Capt. J. Pedersen. Six specimens.

This species is allied to *E. spinulosus* V., from the west coast of Florida. Its rays are not so slender and the dorsal spines are still more numerous.

Ophidiaster pyramidatus Gray, (p. 287).

Several specimens were sent from La Paz by Capt. Pedersen.

The dry specimens in best condition are light straw-color beneath; the poriferous zones are bright orange; the rows of large plates on the back and sides olive-green; madreporic plate large, dark olive-green.

Lepidaster, gen. nov.

Disk small, rays rounded, elongated; whole surface covered with a thin smooth skin, without granules or spines. The skeleton consists, in the rays, of several similar dorsal and lateral rows of rather large, more or less rhomboidal, overlapping plates, so articulated with those of the adjacent rows as to leave a regular row of pores between all the rows of plates, except between the ventral and interambulacral rows. On disk the plates are pentagonal. The interambulacral plates bear an inner row of small slender spines, several to each plate, bordering the ambulacral groove, and outside, but adjacent to these, a row of much larger oblong spines, not more than one to a plate.

This genus is allied to *Tamaria* and *Cistina* of Gray, but in both of those groups the plates bear spines. *Ophidiaster* and *Linckia* are granulated and the plates are arranged quite differently.

Lepidaster teres Verrill, sp. nov.

Rays five, long, round, slender, tapering; disk small. Radii as 1 : 6·3 The rays have three dorsal rows of overlapping rhomboidal plates, with the angles prolonged and sides concave; two lateral rows of similar plates on each side; and a ventral row of much smaller crowded plates, which are united directly to the interambulacral plates, but are joined to the first lateral series by an interrupted row of small squarish plates, between which there are rather large pores. The interambulacral plates bear an outer series of small, round, truncated spines, sometimes one to each plate, but usually only on alternate plates; and an inner series of very slender, small, subequal spines, three to each plate, the middle one usually slightly longest. Each corner of the mouth has a group of four, longer, sharp spines, the two middle ones largest. Anal orifice central, surrounded by numerous minute granules or papillæ; madreporic plate rather large, circular, concave, finely convoluted. Whole surface covered with a soft, thin skin, which allows the plates to be seen distinctly. Color of the dried specimen pale yellow.

Radius of disk ·30; of rays 1·90; diameter of rays at base ·32; length of outer interambulacral spines ·06; diameter of larger dorsal plates ·10 to ·12; of madreporic plate ·11 of an inch.

La Paz,—Capt. J. Pedersen.

Heliaster Kubiniji Xantus, (p. 292).

Three specimens of this species were sent from La Paz by Capt. Pedersen.

The two larger ones have 23 rays. The largest measures 4·15 inches from center to end of longest rays; to edge of disk 2·15; length of rays 1·50 to 2 inches; length of interambulacral spines ·15; of largest capitate dorsal spines ·10; their greatest diameter ·06 to ·08. The smallest specimen has 21 rays; its greatest radius is 2·50 inches; of disk 1·25.

The larger specimens have a median dorsal row of large capitate spines on all the rays, which, with a marginal row of smaller, more blunt spines on each side, extend inward to the central area of the disk; between the dorsal and lateral rows, on the middle of the rays, there are, on each side, one or two less regular rows of capitate spines, some of which often extend inward, more or less, on the disk.

On the upper side, especially near the end, the rays are thickly covered with small oval pedicellariæ, mixed with other very minute ones of similar form.

ECHINOIDEA.

Quite recently I have had an opportunity to compare specimens of most of the following species with those in the Museum of Comparative Zoölogy, in company with Mr. A. Agassiz, who, while in Europe last year, took pains to carefully examine nearly all the typical specimens contained in European museums, and in many cases brought home specimens identified by direct comparison. Therefore I am able, with the approval and through the courtesy of Mr. Agassiz, to correct a few erroneous identifications previously made by him, together with others made by myself in the earlier part of this volume. Other species, described since the earlier articles on the Echinoderms of the Pacific coast were printed, have been introduced in order to render the work more complete.

Cidaris Thouarsii Val. (p. 294).

Numerous specimens were sent by Capt. Pedersen from La Paz.

They show great variation in form, in addition to that due to difference of age. Several specimens give the following measurements:

Diameter, (inches)	2·10	2·05	2·00	1·55	1·50	1·35	1·30
Height,	1·30	1·35	1·50	·85	·80	·75	·75
Actinal area,	·85	·90	·80	·73	·70	·64	·55
Abactinal area,	·70	·70	·68	·58	·56	·50	·43
Anal region,	·38	·40	·33	·30	·30	·28	·22

Astropyga depressa Gray, Proc. Zoöl. Soc. Lond., xxiii, p. 35, 1855.

Astropyga venusta Verrill, these Trans., p. 296; Amer. Jour. Sci., xlix, p. 99, 1870.

Mr. A. Agassiz, who has recently examined Dr. Gray's type and brought home a specimen identified by comparison with it, has compared the latter with specimens sent by me, and regards them as identical with the *A. depressa* of Gray. The latter was described from a young specimen, but considerable changes take place, especially in the arrangement of the tubercles, during its growth, and even after it becomes two or three inches in diameter, as may be seen from the original descriptions of small and medium sized specimens (p. 296).

Capt. Pedersen sent from La Paz two fine large specimens, about 6 inches in diameter, and I have seen a similar one in the Museum of the Chicago Academy, collected at San Salvador by Capt. Dow.

These large specimens have 12 to 14 vertical rows of large, nearly equal interambulacral tubercles on the lower side; the first row from the ambulacra extends on the upper side to within three or four plates from the summit; between this row and the ambulacral pores, a row of secondary tubercles is introduced, which commences a short distance below the periphery and extends nearly as high as the preceding row, usually ceasing about two plates sooner; in young specimens this row is wanting, and the large tubercles of the first row cease sooner; outside of the first row of large tubercles there is another similar row of secondary ones, commencing at about the same place, but extending quite to the genital plates, as in the younger specimens; the second row of large tubercles extends about to the third plate above the periphery; the third ceases at or below the periphery; the fourth extends upward to within one or two plates of the apex of the yellow triangular area; and the remaining rows cease successively sooner, the two median rows scarcely rising above the periphery. The actinal membrane is filled with small, transversely oblong and elliptical, imbedded plates, some of which bear one or two small and very slender spines, which are more numerous on the larger plates near the mouth. The spines of the lower surface are straw-color; the larger ones of the upper surface are tinged and banded with purplish at base, the outer half straw-color; the small ones are very slender and mostly purplish throughout.

The largest specimen from La Paz has the test 5·90 inches in diameter; 2·10 high; diameter of actinal area 1·50; of abactinal area 1·35; of anal region .80; length of longest spines of upper surface 1·80.

Echinodiadema coronatum Verrill (p. 295).

In the Bulletin of the Museum of Comparative Zoölogy, i, p. 282, 1869, Mr. A. Agassiz considered this the young of *Diadema Mexicanum*. On reëxamining the original specimen and comparing it with the genuine young of that species, he is convinced that it is really quite distinct, both generically and specifically.

The existence of spines on the actinal membrane (to which the name refers) is of itself quiet sufficient to distinguish this genus from the young of *Diadema*, in all stages of growth. In all the species of the latter the actinal membrane in young specimens is covered with pretty regular, nearly smooth plates, which later in life become more separated and deeply imbedded, but never bear spines.

The name, *Echinodiadema*, has more recently been used for an entirely different genus by M. Cotteau (Rev. et Mag. de Zool., May, 1869).

Echinocidaris Dufresnii Desmoulins, Echin., p. 306. (p. 344).

Echinocidaris Scythei Philippi, Wiegm. Arch., 1857, p. 131.

According to Mr. Agassiz, who has seen the original specimen of *E. Dufresnii* and others in the British Museum from Str. of Magellan (coll. Cunningham), which are identical with *E. Scythei*, this species belongs to the fauna of Patagonia.

Boletia picta Verrill.

Psammechinus pictus Verrill, these Trans., p. 301, (young).
Lytechinus semituberculatus (*pars*) A. Agassiz, op. cit., p. 301, (*non* Val. sp.).

Capt. Pedersen sent one large specimen of this species from La Paz. It has but few spines remaining and the actinal membrane is wanting.

Diameter 4·10 inches; height 1·80; diameter of abactinal area 1·30; depth of cuts ·25; diameter of abactinal area ·60; of anal membrane ·24; breadth of ambulacral zones at periphery ·98; of poriferous zones, ·22; of interambulacral zones 1·55; length of larger spines of upper surface ·30 to ·35; their diameter ·05 to ·06 of an inch.

The test is very thick and firm for this genus. The outline is somewhat pentagonal, with rounded sides, the ambulacra somewhat bulging, and toward the summit somewhat raised above the concave interambulacra. The lower side is concave; the upper surface depressed, subconical, elevated at the center.

The actinal cuts are deep, their interambulacral margin raised, but not projecting inward beyond the ends of the ambulacral zones. The lower surface is covered by numerous, nearly uniform, large tubercles, which form about eight interambulacral and four ambulacral rows; in the former the two inner rows terminate about half way to the actinal area and are separated by a median region of some width, on which there are several irregular rows of smaller tubercles. On the upper side each of the zones bears two primary rows of large and conspicuous tubercles, which commence at the summit and extend to the actinal area. In the interambulacra the interior secondary rows commence at about the third or fourth plate, as small irregular tubercles at first, becoming about as large as the primaries near the periphery, and extending nearly to the actinal area; the exterior secondary row commences at about the sixth or seventh plate, their tubercles, very small at first, equalling the primaries at the periphery and extending to the actinal area outside of the cuts, where they become small again; the interior ternary row commences at about the ninth or tenth plate, and the tubercles equal the primaries at the margin, but cease at five or six plates from the actinal area; the external ternary rows commence a little above the periphery and extend about half way to the actinal area, alternating irregularly with the external secondaries, but not equalling them in size; these two rows border the poriferous zones, except near the summit; near the periphery there are also interior quaternary rows of small tubercles imperfectly developed, and some still smaller scattered tubercles. The miliary tubercles are rather large and numerous, except along a central, narrow, naked band, which commences at the periphery and becomes depressed and conspicuous, but not wider, toward the summit. In the ambulacral zones the primary tubercles border the poriferous zones throughout; the interior secondary rows are represented toward the summit by small tubercles scarcely distinct from the miliaries, but become regular toward the periphery, where the tubercles are nearly as large as the primaries, but they fade out before reaching the actinal areas; at and below the periphery there are small tubercles scattered in the central region, but on the upper side there is a very narrow naked band. The pores are rather large, forming conspicuous zones above, which become much narrower below. On the lower side the pores are in regular oblique rows of three pairs, but above they appear to form a regular inner vertical row, separated by a row of small tubercles from the two, less regular, alternating, outer rows. The genital plates are thick, with the outer end obtusely rounded, and sunken around the large, round genital orifices. The anal membrane is covered with numerous irregular, separated plates, forming about three irregular outer circles and a central radiating group of smaller ones. The jaw supports are stout and elongated, narrowed toward the end, with an elongated, elliptical foramen. The few larger spines that remain on the upper surface are short, stout, and blunt.

The color of the test is yellowish beneath, this color extending up into the central parts of the ambulacral and interambulacral zones above; the rest of the upper side is brownish, with more or less red, especially on the naked bands; spines pale brown.

This species differs from *B. rosea* in its much thicker test, less depressed form, more prominent ambulacra, much more numerous and larger tubercles, narrower naked bands, less acute genital plates, different anal area, etc.

The specimens formerly described by me as *P. pictus* appear to be the young of this species. Before the large specimen above described was known, a comparison of those with authentic specimens of *L. semituberculatus* had convinced both Mr. Agassiz and myself that they are really quite distinct from the latter.

L. semituberculatus (Val. sp.) Verrill (p. 333) differs from *B. picta*, young, in having fewer and more distant tubercles, and broad, well-defined, naked areas, bearing only small granule-like miliaries in the interambulacral zones of the upper side, instead of the very small and narrow naked areas, encroached upon by the numerous, crowded tubercles, seen in the latter; in the more numerous and regular, crowded plates, which closely cover the actinal membrane; and in the form of the ovarial plates, which are more obtuse outwardly, and have the large genital orifices at the edge, forming notch-like openings in the margin, while in *B. picta* the plates are more pointed at the outer end, and the genital orifices are small, round, and distant from the margin.

Boletia rosea A. Agassiz, 1863.

Lytechinus roseus Verrill. these Trans., p. 302.

A reëxamination of this species, and comparison with *B. pileolus*, the type of the genus, has convinced me that I was wrong in referring it to *Lytechinus*, and that it is a true *Boletia*. The deep actinal cuts, the remarkably large pedicellariae, the few scattered plates of the actinal membrane, and the thinness of the test are sufficient to separate it from *Lytechinus*.

B. depressa, as figured in Voy. Vénus, Pl. 3, figs. 1–1', is a similar species, but differs in having pointed processes bordering the actinal cuts, and in its larger and more numerous tubercles.

Evechinus, gen. nov.

Test thick, circular, thickly covered with tubercles of various sizes. Spines rather short, tapering, very unequal. Ambulacral zones with two principal rows of large tubercles; poriferous zones not widened below; pores beneath, near the actinal areas, arranged in obliquely transverse groups of three pairs, very soon becoming irregular, the inner ones being separated from the others by a vertical row of tubercles, so that throughout the greater part of the extent of the zones, both above and below, the pores form an inner, nearly regular, vertical row, and two irregularly alternating rows, of which the outer is more regular than the median row; in the latter the pores are arranged in a more or less zigzag line.

Actinal area small, with shallow cuts; the membrane is thin and bears a few scattered, rounded, granulated plates; the larger plates, near the mouth, bear minute spines and very small oval pedicellariae. Anal area covered by an outer circle of 8 to 10, larger, often spine-bearing plates, and an inner converging cluster of smaller plates.—Type, *Echinus chloroticus* Val.

Evechinus chloroticus Verrill.

Echinus chloroticus Val., Voy. Vénus. Zoöph., Pl. 7, figs. 2–2d, 1846.
Heliocidaris chlorotica Desml.; Ag. and Des., Ann. des Sci. nat., vi, p. 374, 1846.
Psammechinus chloroticus A. Ag., Bulletin, M. C. Z., i, p. 23, 1863.
Boletia viridis Verrill, these Trans., p. 304, 1867.

The specimen erroneously described by me (page 304) as from Peru, proves to be identical with the New Zealand species, and was undoubtedly collected there by Mr. H. Edwards, and accidentally misplaced while packing the Peruvian collection. As I am unable to refer it to either of the four genera in which it has already been placed, it seems necessary to establish a new genus to include it, together with a smaller undetermined species in our collection.

The arrangement of the pores and the few distant plates of the actinal membrane are sufficient to separate it from *Psammechinus*. *Boletia* differs in having a thin test, deeper actinal cuts, and in being destitute of tubercles in the middle of the interambulacral areas above, etc. *Heliocidaris* has a very different arrangement of pores, and the zones are expanded beneath.

Tripneustes depressus A. Ag.

Verrill, these Trans., p. 375; Amer. Jour. Sci., xlix, p. 99, 1870.

Of this large species there are 24 specimens from La Paz, with their spines partially preserved. They are quite variable in form, but often more elevated than ordinary specimens of *T. ventricosus*. Some are conical, others broadly rounded above. The largest spines on the upper surface of the largest specimen are ·45 of an inch long, ·04 in diameter, and rapidly taper to the acute point; those of the lower surface are often ·60 of an inch long, ·04 in diameter, tapering but little, the end blunt.

Several specimens give the following proportions:

Diameter, (inches)	5·80	5·40	5·35	5·25	5·15	5·10	4·90	4·75	4·60
Height,	3·00	3·40	2·90	3·25	2·60	2·85	2·65	2·85	2·80

One specimen has much larger ovarial plates than the others, and consequently a larger abactinal area. These plates are also more pointed, giving to the abactinal area a more stellate form.

Toxocidaris Mexicana A. Agassiz, (p. 307), (*non Heliocidaris Mexicana* Ag.)

This is a large species, belonging to a group distinct from the typical species of *Toxopneustes* (*T. tuberculatus*), of which Mr. Agassiz has recently brought authentic specimens from Europe. The original *Heliocidaris Mexicana* Ag., according to Mr. A. Agassiz, is a variety of the common West Indian *Echinometra Michelini*. The specimen referred by me to that species (p. 308) proves by comparison with the types of Mr. Agassiz, to be *Toxocidaris crassispina* A. Ag., from Japan, (not the young of *Echinometra Michelini*, to which Mr. Agassiz formerly referred it in the Bulletin M. C. Z., i, p. 260). Since *Anthocidaris* of Lütken is identical with *Toxocidaris* A. Ag., this species was referred by me to the right genus, but the erroneous localities on the labels of two separate lots, led to the mistake as to the species, which in this group of genera have not been described with sufficient care to make them recognizable with certainty, without a comparison with the original types.

The other species of *Toxocidaris*, described from the west coast, are as follows:

T. homalostoma (p. 333) =*Echinus homalostoma* Val., Voy. Vénus, Zooph., Pl. 6, figures 2–2f., Galapagos.

T. erythrogramma (p. 335), =*Echinus erythrogramma* Val., op. cit., Pl. 7, figures 1–1d., Chili.

T. Franciscana A. Ag., (p. 327), California.

The last species, however, appears to agree nearly with *Loxechinus*. The two groups are closely allied and perhaps ought not to be separated. Both have regular arches of numerous pores above, and the poriferous zones expanded beneath, but less so in the latter.

Echinometra Van Brunti A. Ag., (pp. 309, 375).

The numerous specimens of this species sent by Capt. Pedersen from La Paz show great variation in form. Many are quite oblong, while others are nearly circular; most of them are quite depressed, but some are considerably elevated at the center. Some have wider poriferous zones and more oblique arcs of pores above than the typical form, in this respect approaching *E. rupicola*, rendering it possible that the two forms are only variations of one species, but they all have the interambulacral tubercles very unequal and but two rows of the largest ones, with only two, close, alternating rows of secondary tubercles between, differing in this respect very decidedly from *E. rupicola*. The specimens hitherto received, therefore, do not warrant the union of the two species.

Encope grandis Ag. (pp. 310, 375).

Verrill, Am. Journ. Science, xlix, p. 96, 1870.

Of this very distinct species there are several hundred specimens in the La Paz collection, varying in size from 3 inches in length by 3·20 wide, to 4·60 inches by 4·40. There is but little variation in outline and general appearance, and in all the margin is thick, with the five large notches widely open, though in the larger there appears to be a tendency to close the anterior pair. The posterior interambulacral opening is large and broad-oval with thickened borders in all, but there is a variation of more than 50 per cent. in its relative size; the region around it is in all more elevated than the central region and considerably swollen. The form of the ambulacral rosette varies considerably. The three anterior petals are subequal and usually long-oval, obtusely rounded at the end, but in one case they are narrower and more elliptical, especially the odd anterior one, which is widest in the middle, tapering to each end, and in another they are broader and more dilated outwardly than usual; the two posterior ones are much longer, widest outwardly, and curve somewhat around the posterior opening, but they vary considerably in relative width. The following are the proportions in two extreme specimens:

From abactinal center to posterior edge,	2·20	2·20
Center to anterior edge,	1·98	2·00
Center to lateral edge,	2·20	2·10
Length of anterior odd ambulacral petal, from center,	1·28	1·25
Greatest breadth of do.,	·50	·68
Breadth of its enclosed area,	·20	·30
Length of anterior-lateral pair,	1·25	1·15
Breadth of do.,	·50	·65
Breadth of enclosed area,	·16	·27
Length of posterior pair,	1·65	1·55
Breadth of do.,	·45	·62
Breadth of enclosed area,	·12	·20

The branchings of the ambulacral grooves beneath are quite constant in their arrangement, but the relative breadth and form of the enclosed areas are quite as variable as in the dorsal rosette. The region about the anal opening and around the posterior foramen is sometimes deeply concave or excavated; but in most cases slightly, and sometimes not at all so.

Encope Californica Verrill.

American Jour. Science, xlix, p. 97, 1870.

Plate X, figures 5 and 6.

Test broad, thin at the edge, rounded anteriorly, broadest behind the middle, sub-truncate or rounded posteriorly; usually about as broad as long, sometimes broader than long. Apex behind the center. In profile the outline descends from the center to the anterior edge, but rises from the center to the posterior foramen, from which it descends rapidly to the edge. The posterior interambulacrum is, therefore, swollen and the test is most elevated near its foramen. Ambulacral rosette with the petals long-oval, somewhat obovate, broadly rounded outwardly; the anterior pair shortest and most rounded; the odd anterior one somewhat longer and narrower and a little shorter than those of the posterior pair, which are of about the same form and not curved. Posterior foramen variable in form and size, usually rather small, regularly oval or rounded, sometimes long oval, or even narrow and elongated, occasionally quite large and broad oval, often obovate beneath, sometimes constricted in the middle. Ambulacral foramina also quite variable in form and size, but commonly small and rather regularly oval, often at a considerable distance from the margin.

Two specimens, showing the extreme variations, give the following measurements:

Length of test,	4·75	4·30
Breadth,	4·65	4·30
Center to anterior edge,	2·45	2·15
" " anterior foramen,	1·80	1·65
" " lateral edge,	2·35	2·15
" " " foramen,	1·60	1·50
" " posterior edge,	2·45	2·25
" " posterior-lateral foramen,	1·85	1·70
" " posterior foramen,	1·15	1·10
Length of " "	·67	·60
Breadth of " "	·22	·26
Length of anterior ambulacral petal, from center,	1·42	1·32
Breadth where widest,	·65	·50
Breadth of enclosed area,	·30	·18
Length of anterior-lateral petals,	1·28	1·10
Breadth,	·67	·50
Breadth of enclosed area,	·28	·20
Length of posterior-lateral petals,	1·58	1·35
Breadth,	·68	·53
Breadth of enclosed area,	·25	·16

Of this species there are 74 specimens in the collection from La Paz, and I have seen others from Cape St. Lucas.

It varies considerably in outline and in the form of the openings, especially the posterior one; the ambulacral rosette varies somewhat in the form of the petals, as shown by the above measurements; the ambulacral grooves beneath also vary in direction. But all the specimens agree in having their greatest elevation behind the center, or the posterior interambulacral region swollen. This peculiarity, which is found to depend upon a very different internal structure, will readily separate this species from *E. occidentalis* V. In the latter the greatest elevation is in front of the center, and there is a regular slope from thence to the broad, thin, posterior edge, and the sections show that the wide space between the central cavity and the posterior foramen is filled with a pretty firm, alveolar tissue, having comparatively small spaces, but in *E. Californica* the same region is much less extensive (owing to the relatively larger central cavity and jaws) and is filled with a much less firm and more open tissue, with large cavities.

The difference is therefore analogous to that which separates *E. Michelini* from *E. emarginata*.

Mellita longifissa Michelin.

Mellita longifissa Michelin, Revue et Mag. Zool., 1858, No. 8, Pl. 8, fig. 1; Verrill, Proc. Boston Soc. Nat Hist., xii, p. 383.

This species is the Pacific analogue of *M. pentapora* of the Atlantic coast. It is remarkable for the thinness or flatness of the outer portion of its shell, the deeply sunken grooves of the lower surface, and the length and narrowness of its five perforations, and especially of the odd posterior one. The posterior side is somewhat truncate, but a little rounded in the middle, and the posterior lateral perforations are curved. The largest specimen from Gulf of California (Stearns) is 3·8 inches in diameter; another is 2·95 wide, 2·70 long, ·45 high; the anterior pair of perforations ·54 and ·56 long; the posterior pair ·55 and ·60; the posterior odd one ·78 long; ·09 wide.

La Paz,—Capt. Pedersen; Gulf of California,—Robt. E. C. Stearns; Corinto, Nic.,—J. A. McNiel.

Clypeaster testudinarius nob. (*non* Martens).

Echinanthus testudinarius Gray, Proc. Zoöl. Soc. Lond., xix, 1851, p. 35; Cat. Ech. Brit. Mus., p. 6, Pl 1, fig. 1, 1855.
Clypeaster speciosus Verrill, Am. Jour. Science, xlix, p. 95, 1870.

Plate X, figures 7, 7ª.

Depressed, gradually rising toward the apex; the lower side sometimes slightly concave from near the edge of the mouth, in other specimens flat, except close to the mouth, which is much sunken. Outline oblong-pentagonal, with rounded angles and slightly concave sides. The anterior end slightly elongated. Interambulacral regions decidedly concave between the ends of the ambulacral rosette; the ambulacral regions enclosed by the pores slightly raised, narrow, elongated, widening but little outwardly and somewhat acuminate at the end, which is often nearly enclosed by the pores. The interambulacra are broader and decrease much more rapidly toward the apex than in *C. rosaceus*. Anal opening transversely oval, or rounded, situated about its own diameter from the edge of the shell.

Length of largest specimens 4·60 inches; breadth 3·90; height 1·15. Length of anterior petal, from the apex, 1·90; its breadth ·82; breadth of enclosed space ·50; length of anterior petals 1·70; breadth ·85; breadth of enclosed space ·48; length of posterior petals 1·80 and 1·85; breadth ·94; of enclosed space ·58 and ·60; diameter of anal area ·20; of actinal opening ·33.

Thirty-five specimens of this species are contained in the collection. They show but little variation in outline, except what is due to age, though some specimens are more elevated toward the apex than others; in regard to the flatness or concavity of the lower side there is, however, great variation, though Dr. Gray used this character in dividing the genus into sections. The youngest specimens are 2·30 long by 2·10 wide, and are more oval in form and scarcely angular, but have the flatness and form of ambulacral rosette characteristic of the larger specimens, as well as the same position of the anal opening.

From *C. rosaceus* of the Atlantic this species differs widely, the former having a much more elevated and thick form, with broader and more obovate ambulacra, which are much more swollen; the lower side is much more concave, and the anal opening nearer the edge.

La Paz,—J. Pedersen.

Dr. Gray erroneously gave Borneo as the locality of his specimen, which Mr. Agassiz has identified, *by direct comparison* in the British Museum, with specimens sent by me.

Brissus obesus Verrill, (pp. 316, 375).

These Transactions, p. 316, 1867; Proc. Bost. Soc. Nat. Hist., xii. p. 382, 1869.

A larger specimen, with part of its spines, collected by Capt. Pedersen at La Paz, agrees well in form and other characters with the original specimens. The spines are silvery white and slender, on the upper side decreasing regularly in length from the peripetalous fasciole to the margin; the upper ones being ·10 or ·12 long, the lower ones ·25 to ·28. Those near the margin beneath are quite long, ·35 to ·38, those near the mouth being largest. This specimen is 2·65 inches long; 2 broad; 1·40 high.

Meoma grandis Gray.

Meoma grandis Gray, Ann. and Mag. Nat. Hist., vii, p. 132, 1851; Cat. Ech. Brit. Mus., p. 56, Pl. 5, fig. 2, 1855: A. Agassiz. Bulletin Mus. Comp. Zoöl., i, p. 275, 1870.
Kleinia nigra A. Agassiz. Bulletin Mus. Comp. Zoöl., p. 27, 1863.
Meoma nigra Verrill, these Trans., p. 317, 1867; Amer. Jour. Sci., xlix, p. 93. 1870.

Of this interesting species there are ten specimens in the collection from La Paz, which show considerable variation from the type formerly described by me, as well as among themselves.

The largest is 4·85 inches long, 4·25 broad, 2·10 high; the smallest 3·85 long, 3·40 broad, 1·75 high. The outline, as seen from below, varies but little and is broad-oval, somewhat emarginate anteriorly, obliquely truncate posteriorly, and slightly compressed laterally, or, in other words, nearly heart-shaped. The anal area is large, somewhat sunken, and is at the extreme posterior end of the shell, occupying the greater part of the truncated portion. Its form varies from regularly elliptical, acute at each end, to broad-oval, rounded below and acute above; its position varies from nearly vertical to decidedly oblique, and it is so nearly terminal as to produce a posterior emargination in a dorsal view of the shell. In a side view some specimens are decidedly depressed, but most are regularly arched, while one is decidedly elevated at the apex. There is considerable variation in the depth of the anterior ambulacral groove, and also in the number and prominence of the large tubercles, which are more or less restricted to the region enclosed by the peripetalous fasciole. The fasciole itself shows remarkable variations, but does not agree at all with Gray's figure. The portion crossing the anterior interambulacral regions varies less than other parts, but in some the intermediate transverse portion is nearly straight, in others strongly curved and often crooked, in one it is bent up into a right angle on each side of the ambulacral groove; its bend or angle near the antero-lateral grooves is also variable, both in form and extent, it being twice as large in some specimens as in others, and in one an irregular, crooked branch passes from the apex of the angle on the left side to the anterior groove. In the posterior interambulacrum the course of the fasciole is quite variable, in five examples it crosses with a strongly curved upward bend, without any distinct angle, rising highest in four specimens on the right side, in the other forming a nearly straight transverse middle portion; in three specimens it forms a sharp angle on the right side; in one a similar angle on the left side; in another there is a strong median angle, its apex pointing to the anal region, and another to the right of it, pointing to the summit; in all the specimens it bends inward farther than in Gray's figure. The lateral part of the fasciole also varies, especially on the left side; in five (but not the same five that agree in the posterior region) it has but one angle, near the antero-lateral grooves, where it rises highest; in three it has two angles, rising highest at the posterior one, and nearly straight between; in two others, which also have two angles, the transverse part is double. On the other side the fasciole varies in the same way, but not in the same specimens, for some have two angles, both on the right and left; others two only on one side; others one on both sides. The anal fasciole is also variable; usually the subanal branch is wanting or indistinct, though indicated by a band of smaller tubercles, but in one specimen it is well marked and the subanal disk is clearly and perfectly circumscribed. In this the subanal disk is very broad, bilobed, narrowest in the middle, scarcely heart-shaped, the anterior border being nearly transverse, and the posterior border nearly parallel with the anal region and about ·15 of an inch from it. In others the posterior border is more curved. One specimen has but three ovarial openings, the rest four. The proportionate length of the ambulacral grooves varies considerably, both in different specimens and on opposite sides of the same individual, sometimes those on the right being longest, sometimes those on the left, and not uncommonly a longer anterior one is offset by a shorter posterior one on the same side.

My specimens differ widely from Gray's figure, the position of the anal area, especially, is quite different, it being in the figure at a considerable distance from the posterior end, and therefore more ventral and nearer the subanal fasciole. The peripetalous fasciole is also very different from that of any of my specimens.

Mr. A. Agassiz, who has recently examined Gray's type in the British Museum, is fully satisfied that it is identical with *M. nigra*, as he had previously supposed.

The locality given by Gray (Australia) is, therefore, doubtless erroneous.

Metalia nobilis Verrill. (p. 319).

Plagionotus nobilis A. Agassiz, Bulletin Mus. Comp. Zoöl., i p. 302, 1870.

Mr. Agassiz, after an examination of the original specimen, referred this species to *Plagionotus*. In this opinion I cannot concur, unless *Metalia* and *Plagionotus* are to be united, which at present does not seem to be justifiable, although the two groups are evidently closely allied.

Metalia nobilis appears to be much more closely allied to *M. sternalis*, and especially to *M. Garretii*, than to the two typical species of *Plagionotus* (*P. pectoralis* and *P. Africanus*). The two latter species agree in their broad depressed form; in having the peripetalous fasciole convex across the lateral and posterior interambulacra, or *nearly parallel with the margin of the test;* in possessing many very large tubercles, surrounded by a smooth sunken area, bearing large spines, and arranged in oblique transverse rows in all the interambulacra, within the fasciole; and especially in having narrow ambulacra and small ambulacral plates, beyond the petals, while the lateral interambulacral plates are very long transversely and narrow vertically, the latter being six or seven times as long as broad, and five or six times as long as the corresponding ambulacral plates; and in the anterior interambulacra the plates next the anterior ambulacra are only about half the length of those next the lateral ambulacra, and the latter are much bent, and angulated toward the inner end.

In *Metalia* the form is more swollen above; the peripetalous fasciole is curved upward in the lateral and posterior interambulacra, and *not at all parallel with the margin;* there are no *very large tubercles* in the interambulacra, the largest ones, which correspond nearly with the secondary ones of *Plagionotus*, are chiefly found in the posterior zone and near the anterior ambulacra, in *M. nobilis*, but they are not arranged in definite rows, and are not at all conspicuous, while in the lateral zones they are very few and scarcely distinct from the small tubercles; the ambulacra, below the petals, are relatively broad (in *M. nobilis* about half as wide as the lateral interambulacra), and composed of large plates, while the interambulacra are correspondingly narrowed, and composed of fewer plates, which are much broader vertically and shorter transversely than those of *Plagionotus;* in *M. nobilis* these are only two or three times longer than broad, and about three times as long as the corresponding ambulacral plates; in the anterior interambulacra the two rows of plates are nearly equal, and those of both are more regularly curved in the middle.

In *Metalia* the ambulacral petals are more sunken than in *Plagionotus*, and this is notably the case in *M. nobilis*. In the latter and *M. Garretii*, the vertex is more anterior than is usual in *Plagionotus*, but this character is somewhat variable. In the character of the lower surface the two genera do not materially differ.

In *M. nobilis* the actinal area is broadly crescent-shaped, and covered with few, rather large, polygonal plates, which are in close contact. The anal area is also closely covered with angular plates, the outer ones forming a continuous marginal row, in which the lower ones are smallest and oblong or squarish, while the upper ones, filling the acute angle, are much larger and irregular in form. There are four, round, genital orifices, of which the two anterior are largest and nearest together.

Agassizia scrobiculata Val

Voyage de la Vénus. Zoöph., Pl. 1, figures 2-2 f, 1840; Agassiz and Desor, Ann. des Sci. nat., viii, p. 20. 1847; A. Agassiz, Bulletin Mus. Comp. Zoöl., i, p. 276, 1870. *Agassizia subrotunda* Gray, Ann. and Mag. Nat. Hist., vii, p. 133, 1851; Catalogue Echinida of British Mus., p. 63, tab. 3, fig. 2, 1855; Verrill, Proc. Bost. Soc. Nat. Hist., vol. xii, p. 381, 1869; Amer. Jour. Sci., xlix, p. 95, 1870.

A. ovulum Lütken, Vidensk. Medd., p. 134, tab. 2, fig. 8; Verrill, these Trans., p. 320.

Of this species there are from La Paz about a dozen specimens, mostly more or less broken, which show but little variation. They agree well with Gray's figure, but not with those in the Voyage de la Vénus. Mr. A. Agassiz has, however, seen the original of the latter, and finds it identical with the *A. subrotunda* of Gray. The figure is inaccurate. *A. ovulum* Lütk. is the young of the same species, and is more oblong in form than the larger specimens.

One of our larger specimens is 1·70 inches long; 1·55 broad; 1·25 high. A smaller one is 1·50 long; 1·35 broad; 1·05 high.

I have taken several small specimens from the stomach of a fish, collected at Panama by Mr. F. H. Bradley. Mr. J. A. McNiel also sent larger specimens from Panama.

No. 9.—*The Echinoderm-Fauna of the Gulf of California and Cape St. Lucas.*

In order to give a better idea of the fauna of the Gulf of California, I have brought together, in the following list, all the species hitherto recorded from there.* The Holothurians are entirely unknown, and doubtless many additional species of the other orders remain to be discovered, when systematic dredgings shall have been undertaken. All the species hitherto described belong to the littoral and laminarian

---

* Dr. Chr Lütken has informed me by letter that the Museum of Copenhagen has received a collection from Altata. nearly opposite La Paz, which contained *Ophiolepis variegata*; a new species of *Ophioglypha*, allied to *O. Sarsii*; *Heliaster Kubiniji*; *H. microbrachia*; a new genus and species of Star-fish, with 30-35 long arms, and allied to *Acanthaster* and *Pedicellaster*; a second species of *Cidaris*; *Astropyga depressa*; *Boletia rosea*; and *Meoma grandis*. Also from Mazatlan a new species of *Luidia*, with remarkably short marginal spines (*L. brevispina* Ltk). These were probably obtained by dredging in deeper water.

zones, and have been obtained upon the shores at low-water, or by the aid of pearl-divers at depths less than eight fathoms.

In the list I have prefixed letters to indicate the relations of this to the other tropical fauna. Those species indicated by c are represented by closely allied species in the Caribbean fauna; those designated by M are represented in the same way in the Mediterranean; those with A have corresponding species on the west coast of Africa; those with I have representative species in the Indo-Pacific fauna.

The species which I have personally examined are designated by a mark of exclamation (!).

OPHIUROIDEA.

C-M- -I-*Astrophyton Panamense* Verrill! La Paz to Zorritos.
C-M- - -*Ophiura Panamensis* Lyman! Southward to Panama.
C- - - -*O. teres* Lyman! S. to Panama.
C- - -I-*Ophiolepis variegata* Lütken. Altata. S. to Panama.
C-M- -I-*Ophiocoma æthiops* Lütken! S. to Panama.
C- - -I-*O. Alexandri* Lyman! S. to Panama.
C-M- -I-*Ophiactis virescens* Lütken! S. to Panama.
C- - -I-*Ophionereis Xantusii* Lyman. Cape St. Lucas.
C- - -I-*O. annulata* Lyman! S. to Panama.
C-M- -I-*Ophioglypha*, sp. Altata (t. Lütken).
C-M- -I-*Ophiothrix spiculata* LeC.! S. to Zorritos.
C-M- -I-*O. dumosa* Lyman. Cape St. Lucas, San Diego, Guaymas.
- - -I-*Ophiothela mirabilis* Verrill! La Paz to Panama.

ASTERIOIDEA.

C-M-A-I-*Astropecten Ørstedii* Lütken! S. to Panama.
C-M-A-I-*Luidia brevispina* Ltk. Mazatlan.
- - -I-*Gymnasteria spinosa* Gray! La Paz.
Amphiaster insignis Verrill! La Paz.
Nidorellia armata Gray! Guaymas and La Paz to Zorritos.
C- -A-I-*Oreaster occidentalis* Verrill! La Paz to Panama.
- - -I-*Acanthaster Ellisii* Verrill! La Paz to Galapagos and "S. America."
- - -I-*Mithrodia Bradleyi* Verrill! La Paz to Panama.
C-M- -I-*Echinaster tenuispina* Verrill! La Paz.
Lepidaster teres Verrill! La Paz.
C-M- -I-*Linckia unifascialis* Gray! S. to Zorritos.
Do. var. bifascialis Gray! S. to Panama.
C-M- -I-*Ophidiaster pyramidatus* Gray! S. to Zorritos.
Heliaster microbrachia Xantus! Cape St. Lucas to Panama.
H. Kubiniji Xantus! Guaymas, La Paz and Cape St. Lucas.
C-M-A-I-*Asterias sertulifera* Xantus! Cape St. Lucas.

Echinoidea.

C- -A-I-*Cidaris Thouarsii* Val.! Guaymas and La Paz to Panama and Galapagos.
    Cidaris, sp. Altata (t. Lütken).
C-M-A-I-*Diadema Mexicanum* A. Ag.! Guaymas to Acapulco.
    Echinodiadema coronatum Verrill! Cape St. Lucas.
- - -I-*Astropyga depressa* Gray! La Paz to Panama.
C-M-A- -*Echinocidaris stellata* Agassiz! Margarita Bay and Guaymas to Paita and Galapagos.
- - -I-*Boletia picta* Verrill! La Paz and Cape St. Lucas.
- - -I-*Boletia rosea* A. A. Altata (t. Lütken), S. to Panama.
C- - -I-*Tripneustes depressus* A. Ag.! Guaymas and La Paz.
C- -A-I-*Echinometra Van Brunti* A. Ag.! La Paz to Acapulco.
C- -A-I-*Clypeaster testudinarius* Verrill! La Paz.
C- - - -*Mellita longifissa* Mich.! Guaymas and La Paz to Panama.
C- - - -*Encope grandis* Ag.! La Paz and Guaymas.
C- - - -*Encope Californica* Verrill! Guaymas to Cape St. Lucas.
C- - - -*Encope occidentalis* Verrill! S. to Zorritos and Galapagos.
C- - - -*Rhyncholampas Pacificus* Ag.! Cape St. Lucas and Acapulco.
C- - - -*Meoma grandis* Gray! La Paz to Acapulco.
- - -I-*Metalia nobilis* Verrill! Cape St. Lucas and Panama.
C-M- -I-*Brissus obesus* Verrill! La Paz to Panama.
C- - - -*Agassizia scrobiculata* Val.! Guaymas and La Paz to Panama and "Peru."
- - -I-*Lorenia*, sp.! Cape St. Lucas and San Diego.
C- - - -*Mœra Clotho* Mich.! Mazatlan.

In this list there are 50 species. Of these, 28 species extend southward to Panama Bay, or beyond; 8 are known even to reach northern Peru, and doubtless many others will be found to do so when that region becomes better known; 4 species have been found also at the Galapagos; 4 species, which have not been found at Panama, reach Acapulco; 2 species are common to the Gulf and San Diego, but have not been found southward; and 17 species are as yet known only from the Gulf and Cape St. Lucas.

Of the whole number, 35 are represented by allied species in the Caribbean fauna. 24 of these are also represented in the Indo-Pacific fauna, 19 of which are also represented in the Mediterranean or on the west coast of Africa, and may, therefore, be regarded as true cosmopolitan tropical types. 9 additional species, which do not have allies in the Caribbean, are represented in the Indo-Pacific fauna and may be regarded as true Pacific types; 7 species (including Lütken's new genus of star-fishes, not in the list) have no allies elsewhere, so far as known, and for the present may be regarded as peculiar West-American types.

We may, therefore, consider this fauna as made up, approximately, of 11 species, Atlantic in type; 9 Indo-Pacific; 19 cosmopolitan, and 4 others probably so; with 6 species of types peculiar to the west coast.

ERRATA TO PART II.

Page 293, line 16, for *tesselata*, read *tessellata*.
Page 293, line 18, for *Ludia*, read *Luidia*.
Page 294, line 32, for *Mexicana*, read *Mexicanum*.
Page 295, line 30, for *coronata*, read *coronatum*.
Page 297, line 23, for *ambulacra*, read *interambulacra*.
Page 303, line 2 of foot-note, for *depressus*, read *depressa*.
Page 376, line 32, for *Pterogorgia gracilis*, read *Gorgonia gracilis*.
Page 386, last line of foot-note, insert p. 419.
Page 387, last line, for p. 325, read p. 419.
Page 410, line 18, omit Plate VI, figure 8.
Page 413, line 17, for *Phycogorgia fucata*, read *Leptogorgia fucata*. The spicula of *Phycogorgia fucata*, according to Mr. Wm. S. Kent (Trans. Roy. Mic. Soc., iii, p. 91, 1870), agree with those of *Leptogorgia*, to which it should therefore be referred.
Page 514, line 33, for *Stylasteridæ* Pourtales, read *Stylasteridæ* Gray (emended).*
Page 518, line 20, for *Pocilliporidæ* Verrill, read *Pocilliporidæ* Gray (restricted).
Page 519, line 17, for *Astræopsammia*, read *Astropsammia*.
Page 542, line 26, for *Agaricidæ* Verrill, read *Agaricidæ* Gray (restricted).
Page 554, after *Eugorgia multifida*, insert Plate VI, figure 8.

* Annals and Mag. Nat Hist., vol. xix, p. 127, 1847.

INDEX.

Abatus antarcticus, 336.
  australis, 336.
  cavernosus, 336.
Abrolhos Reefs, Brazil, Notice of the Corals and Echinoderms collected by Prof. C. F. Hartt, at the, 351.
Acalephæ, 362.
Acanthaster, 348, 593.
  Ellisii, 332, 333, 343, 576, 594.
  solaris, 576.
Acanthastræa, 355, 365.
  Braziliensis, 355, 357.
Acanthocidaris Mexicana, 308.
  erythrogramma, 335.
Acanthogorgia, 419.
  aspera, 419.
  Atlantica, 419.
  coccinea, 419.
  Grayi, 419.
  hirsuta, 419.
Acis, 449, 450.
Acrocladia, 349.
Act of Incorporation, 5.
Actinacea, 461.
Actinaria, 460, 461, 500, 559, 560, 562, 566.
Actinia, 466, 475, 478, 487, 491.
  artemisia, 470, 471.
  bicolor, 486.
  bimaculata, 469.
  carneola, 469.
  Chilensis, 488.
  clematis, 476.
  coriacea, 469.
  crassicornis, 469.
  crispata, 484.
  cruentata, 467.
  decorata, 481.
  Dowii, 474.
  elegantissima, 469, 470.
  felina, 469.
  florida, 477.
  flosculifera, 464.
  Fuegiensis, 480.
  Holsatica, 469.
  impatiens, 483.
  Krebsii, 473.
  Laurentii, 469, 470.
  lineolata, 483.
  Mertensii, 479, 566.
  nivea, 485.
  nymphæa, 486.
  obtruncata, 469.

Actinia ocellata, 468.
  papillosa, 468.
  Peruviana, 486.
  picta, 493.
  primula, 487, 488.
  pluvia, 468.
  reticulata, 479.
  rubens, 487.
  spectabilis, 469.
  xanthogrammica, 471.
Actiniadæ, 491.
Actiniaires, 461.
Actinidæ, 362, 466, 461, 494.
Actinina, 461, 466.
Actininæ, 461, 466, 491.
Actinines perforées, 477.
Actinines verruqueuses, 466.
Actinocereus, 484.
Actinoids, 460.
Actinoloba, 478.
  reticulata, 479.
Actinopyga Agassizii, 347.
  obscura, 347.
  parvula, 347.
Actinotryx, 462.
Adamsia, 477, 481.
  Egletes, 481.
Addenda to Review of the Corals and Polyps of the west coast of America, 546.
Advertisement, 2.
Agaricia, 352, 543.
  agaricites, 352.
Agaricidæ, 542, 596.
Agassizia, 320, 348.
  excentrica, 346.
  ovulum, 320, 331, 346, 593.
  scrobiculata, 334, 593, 595.
  subrotunda, 593.
Alcyonacea, 458, 455.
Alcyonaria, 359, 378, 559, 560, 566.
Alcyonidæ, 458.
Alcyonides, 458.
Alcyoninæ, 458.
Alcyonium, 459.
  Bradleyi, 459, 562.
  carneum, 459.
  rubiforme, 459, 559.
Allopora, 516, 515.
  Californica, 516, 503, 517, 663.
  venusta, 517, 560.
Alveopora, 502.
Amblypneustes formosus, 333.

Amblypneustes pallidus. 333.
Amphiactis, 462.
Amphiaster, 372.
　　insignis, 372, 594.
Amphipholi-, 261.
　　albida, 341.
　　grisea, 342.
　　Jannarii, 341.
　　subtilis, 341.
Amphiura, 261, 348.
　　Chilensis, 335.
　　geminata, 261, 330, 341.
　　gracillima, 342.
　　hispida, 260.
　　limbata, 342.
　　marginata, 262.
　　microdiscus, 270, 261, 330, 342.
　　occidentali-, 325, 326.
　　örstedii, 270, 262, 340, 341.
　　Pugetana, 325.
　　Punt ,rene, 261, 330, 341.
　　Rüsei, 341.
　　squamata, 341.
　　Stimpsonii, 341.
　　tenera, 341.
　　urtica, 325.
　　violacea, 261, 330, 341.
Anactis, 493.
　　picta, 493, 566.
Anaperus, 322.
　　Briareus, 322.
　　Pernanus, 322, 335, 376.
Anemonia, 491.
Anthea, 491.
Antheadæ, 466, 491.
Anthenia, 349.
Anthocidaris 333, 583.
　　homalostoma, 333.
　　Mexicana, 345.
Anthogorgia, 419.
Anthophyllum, 513.
Anthopleura, 473, 467.
　　Dowii, 474, 562.
　　granulifera, 474.
　　Krebsii, 474, 462.
　　pallida, 474.
Antipathacea, 499.
Antipatharia, 499.
Antipathes, 499.
　　Panamensis, 499, 562.
Antipathidæ, 499.
Antipathina, 499.
Antodon, 365.
　　armata, 341.
　　Braziliensis 341, 365.
　　brevipinna, 341.
　　Cubensis, 341.
　　Dubenii, 365, 341.
　　Hagenii, 341.
　　meridianalis, 341.
　　Milbertii 341.
　　rubiginosa. 341.
Arachnactis, 496.

Araucanian Province, 339.
Arbacia, 301, 348.
　　grandinosa, 334.
　　nigra 301, 334, 335.
　　pustulosa, 344.
Arbaciæ, 344.
Arca, 350.
Archaster, 349.
Arctic Province, Polyps of, 559.
Aspidochir Mertensii, 325.
Asteracanthion, 289.
　　aurantiacus, 293.
　　helianthus, 289.
Asteractis, 464, 492.
　　Bradleyi, 465, 562.
Asterias, 337.
　　æqualis, 327.
　　antarctica, 336, 339.
　　aster, 248.
　　Atlantica, 368, 344.
　　aurantiacus. 293.
　　brevispina, 327.
　　capitata, 327.
　　conferta, 326.
　　Cumingii, 291.
　　echinata, 335.
　　epichlora, 325, 326.
　　fissispina, 326.
　　gelatinosa, 335.
　　Germanii, 335.
　　gigantea, 327.
　　helianthus, 289.
　　hexactis, 326.
　　Katherinæ. 326.
　　lævigata, 285.
　　lurida, 335.
　　Lütkenii, 326.
　　Mexicana, 344.
　　miniata, 324, 326.
　　ochracea, 325. 326, 327.
　　paucispina, 326.
　　regalis, 330.
　　rugispina. 336.
　　rustica, 335.
　　sertulifera, 328, 344, 594.
　　solaris, 333.
　　tenuispina, 344, 369.
　　Troschelii, 326.
　　variolata, 285.
Asteridæ, 344.
Asterina, 250.
　　modesta, 277.
　　regularis, 250.
Asterioidea, 271, 343, 367, 372, 574
Asteriscus. 250, 348.
　　Braziliensis, 343.
　　Chilensis, 334, 335.
　　folium, 343.
　　modestus, 277, 330, 343
　　regularis, 250.
　　stillifer, 343.
Asteroporpa, 349.
　　affinis, 341.

INDEX. 599

Asteroporpa annulata 341.
   dasycladia, 341.
Asteropsis imbricata, 324.
Astræa, 512.
Astræacea. 461, 536.
Astræidæ, 519, 513, 540.
Astrangia, 525, 340, 362. 513, 532, 567.
   astræiformis, 524.
   bella, 530, 531.
   concinna, 528, 563.
   conferta, 530, 563, 564.
   costata, 529, 563.
   Danæ, 524, 530, 531.
   dentata, 528, 563, 565, 566.
   Edwardsii, 526.
   Haimei, 526, 525, 530, 563.
   Marylandica, 530, 531.
   Michelini, 526.
   palifera, 525, 526.
   Pedersenii, 529, 563, 564, 565.
   pulchella, 527, 563.
Astrangiaceæ, 525.
Astrangidæ, 524, 514. 536.
Astranginæ, 525, 514.
Astreinæ reptantes, 525.
Astriclypeus, 311, 348.
   Mannii, 311, 327.
Astrochema, 348.
   affinis, 341.
   oligactes, 341.
Astrochemidæ, 341.
Astrogonium Fonki, 335.
Astrogorgia, 416, 419.
Astropecten, 250, 272, 348.
   Antillensis, 343.
   armatus, 332, 343.
   articulatus, 343
   Braziliensis, 343.
   cœlacanthus, 273.
   ciliatus, 343.
   dubius, 343.
   Edwardsii, 250.
   erinaceus, 332, 343.
   fragilis, 272, 330, 332, 333, 343.
   Örstedii, 274, 328, 330, 343 594.
   Peruanus, 334.
   Peruvianus, 275.
   regalis, 273, 330, 343.
   stellatus, 276.
   Valenciennesii, 276, 343.
   variabilis, 343.
Astropectenidæ, 343.
Astropsammia, 509, 506, 519.
   Pedersenii, 509, 563, 565.
Astropyga, 296, 348.
   depressa, 579, 593, 595.
   venusta, 296, 331, 344, 579.
Astrophytidæ, 341.
Astrophyton, 251, 348.
   Caryi, 325, 326.
   cæcilia, 341.
   Chilensis, 335.
   Krebsii, 341.

Astrophyton muricatum, 341.
   Panamense, 251, 294.
Aulactinia, 474.
Aureliania, 462.
Aurora Borealis at New Haven, Conn., from March, 1837, to Dec., 1853, 9.
Auroral Observations, Summary of, 168, 171.
Auroral Register kept at New Haven, Ct., by Francis Bradley, 139.
Auroras, average number of annually, 172.
Auroras, Notices of, extracted from the Meteorological Journal of Rev. Ezra Stiles, 155.
   extracted from a Meteorological Journal kept at Sharon, Conn., 167.
   extracted from various Journals kept at New Haven, Conn., 164.
Auroras observed by Rev. Ezra Stiles, at Dighton, Mass., 156.
   New Haven, Conn., 156.
   Newport, R. I., 155.
   Portsmouth, N. H., 156.
Average number of Auroras annually, 172.
Axohelia, 515.

Balanophyllia, 511.
   elegans, 511, 560.
Bathycyathus, 538.
   Chilensis, 539, 567.
   Indicus, 538.
   Sowerbyi, 538.
Bebryce, 419.
Bekker's Digammated Text of Homer, 173.
Bergidæ, 494.
Blepharogorgia Schrammi, 419
Bohadschia agglutinata, 347.
   fasciata, 347.
Boletia, 304, 582.
   depressa, 303, 583.
   picta, 581, 595.
   pileolus, 303, 583.
   rosea, 302, 583, 593, 595.
   viridis, 304, 334, 584.
Bolocera eques, 469.
Boston, and New Haven, Summary of Auroral Observations at, 171.
Brachyrhinus creolus, 340.
Bradley, Francis, Extracts from an Auroral Register kept at New Haven, Conn., 139.
Brazilian Coral-fauna, Remarks on the, 364.
Briaraceæ, 454.
Briaraceës, 454.
Briaraceæ, 454.
Briareidæ, 454.
Briareum, 454.
Brissus, 316, 318, 348.
   Columbaris, 316, 345.
   obesus, 316, 328, 345, 375, 589, 595.
   pectoralis, 571.
Brissus Scillæ, 316, 317.
Bunodes, 467, 469, 471, 475, 562.
   cavernata, 473.

Bunodes crassicornis 469.
    cruentata, 467, 567.
    ocellata, 468, 566.
    papillosa, 468, 566, 567.
    pluvia, 468, 566.
    xanthogrammica, 471.
Bunodidæ, 466.
Bunodinæ, 466, 462.

California, Gulf of, and Cape St. Lucas, Echinoderm-fauna of, 593.
Californian Province, 337.
    Polyps of, 566.
Calliactis, 481.
    bicolor, 481.
    decorata, 481, 482.
    Egletes, 481.
    fusca, 481.
    polypus, 481.
    tricolor, 481.
    variegata, 481, 562.
Callipodium, 455.
    aureum, 457, 562.
    Pacificum, 456, 562, 565.
Cape St. Lucas, list of Echinoderms found at, 327.
    and Gulf of Cal., Echinoderm-fauna of, 593.
Capnea, 462.
Capneadæ, 462.
Caribbean and Panamian Faunæ, comparative lists of the Echinoderms of the, 341.
Caryophyllaceæ, 512.
Caryophyllia, 336, 507, 513, 535.
    Smithii, 535.
Caryophyllidæ, 535, 506, 512, 514.
Caryophyllinæ, 535.
Cassidulidæ 345.
Cassidulus, 316, 348.
    Carribæarum, 316, 345.
Cassis sp. 350.
Central America, list of the Echinoderms of the west coast of, 329.
Cereæ, 466
Cereus, 480, 476, 469.
    artemisia, 471.
    bellis, 480.
    coriaceus, 469.
    cruentatus, 467.
    Fuegiensis, 480, 567.
    ocellatus, 468.
    papillosus, 468.
    pluvia, 468.
Chætaster Californicus, 327.
Chilian Province, 338.
    Polyps of, 566.
Chili, list of Echinoderms found on the coast of, 335.
Chirodota, 371, 349.
    discolor, 325.
    pygmæa, 346, 371.
    rotiferum, 346 371.
    verrucosum, 325.

Cidaridæ, 344.
Cidaris, 294, 348.
    annulata, 294, 344.
    Danæ, 327.
    species, 593, 595.
    Thomarsii, 294, 328, 331, 333, 370, 579, 595.
Cistina, 577.
    Columbiæ, 332, 344.
Cladactis, 471, 472, 474.
    grandis, 472, 562, 566.
Cladocora, 365, 513, 524.
Cladocoraceæ, 524.
Cladocorinæ, 514.
Clypeaster, 348.
    Rüsei, 314.
    rosaceus, 345, 589.
    speciosus, 348, 345, 588.
    testudinarius, 588, 595.
Clypeasteridæ, 345.
Cœlasterias, 247.
    australis, 247.
Cœlastræa, 519.
Cœnangia, 530.
    conferta, 530, 563.
Cœnopsammia, 340.
    tenuilamellosa, 508.
Colobocentrotus pediferus, 335.
Columbella sp., 350.
Columnaria, 519.
Comatulidæ, 349.
Comparison of the tropical echinoderm faunæ of the east and west coasts of America, 339.
Connection, oceanic, across the Isthmus of Darien, 349.
Conularidæ, 455.
Corticifera, 495.
Corynactis, 462.
Coral-fauna, remarks on the Brazilian, 364.
Corals and Echinoderms collected by Prof. C. F. Hartt, at the Abrolhos Reefs, Brazil, Notice of the, 377.
Corals and Polyps of the west coast of America, Review of, 377.
Coscinasterias, 248.
    muricata, 249.
Crepidula unguiformis, 339.
Cribrella leviuscula, 326.
Cribrina, 467, 478 480, 482.
    coriacea, 469.
Crinoidea, 341, 349, 365.
Crustacea, common to the east and west coasts of tropical America, 339.
Crustulum gratulans, 311.
Cryptohelia, 515.
Cucumaria, 321.
    frondosa, 327, 346.
Cucumaridæ, 346.
Culcita, 349.
    Schmideliana, 333.
Cuvieria antarctica, 336, 339.
    operculata, 346.

Cuvieria Sitchœnsis, 325.
Cyathinœ, 535.
Cyclopora, 515.
Cyphastræa, 513.
Cystiactis, 473, 472.
  cavernata, 473.
  Eugenia, 473.
  Eydouxi, 473, 566.
  Gaudichaudi, 473.

Dactylosaster gracilis, 332, 344.
Dendraster, 337, 348.
  excentricus, 325, 326, 327.
Dendrophyllia, 507, 513.
  surcularis, 507, 508, 563.
  tenuilamellosa, 508, 563, 565.
Desmophyllum, 539, 536.
  crista-galli, 539.
  Cumingii, 539, 563.
Desoria, 349.
Diadema, 295, 348, 580.
  Antillarum, 295, 344.
  Mexicanum, 294,328,329,344, 580, 595.
Diadematidæ, 344.
Digammated Text of Homer, on Bekker's, 173.
Dighton, Mass., Auroras observed at, 156.
Dimorphous polyps in Renilla, etc., 378.
Diploperideris Sitchœnsis, 325.
Diploria, 365.
Discosoma, 462, 480.
  Fuegiensis, 480.
Discosomæ, 461.
Discosominæ, 461.
Discosomus, 462.
Discotrochus, 536.
Distichipora, 515.
Dysactis Chilensis, 483.

Echinactis, 462.
Echinanthus testudinarius, 588.
Echinaster, 348.
  aculeatus, 331, 343.
  Brazilicusis, 343.
  crassispina, 368, 343.
  Ellisii, 332, 576.
  serpentarius, 343.
  spinosus, 343, 577.
  spinulosus, 343.
  tenuispina, 577, 594.
Echinasteridæ, 343.
Echinidæ, 344.
Echinocidaris, 298, 348.
  Dufresnii, 344, 580.
  incisa, 298.
  longispina, 298.
  nigra, 301.
  punctulata, 344.
  Scythei, 336, 580.
  spatuligera, 300, 334, 335.
  stellata, 298, 328, 329, 331, 332, 333, 334, 335, 338, 344, 595.
Echinocucumis typica, 346.
Echinodermata, 365.

Echinoderm-fauna of the Gulf of California and Cape St. Lucas, 593.
Echinoderm faunæ, comparison of the tropical, of the east and west coasts of America, 339.
Echinoderms, additional observations on, 568.
  and Corals collected by Prof. C. F. Hartt, at the Abrolhos Reefs, Brazil, notice of the, 351.
  notice of a collection of, from La Paz, Lower Cal., 361.
  of Panama and the west coast of America, geographical distribution of, 352.
Echinodiadema, 295, 348, 365, 580.
  coronatum, 295, 328, 344, 580, 595.
Echinoglycus, 312, 348.
  frondosus, 370.
  Stokesii, 312, 331, 332, 334, 345.
Echinogorgia, 387, 413, 419.
  arbuscula, 414.
  arida, 384.
  aurantiaca, 450, 413, 557, 566.
  sasappo, 450, 557.
Echinoidea, 294, 341, 369, 374, 579.
Echinolampus, 349.
  caratomides, 349.
Echinometra, 308, 348.
  lucuntur, 369, 345.
  Mexicana, 307.
  Michelini, 345, 585.
  plana, 308, 345.
  rupicola, 308, 331, 332, 333, 345, 376, 583.
  Van Brunti, 309, 328, 329, 370, 585, 595.
  viridis, 345.
Echinometridæ, 345.
Echinomuricea coccinea, 419.
Echinoporinæ, 540.
Echinothrix 349.
Echinus, 304.
  chloroticus, 304, 583, 584.
  erythrogramma, 585.
  gibbosus, 305, 333.
  grandinosus, 301.
  homalostoma, 585.
  lucuntur, 369.
  Magellanicus, 336.
  niger, 301.
  purpurescens, 301.
  spatuliger, 300.
Edwardsia, 494.
Encope, 309.
  Californica, 345, 586, 595.
  emarginata, 310, 345, 370, 588.
  grandis, 310, 312, 329, 345, 585, 595.
  Michelini, 310, 345, 588.
  occidentalis, 309, 312, 331, 332, 333, 334, 345, 370, 587, 595.
  quinqueloba, 345.
  Stokesii, 312.
  tetrapora, 309.
Endohelia, 515.

Epiactis, 492.
  prolifera, 492, 560.
Epizoanthus, 497.
  crassus, 498, 562.
  elongatus, 497, 562, 565.
  humilis, 498, 562.
Eriphia, 340.
  gonagra, 340.
  squamata, 340.
Errina, 515.
Erythropodium, 454, 455.
  Pacificum, 456.
Eugorgia, 406, 340, 386, 413.
  ampla, 407, 386, 561, 566.
  aurantiaca, 410, 555, 561, 564.
  Bradleyi, 411, 399, 561, 566.
  Daniana, 409, 388, 555, 561, 566.
  excelsa, var., 553, 409, 551, 558, 561, 564.
  Mexicana, 410, 388.
  multifida, 554, 561, 564.
  nobilis, 408, 551, 553, 558, 561, 564, 566.
  purpurascens, var., 408, 561, 566.
  rubens, 411, 566.
  stenobrachis, 393.
Eunicea, 360, 385, 386, 413, 416.
  anceps, 362.
  Castelnaudi, 362.
  humilis, 360.
  Tobagensis, 444.
Eunicella, 386.
Eunicidæ, 413.
Eunuricea, 449.
Euphyllia, 513.
Eupsammidæ, 506, 501, 509, 519.
Eupsamminæ, 506.
Eurychinus, 304.
  chlorocentrotus, 325, 326.
  Delalandii, 304.
  Dröbachiensis, 304, 325, 326.
  gibbosus, 305.
  granulatus, 304.
  imbecillis, 305, 333, 334.
  lividus, 304.
Eusmilidæ, 536
Evactis, 470, 474.
  artemisia, 471, 560.
  xanthogrammica, 471, 559.
Evagora, 455.
Evechinus, 583.
  chloroticus, 584.
Extracts from an Auroral Register kept at New Haven, Conn., by Francis Bradley, 139.

Fabia Chilensis, 306.
Faunæ, Caribbean and Panamian, comparative lists of the Echinoderms of the, 341.
  Comparison of the tropical echinoderm, of the east and west coasts of America, 339.

Favia, 353, 355, 365, 512.
  conferta, 355.
  deformata, 355.
  gravida, 354, 364.
  incerta, 355.
  leptophylla, 353.
Favositidæ, 518, 519.
Favositinæ, 518.
Ferdina Cumingii, 332, 343.
Fishes common to the east and west coasts of tropical America, 340.
Flabellinæ, 539.
Flabellum, 513, 535, 536.
Fungacea, 540, 543.
Fungia, 541.
  elegans, 542, 563, 565.
Fungidæ, 540, 542.
Funginæ, 540.
Galapago Islands, list of Echinoderms from the, 333.
Galapagos Province, 338.
Galaxea, 513.
Gammaria, 497.
  crassa, 498.
  elongata, 497.
  humilis, 498.
Ganeria Falklandica, 336.
Geographical distribution of the Echinoderms of the west coast of America, 352.
  of the Polyps of the west coast of America, 558.
Geological evidence of an oceanic connection across the Isthmus of Darien, 349.
Gerardidæ, 499.
Goniasteridæ, 343.
Goniastræa, 355.
  varia, 355.
Goniocidaris, 349.
Goniodiscus, 284.
  armatus, 280, 372.
  conifer, 372.
  singularis, 335.
  stella, 284, 343, 372.
  verrucosus, 335.
Gorgonia, 384, 340, 359, 385, 386, 387, 406, 407.
  Adamsii, 391.
  alba, 398.
  Agassizii, 388.
  aurantiaca, 410.
  citrina, 360.
  cuspidata, 403.
  dichotoma, 361.
  flabellum, 386.
  fucata, 413.
  fucosa, 417.
  fusco-purpurea, 386.
  gracilis, 359, 596.
  humilis, 394, 396.
  levis, var., 398.
  media, 389.
  palma, 386, 400.

Gorgonia papillosa, 385.
　plantaginea, 444.
　pumicea, 362.
　ramulus, 394.
　reticulata, 405.
　rigida, 398, 401.
　sanguinea, 406.
　stenobrachis, 393.
　stenobrochis, 393.
　ventalina, 391.
　verrucosa, 384, 385, 386.
Gorgonacea, 384.
Gorgonella, 384, 385, 387.
Gorgonidæ, 384, 455, 499.
Guaymas, Polyps collected at, by Dr. E. Palmer, 564.
Gymnasteria, 348.
　iuermis, 330, 343.
　spinosa, 330, 343, 574, 594.

Hadley, James, on Bekker's Digammated Text of Homer, 173.
Halcyonina, 458.
Hartt, Prof. C. F., Notice of the Corals and Echinoderms collected by, at the Abrolhos Reefs, Brazil, 351.
　Remarks on the Brazilian Coral-fauna, 364.
Heliaster, 289, 348.
　Cumingii, 291, 333, 334, 344.
　helianthus, 287, 329, 334, 335.
　Kubiniji, 292, 312, 328, 329, 344, 578, 593, 595.
　microbrachia, 290, 328, 331, 344, 593, 595.
　multiradiata, 333.
Heliastræa, 356, 365.
　aperta, 356, 364.
Heliocidaris, 349, 584.
　chlorotica, 584.
　Mexicana, 583, 307, 308, 584.
Hemipholis, 262, 348.
　affinis, 262, 573.
　cordifera, 263, 342.
　gracilis, 262, 330, 342, 573.
Hepatella amica, 484.
Herrick, Edward C., a Register of the Aurora Borealis at New Haven, Conn., from March, 1837, to Dec., 1853, 9.
Heterocentrotus, 349.
Heterodactyla, 461.
Heterodactylinæ, 461.
Heterogorgia, 450, 419.
　papillosa, 557, 562, 565.
　tortuosa, 452, 562.
　verrucosa, 451, 562.
Heteropsammia, 506.
Heterosynapta, 346.
　viridis, 346.
Hipponoë, 349.
Hipponoidæ, 345.
Holothuria botellus, 331, 346.
　Californica, 327.

Holothuria Floridiana, 346.
　glaberrima, 331, 346.
　grisea, 346.
　languens, 331, 346.
　lepadifera, 346.
　lubrica, 329, 346.
　maculata, 346.
　Peruviana, 322, 376.
　princeps, 346.
　subditiva, 346.
Holothuridæ, 346.
Holothuriohdea, 321, 346, 370.
Homactis, 462.
Homer, Bekker's Digammated Text of, 173.
Hugea, 494.
Hydroidea, 362, 519.
Hymenogorgia, 359, 384, 385.
　quercifolia, 359, 360, 362.

Incorporation, Act of, 5.
Introductory notice to Herrick's Auroral Register, 7.
Isacmaea crassicornis, 469.
　papillosa, 469.
Isaura, 494.
Isthmus of Darien, oceanic connection across the, 349.

Juncella hystrix, 362.

Kleinia nigra, 317, 590.

Laganum, 349.
La Paz, L. Cal., notice of a collection of Echinoderms from, 371.
　Polyps collected at, by Capt J. Pedersen, 564.
Leioptillum, 381.
　undulatum, 381, 378, 546, 560.
Lepidaster, 577.
　teres, 577, 491.
Lepidopsolus antarcticus, 336.
　operculata, 346.
Leptogorgia, 387, 385, 386.
　Adamsii, 391, 392, 551, 561, 564, 565.
　Agassizii, 388, 390, 548, 550, 560, 565.
　ampla, 407.
　arbuscula, 406, 566.
　alba, 398, 401, 412, 561, 564, 566.
　aurantiaca, 413, 410.
　Californica, 398, 561.
　Caryi, 404, 556, 560.
　Chilensis, 406, 566.
　cuspidata, 403, 401, 552, 561.
　diffusa, 397, 561, 566.
　Englemanni, var., 394, 561, 565.
　exigua, 552, 561, 564, 566.
　exilis, 550, 561, 564.
　eximia, 390, 388, 551, 561.
　Floræ, 387, 391, 560.
　flexilis, 400, 561.
　fucata, 596.
　labiata, 552, 561, 564, 565.

Leptogorgia media, 389, 391, 550, 560, 564, 565.
   Peruana, 405, 566.
   platyclados, 406, 566.
   pulchra, 549, 561, 564.
   pumila 396, 561.
   ramulus, 394, 397, 399, 552, 561, 565.
   rigida, 401, 404, 552, 561, 564, 565.
   rutila, 392, 561, 565.
   sanguinea, 406.
   stenobrochis, 393, 403, 561, 565.
   tennis, 551, 561, 564.
   viminalis, 387.
   virgularia, 406.
Leptosynapta, 325.
   hydriformis, 346.
   Pourtalesii, 346.
   tenuis, 325.
   verrucosa, 325.
Linckia, 285, 348, 577.
   bifascialis, 287, 328, 372, 594.
   Columbiæ, 332, 344.
   Guildingii, 344, 367.
   ornithopus, 344, 367.
   unifascialis, 285, 312, 328, 329, 330, 332, 333, 344, 372, 594.
Liosoma arenicola, 327.
   Sitchaensis, 325.
Lissothuria, 322.
   ornata, 322, 331, 346.
List of Echinoderms from
   Sitcha, 324.
   Puget Sound and along the coast to Cape Mendocino, Cal., 325
   between Cape Mendocino and San Diego, Cal., 326.
   Margarita Bay and Cape St. Lucas, 327.
   Acapulco, Mazatlan, and the Gulf of California, 328.
   the west coast of Central America and the Bay of Panama, 329.
   the west coast of Ecuador and the southern part of New Grenada, 332.
   Zorritos, Peru, 333.
   the Galapago Islands, 333.
   the coast of Peru, at Paita and southward, 334.
   the coast of Chili, 335.
   the southern extremity of South America and the neighboring Islands, 336.
List of Polyps of
   Arctic Province, 559.
   Californian Province, 560.
   Chilian Province, 556.
   Sitchian Province, 559.
   Oregonian Province, 559.
   Panamian Province, 560.
   Peruvian Province, 566.
List of Polyps collected at
   Corinto and Gulf of Nicoya by J. A. McNiel, 565.
   Guaymas by Dr. E. Palmer, 564.
   La Paz by Capt. J. Pederson, 564.

Lithodendron, 507.
Litigorgia, 387, 385.
   Adamsii, 391,
   Agassizii, 388.
   arbuscula, 406.
   Californica, 398.
   cuspidata, 403.
   diffusa, 397.
   Englemanni, var., 394.
   eximia, 390.
   levis, 398.
   flexilis, 400.
   Floræ, 387.
   fucosa, 404.
   media, 389.
   Peruana, 405.
   platyclados, 406.
   pumila, 396.
   ramulus, 394.
   rigida, 401.
   rosea, 406.
   rutila, 392.
   sanguinea, 406.
   stenobrochis, 393.
Lobophora, 349.
Lobopsammia, 506.
Lobularia rubiforme, 459.
Loomis, Elias, notices of Auroras, extracted from the meteorological journal of Rev. Ezra Stiles, 155
Loomis, Elias, and H. A. Newton, on the mean Temperature, and on the fluctuations of Temperature, at New Haven, Conn., 194.
Lophactis, 463.
   ornata, 464, 562.
Lophogorgia, 384, 385, 386, 387.
   alba, 398.
   aurantiaca, 410.
   palma, 403.
   Panamensis, 394, 396.
Lophoseridæ, 542.
Lophoserinæ, 542.
Lophoseris, 543.
Lovenia, 329, 346, 348, 595.
Loxechinus, 348.
   albus, 324, 335.
   purpuratus, 327, 337.
Luidia, 271, 348.
   alternata, 343.
   Bellonæ, 293, 332, 334, 343.
   brevispina, 593, 594.
   clathrata, 271, 343.
   Columbiæ, 343.
   Macgravii, 343.
   tessellata, 271, 330, 343.
Lytechinus, 302.
   Atlanticus, 303, 344.
   excavatus, 344.
   roseus, 302, 328, 329, 331, 333, 344, 583.
   semituberculatus, 301, 333.
   variegatus, 344, 369.

Madrepora, 365, 500, 501, 503.
Madreporacea, 500.
Madreporaceæ, 512.
Madreporaria, 352, 500, 556, 562.
　perforata, 500.
Madreporidæ, 501.
Madreporinæ, 501.
Mæandrina, 355, 365, 512.
Malea sp., 350.
Mammillifera, 495.
　auricula, 496.
　conferta, 497, 562.
　Damæ, 496, 562.
　nitida, 497, 562.
Manicina, 365.
Maretia, 349.
Margarita Bay, list of Echinoderms found at, 327.
McNiel, J. A., Polyps collected by, on the west coast of Nicaragua, 565.
Mediaster æqualis, 326.
Melitodes virgata, 572.
Mellita, 348.
　hexapora, 314, 345.
　longifissa, 314, 331, 345, 588, 595.
　Pacifica, 313, 333, 345.
　pentapora, 314, 345, 586.
　testudinea, 345.
Meoma, 317, 348.
　grandis, 317, 590, 593, 595.
　nigra, 317, 329, 345, 590.
　ventricosa, 345.
Merulinaceæ, 540.
Metalia, 318, 348.
　Garretii, 320, 591.
　nobilis, 319, 591, 328, 331, 345, 348, 595
　sternalis, 319, 591.
Meteorology of New Haven, 194.
Metridium, 478, 462, 463.
　concinnatum, 463.
　dianthus, 478.
　fimbriatum, 478, 560.
　marginatum, 478, 560.
　reticulatum, 479, 567.
Millepora, 362, 365, 519.
　alcicornis, 363, 364.
　Braziliensis, 363.
　cellulosa, var., 363.
　digitata, var., 364.
　fenestrata, var., 364.
　nitida, 362.
Mithrodia, 288, 348.
　Bradleyi, 288, 330, 343, 575, 594.
Mœra, 349.
　Atropos, 346.
　Clotho, 329, 346, 348, 595.
Mollusca common to the east and west coasts of tropical America, 339.
Molpadia borealis, 346.
Montipora, 502, 501.
　fragosa, 502, 562.
Montiporinæ, 501.

Morsella Japonica, 572.
Moulinia cassidulina, 345.
Mulleria Agassizii, 347.
　obscura, 347.
　parvula, 347.
Muricea, 418, 450, 340, 384.
　acervata, 419, 424, 449, 561.
　albida, 437, 435, 441, 562.
　appressa, 444, 448, 449, 562, 564, 566.
　aspera, 448, 562.
　austera, 430, 428, 433, 441, 561, 564.
　clavata, 444.
　crassa, 425, 432, 433, 561.
　echinata, 426, 424, 430, 432, 561.
　elegans, 450.
　elongata, 449.
　flabellum, var., 427, 561.
　flavescens, var., 446, 448, 562, 566.
　flexuosa, 450.
　formosa, 434, 517, 561.
　fruticosa, 428, 432, 433, 561, 565.
　hebes, 439, 441, 443, 450, 562, 565.
　hispida, 422, 561.
　horrida, 423, 422, 566.
　humosa, 449, 450.
　laxa, 450.
　lima, 450.
　miser, var., 430, 561, 565.
　muricata, 450.
　nitida, 450.
　pendula, 450.
　purpurea, 441, 437, 450, 562, 565.
　retusa, 432, 443, 561.
　robusta, 436, 441, 450, 562, 565.
　spicifera, 450.
　squarrosa, 423, 435, 561.
　sulphurea, 449, 450.
　tenella, 446, 449, 562, 566.
　tuberculata, 449, 450.
　tubigera, 421, 423, 435, 561.
　vatricosa, 384, 449, 450.
Muricea, Remarks on the subdivisions of the genus, 449.
Muricella, 450.
Museum of Yale College, notes on the Radiata in, 247.
Mussa, 357, 365, 512.
　Harttii, 357, 352, 358.

Nardoa, 285, 349.
Nemactis, 487, 477.
　Chilensis, 488, 567.
　Draytonii, 488, 493, 566.
　primula, 488, 566.
Neoporites, 503.
New Haven, Conn., Auroras observed at, by Rev. Ezra Stiles, 156.
　and Boston, summary of Auroral observations at, 171.
　extracts from an Auroral register kept at, by Francis Bradley, 139.
　register of the Aurora Borealis at, from March, 1837 to Dec., 1853, 9.

New Haven, Mean Temperature and Fluctuations of Temperature at, 194.
Newport, R. I., Auroras observed at, 155.
Newton, H. A., and Elias Loomis, on the Mean Temperature, and on the Fluctuations of Temperature at New Haven, Conn., 194.
New Zealand, new starfishes from, 247.
Nicaragua, Polyps collected on the coast of, by J. A. McNiel, 565.
Nidorellia, 280, 348.
    armata, 280, 284, 312, 328, 329, 330, 332, 333, 343, 372, 574, 594.
Notes on the Echinoderms of Panama and the west coast of America, 251.
    on the Radiata in the Museum of Yale College, 247.
Notice of a collection of Echinoderms from La Laz L. C., 371.
    of the Corals and Echinoderms collected by Prof. C F. Hartt. at the Abrolhos Reefs, Brazil, 351.
    Introductory, to Herrick's Auroral Register, 7.
Notices of Auroras extracted from the Meteorological Journal of Rev. Ezra Stiles, 155.
    of Auroras extracted from various Journals kept at New Haven, Conn., 164.
    of Auroras extracted from a Meteorological Journal kept at Sharon, Conn., 167.

Observations, additional, on Echinoderms, 568.
Oculina, 365, 507, 512, 513, 518.
Oculinacea, 512, 536.
Oculinidæ, 514, 512, 519.
Ophiacantha Pentacrinus, 341.
Ophiactis, 264, 348.
    arenosa, 266, 330, 341.
    asperula, 335.
    Kroyeri, 264, 334, 366, 341.
    Mülleri, 341.
    Örstedii, 266, 264, 330, 341.
    simplex, 266, 264, 330, 341.
    virescens, 265, 327, 330, 372, 341, 594.
Ophiarachna, 348, 349.
    maculata, 574.
Ophiarthrum, 349.
Ophidiaster, 287, 285, 348, 577.
    flaccidus, 344.
    ophidianus, 285.
    ornithopus, 367.
    porosissimus, 287.
    pyramidatus, 287, 328, 330, 332, 333, 344, 577, 594.
    suturalis, 285.
    unifascialis, 285.
Ophidiasteridæ, 344.
Ophioblenna, 348.
    Antillensis, 342.
Ophioceramis Januarii, 343.

Ophiocnida, 260.
    hispida, 260, 330, 342.
    scabriuscula, 342.
Ophiocoma, 258, 348.
    æthiops, 258, 327, 329, 330, 341, 594.
    Alexandri, 259, 327, 329, 330, 341, 594.
    echinata, 258, 341.
    pumila, 341.
    Riisei, 257, 341.
Ophiocomidæ, 341.
Ophioderma Antillarum, 364.
    cinereum, 367.
    Panamensis, 253.
    variegata, 254.
Ophioglypha Lütkenii, 325.
    Sarsii, 593.
    species, 593, 594.
Ophiolepidæ, 342.
Ophiolepis, 256, 348.
    annulata, 259.
    Atcamensis, 335.
    elegans, 367, 342.
    geminata, 261.
    hispida, 260.
    Pacifica, 257.
    paucispina, 342.
    simplex, 266.
    triloba, 259.
    variegata, 256, 330, 342, 593, 594.
Ophiomastrix, 349.
Ophiomyxa, 330, 341, 348.
    flaccida, 366, 341.
Ophiomyxidæ, 341.
Ophionema intricata, 341.
Ophionephthys limicola, 341.
Ophionereis, 259, 348.
    annulata, 259, 328, 330, 342, 594.
    reticulata, 366, 342.
    porrecta, 342.
    triloba, 259.
    Xantusii, 270, 328, 342, 594.
Ophiopeza, 348, 349.
Ophiopholis Caryi, 326.
    Kennerleyi, 325.
Ophiophragmus, 270, 348.
    marginatus, 270, 330, 342.
    septus, 342.
    Wurdemanni, 342.
Ophioplocus, 349.
Ophiopsila Riisei, 341.
Ophiostigma, 270, 348.
    isacanthum, 342.
    tenue, 270, 330.
Ophiothela, 269, 348.
    Danæ, 572.
    mirabilis, 268, 330, 342, 376, 572, 594.
Ophiothrix, 278, 348.
    Caribæa, 342.
    dumosa, 270, 326, 328, 329, 342, 594.
    lineata, 342.
    magnifica, 334.
    mirabilis, 268.
    Örstedii, 342.

Ophiothrix spiculata, 267, 328, 330, 332, 333, 342, 594.
   Suensonii, 342.
   violacea, 267, 342, 346.
Ophiozona, 257, 348.
   impressa, 342.
   Pacifica, 257, 330, 342.
Ophiura, 253, 347.
   appressa, 342.
   brevicauda, 342.
   brevispina, 342.
   cinerea, 342, 367.
   Daniana, 254, 329, 342.
   elaps, 342.
   flaccida, 366.
   guttata, 342.
   Januarii, 342.
   Panamensis, 253, 270, 327, 328, 329, 342, 594.
   paucispina, 367.
   reticulata, 366.
   rubicunda, 342.
   teres, 253, 327, 328, 329, 342, 594.
   variegata, 254, 329, 342, 376.
   sp. nov., 270, 330, 342.
Ophiuridæ, 342.
Ophiuroidea, 251, 341, 366, 372, 572.
Oreaster, 278, 348.
   aculeatus, 343.
   armatus, 280, 372.
   Cumingii, 332, 343.
   gigas, 279, 343, 367.
   occidentalis, 278, 312, 328, 330, 343, 374, 574.
   reticulatus, 343, 367.
Oregonian Province, 337.
   Polyps of, 559.
Orinidæ, 494.
Othilia crassispina, 368.
Oulactis, 463, 462, 464.
   concinnata, 463, 566.
   granulifera, 462.
   flosculifera, 464.
   formosa, 464.
Oulangia, 533.

Pachypsammia, 506.
   valida, 506.
Pachysammia, 506.
Paita, Peru, list of Echinoderms found at, 334.
Palmer, Dr. E., Polyps collected by, at Guaymas, 564
Palythoa, 362, 495, 497.
Panama and west coast of America, Notes on the Echinoderms of, 251.
   list of the Echinoderms of the Bay of, 329.
Panamian and Caribbean Fauna, comparative lists of the Echinoderms of the, 341.
Panamian Province, 337.
   Polyps of, 560.
Paractis 477, 482, 491.

Paractis impatiens, 483.
   lincotala, 483.
   nobilis, 491, 562.
   nymphæa, 486.
   rubus, 487.
Paracyathus, 536, 510, 513.
   caltha, 537, 560.
   humilis, 538, 563.
   Stearnsii, 537, 560.
   Stokesii, 536.
Paragorgia, 454.
Paramuricea, 419.
   clathrata, 419.
Parisis, 572.
Patiria, 276.
   Chilensis, 334, 335.
   miniata, 324, 326.
   obtusa, 276, 330, 343.
Pattalus mollis, 376.
   Peruvianus, 335, 376.
Paulia horrida, 332, 343.
Pavonia, 543, 340, 350.
   clivosa, 544, 563.
   gigantea, 543, 563.
Pectinia, 353.
   Braziliensis, 353.
Pectinura maculata, 574.
Pedersen, Capt. J., Notice of Echinoderms collected at La Paz, Lower Cal., by, 371.
   Polyps collected by, at La Paz, 564.
Pedicellaster, 593.
Pennatula tenua, 382.
   undulata, 546.
Pennatulacea, 378.
Pennatulidæ, 381, 546.
Pentaceros, 574.
   armatus, 280, 372.
   Cumingii, 279.
   occidentalis, 574.
   reticulatus, 367.
Pentacrinus, 348.
   asterias, 341.
   caput-medusæ, 341.
   decora, 341.
   Müller, 341.
Pentacta, 321.
   albida, 325, 326.
   miniata, 325.
   nigricans, 325.
   Panamensis, 324, 331, 346.
   pentactes, 321.
   piperata, 326.
   populifera, 326.
   quinquesemita, 326.
   sp., 335
Peruvian Province, 338.
   Polyps, 566.
Petalster Columbiæ, 272, 330, 343.
Petricola pholadiformis, 531.
Pharia pyramidatus, 287.
Phata in unifascialis, 285.
Phellia 489, 466
   arctica, 490, 559.

Pheltia inornata, 489, 562.
    Panamensis, 490, 562.
    rubens, 489, 562.
Phos, 350.
Phycogorgia, 413, 484.
    fucata, 413, 561, 596.
Phyllacanthus, 349.
Phyllactinia, 462, 461.
Phyllactis, 463,
Phyllangia, 531, 340, 534, 536.
    dispersa, 532, 563, 566.
Phyllogorgia, 384.
    dilitata, 362.
Phyllophorus lepadifera, 346.
Phymactis, 475.
    clematis, 475, 566.
    florida, 475, 566.
Pinnaxodes hirtipes, 306.
Placotrochus, 535.
Plagionotus, 348, 591.
    Africanus, 569, 571, 592.
    Desorii, 571.
    nobilis, 591.
    pectoralis, 571, 345, 592.
Plexaura, 413, 386, 416.
    arbuscula, 406.
    aurantiaca, 413.
    dichotoma, 361.
    fucosa, 404, 405.
    platyclados, 406.
    reticulata, 405.
    rosea, 406.
    sanguinea, 406.
Plexaurella, 361, 413, 416.
    anceps, 362.
    dichotoma, 361.
Plexauridæ, 413, 386, 418.
Pocillipora, 519, 340, 513, 518.
    capitata, 520, 563, 565.
    lacera, 523, 563.
    porosa, var., 521, 563.
    pumila, var., 522, 563.
    robusta, var., 521, 563.
Pocilliporidæ, 518, 514, 512, 596.
Pocillopora, see Pocillipora.
Pocilloporinæ, 518.
Polypi, Brazilian, 352.
Polypiers lamellifera, 500.
Polyps, and Corals, of the west coast of America, Review of the, 377.
    Geographical distribution of, of the west coast of America, 566.
Porites, 503, 358, 365.
    Californica, 504, 564, 562, 565.
    excavata, 504, 562.
    Gaudaloupensis, 358.
    nodulosa, 505, 563, 565.
    Panamensis, 505, 523, 563.
    porosa, 504, 562, 565.
    solida, 358, 364.
Poritidæ 503, 501.
Portsmouth, N. H., Auroras observed at, 156.

Primnoa, 454.
    compressa, 454, 559.
    lepadifera, 454.
    reseda, 454.
Primnoaceæ, 418.
Primnoacées, 418.
Primnoidæ, 418.
Psammechinus, 301, 348, 584.
    aciculatus, 344.
    chloroticus, 584.
    pictus, 301, 344, 581.
    variegatus, 369.
Psammocora, 501.
Psammogorgia, 414, 413, 405.
    arbuscula, 414, 556, 561.
    Dowii, var., 415, 417, 561.
    fucosa, 417, 556, 561.
    gracilis, 417, 561.
    pallida, var., 415, 561.
    teres, 416, 556, 561, 564.
Psilechinus variegatus, 369.
Psolus Sitchaensis, 325.
Pteraster Danæ, 568.
    militaris, 569, 344.
    pulvillus, 569.
Pterogorgia, 359, 385, 386, 387.
    acerosa, 386.
    bipinnata, 360.
    gracilis, 359, 596.
    flabellum, 392.
    petechizaus, 385.
    sarmentosa, 385.
Ptilosarcus, 382.
    Gurneyi, 548, 382, 559, 560.
Puget Sound, list of Echinoderms found at, 324.
Pycnopodia helianthoides, 324, 326, 327.
Pygorhynchus, 315, 348.
    Pacificus, 315, 328, 329, 345, 348.

Radiata, Notes on, in the Museum of Yale College, 247.
Register, Extracts from an Auroral, kept at New Haven, Ct., by Francis Bradley, 139.
    of the Aurora Borealis at New Haven, Ct., from March, 1837, to Dec., 1853, 9.
Remarks on the Brazilian Coral-fauna, 364.
Renilla, 378, 340.
    Americana, 380.
    amethystina, 379, 546, 560.
    Danæ, 362, 516.
    patula, 381, 546.
    reniformis, 381, 546.
    violacea, 362, 546.
Renillidæ, 378.
Review of the Corals and Polyps of the west coast of America, 377.
Rhipidogorgia, 340, 384, 385, 386, 387.
    Agassizii, 388, 391, 392.
    Englemanni, 393.
    flabellum, 385, 340.
    media, 389.

Rhipidogorgia ventalina, 391.
Rhizocrinus Lofotensis, 341.
Rhizopsammia, 510.
    pulchra, 510, 563.
Rhizotrochus, 535.
Rhizoxenia, 455.
    rosea, 455.
    Thalassantha, 455.
Rhodactinia, 469.
    Davisii, 469.
Rhodactis, 462.
Rhyncholampas, 316.
    Pacificus, 595.
Rhyncopygus, 316.
Ricordea, 462.
Rumphia, 349.
Ryssobrissus nigra, 317.

Sagartia, 482, 480, 491, 560, 562.
    Bradleyi, 584, 562.
    carcinophila, 484, 562.
    crispata, 484, 562.
    Fuegiensis, 480.
    Gossei, 485, 486.
    impatiens, 483, 567.
    Lessonii, 486, 566.
    lineolata, 483, 567.
    nivea, 485, 566.
    nymphaea, 486, 567.
    Panamensis, 484, 562.
    Peruviana, 486, 566.
    rubus, 487, 567.
Sagartiadæ, 477.
Sagartidæ, 477.
Sagartinæ, 477, 466, 491, 493.
Salmacis, 349.
Sarcophyta, 458.
Sarcoptilus Gurneyi, 382, 378.
Scutella emarginata, 370.
Scutellidæ, 345.
Scytaster, 349.
Seriatopora, 513, 519.
Sharon, Ct., Notices of Auroras, extracted from a Meteorological Journal kept at, 167.
Siderastræa, 352, 365, 540, 542.
    conferta, var., 353.
    radians, 352.
    stellata, 352, 364.
Sideropora, 513.
Sitcha, list of Echinoderms found at, 324.
Sitchian Province, 336.
    Polyps of, 559.
Smith, John C., Notices of Auroras at Sharon, Conn., 167.
Solaster decemradiatus, 324.
Spatangidæ, 345.
Spatangus pectoralis, 571.
Sphenopus, 494.
Sphenotrochus, 536.
Sporadipes gigas, 347.
Starfishes, new, from New Zealand, 247.
Stephanactis, 462.

Stephanaria, 545, 340.
    stellata, 545, 563, 565.
Stephanocora, 545, 340.
    stellata, 545.
Stichaster aurantiacus, 293, 334, 335.
    striatus, 293.
Stichopus badionotus, 347.
    Kefersteinii, 329, 347.
    rigidus, 347.
Stiles, Rev. Ezra, Notices of Auroras, extracted from the Meteorological Journal of, 155.
Stilifera astericola, 333.
Stoloniclypeus, 314, 348, 350.
    prostratus, 315, 345.
    rotundatus, 314, 329, 331, 345, 350.
Stolus gibber, 346.
    ovulum, 329 331, 346.
Stomphia Churchiæ, 469.
Stylaster, 515.
Stylasteraceæ, 514.
Stylasteridæ, 514, 513, 512, 596.
Stylatula, 382, 340, 548.
    elongata, 384, 548, 560.
    gracilis, 382, 348, 560
Stylina, 513.
Stylinidæ, 514.
Stylophora, 513, 518.
Stylophoridæ, 514, 513, 519.
Summary of Auroral Observations, 168, 171.
Symphyllia, 358, 362.
    Harttii, 358.
Sympodium, 454.
    Pacifica, 456.
Synapta, 325, 349.
    albicans, 326.
    inhærens, 325.
    lappa, 346.
    mammillosa, 325.
    rotifera, 371.
    tenuis, 325.
Synaptidæ, 346.
Synaptula vivipara, 346.
Syndepas, 536.

Tabulata, 519.
Tamaria, 577.
Tealia, 469.
    crassicornis, 469.
Temnopleurus, 349.
    botryoides, 333.
Thalassianthidæ, 461.
Thalassianthinæ, 461.
Thesea, 419.
    exserta, 384.
Thecidæ, 519.
Thyone, 370.
    Briareus, 370.
    Braziliensis, 370.
    Peruana, 322.
Thyonidium conchilegum, 346.
    gemmatum, 346.

Titanideum, 454.
Tonia Atlantica, 293.
Toxocidaris, 305, 584.
　crassispina, 584.
　erythrogramma, 584.
　Franciscana, 327, 337, 584.
　homalostoma, 584.
　Mexicana, 307, 329, 345, 584.
Toxopneustes, 304, 307, 348, 584.
　Franc scana, 327, 337.
　gibbosus, 305.
　Mexicana, 307, 329, 345.
　tuberculatus, 584.
Trichaster, 349.
Tripneustes, 305, 375.
　depressus, 375, 329, 315, 584, 595.
　ventricosus, 345, 375, 584.
Tripylus, 339.
　excavatus, 336.
　Philippii, 336.
Trivia Californica, 512.
Trochosmiliaceæ, 536.
Turbinaridæ, 501.
Turbinolia, 536.
Turbinolidæ, 539, 535.
Turbinolinæ, 539, 536.

Ulangia, 533, 340.
　Bradleyi, 534, 563.
　Stoke-iana, 534.
Urodemas. sp. nov., 346.
Urticina, 469.
　coriacea, 470.
　crassicornis, 469, 559, 560.
　papillosa, 469.

Venus, sp., 350.
Veretillum Stimpsonii, 378.
Verrill, A. E., Notes on the Radiata in the Museum of Yale College, with Descriptions of new genera and species, 247.
　No. 1, Descriptions of new Starfishes from New Zealand, 247.
　No. 2, Notes on the Echinoderms of Panama and the west coast of America, 251.
　No. 3, On the Geographical Distribution of the Echinoderms of the west coast of America, 321.
　No. 4, Notice of the Corals and Echinoderms collected by Prof. C. F. Hartt, at the Abrolhos Reefs, Province of Bahia, 1867, 351.
　No. 5, Notice of a collection of Echinoderms from La Paz, Lower Cal., 371.
　No. 6, Review of the Corals and Polyps of the west coast of America, 377.
　No. 7, On the Geographical Distribution of the Polyps of the west coast of America, 558.
　No 8, Additional Observations on Echinoderms, chiefly from the Pacific coast of America, 568.
　No. 9, The Echinoderm-Fauna of the Gulf of Cal. and Cape St. Lucas, 593.
Virgularia, 383.
　elegans, 548.
　elongata, 384.
　Finm rchien, 548.
　gracilis, 383, 382, 548, 560.
　multiflora, 548.

West coast of America, and Panama, Notes on the Echinoderms of the, 252.
　geographical distribution of the Echinoderms of the, 352.
　geographical distribution of the Polyps of the, 558.
　Review of the Corals and Polyps of the, 377.
West coast of Central America, list of Echinoderms of the, 329.

Xanthobrissus, 318.
Xiphigorgia, 384, 385.

Zoanthacea, 494.
Zoanthaires, 460.
　pierreux, 500.
Zoanthidæ, 493. 494.
Zoanthina, 493.
Zoanthinæ, 495.
Zoanthus, 360.
　Danæ, 496.
　Danai, 496.
Zorritos, Peru, list of Echinoderms found at, 333.

EXPLANATION OF PLATES.

Plate IV.

Figure 1.—Spicula of *Hymenogorgia quercifolia* Edw.; 1*a*, double-spindles; 1*b*, crescent-shaped or scaphoid spicula,—enlarged 150 diameters.

Figure 2.—Spicula of *Gorgonia gracilis* Verrill; 2*a*, double-spindles; 2*b*, scaphoid spicula,—enlarged 150 diameters.

Figure 3.—A part of a branch of the same, natural size.

Figure 4.—Spicula of *Eunicea humilis* Edw.; *a*, spindles from cœnenchyma,—enlarged 50 diameters; *b*, club-shaped spicula,—enlarged 100 diameters.

Figure 5.—Spicula of *Plexaurel'a dichotoma* Köll.; 5*a*, a cross-shaped spiculum, with unequal branches; 5*b*, a cross with two of the branches undeveloped,—enlarged 100 diameters.

Figure 6.—Cross-shaped spicula of *Plexaurella anceps?* Köll.; 6*a*, one of the larger spindles,—enlarged 100 diameters.

Figure 7.—*Echinaster crassispina* Verrill; part of ray, natural size.

Figure 8.—*Thyone Braziliensis* Verrill; *a*, oral plates, natural size.

Figure 9.—*Chriodota rotiferum* Stimp.; calcareous wheels of the skin,—enlarged 150 diameters.

Figure 10.—*Amphiaster insignis* Verrill; ray and part of disk, natural size.

Plate V.

All the figures on this plate are from camera-lucida drawings by the author.

Figure 1.—*Renilla amethystina* V.; triquetral spiculum from the disk,—enlarged 100 diameters.

Figure 2.—*Stylatula gracilis* V.; one of the spine-like spicula, which support the pinnæ,—enlarged 50 diameters.

Figure 3.—*Leptogorgia Floræ* V.; *a*, longer double-spindle; *b*, stouter double-spindle,—enlarged 200 diameters.

Figure 4.—*L. Agassizii* V.; *a* and *b*, longer double-spindles; *c*, stouter double-spindle.—enlarged 200 diameters.

Figure 5.—*L. Adamsii* V.; *a* and *b*, longer double-spindles; *c*, stouter double-spindle.—enlarged 200 diameters.

Figure 6.—*L. diffusa* V.; *a*, longer double-spindle; *b*, stouter double-spindle,—enlarged 200 diameters.

Figure 7.—*L. alba* V.; *a* and *b*, longer double-spindles; *c*, stouter double-spindle,—enlarged 200 diameters.

Figure 8.—*L. pumila* V.; *a*, longer double-spindle; *b*, stouter double-spindle,—enlarged 200 diameters.

Figure 9.—*L. rigida* V.; *a*, longer double-spindle; *b* and *c*, stouter double-spindles,—enlarged 200 diameters.

Figure 10.—*L. Californica* V.; *a*, longer double-spindle; *b*, stouter double-spindle,—enlarged 200 diameters.

Figure 11.—*L. flexilis* V.; *a* and *b*, longer double-spindles; *c*, stouter double-spindle,—enlarged 200 diameters.
Figure 12.—*Eugorgia ampla* V.; *a*, longer double-spindle; *b* and *c*, double-wheels,—enlarged 200 diameters.
Figure 13.—*E. nobilis* V.; *a*, longer, and *b*, stouter double-spindles; *c* and *d*, double-wheels,—enlarged 200 diameters.
Figure 14.—*E. Daniana* V.; *a*, longer, and *b*, stouter double-spindles; *c* and *d*, double-wheels,—enlarged 200 diameters.
Figure 15.—*E. aurantiaca* V.; *a*, longer, and *b*, stouter double-spindles; *c* and *d*, double-wheels.—enlarged 200 diameters.
Figure 16.—*Echinogorgia aurantiaca* V.; scale-club,—enlarged 100 diameters.
Figure 17.—*Psammogorgia arbuscula* V.; *a*, spindle from the polyp; *b*, irregular spindle from the cœnenchyma; *c* and *d*, irregular club-shaped spicula,—enlarged 100 diameters.
Figure 18.—*P. teres* V.; *a*, double-spindle; *b*, irregular stout spindle; *c*, irregular head,—enlarged 100 diameters.
Figure 19.—*P. gracilis* V.; *a*, spindle; *b*, club-shaped spiculum,—enlarged 100 diameters.
Figure 20.—*Leptogorgia eximia* V.: longer double-spindle,—enlarged 200 diameters.
Figure 21.—*L. Caryi* V.; *a*, longer double-spindle; *b*, stouter irregular double-spindle,—enlarged 200 diameters.
Figure 22.—*Callipodium Pacificum* V.; *a*, *b*, *c*, branched spicula from the cœnenchyma,—enlarged 100 diameters.
Figure 23.—*C. aureum* V.; *a*, *b*, *c*, branched spicula from the cœnenchyma,—enlarged 100 diameters.

PLATE VI.

All the figures on this plate and the next are copied from photographs made by the author and Mr. S. I. Smith, and represent branches or terminal branchlets of natural size.

Figure 1.—*Leptogorgia Floræ* V.
Figure 2.—*L. eximia* V.
Figure 3.—*L. diffusa* V.
Figure 4.—*L. Adamsii* V.
Figure 5.—*L. rutila* V.
Figure 6.—*Eugorgia ampla* V.
Figure 7.—*E. Daniana* V.

Figure 8.—*E. multifida* V.
Figure 9.—*Psammogorgia arbuscula* V.
Figure 10.—*P. gracilis* V.
Figure 11.—*Heterogorgia verrucosa* V.
Figure 12.—*Muricea tenella* V.
Figure 13.—*L. squarrosa* V.

PLATE VII.

Figure 1.—*Psammogorgia teres* V.
Figure 2.—*Muricea fruticosa* V.
Figure 3.—*M. robusta* V.
Figure 4.—*M. hispida* V.
Figure 5.—*M. acervata* V.

Figure 6.—*M. purpurea* V.
Figure 7.—*M. tubigera* V.
Figure 8.—*M. hebes* V.
Figure 9.—*M. albida* V.
Figure 10.—*M. crassa* V.

PLATE VIII.

The figures on this plate are all copied from photographs, enlarged 20 diameters, made by the author from spicula prepared by him from the typical specimens. Only the principal forms of the spicula of each species are represented, and especially the larger spindles from the cells and cœnenchyma.

Figure 1.—*Muricea acerrata* V.
Figure 2.—*M. tubigera* V.
Figure 3.—*M. hispida* V.
Figure 4.—*M. squarrosa* V.
Figure 5.—*M. crassa* V.
Figure 6.—*M. echinata* Val.
Figure 7.—*M. austera* V.
Figure 8.—*M. retusa* V.
Figure 9.—*M. robusta* V.
Figure 10.—*M. albida* V.
Figure 11.—*M. hebes* V.
Figure 12.—*M. purpurea* V.
Figure 13.—*M. appressa* V.
Figure 14.—*M. tenella* V.
Figure 15.—*M. formosa* V.
Figure 16.—*Heterogorgia verrucosa* V.

PLATE IX.

All the figures are copied from photographs made by Mr. S. I. Smith.

Figure 1.—*Callipodium Pacificum* V., natural size.
Figure 2.—*Astrangia palifera* V., from Ceylon,—enlarged 2 diameters.
Figure 3.—*Phyllangia dispersa* V., natural size, seen from above; 3a, side view of two corallites, natural size.
Figure 4.—*Stephanaria stellata* V., a small specimen viewed from above, showing the mode of branching; 4a, some of the cells, enlarged 2 diameters.
Figure 5.—*Astrangia concinna* V., a corallite enlarged 2 diameters.
Figure 6.—*A. Haimei* V., a small cluster of corallites, of natural size; 6a, a corallite, enlarged 2 diameters.
Figure 7.—*Pavonia gigantea* V., portion of the surface, natural size.
Figure 8.—*P. clivosa* V., portion of the surface, natural size.
Figure 9.—*Paracyathus caltha* V., natural size; 9a, calicle, enlarged 2 diameters.
Figure 10.—*Ulangia Bradleyi* V., a calicle, enlarged somewhat less than 2 diameters.
Figure 11.—*Pteraster Danæ* V., dorsal surface; 11a, lower surface,—natural size.

PLATE X.

All the figures, except 8 and 9, are copied from photographs made by the author.

Figure 1.—*Fungia elegans* V., upper surface, natural size.
Figure 2.—Another specimen of the same, lower surface, natural size.
Figure 3.—*Balanophyllia elegans* V., calicle, enlarged 2 diameters.
Figure 4.—*Encope occidentalis* V., a section through the center, showing the right side; 4a, left side of the same section,—natural size.
Figure 5.—*E. Californica* V., right side, natural size.
Figure 6.—Another specimen of same, with the spines remaining, left side, natural size.
Figure 7.—*Clypeaster testudinarius* (Gray sp.), left side of a section through the median line; 7a, right side of the same section,—natural size.
Figure 8.—*Allopora Californica* V., one cell, enlarged 12 diameters.
Figure 9.—*A. venusta* V., one cell, enlarged 12 diameters.

www.ingramcontent.com/pod-product-compliance
Lightning Source LLC
Chambersburg PA
CBHW030405230426
43664CB00007BB/753